NIETZSCHE
AND
DEPTH
PSYCHOLOGY

£22.50

CW01095219

NIETZSCHE AND DEPTH PSYCHOLOGY

edited by

JACOB GOLOMB, WEAVER SANTANIELLO, and RONALD L. LEHRER

State University
of New York
Press

Published by
State University of New York Press, Albany

© 1999 State University of New York

Production by Susan Geraghty
Marketing by Patrick Durocher

Printed in the United States of America

For information, address State University of New York
Press, State University Plaza, Albany, N.Y., 12246

Cover photo source: Goethe-Schiller Archiv

Library of Congress Cataloging-in-Publication Data

Nietzsche and depth psychology / Jacob Golomb, Weaver Santaniello,
  Ronald Lehrer, eds.
      p.   cm.
    Includes bibliographical references and index.
    ISBN 0-7914-4139-3 (hardcover : alk. paper). — ISBN 0-7914-4140-7
(pbk. : alk. paper)
    1. Nietzsche, Friedrich Wilhelm, 1844–1900. 2. Nietzsche,
Friedrich Wilhelm, 1844–1900—Psychology. 3. Psychology and
philosophy—Germany—History—19th century. 4. Psychology-
-Philosophy—Germany—History—19th century. 5. Psychologists-
-Germany. I. Golomb, Jacob. II. Santaniello, Weaver, date.
III. Lehrer, Ronald, date.
BF109.N54N54 1999
150'.92—dc21   98-26836
                                                              CIP

10   9   8   7   6   5   4   3   2   1

CONTENTS

CONTRIBUTORS

CLAUDE BARBRE, M. Div., M. Phil., is managing editor of *The Journal of Religion and Health*, and Assistant Director of the Harlem Family Institute in New York City where he works as a child and family psychotherapist and training supervisor. He has edited recently two books by Dr. Esther Menaker entitled *The Freedom to Inquire* (1995) and *Separation, Will, and Creativity: The Wisdom of Otto Rank* (1996). He is a psychotherapist in private practice in New York City. A longer version of his article on Nietzsche's influence on Otto Rank received a 1997 Gradiva Award.

ERIC BLONDEL teaches philosophy and ethics at the Sorbonne University of Paris I. He is a former student of the Ecole normale Supérieur in Paris and has published several books and translations (with commentaries), on Nietzsche, honor, love, and ethics, including *Nietzsche, the Body and Culture* (1986).

JAMES P. CADELLO is Associate Professor of Philosophy at Central Washington University, in Ellensburg. He has published widely in social philosophy, and has a particular interest in Nietzsche. Current projects include a book on Nietzsche's early American legacy and studies of the relationship between Nietzsche and pragmatism.

DANIEL CHAPELLE, Ph.D., is the author of *Nietzsche and Psychoanalysis* (1993). He has recently completed a manuscript on *Myth and Psychotherapy* and is currently composing a book on *The Depth of the Soul: The Paradigm of Psychological Interiority*. His background is in phenomenological and archetypal psychology. He is a practicing clinician in Massachusetts.

DANIEL W. CONWAY is Professor of Philosophy and Director of the Center for Ethics and Value Inquiry at the Pennsylvania State University. He has published widely in Continental philosophy and political theory, and he is the author of two recent books, *Nietzsche & the Political* (1996) and *Nietzsche's Dangerous Game* (1997).

CLAUDIA CRAWFORD is based in Minneapolis. She has taught humanities, and comparative literature at the University of Minnesota, Macalester College, and Metropolitan State University. She is currently teaching philosophy at North Hennepin Community College. Dr. Crawford has published two books, *The Beginnings of Nietzsche's Theory of Language*, and *To Nietzsche: Dionysus, I Love You! Ariadne* (1995), as well as many articles on Nietzsche.

JACOB GOLOMB teaches philosophy at the Hebrew University of Jerusalem, and acts as Philosophical Editor of the Hebrew University Magnes Press. His other vices include his books and editions: *Nietzsche's Enticing Psychology of Power* (1989), *In Search of Authenticity from Kierkegaard to Camus* (1995), and *Nietzsche and Jewish Culture* (1997). He is also co-editor of *Nietzsche: Godfather of Fascism?* (forthcoming).

DEBORAH HAYDEN, an independent scholar, lives in Marin County, California. She is currently working on a book, *Nietzsche's Pox: Syphilis and the 19th Century Aesthetic Sensibility.*

ROBERT C. HOLUB teaches German intellectual, cultural, and literary history in the German department at the University of California, Berkeley. Among his numerous publications on these topics are *Reflections of Realism* (1991), *Jürgen Habermas: Critic in the Public Sphere* (1992), *Crossing Borders: Reception Theory, Poststructuralism, Deconstruction* (1992), and *Friedrich Nietzsche* (1995). Most recently Professor Holub edited *Impure Reason: Dialectic of Enlightenment in Germany* (1995) and *Responsibility and Commitment* (1996).

RONALD L. LEHRER, M.S., Ph.D., is in private psychotherapy practice in Brooklyn, New York, and Associate Professor of Education and Psychology, and Director of the Undergraduate Program in Special Education, Touro College. He has made contributions to *The Psychoanalytic Review, Psychoanalytic Dialogues,* and the *Newsletter of the Association for the Advancement of Philosophy and Psychiatry.* He is the author of *Nietzsche's Presence in Freud's Life and Thought* (1995).

ROCHELLE L. MILLEN, is Associate Professor of Religion at Wittenberg University in Springfield, Ohio. She is the editor of a recently published volume *New Perspectives on the Holocaust: A Guide for Teachers and Scholars.* The author of articles on women and Jewish law, she has presented academic papers on issues of women and religion, Talmudic law, and various aspects of the philosophy of Martin Buber.

DR. GEORGE MORAITIS is a training and supervising analyst at the Chicago Institute for Psychoanalysis. Born in Athens, Greece, he received his M.D. from the University of Athens and had his psychiatric and psychoanalytic training in the United States. During the past twenty years he has been actively involved in studying the psychological aspects of writing biographies, and has developed his own method for pursuing these studies.

GRAHAM PARKES is the editor of *Heidegger and Asian Thought* and *Nietzsche and Asian Thought,* translator of *The Self-Overcoming of Nihilism* by Nishitani Keiji, and *Heidegger's Hidden Sources: East-Asian Influences on His Work* by Reinhard May, and author of *Composing the Soul: Reaches of Nietzsche's Psychology.* He is currently working on a philosophical biography of Nietzsche.

CARL PLETSCH is Coordinator of Academic Technology at the University of Colorado at Denver. He is the author of *Young Nietzsche: Becoming a Genius,* editor of *Introspection in Biography,* and author of essays in European intellectual history.

WEAVER SANTANIELLO is Assistant Professor of Philosophy at Penn State University, Berks. She is the author of *Nietzsche, God, and the Jews* (1994), and has published several articles on Nietzsche. She is currently composing a manuscript on Nietzsche's *Zarathustra,* and editing a volume on *Nietzsche and the Gods.*

OFELIA SCHUTTE is Professor of Philosophy at the University of Florida, Gainesville, where she teaches existentialism and Continental philosophy. She is the author of *Beyond Nihilism: Nietzsche without Masks* (1984), *Cultural Identity and Social Liberation in Latin American Thought,* and many articles on Nietzsche, feminism, and cultural identity issues.

ROBERT C. SOLOMON is Quincy Lee Centennial Professor of Philosophy at the University of Texas at Austin and the author of many articles on Nietzsche and existentialism. He is the winner of several teaching awards and the author of *The Passions* (1976), *In the Spirit of Hegel* (1983), *About Love* (1988), *From Hegel to Existentialism* (1988) and *A Passion for Justice* (1990). With Kathleen M. Higgins, he is the co-editor of *Reading Nietzsche* (1988) and the co-author of *A Short History of Philosophy* (1996) and *A Passion for Wisdom* (1997).

ACKNOWLEDGMENTS

The editors would first like to thank James Peltz (at SUNY) for his patience and invaluable assistance—and for putting up with three intense editors who are in great need of depth psychologists.

We would also like to thank the following for their assistance in many ways: Carola Sautter, for initially recognizing the potential significance of our project; Dr. James Lieberman, for his recommendations; Werner and Evelyn Pluhar, for their advice on computer matters. We also would like to thank Brooklyn College librarians Sherry Warman and Betty Miller for their expert assistance, and the Computer Center at Penn State, Berks (especially Lisa Glass and Chris).

Dr. Lehrer wishes to thank Heinz L. Ansbacher and Edward Hoffman for reading and commenting on his paper on Freud and Adler.

Weaver gives special thanks to her research assistant, Thomas Zerkowski, for helping with final proofs—and going through the last hours of madness with her! Distinct acknowledgment also goes to production editor, Susan Geraghty.

Last but not least, each editor would like to acknowledge the others. Drs. Golomb and Santaniello especially thank Dr. Lehrer for his bibliography.

Weaver would especially like to thank JG for initiating this volume.

Ron and Jacob would like to express their deep gratitude for Weaver's painstaking efforts for most of the technicalities involved.

ABBREVIATIONS

All references to Nietzsche's texts refer to section numbers unless page numbers are specified.

AC   *The Antichrist*(ian)
AO   *Assorted Opinions and Maxims* (*Human, All-Too-Human*, v. II, part 1).
BGE   *Beyond Good and Evil*
BT   *The Birth of Tragedy*
CW   *The Case of Wagner*
D   *Daybreak*
EH   *Ecce Homo*
GM   *Toward the Genealogy of Morals*
GS   *The Gay Science*
HU   *Human, All-Too-Human*
KSA   *Sämtliche Werke: Kritische Studienausgabe*, ed. Giorgio Colli and Mazzino Montinari (Berlin: de Gruyter, 1980).
TW   *Twilight of the Idols*
WP   *The Will to Power*
WS   *The Wanderer and his Shadow* (*Human, All-Too-Human*, v. II, part 2).
Z   *Thus Spoke Zarathustra*

Introductory Essay:
Nietzsche's "New Psychology"

Jacob Golomb

That a psychologist without equal speaks from my writings, is perhaps the first insight reached by a good reader—a reader as I deserve him.

—*Ecce Homo*

In many places Nietzsche referred to himself as the first great and "new psychologist" of the West.[1] In a letter to August Strindberg (in 1888) Nietzsche describes himself proudly: "*Ich bin ein Psychologe*" and hence, not surprisingly, in a letter to Carl Fuchs in the same year, he complained that no one had still characterized him "*als Psychologe.*"[2]

Over a century has passed, yet most Nietzsche interpreters have disregarded his wish for recognition as a psychologist, and have failed to come to grips with the *essential* psychological aspects of his thought.[3] Since the status and function of psychology *within* the framework of Nietzsche's thought was seldom explored, Part 1 of the present collection aims at remedying this situation. In this introductory essay I will argue that psychology, being one of the most significant components of Nietzsche's philosophy, assists him in carrying out the existential project of his teaching, that of enticing readers to reactivate for themselves their creative powers and use them in authentic patterns of life. In attempting to foster authenticity, Nietzsche needed a special type of psychology that would entice his readers into discovering for themselves the genuine roots of their creative powers.

When addressing Nietzsche's psychology we must distinguish between his unique psychological-genealogical *method* that "freezes" our will to believe in life-nihilating values, and the *positive content of his psychology* that had a formative impact on depth psychology and antic-

1

ipated some of its leading ideas, as the essays in Part 2 of this present volume clearly demonstrate. Here I will limit myself to describing Nietzsche's method of psychologizing (part A), as well as his psychology (part B), purported to affect his readers' "transfiguration" toward authenticity (part C). By doing this I hope to elucidate and justify Nietzsche's rather enigmatic claim that his *new* "psychology is now again the path to the fundamental problems"[4]—the problems of morality.

In what follows it should be clear, however, that I do not intend to reduce Nietzsche's philosophy to psychology. Moreover, I do not claim any priority for my perspective, productive though it may be. To be faithful to Nietzsche one must regard various perspectives as legitimate as long as they abjure such claims. And though the present essay serves here as an introductory piece for the collection as a whole, I am in no way presuming to represent faithfully all the multifarious perspectives delineated in the essays below. However, some fundamental beliefs are common to all of the contributors, especially the feeling that Nietzsche's psychology and its formative impact on depth psychology are of such importance that they are worthy to be dwelled upon. Perhaps some of us also share the present editors' conviction that deeper understanding of Nietzsche's psychology will assist some of us to become "what we are."

A. NIETZSCHE'S "UNMASKING" AND "FREEZING" PSYCHOLOGIZING

In *The Birth of Tragedy*, we find the question that constitutes a major methodological principle in Nietzsche's psychological investigations: "what dreadful need was it that could produce such an illustrous company of Olympian beings?"[5]

This question can be paraphrased as: "what is the psychological function of any given area of culture, such as Greek myths, religion, metaphysics, and any other theoretical preoccupation?" The question is not concerned with a rational justification of any given realm, rather it seeks to expose why we are prompted to believe in the existence of such a realm, and what sort of psychological need is fulfilled through it.

Nietzsche's essay "Schopenhauer as Educator" makes explicit Nietzsche's method of psychologizing, which later developed into a comprehensive psychological theory. Nietzsche claims in this essay that a human being is "a thing dark and veiled."[6] Although potentially creative and powerful, we are afraid of expressing ourselves freely, fully, and uniquely, and hide behind various dogmas and ideologies. We typically prefer empty generalizations to our own remarkable particularity. This is the thesis that motivates Nietzsche's method of unveiling one's dependence on external conditioning and internal deception.

One of the main purposes of Nietzsche's psychologizing method was to *"freeze"* our needs to believe in some transcendental agencies at the expense of believing in ourselves and freely creating our selves. Nietzsche realized that psychologizing alone is unable to liberate us completely from our attachments to metaphysical viewpoints since this devotion is sustained by powerful psychic needs. Nietzsche is thus compelled to concentrate on "cooling down" and freezing these needs. To ultimately subdue the metaphysical drive (his own as well as ours) Nietzsche himself adopted—and prescribed for his entire culture—the freezing tactics. Because our intellectual beliefs serve to satisfy certain powerful psychic needs, an attempted refutation would have provoked an emotional resistance motivated by those same needs, resulting in a reinforcement of the very dogmas one wished to refute. For this reason, Nietzsche preferred his psychologizing method to rational and direct refutation:

> Do not deride and befoul that which you want to do away with for good but respectfully *lay it on ice*, and, in as much as ideas are very tenacious of life, do so again and again. Here it is necessary to act according to the maxim: "One refutation is no refutation."[7]

At this point one might argue that Nietzsche's psychologistic "treatment" of metaphysics and other intellectual preoccupations involves a genetic fallacy: it tends to judge the value and validity of any given philosophical position by reference to noncognitive functions and motives. Hence it might be held that his ambitious program of overcoming metaphysics by means of genetic psychologizing is irrelevant to any serious attempt at logical refutation. Thus, the project of uncovering the psychic motives that draw humanity to some preoccupation with certain metaphysical commitments cannot inform questions concerning the truth or falsity of those commitments themselves.

Nietzsche might defend himself by contending that the objective of psychologizing is not intended to produce a rational refutation. The first purpose of the genetic uncovering is to freeze the motivating force or driving power—not to provide proof of their logical invalidity. In any case, he is aware of the danger of genetic fallacy and thus abstains from suggesting that his psychologizing is equivalent to refutation.[8] On the contrary, he explicitly rejects the claim that metaphysical beliefs are strictly (or necessarily) false per se.[9] However problematic the concept of truth may be in Nietzsche's philosophy,[10] it will suffice to say here that the acceptance of Nietzsche's arguments does not depend on their truth-value, for with respect to rational validity they are no more or less preferable than the views he attempts to "put on ice." They are accept-able only if, like Nietzsche, we adopt a certain existential perspective—a lived attitude—that will enable us to exemplify in our own lives a par-ticular pattern; and this pattern, Nietzsche holds, is latent in every individual. If we allow ourselves to be enticed into accepting the pro-posed life perspective, it is not because we recognize it as objectively "true," but because it successfully reactivates the elements of our inher-ent power (*Macht*), previously repressed by other psychological forces. Nietzsche understands that his freezing tactic is distinct from a rational refutation: "if one has a mistrust of metaphysics the results are by and large the same as if it had been directly refuted and one no longer had the *right* to believe in it."[11]

From this (and other quotations)[12] it becomes clear that Nietzsche's main concern in his applications of the psychologistic method is to evoke a mood of deep suspicion and distrust toward metaphysics (and other dogmatic views as well).

The appropriate affective mood would, in his view, be tantamount in practice to a direct refutation: its lived consequences would be the same. The evocation of a psychic (rather than strictly philosophical) doubt in the viability of metaphysics (or religion and any rational-objec-tive ethics), would freeze our motivation for believing in them and would check our efforts to repeatedly resurrect their various manifesta-tions. An authentic and healthy culture would then emerge, a culture no longer relying on metaphysical comforts, able to function creatively without the traditional philosophical crutches.

Nietzsche's method found a powerful contemporary ally; namely, the world historical process that was bringing about "the death of God"—a "metaphysical Being"—who had functioned as the main source of inspiration for constructing metaphysical philosophy. How-ever, the shadows of the deceased God (including metaphysics itself) were extremely slow to disappear, as they still served powerful and per-vasive psychic needs. Although our belief in God as such had subsided, the need for God remains quite alive. In order for humanity to take its fate and future into its own hands, it had to dispel these lingering shad-ows. The constitution of a new metaphysics could not accomplish this, as it would only create yet a further shadow. Psychology, on the other hand, might function to support humanity's aspirations for achieving complete spiritual autonomy. Here, one can locate another reason for Nietzsche's indirect tactic of attack: to engage in a direct confrontation with metaphysics would have required the development of some new metaphysical doctrine. Any potential success it might have enjoyed would have left Nietzsche with his destructive instrument still in hand; another metaphysical system, another illusionary consolation, another redundant shadow of the dead God. Of metaphysical needs, Nietzsche writes: "A philosophy can be employed either to satisfy such needs or to *set them aside.*"[13] The second route is clearly preferable by Nietzsche: "the ideal is not refuted—it *freezes* to death."[14] This freezing of emotions is the objective of Nietzsche's method of psychologizing. Hence there is no basis for the accusation of genetic fallacy, which applies only in an argumentation explicitly attempting to refute the rational validity of any given statements by psychological means.

However, Nietzsche's psychologizing is much more than a means of overcoming metaphysics or revaluating all values. It also fulfills a specifically existential function by addressing the psychic needs of humans, easing the burden of our life, giving us peace of mind and "cooling" us.[15] These existential effects flow directly from the capacity of psychologizing to freeze the metaphysical need that has never been adequately satisfied by metaphysics itself: every "metaphysical comfort" was subsequently shattered by the collapse of the system that provided it. A state of disquiet and discontent naturally ensues, perpetuated by the individual's skepticism about the adequacy of any system. This has been the historical predicament of philosophy, but if Nietzsche's method can successfully freeze the need for metaphysical consolation and support, he will have helped to relieve us of a profoundly distressing condition. In this respect, then, Nietzsche offers a kind of existential salvation precisely by redeeming us from our need for salvation. The salvation from salvation was to become a central motif of Nietzsche's mature philosophy.

Nietzsche expounds the many personal benefits and "blessings" conferred on us when the psychologistic "axe" finally eradicates the metaphysical need and a liberation ensues.[16] Our present condition is conceived as a state of illness, and that need—as a primary symptom— requires the treatment of "icepacks" that can enable us to be "steady, inoffensive, moderate."[17] Psychologizing is a personal therapy prescribed for anyone suffering a perturbing intellectual or ideological fever; it is a prescription for the restoration of a healthy tranquility through personal emancipation.[18]

We should not, however, ignore the fact that the very process of freezing our belief in most of the prevalent values is founded on the assumption that the "frozen" personality will reject certain values and accept other norms, which already exist both in our social surroundings and within ourselves. Hence the striking similarity between the procedure of "coolly placing on ice"[19] and the aporetic tactics employed by Socrates, whom Nietzsche ambivalently admired. Socrates "froze" by logical means, whereas Nietzsche does so by means of genetic psychologizations. In his dialogues, Socrates seeks to freeze the listener's belief in

X, for example, by showing that this logically entails a belief in Y. The listener is not ready to endorse belief in Y because of their belief in the set of values: p, s, t . . . which they share with Socrates.

Nietzsche employs almost the same method. He shows his readers that their most "sacred" values have negative roots, and the "effects" of their endorsement are stagnation, repression, inhibition of creativity, depression, regression, and so on. Most of us typically consider these effects undesirable and wish to eliminate them; yet on the other hand, we often blindly adhere to the same "ideals" that propagate these states. Thus the freezing process is employed indirectly by means of a genealogy, revealing the negative origins of prevalent norms, arguing that the effects of our accepting these norms are psychologically and existentially destructive.

B. NIETZSCHE'S PSYCHOLOGY OF POWER

Nietzsche's subsequent exercise of psychologizing in the sphere of morality issues in a set of positive principles: the psychology of the weak and their "slave-morality"; the psychology of the powerful and their "master-morality"[20] and underlying them, the principle of the will to power. All these elements constitute a quite comprehensive psychology.

This transformation from psychologizing to psychology is mainly implicit and *a posteriori*; it occurs only when Nietzsche recognizes that he requires a positive psychological doctrine to successfully substantiate and intensify its therapeutic aims. Specific principles and criteria must be made explicit if the method is to be practically viable and coherently applied. In articulating his method Nietzsche already appealed to certain psychological principles, that is, the unconscious, sublimation, and repression.[21] He now perceives that this assortment of positive ideas may combine into an organic whole which, if not consistent *de jure*, may nonetheless endow his "science" of psychology with a *de facto* applicability.

Nietzsche's psychological findings are not accidental or particularistic: his theses are consolidated and unified by a pivotal principle of mental life—the concept of *Macht*. It is the discovery, explication, and consistent application of this principle that represents the culmination of Nietzsche's psychology. It follows that the specific object of the psychologist's task is power and its appearance in culture and history; we can say that Nietzsche-as-psychologist is actually a philosopher dealing with power and its exhibitions. And thus, Nietzsche's "new psychology," which—unlike others—"dared to descend into the depths," became what he called "the doctrine of the development of the will to power."[22] In so doing, it unmasks the basic instinct of the human-all-too-human soul: its power. This power has two diametrically opposed psychological manifestations: the negative and the positive.

> There are recipes for the feeling of power, firstly for those who can control themselves and who are thereby accustomed to a feeling of power; then for those in whom precisely this is lacking.[23]

This is the hard core of Nietzsche's psychology or, to be more exact, of his theory of personality. Negative power does not express itself spontaneously, but derivatively: it is fundamentally deficient and defective, striving to encourage and fortify itself by enjoyment obtained from abuse and cruelty.

The tendency of certain individuals to excel at all costs, moved by the *"drive to distinction,"*[24] also belongs to this negative pattern. The ambitious, competitive personality lacks the "feeling" of genuine power, and struggles to attain it through overpowering their rivals. By contrast, one who possesses positive power needs neither the approbation of their external surroundings, nor medals and decorations their culture often affords. They do not require the various satisfactions stemming from abusive domination to intensify their *"feeling of power"*—for it is already intrinsic to them.

Nietzsche employs this characterology to his criticism of moral patterns prevalent in his culture and throughout history. Thus he proposes an active morality of positive power *against* the traditional passive type, opting for courageous creativity and autonomy based on the acquired selfhood of the moral agent. The mechanism for adopting the prevalent morality includes a passive internalization of external maxims, making them into a habit, an acquired "second nature" or, to use a Freudian notion, the superego, which Nietzsche anticipated.[25] This habitual morality, conditioned in childhood, stands in contrast to the evaluations made by a mature "selfhood."

The transmitted "morality of tradition," which mechanically and arbitrarily conditions our "highest selves," is in fact anti-individualistic, obscuring and repressing the original personality. Hence this morality (generally conceived as altruistic), actually suppresses the ego and directs excessive violence against the *"individuum,"* making us into a *"dividuum."* Nietzsche proposes morality that instead springs out of the ego's power and self-expression. The violence of the "highest self" against the ego explains the impoverishment, pessimism, and depression of the individual. Their vitality withers away, leaving a feeling of weakness, discontent, and "the profoundest misery" (D 106). This moral wretchedness, and other expressions of the traditionally accepted ethos, are all manifestations of power. However, this is only the supreme expression of negative power, characterized by fear and weakness. The power impelling traditional morality is not sufficiently strong or independent; thus, the person suffers from a perpetual anxiety that it may be undermined. This causes us to develop defense mechanisms by means of which we seek to guard and intensify our doubts and instabilities. Nietzsche therefore maintains that the supporters of authoritative morality are directed by "an obscure anxiety and awe"[26] of losing their influence and authority. In consequence, their "moral commands" must be oppressive, attempting to enhance and reinforce power by exploiting other human beings.

In contrast to oppressive culture, Nietzsche draws an ideal picture of an entire culture conducted by powerful individuals: independent, unprejudiced, creative, gentle, and courageous, lacking any desire for expansion or domination.[27] What is novel in his morality of positive power is not the specific content of its values but their origin. Not "what" but "how" is of importance here, and Nietzsche seeks to overcome the prevalent moral patterns not because of their content, but because they originate in (and serve to perpetuate) a negative, impotent, and cowardly drive.

Until now, Nietzsche's criticism of current morality has been based on the concepts of positive and negative power. He offers another critique, which originates from his psychological interpretation of human consciousness as "a more or less fantastic commentary on an unknown, perhaps unknowable text."[28] Nevertheless, the concept of the will to power assumes an unconscious mental agency that urges us to action, although we are unaware of the nature and content of its underlying drives. Will to power, especially negative power, drives the weak to establish moral patterns that lend them support. But we are not typically aware that by pursuing power we are being driven to dominate others through a "refined cruelty" obscured in authoritative standards of "duty and guilt." Hence Nietzsche requires the notion of active, but unconscious, mental life, to present the idea of power while rejecting those moral patterns it has invented through ethical rationalizations.

Nietzsche's shift in emphasis in moral theorizing follows directly from the role his psychology ascribes to the unconscious dimensions of the human character.[29] In place of the naive Socratic demand to "know thyself," Nietzsche asks us to explore and come to terms with our unconscious realm of interests, wishes, and motives. Thus an additional element is introduced into the essential process of self-overcoming: the overcoming of the unconscious by uncovering, mastering, and creatively utilizing it within a free, conscious moral context.

Negative power is externalized in negative morality, driven by unconscious, antimoral motives disguised in various pseudomoralistic rationalizations. The morality of guilt also belongs to this category, for it originates in "a new excitation of the *feeling of power*."[30] A frustrated, impotent personality exploits guilt in order to avenge itself on others and intensify its own sense of superiority. Allegedly altruistic patterns likewise may be manifestations of negative morality inasmuch as self-sacrifice can be a means of providing oneself with the sense of a "positive enhancement of the general feeling of human *power*."[31] By exposing the unconscious motives underlying the "altruistic" morality, Nietzsche reveals that these deficient virtues cannot generate an authentic altruism.

From this all it follows that a perceptive depth psychologist must contend with these unconscious processes and subject them to an exhaustive genealogical analysis. The shift in Nietzsche's attitude faithfully reflects his altered approach to the purpose of psychologizing: it is in fact derived from it. As long as the purpose of psychologizing was basically negative—to expose unconscious motives—Nietzsche needed only to commit himself to the position that we are unconscious of certain mental processes. But in entrusting to psychology a positive role in fostering an authentic morality, he is obliged to view the unconscious not merely as functional but as a structural substratum of the mental life. In order to activate authentic morality, Nietzsche has to affirm that such a power potentially exists and should be reactivated, and that this potential has lain dormant within the realm of our unconscious mind.

This change from negative psychologizing to positive psychological doctrine was not made instantaneously, but gradually. So too, the transition from a functional description of the unconscious to ontological structuralism is a developmental process, beginning in Nietzsche's first works where he speaks of the "Dionysian barbarian" forces that are quite similar to what Freud later categorized under the concept of the *id*. Freud too initially spoke of the unconscious merely from a functional economical and epistemological point of view; but at a later stage he committed himself to an ontological structure, postulating the existence of the id as a viable component of our mental lives.[32]

In short: the emergence of Nietzsche's notion of an authentic morality required a deeper understanding of the ontological status of the unconscious. It demanded a knowledge of its formation, its sublimation, its rise to consciousness, and its employment in reactivating the morality of power.

C. NIETZSCHE'S "NEW PSYCHOLOGY" AS THE ENTICING MEANS TOWARD AUTHENTICITY

The fundamental raison d'être of Nietzsche's philosophical psychology is to be influential in the work of enticement to positive power. This is the basic function and objective of his psychology. This objective, that is, the enticement toward personal authenticity is what endows his "new psychology" with a moral dimension and turns it into a vital "ladder" of his existentialist philosophy. I will end this concise exposition of Nietzsche's "new psychology" by dwelling upon its enticing function and the objective of this enticement, namely authentic patterns of positive power.

1. Nietzsche's Enticing Psychology

Nietzsche's philosophy, and the psychological means he employs, purports to move us closer to the "great spirits"[33] who—like Zarathustra—are skeptics out of an abundance of power, and who sustain their skepticism in all vitality and creativity.

To dance "even near abysses" is the only alternative left after the "Death of God"; the ability to embrace this alternative is the free spirit's "proof of strength." Nietzsche's objective is thus to provide and prepare modern's with an intellectual therapy, a creative life in a world without dogmatic beliefs. The death of dogma will not lead to the end of humanity and culture, but will unleash the resources heretofore constrained by repressive morality. It will open new horizons to new beliefs, that now will function as life-enhancing "perspectives." Once they lose their usefulness, such beliefs will be discarded and easily exchanged for other perspectives.

Nietzsche's own psychology should be regarded as just such a belief—a temporary perspective—to be left behind once it has fulfilled its therapeutic aim. Hence, Nietzschean psychology is a means, "a mere instrument"[34] to lure us to touch and freely employ our positive powers. In view of this, Nietzsche unquestionably belongs to "these philosophers of the future" who may have a right to be called "*Versucher*": "This name is in the end a mere attempt and, if you will, an enticement."[35]

Versuchung is an "experiment," an "enticement," and an "hypothesis" directing our efforts toward positive power, and testing our ability to reach and activate it. These "tests" are Nietzsche's psychology of power, which becomes his principal "instrument" for attaining his philosophically existential goals.

Nietzsche is aware that his therapeutic enticement is not appropriate for everyone. In fact, he considers our reaction to his therapy as an additional criterion of distinction between different patterns of power. He suggests that if we fail to respond to him and to his books, this is not because of any inner flaws in the therapy or because it lacks any moving appeal. Such failure would be a consequence of our own inability to raise ourselves to the level of its demands:

What serves the higher type of men as nourishment or delectation must almost be poison for a very different and inferior type.[36]

This passage suggests three kinds of responses or challenges to entice-ment. The challenges stand in direct correspondence to the psychologi-cal type at whom they are directed: (1) the "inferior type" (of negative power) rejects the enticement, is confused by it and escapes from its con-sequences, (2) the "higher type" (of positive power) accepts the doctrine and becomes more powerful, independent, and authentic, and (3) the "*Übermenschen*" of optimal power do not respond to this enticement since they do not require it. They are already endowed with the highest capacity for self-creation, and overcome even this Nietzschean entice-ment by creating their own perspectives and values. Here the rejection of Nietzsche's challenge does not stem from cowardliness or weakness (as in the first case), but out of a surplus of power and an abundance of self that requires no psychologistic crutches—not even Nietzsche's.

Psychology thus becomes the path to the fundamental patterns of positive power. However, being only a path, it is naturally abandoned once it has come to an end. Nietzschean psychology will then have become a type of temporary scaffolding, a provisional hypothesis to be abandoned once it has served its purpose.

One may think of Nietzschean psychology as being simultaneously an instrument for freezing repressive ideologies and a means for enticing and intensifying the will. In the preliminary stages of maturation, power still needs therapeutic and psychological crutches. But with the full ripening of power—with the attainment of Nietzsche's "self-creation"—our authentic power must shed its supports and prove its authenticity by being able to thrive without them. So the way leading to power must already include this very power; it carries this power as a potential for full actualization through a painful and gradual process of reactivation. The psychological ladder does not create the power or its positive pat-terns and pathos *ex nihilo*. It merely explicates and activates this power. This is the meaning of the Nietzschean conception of the philosopher's "thinking," which is, in fact, far less a discovery than a recognition, "a remembering, a return and a homecoming to a remote, primordial, and inclusive household of the soul."[37]

This explicative-descriptive dimension of the ladder also includes a personal meaning clearly indicated by Nietzsche's mention of "the per-sonal confession" and "*memoire*."[38] His instrumental psychology is intended to fulfill Nietzsche's needs as well as our own; his explication of power becomes at the same time a kind of self-psychoanalysis. Freud was probably well aware of this.[39] Nietzsche's analysis of power and self-analysis are parallel and complementary processes, but they are not derived from one another. For while it is true that in his enticing psychology Nietzsche himself is enticed, and that in giving directives for our maturation Nietzsche himself matures and becomes powerful, these two processes are nonetheless clearly distinct. Both of them are separate manifestations of Nietzsche's one "common root," of his "fundamental will" (*GM,* preface, 2). The "common root" is always power, whether used for self-overcoming or for the overcoming of one's epoch. More precisely, this power is used to overcome all these patterns of life and their cultural rationalizations that hinder the spontaneous and creative use of positive powers hidden in Nietzsche and his contemporaries.

This self-psychoanalytic component of Nietzsche's thought accounts for his personal manner of writing and for its partially aphoristic and associative form. This form closely resembles the psychoanalytic treatment that employs spontaneous outburst of primary associative processes, as well as more objective interpretations and theoretical reflections upon these processes. Both evoke and nourish these processes and are in turn elicited by them again and again.[40] And hence the legitimacy of our efforts in this present collection to introduce part 3 below, which deals with "The Psychology of Nietzsche." Nietzsche himself provided us with the example and the clues for undertaking such research on his own personality as far as it does not reduce it to merely a psychoanalytical patient but, on the contrary cultivates an authentic individual.

2. Nietzsche's Ideal of Authentic Life

Nietzsche did not use the term *authenticity* explicitly, but it is possible to locate its origin in his recurrent distinctions between *Wahrheit* (truth) and *Wahrhaftigkeit* (truthfulness): "a proof of truth is not the same thing as a proof of truthfulness . . . the latter is in no way an argument for the former."[41] The shift from philosophy to philosophers and that from the traditional meaning of truth to personal authenticity show up repeatedly in Nietzsche's writings. After the "Death of God" one has to adopt for oneself the Godlike role of being the originator of truth and of one's own self. The absence of a "pre-established harmony" between our cognitions and reality permits us to shift our emphasis to the creation of our own genuine selves.

It appears that two seemingly contradictory models of authenticity are in Nietzsche's thought. The first model derives its inspiration from the biological metaphor of a plant actualizing the potential of the seed. One becomes authentic, according to this model, if one manages to fully manifest this complex in one's lifetime. The second model employs the metaphor of art and artistic creation. The search for authenticity is seen as the wish to reflect one's own indeterminancy by spontaneous choice of one out of the many possible ways of life. Individuals are types of artists who freely shape themselves as works of art.

It would be a mistake, however, to think that Nietzsche embraced these two models equally. The second conception, that of artistic creation, is surely primary. Nietzsche rejects crude naturalism and determinism and does not believe that the innateness of one's individualistic nature completely determines one's self. Nietzsche is less concerned with biological nature and more concerned with cultural conditioning and formative influences that blindly shape one's character. To become "what we are" is not to live according to our so-called "innate nature," but to create ourselves freely. To that end we have to know ourselves to distinguish what we can change in ourselves and in the external circumstances that have shaped us; we must realize what we have to accept as inevitable, and must do so in the heroic manner of *amor fati*.[42]

Nietzsche's use of an artistic model of authenticity begins in *The Birth of Tragedy*, where he delineates an "Apollonian principle" that exercises its drives in direct opposition to the "Dionysian barbarian" instincts. It does this through the creation of sophisticated images, and the imposition of order and a causal network onto the world.

The subjugation by Apollo of the unrestrained drives of the Dionysian barbarian is the source of art in general. This synthesis provides "the metaphysical comfort" that allows humans to affirm existence despite its horrors. By this process, where humans are purified of their cruder components, one is transformed into an object of art, into an artistic sublimation: "He is no longer an artist," Nietzsche tells us, "he has become a work of art" (*BT* 1). This is the image of the authentic individual who individualizes and creates himself. In this act of creation, creator and creation merge and any possible alienation between man and his created objects is overcome, since these objects become an integral part of his own self.

Nietzsche is well aware of the strong pressure exerted by social convention and educational systems. Hence the road to authenticity and spontaneous creativity requires the three "stages" described by Nietzsche's Zarathustra: "the spirit becomes a camel; and the camel, a lion; and the lion, finally, a child."[43] The individual ("the lion") must liberate oneself from "the camel," that is, from all the external layers imposed by institutional conditioning. Only then, after attaining a childlike state of "innocence,"[44] can one proceed to the second stage, in which one consciously adopts and assimilates moral norms. These norms may well reflect the traditional values discarded in the first stage; it is not their content that matters, but the unconstrained manner in which they are chosen.

Nietzsche was not searching for new, esoteric values; he sought to reactivate authentic modes of living. This can easily be seen by looking at some of the descriptions of positive power in his writings. We do not find any original or new values there but rather values that have already appeared in traditional philosophical ethics: self-sufficiency, heroism, creative sublimation of instinct, intellectual tolerance, generosity, nobility, courage, vitality, self-control, faith in oneself, the ability to accept contradiction, the lack of bad conscience, and the like. Most of these values can be found in the ethics of Plato, Spinoza, and Kant. By the term *ethic*, I mean a doctrine aiming at a rational justification of moral norms. However, Nietzsche did not believe that we are capable of providing any such rational foundation, especially when it comes to the value of authentic life, which denotes, among other things, a subjective pathos of inwardness that in principle cannot be judged by any external and objective criterion. Nietzsche is well aware that only the individual who strives to attain authentic life is able to feel whether he or she has been successful (*BGE* 41).

This strive for authenticity appears at the twilight of the rational ethic—at the "twilight of the idols." It is an explicit expression of revolt against the spirit of objectivity. Thus it is inconceivable to have a fully authentic individual living in society, which by nature is founded upon a set of objective norms and a common ethos. To clarify this point let me draw an analogy from the domain of psychoanalysis. If neurosis is, as Freud claims, a natural outcome of the repressive society that is founded upon such repression, can we imagine a society where there are no neurotic people? This question remains valid even for a society in which all neurotic individuals have successfully undergone a psychoanalytic treatment. But once they try to live in that society under—more or less—the same conditions that caused their neurosis in the first place, will they not to some degree regress? The same consideration is relevant to the individual whose quest for authenticity is supposedly finally fulfilled. Since such a person continues to be a member of the society, the processes of social conditioning and leveling will continue to exert their inauthenticating effects. Hence the search for authenticity faces what seems to be a paradoxical situation: it cannot be materialized without society, nor can it be lived within its framework.

Nietzsche, I think, was well aware of the difficulty of trying to allow for the "ought" of authenticity within the social "is." The fact is that he leaves this issue intentionally vague in the closing sentence of his book, where Zarathustra, who personifies the ideal of authenticity, leaves his "cave" in order to do—what? To return to society?

> Thus spoke Zarathustra, and he left his cave, glowing and strong as a morning sun that comes out of dark mountains.[45]

The metaphor of a "sun" implies that Zarathustra, not being able to become part of the human-social nexus is like the sun, which not being part of the earth, only warms it from above. Zarathustra can only inspire us to try and become authentic, to be what we really are. Authenticity is a kind of regulative and corrective ideal rather than a manifestly viable norm.

Hence we must understand Nietzsche's basic idea of the "transfiguration of all values" not as radical abolition of the inauthentic ethic but as a gradual approximation to authenticity. This process is constantly taking place "within a *single* soul" (*BGE* 260) vacillating between opposed modes of living. Here I must stress once again that Nietzsche does not reject the "negative" (inauthentic) types of power because they are less "true." They are rejected as detrimental and destructive to his ideal of authenticity, which is concretized in the notion of the *Übermensch*. Nietzsche is aware that such a personality cannot be realized completely; the *Übermensch* provides only a regulative idea, a suprahistorical model to approximate and emulate. It is a corrective to the overemphasis on the equality, the objectivity, the leveling processes of modernity that result in dissolution of the self.

Authenticity does not attach itself to fixed values. Rather, as Nietzsche stresses (*BGE* 41), drawing a model of authentic life-patterns, it is determined by impermanence. At every stage of his philosophizing, Nietzsche is conscious that this stage is actually only a "step" to overcome and proceed further:

> Those were steps for me, and I have climbed up over them; to that end I had to pass over them. Yet they thought that I wanted to retire on them.[46]

Here, however, we reach the limits of our capacity to speak rationally in a world without a *logos*. And perhaps Nietzsche intended to bring us to this ultimate boundary in order to help us transcend his own thought as well, thereby assisting us to reach real maturity of positive power: standing on our own feet and throwing away all crutches, including Nietzsche's psychology.

Nietzsche's Zarathustra incites us as follows:

> This is *my* way; where is yours?—thus I answered those who asked me "the way." For *the* way—that does not exist.[47]

And thus, Nietzsche's psychological-philosophical therapy is a dialectical one: the more efficiently power is uncovered and reactivated, the greater the likelihood that the individual will persevere through the more advanced stages, being able to withstand the reality looming at every step on the road to authenticity. If we have already reached this point, our power will have been most favorably revealed. Only then will Nietzsche be able to throw away his psychological crutches he has given us and send us to our own walks of life and their authentic manifestations.

NOTES

1. Friedrich Nietzsche, *Beyond Good and Evil*, trans. Walter Kaufmann (New York: Random House, 1966), 12. Cf. also Nietzsche's *BT*, preface, 2; *HU*, preface, 8; *GS*, preface, 2; *BGE* 45; *GM* I:1; II:11; and III:9, 19, and 20; *TW*, preface; "Maxims and Arrows," sec. 35; "What I Owe to the Ancients," sec. 3 and 4; *AC*, 24, 28 and 29; *NCW*, preface; *EH*, preface, 3, and "Why I Am So Wise," sec. 8. Most notably, see Nietzsche's remarks in *EH*, "Why I Am a Destiny," sec. 6:

> Who among philosophers was a psychologist at all before me, and not rather the opposite . . . ? There was no psychology at all before me. To be the first here may be a curse; it is at any rate a destiny.

2. *Friedrich Nietzsche Werke*, ed. Karl Schlechta (Frankfurt am Main: Ullstein, 1972–80), 4:930, 900.

3. Walter Kaufmann suggests rightly that the psychological aspects of Nietzsche's thought are no less significant than the philosophical: "Nietzsche als der Erste Grosse Psychologe," *Nietzsche-Studien* 7 (1978): 261–75. However, in his well-known work *Nietzsche: Philosopher, Psychologist, Antichrist* (Princeton: Princeton University Press, 1968) referring to Nietzsche's psychological leanings, he proceeds largely to ignore them. Apart from several insights and lengthy aphorisms little is offered in this pioneering study to justify the word *Psychologist* in the title. Moreover, Nietzsche's "psychological inquiries" were presented by Kaufmann as side effects and temporary digressions from the main issues of values and happiness.

4. *BGE* 23.

5. Friedrich Nietzsche, *The Birth of Tragedy*, in *The Basic Writings of Nietzsche*, trans. Walter Kaufmann (New York: Modern Library, 1968), 3. I translate "*ungeheures Bedürfnis*" as "dreadful need," and not as Kaufmann's colloquial "terrific need."

6. Friedrich Nietzsche, "Schopenhauer as Educator," *Untimely Meditations*, trans. R. J. Hollingdale (Cambridge: Cambridge University Press, 1983), 129. Cf. my "Nietzsche's Early Educational Thought," *Journal of Philosophy of Education* 19 (1985): 99–109.

7. Friedrich Nietzsche, *The Wanderer and His Shadow* in *Human, All-too-Human*, 2 vols., trans. R. J. Hollingdale (Cambridge: Cambridge University Press, 1986), 211. And see Nietzsche's description of his "free-thinking" as consisting of "a highly perilous wandering on glaciers and polar seas" (*WS* 21); and also his declaration that *Human*—as a book "for free spirits"—expresses the "inquisitive coldness of the psychologist" (*WS* p, 1).

8. Moreover, he is not blind to the possible abuse of psychologizing by people who might try to evade a direct intellectual confrontation with a viewpoint they find unacceptable (see *WS* 39). The very fact that Nietzsche himself

persistently uses this method indicates, at least, his belief that he does not abuse it. His warning against the danger of genetic fallacy, and his confidence that he has avoided it is even more pronounced in the following passage:

> If there is anything in which I am ahead of all psychologists, it is that my eye is sharper for that most difficult and captious kind of backward inference in which the most mistakes are made: the backward inference from the work to the maker, from the deed to the doer, from the ideal to him who needs it, and from every way of thinking and valuing to the want behind it that prompts it. (*Nietzsche Contra Wagner*, in *The Portable Nietzsche*, trans. Walter Kaufmann [New York: Viking Press. 1968], "We Antipodes"; see also *GS* 370)

9. *HU* 20.

10. With which I had dealt with in chapters 4 and 7 in my *Nietzsche's Enticing Psychology of Power* (Jerusalem and Ames: The Hebrew University Magnes Press and Iowa State University Press, 1989).

11. *HU* 21. Therefore I concur with David E. Cooper's observation in *Authenticity and Learning* (London: Routledge & Kegan Paul, 1983), that "Nietzsche, incidentally, is not guilty of any 'genetic fallacy' (at least in any crude form)," 24.

12. Like, for example section 254 of *The Will to Power*, ed. and trans. Walter Kaufmann and R. J. Hollingdale (New York: Vintage Books, 1968).

13. *HU* 27.

14. *EH*, "Human," 1.

15. *HU* 56 and 35.

16. *HU* 37.

17. *HU* 38.

18. Actually Nietzsche's method of psychologizing aspires also to become a kind of group therapy, treating the cultural neurosis of his period, *HU* 244.

19. *EH*, "Human," 1.

20. *BGE* 260.

21. See part 1 of my *Nietzsche's Enticing Psychology of Power*, and some of the essays of part 2 below.

22. *BGE* 23.

23. *Daybreak*, trans. R. J. Hollingdale (Cambridge: Cambridge University Press, 1982), 65.

24. *D* 30.

25. In his essay "Schopenhauer as Educator," Nietzsche posits the existence of a mental agency functioning as a focus for the process of identification. This agency is also the locus of internalization of the moral patterns and values of our various educators (parents, teachers, historical heroes, and intellectuals):

> Your true nature lies, not concealed deep within you, but immeasurably high above you, or at least above that which you usually take yourself to be. (p. 129)

In an aphorism entitled "Traffic with one's higher self *(Verkehr mit dem höheren Selbst)*" Nietzsche writes:

> Many live in awe of and abasement before their ideal and would like to deny it: they are afraid of their higher self because when it speaks it speaks imperiously. (*HU* 624)

These self-abasing traits of the "higher self" are the origin of our conscience. For this reason Nietzsche thinks it necessary to somewhat weaken and placate this tyrannical faculty, thereby opening a space for the expression of a spontaneous, free, and creative morality.

This idea of the higher self has received far less attention than it deserves. It anticipates Freudian psychoanalytic theory by introducing and defining one of its key terms: the superego (*Über-Ich*). For a more detailed elaboration of this comparison, see chapter 3 of Golomb, *Nietzsche's Enticing Psychology of Power*.

26. *D* 107.

27. *D* 163, 164, 546.

28. *D* 119

29. See also *D* 129, where Nietzsche speaks about "the actual 'conflict of motives':—something quite invisible to us of which we would be quite unconscious."

30. *D* 140.

31. *D* 146.

32. For a more detailed comparison between Nietzsche's notion of the "Dionysian barbarian" and the Freudian *id* see my *Nietzsche's Enticing*, chapter 1. Here it is sufficient to point out that the adjective "*unbewusste*" was initially used by Freud to describe mental elements outside the field of the conscious at any given moment. This usage was merely "descriptive" and not yet clearly topographical. In the ontological structural sense the concept "*das Unbewusste*" began to be used by Freud to describe one of the mental systems, that which contains all the repressed elements whose conscious reappearance is prevented. Freud arrived at this later concept as a consequence of his rich experience in psychoanalytical treatment, which showed him that the mind cannot be reduced to the area of the conscious alone, and that certain of its elements can only be uncovered and revealed when the patient's resistance has been overcome. This brought Freud to postulate the existence of an independent mental realm and to affirm that the unconscious belongs to a special place in the mind, which cannot be described as a secondary consciousness, but as a complete autonomous system containing its own elements, mechanisms, and energy. See Freud, *The Standard Edition of the Complete Psychological Works of Sigmund Freud*, 24 vols., ed. and trans. James Strachey (London: Hogarth Press, 1953–74), 1:233; 2:262ff.; 14:148ff., 181ff.

33. *AC* 54.

34. *BGE* 6.

35. *BGE* 42 (my slightly revised translation). See also the statement that "the genuine philosopher feels the burden and the duty of a hundred attempts (*Versuchen*) and enticements of life (*Versuchungen*)," *BGE* 205 (my translation). Nietzsche's play on the words "*Versuch*" (hypothesis or experiment) and "*Versuchung*" (seduction or enticement) is far from unintentional; it clearly points to one of the most significant features of Nietzsche's psychological philosophy, namely that it is a sophisticated mode of enticement.

36. *BGE* 30.
37. *BGE* 20.
38. *BGE* 6.
39. Witness his biographer Ernst Jones, who in describing the meeting of the Vienna Psychoanalytic Society of October 28, 1908, devoted to the analysis of *Ecce Homo*, remarks that Freud several times referred to Nietzsche as the man who "had a more penetrating knowledge of himself than any other man who ever lived or was likely to live," E. Jones, *Sigmund Freud: Life and Work* (London, 1955), 2:385. Coming from the founder of psychoanalysis this is no small compliment. Moreover, Freud and his followers believe that humans are able to reach deep self-knowledge only by following a long and intensive psychoanalysis. Freud therefore implies in this passage that Nietzsche, who possessed self-knowledge "more than any other man who ever lived" (including Freud himself, who, as is well known, performed self-psychoanalysis while writing *Die Traumdeutung*), had acquired such knowledge through a painful process of introspection, similar to Freud's. That this is the case appears from several comments made by Freud at the same meeting: "He makes a number of brilliant discoveries in himself. . . . The degree of introspection achieved by Nietzsche had never been achieved by anyone, nor is it likely to be reached again." *Minutes of the Vienna Psychoanalytic Society* (New York, 1967), 2:32. And see also Freud's other observation concerning Nietzsche in his 1934 letter: "In my youth he signified a nobility to which I could not attain," quoted in Jones (New York, 1953–57), 3:460.
40. The interlocking of Nietzsche's self-analysis with the wider, theoretical context of his thought is manifested also in the sporadic nature of his writing. His is not an ordered and established style, but rather one resulting from thoughts composed while walking, written in various notebooks, on scraps of paper, in sudden eruptions, and in fragmented flashes of intensive creativity. And see Hollingdale's description of Nietzsche's characteristic solitary monologues in *Nietzsche: The Man and His Philosophy* (London: Routledge & Kegan Paul, 1965), ch. 8.
41. *D* 73. See also *GS* 357; *BGE* 1; and my *In Search of Authenticity from Kierkegaard to Camus* (London and New York: Routledge, 1995), ch. 4.
42. Love of fate. And see *EH*, "Clever," 10 where he says: "My formula for greatness in a human being is *amor fati*: that one wants nothing to be different. . . . Not merely bear what is necessary, still less conceal it . . . but *love* it."
43. *Thus Spoke Zarathustra*, in *The Portable Nietzsche*, pt. I, "On the Three Metamorphoses."
44. Z I, "On the Three Metamorphoses."
45. Z IV, "The Sign."
46. *Twilight of the Idols*,"Maxims," sec. 42 in *The Portable Nietzsche*.
47. Z III, "On the Spirit of Gravity," sec. 2.

PART 1

Psychology in Nietzsche

CHAPTER 1

Psychology as the "Great Hunt"

James P. Cadello

The human soul and its limits, the range of human inner experiences reached so far, the heights, depths, and distances of these experiences, the whole history of the soul *so far* and its yet unexhausted possibilities—that is the predestined hunting ground for a born psychologist and lover of the "great hunt." But how often he has to say to himself in despair: "One hunter! alas, only a single one! and look at this huge forest, this primeval forest!" And then he wishes he had a few hundred helpers and good, well-trained hounds that he could drive into the history of the human soul to round up *his* game. In vain: it has proved to him again and again, thoroughly and bitterly, how helpers and hounds for all things that excite his curiosity cannot be found. What is wrong with sending scholars into new and dangerous hunting grounds, where courage, sense, and subtlety in every way are required, is that they cease to be of any use precisely where the *"great hunt,"* but also the great danger, begins: precisely there they lose their keen eye and nose.

—*Beyond Good and Evil*, 45

Nietzsche's image of psychology as the "great hunt," described in the first aphorism of part 3 of *Beyond Good and Evil*, provokes a series of questions about the character and status of psychology, and derides scholars who have so far investigated the psychological landscape. These scholars fail to be helpers, according to Nietzsche, because when the "great hunt" is to begin, at the point of great danger, these scholars lose their keen eye and nose. But for what do these scholars lose their eye and nose? For "the range of human experiences reached so far, the heights, depths, and distances of these experiences, the whole history of the soul so far and its yet unexhausted possibilities." Let us take a moment to investigate the failure of these scholars, the ones not ready for the great danger, hoping that this may allow us to avoid their failures and locate our prey in the search for the meaning of Nietzsche's "great hunt."

The region of the psychological hunt is for Nietzsche the whole history of the soul so far and its yet unexhausted possibilities. It is all that the human soul has been and is now, as well as all that it could possibly be. Though on the surface this scope seems to coordinate well with many contemporary characterizations of the reach of the psychological enterprise—both popular and scholarly—it may be that Nietzsche is doing more than merely outlining a field that remained (and remains) unexplored. That is, Nietzsche may be suggesting not merely that such ground has not been explored, but rather that it has not been explored in a manner appropriate for one undertaking a great hunt. Does Nietzsche mean to suggest that scholarly hunters of the psychological terrain have lost their keen eye and nose when entering these dangerous new hunting grounds? Nietzsche says: "helpers and hounds for all things that excite his curiosity cannot be found." Do scholarly hunters of this ground fail to become excited by, curious about these hunting grounds—the whole history of the human soul so far and its yet unexhausted possibilities? On the surface anyway, this seems ridiculous: many have been excited by and curious about the history and the future of human inner experience. But Nietzsche does not deny curiosity and excitement on the part of failed hunters; he merely points to a lack of co-workers who are excited by the things about which the born psychologist and lover of the great hunt is curious. Thus, it does not appear that evidence of an excited curiosity for inner human experience is enough to be considered a helper in the great hunt. One must also have a keen eye and nose to have excited one's curiosity about the heights, depths, and distances—the full range—of human experiences. And, Nietzsche offers, such a hunt is dangerous. But what is the character, the nature of the danger associated with the activity of hunting and the grounds to be hunted? We probably have to make some progress in sorting all of this out before we can fathom what Nietzsche might have meant by the great hunt.

Let us return to Nietzsche's text to find a possible helpmeet in our preliminary hunt. The preface and the first aphorisms of part 1 of *Beyond Good and Evil*—in which Nietzsche discusses philosophers, their problems, projects, and prejudices—raise questions and concerns that parallel those located in the aphorism describing the great hunt. Nietzsche begins the preface:

> Supposing truth were a woman—what then? Are there not grounds for the suspicion that all philosophers, insofar as they were dogmatists, have been very inexpert about women? That the gruesome seriousness,

the clumsy obtrusiveness with which they have usually approached truth so far have been awkward and very improper methods for winning a woman's heart?

Next, Nietzsche takes up the prejudices of philosophers, finding the metaphysics of truth to be foremost among these.

> The will to truth which will still tempt us to many a venture, that famous truthfulness of which all philosophers so far have spoken with respect—what question has this will to truth not laid before us? What strange, wicked, questionable questions! This is a long story even now—and yet it seems as if it had scarcely begun. Is it any wonder that we should finally become suspicious, lose patience, turn away impatiently? that we should finally learn from this Sphinx to ask questions, too? *Who* is it really that puts questions to us here? *What* in us really wants "truth"? . . . And though it scarcely seems credible, it finally almost seems to us as if the problem had never been put so far—as if we were the first to see it, fix it with our eyes, and *risk* it. For it does involve a risk, and perhaps there is nothing that is greater. (*BGE* 1)

Numerous resemblances between philosophers pursuing the metaphysics of truth and psychologist-scholars hunting human experience abound. A single of these similarities can be spotted in Nietzsche's charge that philosophers and psychologist-scholars have failed to attain their object. A second correlation can be found in their mutual lack of subtlety, refinement, their weakness of eye and nose that resulted in their failure. And a third likeness is to be found in their shortage of courage, that they have been unable or unwilling to take a risk.

These correspondences alone suggest that Nietzsche's elaboration of the great hunt might overlap in part his discussion of the prejudices of philosophers. Up to this point we have begun with an investigation of the failures of psychologist-scholars in our attempt to understand better Nietzsche's characterization of psychology as the great hunt, and have been drawn in this task to the failures of philosophers; let us pursue some parallels we have located between philosophers as metaphysicians of truth and psychologist-scholars to see how far these will take us in our quest to flesh out Nietzsche's picture of both. Let us first focus on Nietzsche's discussion of philosophers.

In these discussions from the beginning of *Beyond Good and Evil*, one could envision the work of Nietzsche to be not about truth at all. I mean that Nietzsche's just-quoted comments could be seen *neither as concerned with the character of truth, nor as attempting to establish any particular truths*. It seems possible that Nietzsche is not questioning the specific truths that we hold, that is, he is not questioning the value or accuracy of such truths. Nietzsche might not even be questioning the

character of truth, that is, he might be not concerned with the correct-
ness or the appropriateness of the general conceptions of truth with
which we have attempted to establish our particular truths. Rather,
Nietzsche could be proposing to us another set of questions entirely,
questions about the motivation toward truth itself, about the "will to
truth," that impulse that has and "will still tempt us to many a venture,
that famous truthfulness of which all philosophers so far have spoken
with respect." These interrogations undertaken by Nietzsche are questions about philosophers' inclination toward truth, their desire to attain
truth, their valuing of truth itself.

This "will to truth," proposes Nietzsche, "constitutes the typical
prejudgment and prejudice which give away the metaphysician of all
ages" (BGE 2). This seemingly inevitable and unavoidable inclination of
all philosophers, the "will to truth" that stamps all metaphysicians,
what is to be made of it? What questions and problems has it generated—and, *maybe even more interestingly, what questions and problems has it kept suppressed, hidden, completely outside of truth*? How
has the "will to truth" vetoed any *suspicion* that might have arisen
about *the value of truth*? Nietzsche submits—and the truth-status of the
proposal he here puts forward must, like all other philosophical propositions, already be put into question—that the metaphysicians' pre-
formed valuation of/by/through truth has never been questioned, has
never been doubted, has never been that about which philosophers in
their fundamental questioning have thought to question.

> [T]his kind of valuation looms in the background of all [metaphysi-
> cians'] logical procedures; it is on account of this "faith" that they
> trouble themselves about "knowledge," about something that is finally
> baptized solemnly as "the truth." The fundamental faith of the meta-
> physicians is *the faith in opposite values*. It has not even occurred to
> the most cautious among them that one might have a doubt right here
> at the threshold where it was surely most necessary—even if they
> vowed to themselves, "All is to be doubted." (BGE 2)

The metaphysician appears, therefore, as the one who does not question
his faith in opposite values, paramount among these being the opposing
values of "true" and "false." With this suggestion in hand, any number
of potentially troubling inquiries spring forth, queries, because of their
character, for which it is unclear what would or could serve as possible
responses. Do the opposite values "true" and "false" exist? Might the
assertion of such oppositions as "true" and "false," in whatever conceptual form they may take, be already limited, provisional, wholly
unnecessary and superficial perspectives? Might not other values, more
valuable values, be possible if we could learn to see otherwise than

within this and other oppositional pairs? Are such oppositions even oppositions at all, or might the privileged pole—in this particular case, "truth"—always be linked to, tied up with, involved with its opposite, unable to be distinguished from its opposite, maybe even identical with it?

> For all the value that the true, the truthful . . . may deserve, . . . [it] might even be possible that what constitutes the value of these good and revered things is precisely that they are insidiously related, tied to, and involved with these wicked, seemingly opposite things—maybe even one with them in essence. Maybe! (*BGE* 2)

What if any, or all, of these questions had merit? If any, or all, of these suggestions were worthy of consideration?

Before we attempt to respond to such interrogations, we need to attend carefully to what an "acceptable" response might look like, especially in the light of the suspicions these interpolations "between" truth and falsity might raise about the very character of "truth"—the standard in accordance with which one might "normally" be tempted to measure answers. Are rejoinders to the interpolations Nietzsche inserts into the regime of truth to be judged as either "true" or "false"? What other ways might one evaluate responses to Nietzsche's interpositions into the discussion of truth? Do Nietzsche's questions call for an answer, or answers, at all? Does it make sense to ask questions without expecting an answer? Without expecting an answer that could be judged as either "true" or "false"? What would it mean to ask such questions, and what could it mean to *answer* such questions? This much, at least, remains *un*clear; Nietzsche asks:

> But who has the will to concern himself with such dangerous maybes? For that, one really has to wait for the advent of a new species of philosopher, such as have somehow another and converse taste and propensity from those we have known so far—philosophers of the dangerous "maybe" in every sense. (*BGE* 2)

Thus, again to put the questions at hand: Are such questionable questions reasonable? Possible? Can one even formulate such questions sensibly within the language of our oppositionally determined grammar? *Are* such doubts the sort we should follow? *How* do we hunt such "dangerous maybes"? *Can* we track such doubts and questions?

The meaning of this pursuit might well remain unclear as long as we persist as philosophers of the sort we have always been, carrying forward the metaphysics, the logics, the grammars, the discursive practices, of truth and falsity. Could Nietzsche be suggesting to us that these logics, these grammars, themselves already unargued-for arguments, might have been the unconditioned conditions of philosophical possibility as we have known them so far? What if this dominant philosophical prejudice, characterized as faith in the oppositional pair "true" and "false"—a prejudice that has given away the metaphysicians of all ages, that has been fundamental to the determination of philosophical activity, that has determined in advance *how* we can speak and, therefore, *what* we can talk about—what if this prejudice has been no more than a *fore*thought, an *in*expertness, or a *mis*take?

What if we were to pursue such "dangerous maybes"? What would it mean for "truth"? What would result from a questioning of the metaphysicians' faith in their unquestioned valuing of truth? What kinds of blindness might have been caused by the inability on the part of metaphysicians of truth to consider such "dangerous maybes"? Are these the questions Nietzsche addresses to the metaphysicians of truth, to the philosophers who have never questioned their questionable valuing of the truth-falsity opposition?

Thus, maybe neither the falsity of truth, nor the truth of falsity, would be Nietzsche's concern. Maybe the doubtfulness about the opposition of truth and falsity, the questionable questions associated with this pair, and the unreflective value attributed by philosophers to this opposition, prompted Nietzsche to be a philosopher of "dangerous maybes." Maybe! Not truth or a conception of truth, not a solution or an assertion, but "dangerous maybes," questions, possibilities, provocations: What if these were Nietzsche's concerns, the topics of his doubts and suspicions? Not some particular set of truths, but questions about truth's questions, values, silences: what if these are Nietzsche's business? And where, and how, does psychology conceived of as the great hunt fit among all these "dangerous maybes" and questionable question marks?

The relationship of the great hunt to these discussions of truth—the foremost prejudice of philosophers—perhaps may be found two aphorisms after Nietzsche introduces the conception of psychology of the great hunt. In his discussion of saintliness, Nietzsche says:

> The psychology we have had so far suffered shipwreck at this point: wasn't this chiefly because it had placed itself under the dominion of morals, because it, too, *believed* in opposite moral values and saw, read, *interpreted* these opposites into the texts and facts? (*BGE* 47)

The continuity at this point is evident; the metaphysical faith of philosophers and the moral faith of psychologists—a coincidence made unmistakable by a shared faith in opposite values—is declared by Nietzsche to be the prejudice that has produced the shipwreck of psychology. Thus, the traditional philosopher is like the traditional psychologist: both have a faith in opposite values, both have been influenced by the grammar and logic of opposition, both suffer from the metaphysical prejudice. Of the philosopher as metaphysician, Nietzsche says:

> For one may doubt, first, whether there are any opposites at all, and secondly whether these popular valuations and opposite values on which the metaphysicians put their seal, are perhaps not merely foreground estimates, only provisional perspectives, perhaps even from some nook, perhaps from below, frog perspectives. (*BGE* 2)

Of the psychologist-scholar unwilling or unable to undertake the great hunt, Nietzsche says:

> Countless dark bodies are to be *inferred* beside the sun—and we shall never see them. Among ourselves, this is a parable; and a psychologist of morals reads the whole writing of the stars only as a parable- and sign-language which can be used to bury much in silence. (*BGE* 196)

Like the metaphysician, the psychologist-scholar develops a language of inference, of light and dark bodies whose co-presence is never fully conspicuous, and whose existence as co-present is, therefore, always only inferred. Requisite to the psychologist-scholar—who is fearful of the dangers associated with the great hunt—is developing and implementing the moral language of oppositions. For the psychologist-scholar, this is the language of light and dark, apparent and hidden, healthy and sick, presence and absence, each of which is used to bury much of the full range of human inner experience in silence. Nietzsche does not suggest here that the moral language of psychology is in fact immoral: that is, he does not assert that the language of psychology as we have known it so far has failed because it has not sufficiently brought to light the dark and hidden dimensions of human inner life that remain secluded and out of reach. Nor does Nietzsche suggest that a remoralization of psychology is the key to finally completing the psychological task of bringing light to the bowels of the soul, and composing whole the dark and the light comprising the complex phenomena of inner experience. Such typifications of psychological knots and puzzles stem from the psychologist-scholars who hopefully and confidently invoke oppositional parable- and sign-languages intended to illuminate and elaborate the shining suns and the darkest bodies of the psychic solar system. The failure of the psychologist-scholars who speaks parable- and sign-languages is not that they have not placed all aspects of inner life in "right order," is not that they have gotten something "wrong." The psychologist-scholars fail in speaking the moral-psychological language unquestioningly taken over from the metaphysics of truth. For Nietzsche, the unquestioned faith in opposite values evidenced by psychologist-scholars is still moral;

to one with keen eye and nose, the moral-psychological language manifesting the faith of psychologist-scholars appears to bury the "immense and almost new domain of dangerous insights" open to psychology. This may shed light on Nietzsche's proclamation: "All psychology so far has got stuck in moral prejudices and fears; it has not dared to descend into the depths" (23).

But what exactly does Nietzsche mean by this? What does he have in mind when he declares that, free of morality and the oppositional valuations characteristic of it, "psychology is now again the path to the fundamental problems"?

> To understand [psychology] as morphology and *the doctrine of the development of the will to power*, as I do—nobody has even come close to doing this even in thought—insofar as it is permissible to recognize in what has been written so far a symptom of what has so far been kept silent. The power of moral prejudices has penetrated deeply into the most spiritual world, which would seem to be the coldest and most devoid of propositions, and has obviously operated in an injurious, inhibiting, blinding, and distorting manner. (*BGE* 23)

Psychology as the great hunt, psychology that pushes past moral prejudices to the depths, nonoppositional psychology that is fundamental—as morphology and the development of the will to power. At present, only the latter of these will be taken up explicitly.

Psychology as the doctrine of the development of the will to power. What does this mean? Despite the attempts that have been made by scholars of Nietzsche to present will to power in metaphysical nomenclature, Nietzsche often seeks to describe will to power in conflicting, contradictory terms that challenge the authority of the truth-falsity opposition. Nietzsche's conflictual play of contradictions can only take place within the sphere determined by the oppositional pair "true" and "false"—for without this discord no contradiction, no conflict could appear. Yet the oppositional pair, of which truth has traditionally held sway, does not control Nietzsche's play of opposites, does not determine or resolve the play. In short, "truth" does not master Nietzsche's discussions. Neither does the "false" serve as Nietzsche's substitute for "truth," for such a move would reverse, and thereby reinscribe, the oppositional expectations and demands at which Nietzsche looks warily. Contrary to those who have sought to control Nietzsche's texts by the moral-metaphysical logic and grammar about which Nietzsche ceaselessly raises questions and suspicions, I offer that there is much to suggest the oppositional pair "true" and "false" inherited by Nietzsche from the moral-metaphysical legacy does not determine for him the system of relations according to which decisions must be made. This pair sets out one of the many oppositional conditions of positive interpretation in which Nietzsche speculates that the revered, privileged member of the pair (or the dishonored, diminished member—it makes no difference) is "insidiously related to, tied to, and involved with [its] wicked, seemingly opposite . . . —maybe even one with [it] in essence" (*BGE* 2). Positive interpretation seeks not the attainment of truth, but the never-ending rend(er)ing of possibilities permitted, forced, required by the truth-falsity opposition. And by these means does Nietzsche discuss the development of will to power, which must undermine the undisputed confidence one might have in it as a meaningful, identifiable, legitimate grounding principle.

Perhaps will to power for Nietzsche represents his mockingly moral attempt to derive several kinds of causality from a single one in order to explain our entire instinctive life as the development and ramification of one basic form of the will: "suppose all organic functions could be traced back to this will to power and one could also find in it the solution of the problem of procreation and nourishment—it is *one* problem—then one would have gained the right to determine *all* efficient force univocally as—*will to power*" (*BGE* 36). Might will to power be Nietzsche's parodic postulation of the monster of energy without beginning or end, that is characterized not by increase or decrease but transformation, at all times one and many, simultaneously increasing and decreasing, flowing apart and rushing together, concurrently simple and complex, self-contradictory and self-identical?[1] But such a self-identical will to power is marked only by its self-contradictory nature; it is a fundamental reality that is impossible; the logic of will to power is paralogical. Nietzsche is explicit: will to power represents the culmination of his effort to push the metaphysical enterprise to its ultimate conclusion; it is the accumulation of all the oppositions that have marked the moral history of philosophical metaphysics—including efforts of the psychologist-scholar—and portrays their preposterous reconciliation. Will to power is a conclusion reached not because Nietzsche's sagacity allows him to overcome philosophy in the sense of finally getting the house of metaphysics in order. Instead, it is the climax of metaphysics as we have come to have it present itself to us *today*; it is a conclusion reached because the history of metaphysics has compelled it. And as a conclusion, a product, a finality, a foundational cause, will to power is foolishness, *niaiserie*.

> Not to assume several kinds of causality until the experiment of making do with a single one has been pushed to its limit (*to the point of nonsense, if I may say so*)—that is a moral of method which one may not shirk today. Suppose, finally, we succeeded in explaining our entire instinctive life as the development and ramification of *one* basic form

of the will the world defined and determined according to its "intelligible character"—it would be "will to power" and nothing else. (36, first italics mine)

Will to power, says Nietzsche, is the end of this nonsense in its most inevitably extreme form, the moral method of metaphysics unfolded to its acme. The moral oppositional language of philosophy is not rejected—what would that mean? another opposition?!—but pushed to its utmost limit. The binarisms of philosophy and psychology are overcome, but not in the sense that they are surpassed; rather, their inevitable conflation and mutual implication are recognized as the outcome and upshot of the moral-metaphysical enterprise. But this does not mean such oppositions are left behind, that they could be left behind: the splits evidenced in such talk, such as past/future, old/new, if taken seriously, reconstitute and re-commend the moral valuations that have marked the tradition that, according to Nietzsche, incessantly plays itself out in will to power. *Thus, will to power does not transcend the history of metaphysics, but is the culmination of its logic. It cannot exceed metaphysics, but it does not, cannot have the requisite faith in metaphysics.* Yet it is this will to power, once understood (really? maybe!), which will allow us to avoid becoming stuck in moral prejudices and fears, that will allow us to descend to the depths of psychology, to pursue the great hunt.

So for Nietzsche psychology must be understood as development of will to power, even if it is absurd and absent, in order "to recognize in what has been written so far a symptom of what has been kept silent." The moral prejudices that have marked philosophy and psychology, first and foremost among these being the faith in opposite values, "has obviously operated in an injurious, inhibiting, blinding, and distorting manner." Psychology must be grasped as the development of will to power if the silences that have marked psychology, silences that are the symptoms of oppositional thinking, are to be seen as silences. Psychology as the great hunt, psychology as the development of will to power: these are not "solutions" to the "problems" of psychology; these are not opposed to "wrong" answers to questions about the nature of the psyche or presented as "alternative" conceptions of the psychological enterprise that better capture the inner workings of human experience. Psychology as the great hunt is an interpretive strategy, giving one the keen eye and nose both to seek out the history of the human soul that has been obscured by our moral prejudices and to investigate the yet unexhausted possibilities of human experience. Psychology as the development of will to power descends into the depths not in the sense of locating a deep structure of human psychic life or burrowing beneath the superficial accounts that have so far been given in order to unearth a more profound account of conscious and unconscious phenomena. Instead, Nietzsche's psychology appears as an invitation to positive readings and multiple interpretations, to multiform play of self-referring inevitabilities, to suspicious questioning of the logics, grammars, and truths that have so far claimed authority over thought. Even the tendency to codify his own psychological conceptions is resisted by Nietzsche: "yet even this hypothesis is far from being the strangest and most painful in this immense and almost new domain of dangerous insights" (*BGE* 23). Even will to power as the nonsensical "ground" of positive interpretation circles back upon itself, and is revealed to be at odds with itself: "Supposing that this also is only an interpretation—and you will be eager enough to make this objection?—well, so much the better" (*BGE* 22).

Nietzsche's psychology of the great hunt does not attempt to cancel the oppositional thinking that has characterized the moral-metaphysical projects of philosophy and psychology up to this point. Such a cancellation and exceeding of the moral-metaphysical enterprise would be no more than its reconstitution. The reversal of metaphysics remains metaphysics. Rather, the great hunt offers one of many prototypes to be found in Nietzsche, models that investigate the appearance of truth as a symptom, that seek to displace entrenched moral-metaphysical habits by means of active reinterpretation. Without believing it possible to extricate himself from oppositional interpretation, Nietzsche sought to subvert the moral-metaphysical faith that contrary values could be ranked on the basis of whether or not they adequately demarcated significant, identifiable differences. A psychology that is able to descend to the depths is so because it does not mistake symptomatology for truth. But neither does Nietzsche's psychology attain truth: the great hunt is positive interpretation, actively exchanging the moral-metaphysical task for interminable interpreting, ceaseless explicating, and unrelenting decoding. Confidence in the authority of moral-metaphysical dualisms—of which the truth-falsity binarism is paramount—to announce reality is relinquished. Oppositions lacking ground, images wanting frames— these stamp Nietzsche's "depth," which is unhinged from the symptomatology of moral-metaphysical psychology.

The psychologist-scholar who seeks to understand Nietzsche in the moral-metaphysical tradition has been, and continues to be, dominant among Nietzsche commentators. Most scholars continue to find some kind of truth in what Nietzsche had to say about this or that psychological concept, for example health[2] or *ressentiment*.[3] Others have taken up the whole of his psychology and offered comprehensive accounts of Nietzsche's views about "burgeoning psychological health," which is the product of a "self-discipline" and control that will result in a life "spontaneously" coordinated and moving "in the appropriate ways."[4] Unlike the account I have tendered, these thinkers are looking for the genuine meaning of Nietzsche's texts, for the psychological truths they might bear. As psychologist-scholars and moral-metaphysicians they seek to discover Nietzsche down paths cut between the trees of normal and abnormal, healthy and sick, noble morality and slave morality, conscious and unconscious, manifest and subterranean. These contraries are used by the psychologist-scholar and moral-metaphysician supposedly to establish the foundations of personal identity; however, in Nietzsche's words, these ventures "bury in silence" what he calls the "fundamental problems" of psychology. Crusades for the truths of psychology are disabled through Nietzsche's conception of psychology as the great hunt.

I have chosen to see Nietzsche slip between truth and falsity, neither in nor out of the moral-metaphysical tradition he appropriates, critiques, and shows to be laced with inevitable interdependencies and perpetual mutual implications. Nietzsche, depicted as the great hunter, undertakes the dissipation and proliferation of psychological causes. The great hunt multiplies the numerous intersections and competitions that have "so far been kept silent" by the usual moral-metaphysical prejudices of psychologist-scholars. The great hunt seeks its prey both *in what it has been impossible to know about what we've been and who we are*, and *in the possibilities of no longer being who we are, thinking as we do, or doing what we've done*. The psychology of the great hunt does not attempt to sort out correctly or finally who we are or how we are constituted and composed psychologically; it gives up the quest for psychological identity, sacrificing the belief that there is a psychic world that can be made present, accessible, attainable, available, that can be exposed and decisively secured by the supposedly appropriate moral-metaphysical (set of) binarisms used to access it.

The great hunt is experiential, but also experimental. That is, it is transformative, but not just in the sense of describing psychic life as being able to transform itself. Such a description, if it claims to truthfully characterize human inner experience as transformative, reinscribes moral-metaphysical tendencies in the form of philosophical and psychological prejudices. My proposal is that Nietzsche risks the very transformation of philosophy and psychology themselves, of the moral-metaphysical campaign, not by offering options to be considered as alternatives to already established methods, but by exploring aspects of inner experience that have been made indefinite or indistinct by the moral-metaphysical prejudices, by investigating the yet unexhausted possibilities of human experience inaccessible to psychologist-scholars.

These, then, are the fundamental problems laid bare by the psychology of the great hunt, namely, *the problems traced by psychology*, the problematic character of psychology itself, a problem that is kept silent so long as the psychologist-scholar strives to control and synthesize inner experience by any series of moral-metaphysical contraries. Thus, the psychologist of the great hunt attempts the dislocation of traditional psychology, ascertaining the chicanery involved in all bids to master, synthesize, enclose, or encapsulate the truth of psychic life by any set of conceptual oppositions. The great hunt is a matter of inquisitiveness and novelty, of possibility and playfulness, and of antagonisms not governed by the order or rule of truth.

I'd like to conclude by returning to an earlier issue: the fear of the psychologist-scholar. The fears generated in the sense-impaired moral-metaphysician are a consequence of the danger associated with the great hunt; its playful attitude lacks appropriate respect for the reign of truth. This danger, however, appears as a threat only to those who are involved with and who lay claim to the authoritative control of the moral-metaphysical tradition. But such control wavers even today, made evident by the appearance of a dangerous curiosity that is increasingly perceived as threatening by defenders of the metaphysics of truth. Nietzsche is not oblivious to all of this. Closing the aphorism in which he discusses the great hunt, Nietzsche contrasts his own psychological enterprise and attitude with those psychologist-scholars who lack the keen eye and nose for the dangerous hunt where courage, sense, and subtlety are required. Recognizing fears and perceived threats, though showing only a taunting respect for them, in obvious irony Nietzsche concludes:

> But a curiosity of my type remains after all the most agreeable of all vices—sorry, I meant to say: the love of truth has its reward in heaven and even on earth. (*BGE* 45)

NOTES

1. Friedrich Nietzsche, *The Will to Power,* trans. Walter Kaufmann and R. J. Hollingdale (New York: Vintage, 1967), 1067 and elsewhere throughout Nietzsche's works.

2. Bernd Magnus, "Self-Consuming Concepts," *International Studies in Philosophy* 21.2 (1989), and "Deification of the Commonplace: *Twilight of the Idols,*" in *Reading Nietzsche,* ed. Robert Solomon and Kathleen Higgins (New York: Oxford University Press, 1988).

3. Rudiger Bittner, "*Ressentiment,*" in *Nietzsche, Genealogy, Morality,* ed. Richard Schacht (Berkeley: University of California Press, 1994).

4. Graham Parkes, *Composing the Soul* (Chicago: University of Chicago Press, 1994), specifically 346–62.

CHAPTER 2

Nietzsche and Psychoanalysis: From Eternal Return to Compulsive Repetition and Beyond

Daniel Chapelle

Nietzsche's thought of the eternal return of all things, is first introduced in aphorism 341 of *The Gay Science*: "This life as you now live it and have lived it, you will have to live once more and innumerable times more; and there will be nothing new in it."[1] This thought is arguably, and according to Nietzsche himself, the central and most significant notion in his writings. As a thought that challenged its thinker it also became Nietzsche's personal destiny, something he took upon himself as his historical task. And as a thought that, in Nietzsche's own assessment, divides history in half, overcoming everything that came before it, all the way back to Heraclitus, and opening up a new historical horizon for a wholly new kind of human being and human existence, it is indeed as powerful as dynamite, as he sometimes liked to think of himself. At the level of the West's religious history it is as potentially disturbing as the teachings of an antichrist who teaches that God is dead are bound to be to a civilization that is Judeo-Christian to the bone. Lastly, as a topic of academic reflection and scholarly commentary it is, to say the least, a thorny matter. Everything about it gets intertwined with everything else in Nietzsche, and it can easily sting and draw blood from whoever takes it up. Many Nietzsche commentators have tried to argue, perhaps for that very reason, that it can and should be dismissed as much ado about nothing, an idea out of left field with little, if any, ultimate significance.

Dismissing the thought in this manner can be done, and not without seeming successful, by demonstrating that it is logically untenable or empirically unverifiable or practically irrelevant even if it were proven possible or true. It must be admitted here, though, that Nietzsche himself never reached a point, neither in his published writings nor in his privately penned reflections, of being satisfied with the way he had worked out what had often seemed to him the great promise of a new philosophy based on eternal return. As he wrote in a letter to his friend Franz Overbeck, dated March 8, 1884: "I have had to produce courage for myself since discouragement approached me from all sides: courage to bear that thought. For I am still far from able to speak and describe it. *If it is true*—or rather, if it is believed to be true then everything changes and turns around and all previous values are devalued."[2] Nietzsche's remaining productive years, after this confession, did not bring him closer to finishing the task. So if academic philosophy has not taken eternal return far beyond the point where Nietzsche himself left it, that should perhaps come as no surprise.

Elsewhere, in my book on *Nietzsche and Psychoanalysis*,[3] I have argued in detail that the thought of eternal return is indeed acutely relevant and is, just as Nietzsche claimed, of rather momentous significance. Specifically, I have argued that the whole psychology of unconsciously, compulsively repeated experience patterns—which is the primary source of anguish that brings people all over the world to psychotherapists' offices—is an arena in everyday life where the whole of Nietzsche's philosophy of eternal return is made relevant by being enacted in the lives of everyday men and women. Wherever and whenever unconscious, compulsive repetition of fixed experience patterns is thought to be at play, there Nietzsche's philosophy of eternal return is at work—with all the specifically philosophic implications that go hand in hand with it.

This psychology of the so-called "repetition compulsion" includes most prominently the insights of Freudian psychoanalysis and those of its derivatives that remain focused on the fixed patterns inherent in every individual's personal unconsciousness. But beyond that it also includes the Jungian and post-Jungian psychology of collective or archetypal themes of meaningfulness that are spontaneously repeated everywhere in the lives of individuals and throughout the world's endlessly varied cultures and subcultures.

When viewed in the light of Nietzsche's philosophy of eternal return this entire psychology of spontaneous and inescapable unconscious repetition acquires the significance of a concretely enacted exercise in philosophizing in a Nietzschean key, in Nietzschean terms, and on Nietzschean themes. Or again, and cast in the form of Nietzsche's own way of thinking, by being made practically relevant, in the form of a psychology of repetition in the lives of everyday men and women, the philosophy of the eternal return of all things becomes a truth people can and do live by. Eternal return thus becomes a relevant myth that shapes and that informs human lives—with myth understood not as fallacy to be corrected but as inherent structure of intelligibility and meaningfulness.

Viewed in this manner a psychotherapy that concerns itself with unconscious and compulsive repetition becomes a process of philosophizing based on arguments found in the patient's personal life. This philosophizing starts off at the level of private experiences and everyday events, but it ultimately reaches for a level of significance that, like Nietzsche's thought, involves nothing less than the history of Western philosophic thought. Nietzschean thought is thereby made acutely and concretely relevant. Conversely, every man and woman in the grip of unconscious, compulsive repetition—and that means all of us, for it is an essential part of ordinary life as well, not just of the life of the patient in treatment—thereby becomes what he or she always was and is and will be in any case, a world philosopher.

Put yet another way, treating the life of unconsciously repeated fixed patterns of experience in a Freudian, post-Freudian, Jungian or post-Jungian way becomes a case of philosophizing in a manner that, following the movements of Nietzsche's thought, recapitulates in the life of the individual the collective history of Western philosophic tradition, from Heraclitus through Judeo-Christendom and into the postmodernism that is our present cultural, philosophic, and psychological heritage, destiny, task, and opportunity.

Eternal return is nothing if not a matter of the ultimate valuation of existence. As Nietzsche puts it: "The question in each and every thing, 'Do you desire this once more and innumerable times more?' would lie upon your actions as the greatest weight."[4] The implication is momentous: "How well disposed would you have to become to yourself and to life to crave nothing more fervently than this ultimate eternal confirmation and seal?"[5] There are essentially only two possible responses. Either you "throw yourself down and gnash your teeth and curse the demon" who proposes the thought of eternal return, or because of some "tremendous moment" or other you have once experienced you want to say to the demon: "You are a god and never have I heard anything more divine."[6] Either way: "If this thought gained possession of you, it would change you as you are or perhaps crush you."[7] Just think: "The eternal hourglass of existence is turned upside down again and again, and you with it, speck of dust."[8] You would indeed have to value existence *as is*, whatever that involves in your particular case and case history, in an affirmative manner, and without wanting to change anything about it, if the thought of eternal return is to be at all bearable, let alone desirable, as desirable as "the ultimate confirmation and seal?" By implication—

and this is where Nietzsche and his Zarathustra become profoundly and essentially antichrist—eternal return would do nothing less than challenge the fundamental value judgment inherent in Judeo-Christendom. For that value judgment holds that the world as it has been and is and will be is simply not good enough, is indeed so pathetically imperfect that it needs the miracle of redemption by external and divine means.

The notion of not seeking to change life as is, and of seeking instead to affirm things as they are and have been and will be, acquires a special significance in the case of modern psychotherapy. For in general almost all of modern humanity's activities, but psychotherapy in particular, are driven by the dream of change. And all this aspiring toward change is done in the name of the improvement of humankind or of life or of the world. Such an enterprise seems noble enough in itself, so that, surely, it requires no justification. And yet there is perhaps nothing more demoralizing than the notion that something has to be changed and improved first before it can be good enough. For such a notion implies that things are ultimately not valuable in themselves as they are and have been and will likely be. Ultimate positive value, held to be inherently missing from them, needs to be bestowed on them from the outside, and through a process that changes them.

Nietzsche refers to this implied negative value judgment as a spirit of slander against existence, a spirit of fundamental hatred against life itself. Hence the great agenda he sets for himself: to work out a philosophy, based on the thought of the eternal return of all things, that would overcome the negative valuation of existence and its hatred of life. It is in this spirit, and with this agenda in mind, that he has his Zarathustra, the teacher of eternal return, say: "To be sure: except ye become as little children, ye shall not enter into *that* kingdom of heaven. (And Zarathustra pointed upward with his hand.) But we have no wish whatever to enter into the kingdom of heaven: we have become man—*so we want the earth.*"[9]

Henry David Thoreau wrote: "Beware of all enterprises that require new clothes."[10] This eminently practical and decidedly unphilosophic sounding advice is perfectly in line with Nietzsche's less than immediately practical thought, and psychotherapy theorists ought to bear it in mind. For in their enthusiasm to help improve humankind and life, and in their implicitly disapproving recommendation that people change and improve themselves in order to undertake the enterprise of life as it were with "new clothes," they participate in the great slander against existence as it is, which means they slander life itself. So the obsession with changing lives for the better that keeps the psychotherapy industry going is, quite paradoxically, life's worst enemy. This means nothing less than that the whole psychotherapy enterprise has to be rethought to such a profound depth that the very value in the idea of changing things for the better is itself re-evaluated. This can be done with the help of Nietzsche's formula of eternal return.

Rethinking psychotherapy at this fundamental level, under the sign of the myth of eternal return, can be done by revisioning it in the light of what in Nietzsche appears as *"amor fati."*[11] *Amor fati*—literally the "love of fate"—is, at the practical level, the love of whatever is *as it is* and *for the sake of the way it is.* And this is Nietzsche's great new year's resolution, a resolution not only for *Herr Nietzsche* at the beginning of a new calendar year but for an altogether new form of human life in a new world with a new philosophic horizon and future. In Nietzsche's words: "I want to learn more and more to see as beautiful what is necessary in things; then I shall be one of those who make things beautiful. *Amor fati*: let that be my love henceforth! I do not want to wage war against what is ugly. I do not want to accuse. I do not even want to accuse those who accuse. . . . And all in all and on the whole: some day I wish to be only a Yes-sayer."[12]

By a Yes-sayer he means an altogether new kind of human being, a new philosophic and psychological species that has learned to affirm all of existence *on its own terms and its own terms only*, without the need for or the introduction of any kind of redemption from without.

The significance of such a Yes-saying spirit is perhaps best appreciated in the light of a thought that appears in the pre-Socratic philosopher Heraclitus. Nietzsche thought of Heraclitus as the only figure in Western history who may perhaps have appreciated some of the momentous matters associated with a philosophy based on eternal return. Heraclitus said that, to the gods, all things are beautiful, and that it is men who consider some things beautiful and others ugly. By converse implication this says that life on earth can begin to look, and therefore be, divine only to the extent that the human, all too human dichotomy of beautiful versus ugly, of good versus evil, can be overcome. It is the formula of eternal return that would accomplish this affirmation of life that reaches beyond even the very category of good and evil. In the end this means overcoming the division that separates human from divine, sacred from profane. For Nietzsche's so-called "overcoming" of Platonism is not so much for the sake of overcoming the Platonic epistemology in Plato but the hatred of life that puts all divinity or sacredness at such a great and unbridgeable distance from the earth that it is no longer relevant to it due to practical indifference.

Making *amor fati* into an operational formula for a psychotherapy based on eternal return is done by seeing as beautiful what is necessary in things. This requires an understanding of what Nietzsche means by necessity. Necessity, in Nietzsche, is antiteleological: he rejects any and all notions according to which the value of a thing or event derives from the goal or purpose or end—that is, the *telos*—it serves. Goals and purposes and ends, so he suggests, do not exist per se but are man-made illusions: "We have invented the concept 'end': in reality there is no end."[13] Goals, purposes, and ends must be rejected because they serve as a means of devaluating events or processes as unjustified on their own terms and as needing to be justified by something that is external to them. Nor is necessity something that must be understood as a regulative principle existing somewhere, and somehow, outside the world and independently of it: "'Necessity' not in the shape of an overreaching, dominating total force, or that of a prime mover. . . . To this end it is necessary to deny a total consciousness of becoming, a 'God'."[14] Yet necessity is not to be viewed as a regulative principle existing objectively inside the world and its history either: "Necessity is not a fact but an interpretation."[15] This rejection of an earthly and historical regulative principle that can be pointed at as an objective fact includes as well the rejection of causality, on which the West, especially the rational and scientific West, has become so dependent.

Nietzsche refutes the idea of causation by rejecting the habit of separating every event or deed from the agent or doer performing the deed. It is "this ancient mythology"—the habit of separating the doer from the deed, or the subject from its predicate—"that established the belief in 'cause and effect'."[16] For the belief in cause and effect is itself a result of "the metaphysics of language."[17] "Everywhere it sees a doer and doing; it believes in will as the cause; it believes in the ego, in the ego as being, in the ego as substance, and it projects this faith in the ego-substance upon all things."[18]

By supplying a metaphysics of doer and deed, language answers a deeper human need, the need to give to individual human lives a sense of permanence, a sense of a constant ego. And this is itself a reflection of what is at the heart of the devaluation of existence: the "ill will against time and its 'It was,'"[19] by which Nietzsche means the resentment against the temporality in all things of this world. But just as Nietzsche rejects the metaphysics that separates deed and doer, he also rejects the idea of a permanent and essential ego that is associated with it: "As for the *ego*! That becomes a fable, a fiction, a play on words."[20] And he concludes: "There are neither causes nor effects. Linguistically we do not know how to rid ourselves of them. But that does not matter."[21] This has a further implication. By rejecting causality Nietzsche also rejects every form of mechanistic determinism, which rests on it, and which is dismissed as "the principle of the greatest possible stupidity."[22] Overall the rejection of causality deals a blow to the capacity to explain anything at all: "One cannot 'explain' . . . one has lost the belief in being able to explain at all, and admits . . . that description and not explanation is all that is possible."²³ Or, all we can say is that things are as they are because that is how they are.

If necessity is not an objectively given fact but an interpretation, and if it lies neither in an overreaching force that belongs outside the world, nor in causality and mechanistic determinism, where then does it lie for Nietzsche? His answer is essentially this: in the thing itself, and it is reflected in the eye of the beholder. Ultimately the necessity of a thing or event is equated with and reflected in the value it holds *in the way it is and for the way it is.* Value, understood as inherent necessity, is any thing's or event's bottom-line fact and truth because man is, first and last, the creature that *esteems*: "To esteem is to create: hear this, you creators! Esteeming itself is of all esteemed things the most estimable treasure. Through esteeming alone is there value: and without esteeming, the nut of existence would be hollow."²⁴ At the practical level of living, the necessity or value of a thing or event is reflected in the love declaration of *amor fati.* This love declaration originates in a spirit of affirmation that is best summed up in the words of Zarathustra, the teacher of eternal return. No matter what the world throws at him, for the sake of its ultimate valuation—a valuation that is to be based on affirmation—he learns to respond with these words: "But thus I willed it. . . . But thus I will it; thus shall I will it."²⁵ By willing backward in order to will forward the new species of man, with the help of the formula of *amor fati,* turns eternal return into a myth to believe in and live by.

What makes it possible for modern humans to experience the thought of eternal return as an actual occurrence and reality is what Freud describes in his psychoanalysis of "The Uncanny" (*Das Unheimliche*).²⁶ Something is uncanny, Freud writes, when it involves the double impression of being at the same time new yet also familiar but old and forgotten and associated with things that had been pushed out of consciousness a long time ago. Freud's analysis of the uncanny touches upon a number of seemingly unrelated areas. These include findings from clinical psychology but also from such other fields as etymology, early childhood development, and beliefs in magical sources of meaningfulness such as found in superstitions of all kinds, whether of ancient peoples, of so-called primitive tribes, or of contemporary persons. In each case, and cutting across all areas where the uncanny occurs, there is the same finding. Something appears uncanny when an old and forgotten or otherwise abandoned event or experience or thought or impression seems to have come to life again in the form of a new and at first sight unrelated and possibly even totally dissimilar contemporary situation.

The uncanny is easily exemplified by the case of what occurs in transference, which makes it particularly relevant in the context of a study of Nietzsche's eternal return and the tradition of depth psychology. Transference, so Freud and Jung already agreed in their first meeting in 1907, is not merely a secondary phenomenon of analytic therapy but its very essence, its alpha and omega.[27] Even when Jung later departed from Freudian theory to go his own way he maintained the emphasis on transference as the essential substance, if not method, of therapeutic activity.[28] As Paul Ricoeur writes, in *Freud and Philosophy*, it is "not an accidental part of the cure, but its necessary path."[29] Freud himself goes so far as to say that the presence or absence of transference makes the difference between truly psychoanalytic treatment and nonpsychoanalytic treatment.[30] In other words, the occurrence of transference is what defines treatment of unconsciousness.

Ricoeur succinctly describes transference as the process in the relationship between psychotherapist and patient "in the course of which the patient repeats, in the artificial situation of analysis, important and meaningful episodes of his affective life."[31] *It is the process in which individual history is compelled to repeat itself within the artificial containment of the therapeutic situation.* Here then, in the world of transference and resistance, eternal return is not only a fact of life but the fundamental fact, the bottom-line reality, both in theory and as a concrete experience. It confirms what the Nietzschean demon who proposes the thought of eternal return says: "This life as you now live it and have lived it, you will have to live once more and innumerable times more . . . every pain and every joy and every thought and sigh and everything unutterably small or great in your life will have to return to you."[32] Freud emphasizes the striking sense of complete identity between every repetition and that which it repeats.[33] He also speaks of new editions of old history.[34] Thus if the repetition compulsion that animates transference and that makes for its uncanniness could be given a voice it might say, as if with Zarathustra's words: "I come again, with this sun, with this earth, with this eagle, with this serpent—not to a new life or a better life or a similar life; I come back eternally to this same, selfsame life, in what is greatest and in what is smallest, to teach again the eternal recurrence of all things."[35]

Here then, in the uncanny repetition compulsion of transference, we are, as if by some sort of magic, transported into an altogether different cosmic dimension. For time—which for modern human beings in their daily lives exists only as a linear progression, and which modern human beings typically cannot even imagine otherwise—is, in the repetition compulsion of transference, thwarted in its linearity. It suddenly becomes a circular process that seems to go nowhere but around and around. Things and events from personal history now appear to have led nowhere but to their own inevitable recurrence. Transference, in its uncanny repetition compulsion, captures persons and in dramas that have nothing but themselves and their eternal recurrence for ultimate destination and destiny.

But it is not only at the descriptive level that the repetition compulsion of transference enacts Nietzsche's thought of eternal return. At the dynamic level as well the similarity exists. For just as Nietzsche's philosophy of eternal return is preoccupied with overcoming the long philosophic tradition of resentment against the passage of time, and with the devaluation of everything of this immanent world because of its impermanence, so too is the psychology of unconscious repetition in transference intimately related to the discovery of mortality, and especially to the repression of that discovery. To be precise, in transference the patient unconsciously fights against the conscious memory of the traumatic and repressed experience that presented him with the discovery that he is vulnerable and that his existence can be threatened—not only with pain but ultimately with the ultimate pain, namely, annihilation. For what is most traumatic about so-called trauma is the message of mortality it brings home. And what is most repressive about the repression that would wipe out any and all recollection of the pain of trauma is the refusal to accept the fact of death. In every unconscious repetition in transference this scenario of the discovery of impermanence and of that discovery's repression is repeated.

And just as Nietzsche's thought of eternal return is aimed at overcoming the philosophic resentment of "ill will against time and its 'it was,'" so too is the therapy process of transference analysis aimed at overcoming the repression of the discovery of mortality. For this is ultimately the painstaking work of overcoming repression: to become once more fully cognizant, and, for the first time, tolerant, of the painful fact of vulnerability, which is the harbinger of the ultimate in vulnerability, one's inevitable annihilation.

In his autobiographical *Ecce Homo* Nietzsche describes his and Zarathustra's sense of their task: "Zarathustra once defines, quite strictly, his task—it is mine too—and there is no mistaking his meaning: he says Yes to the point of justifying, of redeeming all of the past."[36] This formulation may well serve as a working definition of the task psychoanalysis and its derivatives set for themselves. Thus Nietzsche's philosophy of eternal return and the psychological analysis of the repetition compulsion in transference aim at the same transformation. Without wanting or trying to change anything that was or is or will be, both would achieve a revaluation of the value judgment placed on the experience of the past, and of the negative value judgment placed on the passage of time. Both would try to end up with a revaluation of all that was and is and will be that is affirmative and nothing but affirmative.

Looking at the psychological analysis of the repetition compulsion in the light of Nietzsche's thought of eternal return gives a new meaning to the notion of psychological convalescence through psychotherapy. For the definition of psychological convalescence is now broadened beyond the scope of removing psychopathological symptoms, and also beyond any limits of significance and relevance that are set by uniquely individual life history. It now not only addresses the affective wound associated with impermanence in the life of the individual. Even at the microcosmic level of the individual's life it now also addresses the cultural, historical, and philosophic *pathos* of metaphysical resentment about life as permanent impermanence that marks the entire tradition of Western humanity's reflection.

From a philosophy and a psychology of eternal return it takes only a small step to arrive at a cosmology of eternal return—a cosmology that is ancient and to all appearances outdated but also, and contrary to what historians say, perfectly contemporary. Before the notion of linear time became as pervasive and exclusive as it now is, men and women lived and understood their daily lives, and all the events taking place in them, in terms of an archetypal ontology that was itself based on a cosmology of eternal return. According to it, and as Mircea Eliade describes it, "neither the objects of the external world nor human acts, properly speaking, have an autonomous intrinsic value. Objects or acts acquire a value, and in so doing become real, because they participate . . . in a reality that transcends them."[37] Things and actions have a significance that is larger than themselves or than the immediate purpose they serve. They are identifiable with this larger significance through participation in it, which is accomplished through a principle of repetition. Everything acquires its meaning, and hence its reality, by being a renewed manifestation or enactment of timeless and unchanging, that is, archetypal, things and events. Archaic man "acknowledges no act which has not been previously posited and lived by someone else, some other being who was not a man. What he does has been done before. His life is the ceaseless repetition of gestures initiated by others."[38] These patterns or prototypes are imagined as sacred, divine, or celestial models. Thus the basic ontological fact behind every event is "an extraterrestrial archetype, be it conceived as a plan, as a form, or purely and simply as a 'double' existing on a higher cosmic level."[39] By repeating an archetypal essence everything becomes "'animated,' . . . endowed with a 'soul.'"[40] The place and context where an event or situation occurs is thereby transformed into a sacred place and scene, and the moment itself becomes a mythic moment.[41] Thus all things profane, all events of history, participate in the sacred by repeating it. More accurately, there is no strictly profane history, since everything participates in the sacred.

There is an inherent paradox in this archetypal ontology. For archaic man attributes a sense of reality to himself and his acts only insofar as he disclaims ownership of himself and his acts. He is himself insofar as he is not himself but equated with another, and autonomous, figure.

Here then, in this ancient cosmology that is based on a myth of eternal return, we see a view of reality that is today spontaneously rediscovered by the contemporary psychotherapy patient who, in the uncanniness of transference, recognizes himself to be reenacting the ancient and unchanging content of a repetition compulsion. Like archaic man the modern psychotherapy patient sees and experiences a kind of doubling of his most intimate experience: everything that at first seemed novel and unique to the psychotherapy situation stands suddenly revealed as a repetition of a pattern that is itself timeless, and independent of the linear progress of time, in the midst of one's seemingly personal psychosocial history.

Nietzsche's Zarathustra describes this sense of the revelation of an autonomous force governing the events of a life as follows: "What the sense feels, what the spirit knows, never has its end in itself."[42] He continues: "But sense and spirit would persuade you that they are the end of things: that is how vain they are. Instruments and toys are sense and spirit: behind them lies the self." He explains: "Behind your thoughts and feelings, my brother, there stands a mighty ruler, an unknown sage—whose name is self." Elsewhere he goes a step further and links this self with personal destiny: "My own necessity! Thou destination of my soul, which I call destiny! Thou in-me! Over-me!"[43]

All this is summed up in a passage that describes Zarathustra on the verge of making a series of profound discoveries—about the idea of eternal return and the facts of a personal repetition compulsion, and about their significance for the human sense of a personal self and a personal destiny:

> As Zarathustra was climbing the mountains he thought often since his youth he had wandered alone and how many mountains and ridges and peaks he had already climbed. I am a wanderer and a mountain climber, he said to his heart; I do not like the plains, and it seems I cannot sit still for long. And whatever may yet come to me as destiny and experience will include some wandering and mountain climbing: in the end, one experiences only oneself. The time is gone when mere accidents could still happen to me; and what could still come to me that was not mine already? What returns, what finally comes home to me, is my own self and what of myself has long been in strange lands and scattered among all things and accidents.[44]

Anybody caught in a repetition compulsion—whether as psychotherapy patient discovering the uncanniness of transference, or as nonpatient caught up in any recurring archetypal theme or motif, from the level of fixed personality traits to that of cultural events—could make Zarathustra's discoveries. And so these discoveries place modern humanity alongside Zarathustra at the threshold of a contemporary affirmative ontology and cosmology that are based on the notion that all things are archetypal.

It is by and large, and beyond any doubt, the "archetypal psychology" developed by James Hillman, Jung's most inspired student, that has given the field of depth psychology its strongest impetus toward such an archetypal ontology of everyday life. This archetypal psychology, in line with Nietzsche (even though not explicitly acknowledging or even consciously realizing the parallel), has the notion of value as its most fundamental ontological fact. As Hillman writes: "The word 'archetypal' . . . points to something, and this is value . . . by archetypal psychology we mean a psychology of value."[45] Archetypal psychology "is aimed to restore psychology to its widest, deepest, and richest volume. . . . Archetypal here refers to a move one makes rather than to a thing that is."[46] That move is always aimed at recognizing that behind all the so-called facts of life there are eternally recurring mythic images being reenacted in them. Hillman adds: "By emphasizing the valuative function of the adjective 'archetypal,' . . . [archetypal psychology] restores . . . [to these eternally recurring mythic images] . . . their primordial place as that which gives psychic value to the world. Any image termed 'archetypal' is immediately valued as universal, transhistorical, basically profound, generative, highly intentional, and necessary."[47] From the point of view of such a depth psychology, one that would ground itself in the archetypal dimension of all things and events, *Dasein* means *esse in anima*—existence as grounded in the archetypal essences of the soul, its images and imagination.[48]

Viewed in this way archetypal psychology, by applying the principle of eternal recurrence to the facts of everyday life, is a method of Yes-saying that affirms every form of experience as valuable. In this respect it is a method of redemption. It works in the opposite direction of moral slander or psychological repression. In doing so it sides with Nietzsche's great philosophic New Year's resolution and offers a practical application of the formula of *amor fati*, making of archetypal psychology a fulfillment of Nietzsche's project for a revaluation of all values.

NOTES

1. Friedrich Nietzsche, *The Gay Science*, trans. Walter Kaufmann (New York: Random House, 1974), 341.

2. Quoted in Joan Stambaugh, *Nietzsche's Thought of Eternal Return* (Baltimore: Johns Hopkins University Press, 1972), 70.

3. Daniel Chapelle, *Nietzsche and Psychoanalysis* (Albany: State University of New York Press, 1993).

4. *GS* 341.

5. Ibid.

6. Ibid.

7. Ibid.

8. Ibid.

9. Friedrich Nietzsche, *Thus Spoke Zarathustra*, in *The Portable Nietzsche*, trans. Walter Kaufmann (New York, Penguin Books, 1954), part 4, "The Ass Festival," sec. 2.

10. Henry David Thoreau, *Walden*, in *The Portable Thoreau*, ed. Carl Bode (New York: Penguin Books, 1975), "Economy," 278.

11. *GS* 276.

12. Ibid.

13. Friedrich Nietzsche, *Twilight of the Idols*, in *The Portable Nietzsche*, "The Four Great Errors," sec. 8.

14. Friedrich Nietzsche, *The Will to Power*, trans. Walter Kaufmann and R. J. Hollingdale (New York: Random House, 1968), 708.

15. Ibid., 552.

16. Ibid., 631.

17. *TW*, "'Reason' in Philosophy," sec. 5.

18. Ibid.

19. *Z* II, "On Redemption."

20. *TW*, "The Four Great Errors," sec. 3.

21. *WP* 551.

22. Ibid., 618.

23. Ibid.

24. *Z* I, "On the Thousand and One Goals."

25. *Z* II, "On Redemption."

26. Sigmund Freud, "The 'Uncanny,'" in *The Standard Edition of the Complete Psychological Writings of Sigmund Freud*, trans. and ed. James Strachey (London: The Hogarth Press, 1955), 17:219–52.

27. James Hillman, *The Myth of Analysis* (Evanston, Ill.: Northwestern University Press, 1972), 107.

28. Ibid.

29. Paul Ricoeur, *Freud and Philosophy: An Essay on Interpretation* (New Haven: Yale University Press, 1970), 438.

30. Sigmund Freud, "On Beginning the Treatment," *Standard Edition*, 12:143.

31. *Freud and Philosophy*, 474.

32. *GS* 341.

33. Sigmund Freud, *Beyond the Pleasure Principle* in the *Standard Edition*, 18:1–64.

34. Sigmund Freud, *The Complete Introductory Lectures on Psychoanalysis*, trans. and ed. James Strachey (New York: Norton, 1966).

35. *Z* III, "The Convalescent," 2.

36. Friedrich Nietzsche, *Ecce Homo*, in *Basic Writings of Nietzsche*, trans. Walter Kaufmann (New York: Random House, 1966), "Thus Spoke Zarathustra," sec. 8.

37. Mircea Eliade, *Cosmos and History: The Myth of Eternal Return*, trans. Willard R. Trask (New York: Harper & Row, 1959), 3–4.

38. Ibid., 5.

39. Ibid., 9.

40. Ibid., 20.

41. Ibid., 20–21.

42. Z I, "On the Despisers of the Body."

43. Z III, "On Old and New Tablets," sec. 30.

44. Z III, "The Wanderer."

45. James Hillman. *Archetypal Psychology: A Brief Account* (Dallas: Spring Publications, 1983), 12.

46. Ibid.

47. Ibid, 13.

48. Ibid, 17.

CHAPTER 3

The Birth of the Soul:
Toward a Psychology of Decadence

Daniel W. Conway

> That a *psychologist* without equal speaks from my writings, is perhaps the first insight gained by a good reader—a reader as I deserve him.
>
> —*Ecce Homo*

> Nothing has preoccupied me more profoundly than the problem of *décadence*—I had reasons.
>
> —*Case of Wagner*

Throughout his post-Zarathustran writings, Nietzsche advertises himself as a psychologist without peer or precedent.[1] Unlike those clumsy "English [*sic*] psychologists" (*GM* I:1), for example, who artlessly project their own pet categories of explanation onto the entire history and prehistory of morality,[2] Nietzsche claims to undertake a ruthlessly naturalistic investigation of the human psyche. Attesting to his "destiny" in his *faux* autobiography, he immodestly describes his "immoralism" as "requir[ing] a height, a view of distances, a hitherto altogether unheard-of psychological depth and profundity."[3] Having (rhetorically) asked his readers, "Who among philosophers was a psychologist at all before me?," he definitively answers that "There was no psychology at all before me."[4]

Even by Nietzschean standards, however, this sort of self-congratulatory hyberbole seems excessively grandiose. What is its possible warrant? What are the psychological theories and insights that compel him to describe himself in such flattering terms? Although Nietzsche lays claim to an unprecedented understanding of psychology, he also understands human physiology to be continuous with, if not finally indistinguishable from, human psychology. "All psychology so far," he insists, "has got stuck in moral prejudices and fears; it has not dared to descend into the depths" (*BGE* 23). In order to precipitate this daring descent, he attempts to account for the whole of human interiority as a development and ramification of the basic organic principles of "animal psychology." Indeed, the insights of which he boasts so immodestly revolve around his pioneering work in *depth psychology*:

> Who before me climbed into the caverns from which the poisonous fumes of this type of ideal—slander of the world—are rising? Who even dared to suspect that they are caverns?[5]

Since Nietzsche is the first philosopher to embrace spelunking as his signature method of psychological analysis, we might fruitfully ask how he arrived at his unique depth-psychological model of the soul. Toward this end, I wish to investigate the most original and controversial result of his experiments in depth psychology: his diagnostic theory of decadence.[6]

THE PSYCHOPHYSIOLOGY OF DECADENCE

In his writings from the year 1888, especially *Twilight of the Idols*, Nietzsche consistently defines decadence as a systemic organic disorder that afflicts the instincts on which human beings prereflectively rely for guidance and regulation. Decadence thus involves what he calls "the degeneration of the instincts"[7] or "the disgregation of the instincts."[8] This systemic organic disorder characteristically manifests itself as an instinctive, involuntary enactment of self-destruction and self-dissolution. He thus offers the following two "formulae of decadence": "Instinctively to choose what is harmful for *oneself*";[9] and the *need* to "fight the instincts."[10] Elaborating on this theme of ineluctable self-destruction, he goes so far as to claim that

> Every mistake in every sense is the effect of the degeneration of instinct [*Instinkt-Entartung*], of the disgregation of the will: one could almost define all that is *bad* in this way. (*TW* 6:2)

In all of these passages, Nietzsche presents decadence as involving a corruption or clash of the instincts. But what exactly does he mean by this reference? What role does instinct play in determining the range and depth of human interiority? While it is true that diagnoses of pandemic corruption inform virtually all of his published writings, he deploys the term *décadence* (as well as the eponymous theory) only in the writings from his final year of sanity.[11] And although he relies throughout his career on similar evaluative terms and categories, including *Entartung*,

Niedergang, Verdorbenheit, and *Verfall,* it is only with the appearance of the term *décadence* in 1888 that he finally gathers his scattered criticisms of Western culture into a unified—albeit inchoate—diagnostic theory. It is no exaggeration to claim, in fact, that the critical dimension of Nietzsche's philosophy is finally realized only in 1888, as a theory of decadence. The belated emergence of an incomplete theory of decadence thus serves to unify the otherwise fragmented critical dimension of his post-Zarathustran thought, such that he can finally articulate the critique of modernity toward which he has gestured throughout his career.

Like most of the themes and topics that dominate Nietzsche's post-Zarathustran writings, however, "decadence" receives neither a formal introduction nor a sustained analysis. Although he believes that decadence afflicts ages, epochs, peoples, and individuals, he nowhere manages to provide his readers with a detailed account of the phenomenon of decay. Indeed, he occasionally employs the term so loosely as to convey nothing more than his general sense of disgust and disapprobation. Despite a late burst of creative productivity in 1888, his theory of decadence remains both largely implicit and incomplete. In order to measure his contributions to depth psychology, we must first reconstruct and render explicit the account of decadence that informs his post-Zarathustran writings. Indeed, his peculiar understanding of the instincts (and their inevitable decay) becomes intelligible only when situated within the framework of his depth-psychological model of the soul.

Nietzsche's evolving depth-psychological model of the soul is perhaps best understood as an articulation of his provocative hypothesis that human psychology is merely a complicated instance of "animal psychology." His unprecedented turn inward reveals to him that animal activity, of which human activity is merely a complicated instance, is always the encrypted surface expression of the operation of primal drives and impulses:

> Every animal . . . instinctively strives for an optimum of favorable conditions under which it can expend all its strength [*Kraft*] and achieve its maximal feeling of power [*Machtgefühl*]; every animal abhors, just as instinctively and with a subtlety of discernment that is "higher than all reason," every kind of intrusion or hindrance that obstructs or could obstruct this path to the optimum. (*GM* III:7)

This postulate, of a primal, instinctual life-activity common to all animal species, thus anchors Nietzsche's depth psychology in the naturalism that ostensibly frames his post-Zarathustran critical project.[12] Rehabilitating his useless training in classical philology, he now characterizes the psychologist as "a reader of signs."[13]

Hoping to distance himself from all predecessor philosophers and psychologists, Nietzsche vows to account for the whole of human interiority as a development and ramification of the basic organic principles of animal vitality. He thus charts the range and depth of the human soul by appealing exclusively to the naturalistic, empirical principles of animal psychology. Throughout his post-Zarathustran writings, he consequently treats conscious intentions, volitions, and actions as derivative manifestations of a more basic, vital core of animal agency:

> Man, like every living being, thinks continually without knowing it; the thinking that rises to *consciousness* is only the smallest part of all this—the most superficial and worst part—for only this conscious thinking *takes the form of words, which is to say signs of communication*, and this fact uncovers the origin of consciousness. (GS 354)

Thus interpreted, the "surface- and sign-world" of consciousness not only surrenders its privileged position within the domain of human interiority, but also bespeaks the depth—hitherto unacknowledged and unexplored—of the human psyche. Having exposed consciousness as the surface expression of an underlying deep structure, Nietzsche consequently locates the real source of "thinking," and of all human endeavors, in the invisible, unconscious drives and impulses that animate all of animal activity. From (at least) 1885 onward, in fact, he unwaveringly cleaves to a drive- and impulse-based model of human agency.[14] As we shall soon see, this depth-psychological model of human agency serves as the basis and foundation for his account of decadence as an internecine clash of instincts.

Nietzsche derives indirect support for this evolving depth-psychological model of agency (and so for his emerging theory of decadence) from his speculative forays into philosophical anthropology. Intending to deliver a strictly naturalistic account of the origin of consciousness, he directs our attention to

> the most fundamental change [man] ever experienced—that change which occurred when he found himself finally enclosed within the walls of security and peace. (GM II:16)

Describing the response of human animals to the (repressive) demands of civil society, he explains that

> in this new world they no longer possessed their former guides, their regulating, unconscious and infallible drives: they were reduced to thinking, inferring, reckoning, co-ordinating cause and effect, these unfortunate creatures; they were reduced to their "consciousness," their weakest and most fallible organ! (GM II:16)

In exchange for the peace and security promised by civil society, that is, human animals must forfeit the natural state of well-being (and internal regulation) associated with the instantaneous discharge of their primal drives and impulses. In order to honor the founding taboos of civil society, they now must rely primarily on consciousness, a feeble organ of relatively recent emergence, to regulate their animal vitality. In an effort to simulate natural principles of regulation within the walls of civil society, human beings preside over the implementation of instinct systems, which impose an artificial order upon the amoral drives and impulses.

Nietzsche famously avers that consciousness has proven to be an extremely inefficient organ of internal regulation. Consciousness "is in the main *superfluous*" (*GS* 354), involving "an exertion which uses up an unnecessary amount of nervous energy" (*AC* 14). Indeed, human animals must pay dearly to afford, even temporarily, the extravagant luxury of renouncing the unconscious regulation provided them by Nature:

> All instincts that do not discharge themselves outwardly *turn inward*—this is what I call the *internalization* of man. Thus it was that man first developed what was later called his "soul." The entire inner world, originally as thin as if it were stretched between two membranes, expanded and extended itself, acquired depth, breadth and height, in the same measure as outward discharge was *inhibited*. (*GM* II:16)

Nietzsche's genealogy thus identifies the birth of the soul as a contingent event in the natural development of the human species. As a consequence of this "forcible sundering from [their] animal past," newly civilized human animals were obliged to participate, schizophrenically, in the taboo pronounced by civil society on "all those instincts of wild, free, prowling man."[15]

While his terminological preference is both anachronistic and potentially misleading, his attention to the *soul* is perfectly consistent with the naturalistic orientation of his post-Zarathustran philosophy. He explains, for example, that his prepotent critique of subjectivity banishes only the "soul atomism" that has stalled the progress of psychological investigation hitherto, and not the "soul-hypothesis" itself (*BGE* 12). He consequently proposes, as alternative formulations of this hypothesis, the "mortal soul"; the "soul as subjective multiplicity"; and the soul "as social structure of the drives and affects."[16]

In his account of the birth of the soul, Nietzsche applies a naturalistic twist to the traditional Christian doctrine of original sin. Born of the tumultuous implosion of a formerly healthy animal organism, the human soul exists only in fragmentation and self-division. In perhaps his most outrageous reversal of the psychological model underlying Christian morality, Nietzsche interprets the ensoulment of the human animal as a type of incurable illness, which he calls the *bad conscience*:

Thus began the gravest and uncanniest illness, from which humanity has not yet recovered, man's suffering of man, of himself—the result of a forcible sundering from his animal past, as it were a leap and plunge into new surroundings and conditions of existence, a declaration of war against the old instincts upon which his strength, joy, and terribleness had rested hitherto. (*GM* II:16)

Although Nietzsche immediately adds, in what his readers typically interpret as a positive gesture of recuperation, that the bad conscience has impregnated the human soul "with a future,"[17] we would do well to resist the maieutic optimism he expresses in his diagnosis of this troubled pregnancy. Where Nietzsche detects "an interest, a tension, a hope, almost a certainty, as if with [humankind] something were announcing and preparing itself, as if man were not a goal but only a way, an episode, a bridge, a great promise,"[18] there may in fact lie only the portents of impending dissolution and demise. By the time he writes *Twilight*, in fact, he is fully convinced that the pregnancy induced by the bad conscience is destined for miscarriage:

To say it briefly (for a long time people will still keep silent about it): What will not be built any more henceforth, and *cannot* be built any more, is—a society [*Gesellschaft*] in the old sense of that word; to build that, everything is lacking, above all the material. *All of us are no longer material for a society.* (*GS* 356)

Nietzsche's naturalistic account of the birth of the soul has important consequences for his inchoate theory of decadence. Indeed, he locates the ultimate source and necessity of decadence in the illness of the bad conscience, which obliges individual human beings to exhaust their native vitality in the struggle to refuse the incessant demands of their natural, instinctual heritage. In order to enjoy the fruits of civil society, that is, the human animal must expend a great deal of its native vitality simply to sustain the artificial introjection of its natural instincts, which in turn exerts an inordinate strain on the newborn soul. Compensating on the one hand for the deficiencies of consciousness as a regulative organ, while enduring on the other hand the inwardly directed discharge of its ever-active drives and impulses, human animals prematurely exhaust their store of native vitality in an attempt to regulate the overtaxed economy of their natural organisms.

The clash of instincts that Nietzsche associates with decadence is therefore the inevitable result of the artificial mode of internal regulation required by civilization and imposed by consciousness. Healthy peoples and individuals can temporarily enforce this artificial mode of regulation, but the eventual cost to them—and their successors—is enormous. Indeed, decadent peoples and individuals must bear the expense of the squandered vitality of their predecessors, in the form of an instinctual discord they cannot afford to quell:

> Such human beings of late cultures and refracted lights will on the average be weaker human beings: their most profound desire is that the war they *are* should come to an end. (*BGE* 200)

By tracing the etiology of decadence to the illness of the bad conscience, Nietzsche thus accounts for the fatalism that pervades his 1888 writings. The bad conscience is the ineliminable, non-negotiable opportunity cost of civilization itself; it is the very condition and ground of human interiority as we now know it. Although some peoples and cultures can successfully mitigate its effects, thereby postponing the onset of decadence, no people or culture can opt out of the illness that constitutes and defines the human species. Death alone can free the human animal from the pain of the bad conscience. For this reason, Nietzsche remains sanguine about our prospects for reversing or arresting the decadence that afflicts the peoples and cultures of late modernity:

> Nothing avails: one *must* go forward—step by step further into decadence (that is *my* definition of modern "progress"). One can check this development and thus dam up degeneration, gather it and make it more vehement and sudden: one can do no more. (*TW* 9:43)

In order to resist or reverse the advance of decadence, that is, a people or culture would need to rid itself of its besetting bad conscience. In perhaps his most hopeful comment on the possibility of humankind "curing" itself of its bad conscience, Nietzsche hypothesizes,

> Man has all too long had an "evil eye" for his natural inclinations, so that they have finally become inseparable from his "bad conscience." An attempt at the reverse would *in itself* be possible—but who is strong enough for it?—that is, to wed the bad conscience to all the *unnatural* inclinations, all those aspirations to the beyond, to that which runs counter to sense, instinct, nature, animal, in short all ideals hitherto, which are one and all hostile to life and ideals that slander the world. (*GM* II:24)

The question he inserts into this otherwise promising passage conveys the enormity of the reversal he envisions: *Who* would be "strong enough" to turn this "evil eye" against itself and impress the bad conscience into the service of the "natural inclinations"? Although his answers to this important question vary throughout the post-Zarathustran period of career, citing the redemptive power of the free spirits, the philosophers of the future, the *Übermensch*, and even Dionysus himself, Nietzsche consistently asserts that late modernity itself lacks the resources to complete the redemptive task at hand.

Nietzsche consequently exposes the folly of all moral and political schemes designed to reverse or "cure" the decadence of a people or culture. A decadent age *must* move inexorably toward the exhaustion of its vital resources. Any attempt to defy this economic law threatens instead to accelerate the degenerative process:

> It is a self-deception on the part of philosophers and moralists if they believe that they are extricating themselves from decadence when they merely wage war against it. Extrication lies beyond their strength . . . they change its expression, but they do not get rid of decadence itself. (*TW* 2:11)[19]

In the face of the escalating chaos that Nietzsche forecasts for the remainder of the modern epoch, one thing remains certain: The decadence that attends the twilight of the idols must run its inexorable course. Modernity will not be redeemed from within. As Heidegger would conclude nearly a century later, only a god can save us now[20]— but only, Nietzsche would add, if the god in question is Dionysus.

INSTINCTS AND DRIVES

Nietzsche's genealogical account of the birth of the soul thus suggests that he equates the instincts with the unconscious drives and impulses that collectively propagate the primal organic vitality that is shared by natural and human animals alike. On this interpretation, decadence would involve a self-destructive, internecine clash among the animal drives that engender human agency. Strictly speaking, however, this equation is not entirely accurate. Indeed, the emergence of Nietzsche's theory of decadence coincides with an important refinement of his evolving depth-psychological model of the soul: his distinction between drive or impulse (*Trieb*) and instinct (*Instinkt*). The articulation of this distinction enables him to claim indirect empirical access to the "social structure" of the drives and impulses through his observation of discernible patterns of instinctual behavior.

Up until 1888, Nietzsche treats the terms *Trieb* and *Instinkt* as roughly synonymous, and faithful Anglophone translators have honored this convention. He employs both terms in contradistinction to the faculties and operations traditionally associated with human consciousness, for he intends both terms to refer in general to the primal, unconscious vitality that human beings share (and discharge) in common with all other members of the animal kingdom. In his account of the "origin of the bad conscience," for example, he employs the two terms interchangeably to refer to the unconscious animal activity that is forced inward at the onset of civilization (*GM* II:16).²¹ He consistently maintains this use of *Trieb* throughout his career, but his writings from the year 1888 suggest the development of a subtle distinction between *Instinkt* and *Trieb*. While the two terms remain extensionally equivalent in the writings of 1888, denoting the unconscious drives that discharge themselves in the natural propagation of animal vitality, they are no longer treated as intensionally equivalent. In *Twilight*, Nietzsche consistently reserves the term *Instinkt* to refer to any specific organization of the drives and impulses, as determined by the dominant mores of the particular people or epoch in question. It is precisely this task of cultivating instincts, of ruthlessly imposing order and rule onto the natural, spontaneous discharge of the drives and impulses, of creating a "morality of mores," that occupied the entire prehistory of the human animal (*GM* II:2).

Nietzsche's precise use of the term *Instinkt* in 1888 thus designates any specific set of conditions, imposed by and inculcated through civilization, under which the drives and impulses are trained to discharge their native vitality. The aim of this process of acculturation is to provide individual souls with the cultural (i.e., artificial) equivalent of those natural instincts that the human animal has forsaken in exchange for the peace and security of civil society. Disciplined to enact a trusty set of prereflective patterns of response to foreseeable exigencies, individuals might minimize their vexed reliance on a conscious regulation of their animal organisms. Nietzsche consequently applauds Manu's attempt

> step by step to push consciousness back from what had been recognized as the right life (that is, *proved* right by a tremendous and rigorously filtered experience), so as to attain the perfect automatism of instinct—that presupposition of all mastery, of every kind of perfection in the art of life. (*AC* 57)

While philosophers and moralists hitherto have been satisfied simply to cultivate any kind of instinctual organization of the soul, usually settling for some heavy-handed regime of castratism, Nietzsche undertakes an evaluation and rank ordering of the various systems of instinctual order that have prevailed throughout the course of human history.

This distinction between *Trieb* and *Instinkt* thus enables Nietzsche to incorporate into his evolving model of the soul an additional dimension of complexity. The unconscious drives and impulses compose the circulatory network of the soul, while the instincts constitute the patterns of regulation that govern the internal operations of this network. On this amended model of the soul, the drives and impulses themselves remain invisible, but the instincts admit of indirect empirical observation by virtue of the traces they manifest in detectable, public patterns of behavior.

Nietzsche's late distinction between *Trieb* and *Instinkt* thus serves the further purpose of supplying his critical philosophy with a more solid, empirical foundation. While he claims no direct access to the basic network of unconscious drives and impulses, he believes that an indirect access to them is available through a "scientific" interpretation of the observable patterns of behavior through which the instincts invariably express themselves. His writings from the year 1888 consistently treat the instincts as manifesting themselves in acculturated, habitual, prereflective patterns of behavior. He consequently applauds the methods and findings of Zopyrus, the itinerant physiognomist who (correctly) diagnosed the ugly Socrates as a "cave of bad appetites" (*TW* 2:9).

By carefully observing an individual's outward, instinctual behavior, Nietzsche can similarly deduce the principle of organization (or lack thereof) that governs the individual's underlying substructure of drives and impulses. Although instincts do not admit of direct observation, their surface traces function as signs of the "social structure" that prevails within the invisible body. He thus insists that "the values of a human being betray something of the *structure* of his soul" (*BGE* 268). As Freud would similarly conclude several years later, a "scientific" defense of depth psychology must establish an empirical link between the invisible activity of the unconscious drives and an established data base of observable phenomena. Just as Nietzsche points to "instinctive" patterns of behavior as reliable signs of the principle of organization that governs underlying drives and impulses, so Freud tirelessly documents the empirical data furnished by dreams, mischievements, parapraxes, and the like.[22]

DECADENCE AND/AS THE
STRUCTURAL COLLAPSE OF THE SOUL

Nietzsche's 1888 distinction between *Trieb* and *Instinkt* also enables him to specify the precise locus of decay within the invisible body. When he describes decadence as the loss or disintegration of the instincts, he does not mean that the underlying drives have somehow decomposed, but that their previous configuration has been compromised.

Decadence thus pertains not to the drives and impulses in themselves, but to the instincts, to the systems of internal organization that regulate the discharge of the drives and impulses: "I call an animal, a species, or an individual corrupt [*verdorben*] when it loses its instincts, when it chooses, when it prefers, what is disadvantageous for it" (*AC* 6).[23] Only the instincts undergo decay and become "reactive," which means that the drives and impulses no longer work harmoniously toward a collectively desirable end. As an instinctual system decays, its constituent drives and impulses fall—amorally and indifferently—under a successor principle of organization, continuing all the while their natural activity of propagating and discharging the native vitality of the organism. For this reason, Nietzsche occasionally equates the decay of a system of instincts with the *disgregation* (rather than the deterioration) of its constituent drives and affects.

Instinctual decay involves either the reconfiguration of the drives and impulses under a novel, unhealthy principle of organization or the "anarchy" that ensues when no single system of instincts emerges as dominant. Nietzsche more regularly associates the decadence of modernity with this latter model, pointing to the internecine clash between fragmentary instinctual systems, but both alternatives are equally unappealing. In either event, the soul is guided by a principle of organization that properly belongs to another time or place, perhaps to another people or race altogether. The ensuing clash of atavistic instinctual systems riddles the soul with open sumps and circuits, which introduce an additional element of endogenous wastage into the strained economy of the soul. Rather than discharge its vitality in outward creative expressions, the discordant soul largely exhausts itself in an internal conflict between competing instinctual systems.

Nietzsche does not mean to imply, however, that it is somehow possible to restore the drives and impulses to their "original" or "raw" form, independent of all acquired patterns of organization. As a creature uniquely reliant for survival upon its nascent interiority, the human animal is defined by the mediated, principled expression of its native vitality. Although Nietzsche occasionally employs "instinct" as a term of valorization to designate those rare, "aristocratic" principles of organization that merit his approval, the absence of instinctual organization in a human soul is in fact unintelligible to him. As an afterbirth of civilization itself, the human soul exists *only* as the product of training and cultivation, in accordance with the repressive demands of civilization. Nietzsche roundly (and unfairly) ridicules Rousseau for believing that some untamed "noble savage" lurks within the human breast, hungrily awaiting its release from the chains of culture and convention. The decay of a regnant system of instincts does not unleash our primal animal nature in its pure, unbridled fury, but simply enables the regency of another system (or of a bricolage of system fragments), ad infinitum.

Nor does Nietzsche mean to imply that the decay or imposition of any single instinctual system is particularly disastrous or beneficial for its constituent drives and impulses. The invisible body is an irresistibly active engine of propagation and discharge, and it continues its animal activity in utter indifference to the instinctual systems imposed upon it. The overworked distinction between "active" and "reactive" forces thus pertains not to the drives and impulses themselves, but to the instinctual systems under which the drives and impulses are organized.[24] Indeed, the drives and impulses do not distinguish, as Nietzsche does, between "healthy" and "decadent" configurations of their enabling networks, or between active and reactive systems of instinctual organization. Despite his occasional wishes to the contrary, the human soul displays neither a natural affinity for healthy instincts nor a natural aversion to decadent instincts. Whereas an instinctual system is a human artifice, perfected and imposed by human beings in an attempt to orchestrate a temporary convergence between *nomos* and *physis*, the unconscious drives and impulses belong exclusively to Nature, from which they inherit their implacable indifference to human design.[25]

For all of Nietzsche's confidence in pronouncing the decadence of various peoples and ages, however, his forays into depth psychology stray dangerously far from the naturalism that supposedly anchors his post-Zarathustran critical philosophy. While he consistently couches his symptomatology in empirical, naturalistic terms, his constant appeal to the unconscious drives and regulatory instincts remains to some extent speculative. Because the invisible body, by definition, defies direct empirical observation, the very existence of the unconscious drives and impulses remains to some extent hypothetical. The only observable traces of physiological decay lie in those mysterious encrypted symptoms that Nietzsche alone can interpret.

He insists that the native vitality of the invisible body can be measured with a "dynamometer" (*TW* 9:20), implying that such measurements would help to secure the tenuous empirical grounding of his critical philosophy. The precise calibration he has in mind for this wondrous instrument, however, such that it might accurately detect instinctual disarray, remains a secret to all but him.[26] In any event, he advances no reproducible method or system whereby others might scientifically confirm or dispute the findings on which he bases his diagnoses. That the human body is amenable to the semiotic strategies he introduces follows only from his postulate—untested and unproved—that human beings rely indirectly on the drives and impulses characteristic of all animal life. If we were to reject this postulate or even suspend it in skeptical abeyance, then Nietzsche's appeal to the invisible body, as well as the symptomatological turn it enables, would probably hold little scientific credence.

THE DISGREGATION OF THE WILL

Having investigated Nietzsche's distinction between *Trieb* and *Instinkt*, we are now in a position to undertake a more precise reconstruction of the inchoate theory of decadence that informs his post-Zarathustran writings. Whereas healthy souls are instinctually fortified to maintain strict control over their patterns of influx and expenditure, decadent souls lack the structural organization and integrity provided by a single, dominant instinctual system. Hence Nietzsche's account of decadence as an inexorable march toward dissolution: "*instinctively* they prefer what disintegrates, what hastens the end" (*TW* 9:39).

As we have seen, Nietzsche hopes to articulate a starkly naturalistic account of the soul, an account that makes no appeal—overt or surreptitious—to supernatural principles of explanation. Experimenting with alternative versions of the "soul-hypothesis," he consequently figures the soul as a transient, self-regulating subsystem sheltered within the undifferentiated plenum of will to power. Hoping to purge his philosophy of its residual anthropocentrisms, he occasionally presents the soul as an embodied energy circuit, through which undifferentiated forces circulate and flow in accordance with amoral principles of internal self-regulation. For Nietzsche, the soul is no inert container, but a surging, pulsating capacitor, which continuously propagates and discharges its native holdings of forces.

As the figure of the capacitor suggests, the natural activity of the soul extends no further than the spontaneous expenditure of native forces in bursts of creative self-expression. This is its sole function, which it involuntarily performs in utter indifference to external obstacles and internal constraints. Even the self-preservation of the organism is subordinated to the maintenance of the soul's natural, unconscious rhythm of propagation and discharge:

> [T]he really fundamental instinct of Life . . . aims at *the expansion of power* and, wishing for that, frequently risks and even sacrifices self-preservation. . . . The struggle for existence is only an *exception*, a temporary restriction of the will to Life. The great and small struggle always revolves around superiority, around growth and expansion, around power—in accordance with the will to power which is the will to Life. (*GS* 349)

Nietzsche thus conceives of the soul as the human animal organism functioning in its most primal, uncomplicated and rudimentary form, as a pure, amoral engine of will to power.[27] Hewing strictly to the stringent naturalism of his post-Zarathustran philosophy, he accords the soul no justificatory *telos* or metaphysical birthright, vowing instead to scour the "eternal basic text of *homo natura*" of its supernatural accretions (*BGE* 230).

In perhaps the most controversial element of his depth-psychological model of the soul, Nietzsche attempts to derive normative judgments from his empirical analysis of the soul as an amoral engine or energy circuit.[28] What metaphysicians have characteristically hypostatized as the "will," he explains, is simply the enhanced feeling of power [*Machtgefühl*] that gives rise to an experience of causal efficacy.[29] This enhanced feeling of power, in turn, is an epiphenomenal result of the configuration of the soul under a specific principle of organization, or set of instincts:

> In this way the person exercising volition adds the feelings of delight of his successful executive instruments, the useful "underwills" or undersouls—indeed, our body is but a social structure composed of many souls—to his feelings of delight as commander. (*BGE* 19)

It is this enhanced feeling of power that alone assures the human animal that its threshold level of vitality has been attained; it thus functions to alert the human animal that it currently operates under a viable principle of internal regulation. Nietzsche's appeal to this feeling of power as a standard of relative health (or decay) thus reflects, or so he believes, the naturalism that guides his symptomatological investigations.

Indeed, the soul experiences itself as a unified, efficient force only when its constituent drives and affects work together to ensure an unimpeded propagation of agency:

> *L'effet c'est moi*: what happens here is what happens in every well-constructed and happy commonwealth; namely, the governing class identifies itself with the successes of the commonwealth. (*BGE* 19)

Because the "invisible" body is a "social structure composed of many souls" (*BGE* 19), the appropriate "political" organization of these souls (or undersouls) will enable the enhanced feeling of power that accompanies a robust propagation of agency.[30] He consequently insists that

> The "unfree" will is mythology; in real life it is only a matter of *strong* and *weak* wills. (*BGE* 21)

Hence the importance for Nietzsche of cultivating strong, monopolistic instincts: only when properly organized and configured do the unconscious drives and impulses attain a propagation of vitality that is commensurate with the feeling of power that he associates with willing. The decay of instinct thus results in a "weakness of the will," which he defines as "the inability not to respond [impulsively] to a stimulus" (*TW* 5:2). A capacitor is damaged not by a quantitative shortage of vital resources, but by an internal structural incapacity to channel these resources effectively and efficiently. He consequently defines decadence in terms of the "disgregation of the will" (*TW* 6:2), a process whereby the drives and affects become (dis)organized in such a way that their subsequent "aggregation" can no longer produce a feeling of power.[31] The disgregation of the will instead produces a "feeling of physiological inhibition," which he associates with "deep depression, leaden exhaustion, and black melancholy" (*GM* III:17).

Nietzsche occasionally attempts an even more fundamental analysis of decadence, explaining the "disgregation of the will" in terms of an entropic deformation in the circulatory system of the soul. Although he conceives of the "world" of will to power as a boundless, undifferentiated plenum, he also believes that this "powerful unity . . . undergoes ramifications and developments in the organic process" (*BGE* 36). The entirety and complexity of human psychology, he consequently insists, can be understood in terms of the organic differentiation and diversification of the will to power (*BGE* 23). He consequently refers to the will to power as a "*pre-form* [*Vorform*] of Life," and to the "life of the drives" [*Triebleben*] as a "ramification" of the will to power (*BGE* 36).[32]

Nietzsche's "morphology" of the will to power thus furnishes the context for his account of the "disgregation" of the will. At the organic level of ramification and differentiation of will to power, the soul propagates quanta of force through its circulatory network of drives and impulses.[33] The internal flow of these quanta of force, which is determined in volume and regularity by the regnant configuration of the instincts, thus accounts for the vitality embodied by "individual" human beings. By means of an efficient propagation of quanta of force, a system of instincts thus enables the phenomenal sensations of empowerment and efficacy.[34] He consequently explains that

> A quantum of force [*Kraft*] is equivalent to a quantum of drive, will, effect—more, it is nothing other than precisely this very driving, willing, effecting. (*GM* I:13)[35]

The enhanced feeling of power associated with willing thus signifies (to the Nietzschean symptomatologist) an unimpeded flow of these quanta of force through the circulatory system of the healthy capacitor. "Willing" thus refers to a specific disposition—both quantitative and qualitative—of the quanta of force propagated and discharged by the capacitor.

Embracing Lange's principles of the "conservation of energy" and the "indestructibility of matter," Nietzsche insists that these basic quanta of force cannot be destroyed.[36] They can, however, fall under anarchic or ochlocratic principles of aggregation in the "social structure of the drives and affects," which invariably occasion a vital entropy. The quantity of vital forces within the soul remains constant, but in the event of a clash of competing instinct systems, these quanta of force become (dis)aggregated in configurations that are qualitatively incapable of sustaining a feeling of power. He consequently equates decadence with "the anarchy of atoms" (*CW* 7), which in turn occasions the experience of weakness of the will.[37]

The advance of decadence thus cripples the soul as an efficient capacitor. Bereft of the instinctual reinforcement that hitherto ensured its structural integrity, the soul devolves into a distended, flaccid casing for the vital forces that now course aimlessly throughout it:

> Everywhere paralysis, arduousness, torpidity or hostility and chaos: both more and more obvious the higher one ascends in forms of organization. The whole no longer lives at all: it is composite, calculated, artificial, and artifact. (*CW* 7)

While the disgregation of the will signals a crisis in the "invisible" body, a vigilant symptomatologist can indirectly detect this crisis by charting its symptoms in the "visible" body. As "the typical signs" of decay, Nietzsche lists selflessness, depersonalization, the loss of a center of gravity, and neighbor love (*EH*, "Destiny," 7).

The disgregation of the will leaves the soul a sclerotic capacitor, which becomes increasingly unable to propagate and discharge its native vitality. Decadence consequently manifests itself as a volitional crisis, or *akrasia*, which prevents individuals from acting in their own best interests.[38] The decadent soul must therefore accommodate within its collapsing economy an ever-widening gulf between the cognitive and volitional resources at its disposal, and it must compensate for the relative deficiency of will that ensues. Indeed, decadent individuals are not typically unaware of their condition, or of the mistakes they involuntarily commit; they simply lack the volitional resources needed to implement their cognitive insights. They often know their destiny, but they are powerless to alter it.

Nietzsche consequently locates decadence in the natural, inevitable failure of the "invisible" body to sustain an efficient propagation through itself of the will to power. He refers to Life as the "foundation [*Grundbau*] of the affects" (*BGE* 258), and he subsequently equates "the decline of Life" with "the decrease in the power to organize" (*TW* 9:37). A tremendous (and eventually mortal) collision transpires at the interface of will to power, or Life, and its transient human capacitors. Like a raging torrent that is temporarily channeled and tamed, the will to power gradually wears down its capacitors with a relentless surge of vitality, eventually obliterating the locks and dams that were engineered to harness its boundless power. Bereft of the structure and organization supplied hitherto by an effective system of internal regulation, the "invisible" body continues to channel and discharge quanta of will to power, but now at the expense of its own structural integrity and "health." The disgregated drives and impulses of a decadent soul are (dis)organized in such a way that any further propagation of quanta of force threatens to cripple the soul as a capacitor. Of course, the will to power itself is oblivious to all such qualitative "limitations" of its natural sumptuary expression. Unlike Nietzsche, the amoral will to power does not distinguish between "healthy" and "decadent" bodies; it expresses itself indiscriminately through either type of engine and eventually exhausts both.

CONCLUSION

As the greatest critic of the transformative power of the will, Nietzsche is egregiously miscast as a (failed) radical voluntarist. To the healthy, prescriptions of health are superfluous, while to the sick they are cruel. Contrary to popular prejudice, he offers no plan for restoring decadent souls to a more robust standard of vitality. He is interested neither in prescribing a recuperative system of instincts, nor in rallying the anemic and infirm to unlikely feats of heroism and nobility. Decadent souls can do nothing but enact their constitutive chaos, expressing themselves creatively in their own self-destruction.

Human flourishing is therefore a remote and attenuated expression of one's physiological destiny. While individuals enjoy limited control over the precise expression of their native vitality, they can neither alter nor augment the vital resources at their disposal. Decadent individuals, for example, cannot help but enact their constitutive contradictions:

> Instinctively to choose what is harmful for *oneself*, to feel attracted by "disinterested" motives, that is virtually the formula of decadence. (*TW* 9:35)

To the decadent souls whom he diagnoses, Nietzsche offers no cures, no therapies, and no hopes for a regimen of self-constitution that might make them whole. In a notebook entry, he ridicules the idea that we might combat decay simply by easing the experience of discomfort that attends it:

> The supposed remedies of degeneration are also mere palliatives against some of its effects: the "cured" are merely one type of the degenerate. (*WP* 42)

Socrates' ugly face betrays not only an ugly character, but also the fatality of an ugly character. So for modern decadents as well: cosmetic surgery can perhaps salvage a misshapen face, but not a broken soul. Decadent individuals can hope at best to rechristen their constitutive ugliness as an alternative form of beauty; in order to receive this dubious service, they must consult their local philosophers and priests.

Decadence *must* run its inexorable course, gradually exhausting those protective instincts that might otherwise have resisted its advance (*EH*, "Wise," 6). Any recuperative scheme that claims otherwise is guilty of confusing the effects (or signs) of decay for its cause:

> This young man turns pale early and wilts; his friends say: that is due to this or that disease. I say: that he became diseased, that he did not resist the disease, was already the effect of an impoverished life or hereditary exhaustion. (*TW* 6:2)

Like all decadents, this young man must enact the mortal drama scripted for him: "one anti-natural step virtually compels the second" (*EH*, "Human," 3). It matters not that he acknowledges his role, discerning perhaps the familiar trajectory of the advancing plot, for his crippled will can muster no effective protest. Nor can he rely on his instincts to guide him to a healthier form of life, for it is precisely the failure of his instincts to collaborate harmoniously that has sealed his demise. In Nietzsche's post-Zarathustran writings, in fact, "physiology" becomes destiny.

NOTES

1. With the exception of occasional emendations, I rely throughout this essay on Walter Kaufmann's translations/editions of Nietzsche's books for Viking Press/Random House. For further discussion of the issues raised here in this essay, see my *Nietzsche's Dangerous Game* (Cambridge: Cambridge University Press, 1997).

2. *GM*, preface, 4.

3. *EH*, "Destiny," sec. 6.

4. Ibid.

5. Ibid.

6. For the most part, Nietzsche's post-Zarathustran theory of decadence has been either ignored by scholars or conflated with his treatment of nihilism. Notable exceptions to this rule include Daniel Ahern, *Nietzsche as Cultural Physician* (University Park: Pennsylvania State University Press, 1995), especially chapters 1–2; Brian G. Domino, "Nietzsche's Republicanism" (Ph.D. diss., Pennsylvania State University, 1993); Jacob Golomb, *Nietzsche's Enticing Psychology of Power* (Ames: Iowa State University Press, 1989), especially chapter 1; and Henning Ottman, *Philosophie und Politik bei Nietzsche* (Berlin: de Gruyter, 1987), especially part C, section 4.

7. *TW* 9:41.

8. *TW* 9:35.

9. *TW* 9:35; cf. *TW* 9:39, *AC* 6.

10. *TW* 2:11.

11. For a thorough account of Nietzsche's reliance on the imagery and vocabulary of *décadence*, see Domino, "Nietzsche's Republicanism," 133–44.

12. For a succinct and sympathetic account of the naturalism that informs Nietzsche's critical philosophy, see Richard Schacht, "Nietzsche's *Gay Science*, Or, How to Naturalize Cheerfully," collected in *Reading Nietzsche*, ed. Robert C. Solomon and Kathleen M. Higgins (New York: Oxford University Press, 1988), 68–86.

13. *Human, All-Too-Human*, trans. R. J. Hollingdale (Cambridge: Cambridge University Press, 1986), preface, 8. On Nietzsche's ingenious transformation of philology, from the science of interpreting "dead" texts into the science of interpreting "live" bodies, see Eric Blondel, *Nietzsche, The Body and Culture: Philosophy as a Philological Genealogy*, trans. Seán Hand (Stanford, Calif.: Stanford University Press, 1991), chapter 8.

14. On the development of Nietzsche's reliance on a drive-based model of agency, see the excellent study by Graham Parkes, *Composing the Soul* (Chicago: University of Chicago Press, 1994), especially chapters 7–8.

15. *GM* II:16.

16. For Nietzsche's attempt to explain what the soul is *like* (rather than what it *is*), see Parkes, *Composing the Soul*, 7–8, 171–73.

17. *GM* II:16.

18. Ibid.

19. A persistent theme of Nietzsche's notes from 1888 is the belief that philosophers, moralists, and statesmen regularly mistake the consequences of decadence for its causes (cf. *WP* 38–48). Hence the failure of all prescriptive measures for "treating" decadence: "But the supposed remedies of degeneration are also mere palliatives against some of its effects: the 'cured' are merely one type of the degenerates" (*WP* 42).

20. Martin Heidegger, "*Nur noch ein Gott kann uns retten*," *Der Spiegel*, 23 (1976):193–219.

21. In the context of the Darwinesque analogy he proposes to explain the origin of the bad conscience, he describes the loss on the part of the first land animals of "their former guides, their regulating, unconscious and infallible drives [*Triebe*]" in apposition to the disvaluation and suspension of their "instincts [*Instinkte*]" (GM II:16).

22. On the question of Nietzsche's multiple influences on Freud, see Golomb, *Nietzsche's Enticing Psychology of Power*, chapter 1.

23. Although Nietzsche does not use the term *decadence* in this passage, his definition here of *corruption* is virtually the same as his definition of *decadence* at *TW* 9:35 and 9:39.

24. The currency of this distinction is most directly attributable not to Nietzsche himself, but to Gilles Deleuze, *Nietzsche and Philosophy*, trans. Hugh Tomlinson (New York: Columbia University Press, 1983), especially chapter 2. Deleuze proposes this distinction as the guiding typology of Nietzsche's thought, and he often employs it in synonymy to Nietzsche's own distinction between "health" and "decadence."

25. For a compelling account of the psychological conditions under which the (self-)creative individual might "return to Nature," see Parkes, *Composing the Soul*, 363–71. Parkes persuasively suggests that if one assiduously disciplines one's multiple drives and impulses, then eventually "control can be relaxed, one

can dare to be natural, and the multiplicity will spontaneously order itself" (377).

26. Nietzsche insists that "one can measure the effect of the ugly with a dynamometer. . . . The ugly is understood as a sign and symptom of degeneration: whatever reminds us in the least of the degeneration causes in us the judgment of 'ugly'" (*TW* 9:20). In his notes, he similarly maintains that "the muscular strength of a girl increases as soon as a man comes into her vicinity; there are instruments to measure this" (*WP* 807); *Friedrich Nietzsche: Sämtliche Werke, Kritische Studienausgabe in 15 Bänden*, ed. G. Colli and M. Montinari (Berlin: de Gruyter/Deutscher Taschenbuch Verlag, 1980), vol. 13, 17[5], pp. 526–27.

27. *BGE* 13.

28. Golomb offers a persuasive account of how Nietzsche's depth-psychological method enables "a morality of positive power" (*Nietzsche's Enticing*, 225). See especially chapter 6, in which Golomb articulates his illuminating distinction between "negative" and "positive" power.

29. While outlining "a psychology of the artist," for example, Nietzsche maintains that "What is essential in [the frenzy of an overcharged and swollen will] is the feeling of increased strength and fullness" (*TW* 9:8).

30. My attention to Nietzsche's reliance on political metaphors for soulcraft, and to its Platonic provenance, are indebted to Parkes, *Composing the Soul*, 346–62.

31. For a provocative investigation into the potentially affirmative consequences of decadence, especially for the possible reconfiguration of individual agency, see Werner Hamacher, "'Disgregation des Willens': Nietzsche über Individuum und Individualität," *Nietzsche-Studien* 15 (1986):306–36.

32. Influenced by the antimaterialist atomisms promulgated by Boscovich, Lange, and others, Nietzsche presents the "world" of will to power as a dynamic whirl of quanta (or "centers") of force. Each quantum of force is defined not in terms of a material essence or substratum, but only in terms of its differential "effects" on other quanta of force within the plenum. He thus proposes, in a famous notebook entry, that "a 'thing' is the sum of its effects, synthetically united by a concept, an image" (*WP* 551). His hypothesis of will to power thus suggests an account of the world as an immeasurably dense, undifferentiated whole, which is *not* the sum of the constituent "parts" inhabited (and hubristically "explained") by human beings. If quanta of force are isolated and defined only in terms of their differential relations to other quanta of force (*WP* 1067), then any attempt to measure the world itself, through an aggregation of all known quanta of force, is doomed to failure and folly.

33. In his letter to Köselitz on March 20, 1882, Nietzsche credits Boscovich with replacing matter with force [*Kraft*] as the central focus of physics and cosmology. *Friedrich Nietzsche: Sämtliche Briefe, Kritische Studienausgabe in 8 Bänden*, ed. G. Colli and M. Montinari (Berlin: de Gruyter/Deutscher Taschenbuch Verlag, 1986), vol. 6, no. 213, pp. 183–84. For a definitive reckoning of Nietzsche's debts to Boscovich and Lange, see George J. Stack's seminal study, *Nietzsche and Lange* (Berlin: de Gruyter, 1983), especially chapter 9.

34. In a notebook entry from 1887, Nietzsche thus scribbles: "What determines rank, sets off rank, is only quanta of power, and nothing else" (*WP* 855).

In the following year he adds, "What determines your rank is the quantum of power you are: the rest is cowardice" (*WP* 858).

35. In a notebook entry from 1888, Nietzsche thus insists that "If we eliminate these additions, no things remain but only dynamic quanta, in a relation of tension to all other dynamic quanta: their essence lies in their relation to all other quanta, in their 'effect' upon the same" (*WP* 636).

36. See Stack, *Nietzsche and Lange*, 35–36.

37. For a detailed study of Nietzsche's various experiments with atomism, see James Porter, "Nietzsche's Atoms," in *Nietzsche und die antike Philosophie*, ed. Daniel W. Conway and Rudolf Rehn (Trier: Wissenschaftlicher Verlag, 1992), 47–90.

38. Mark Warren has persuasively demonstrated the centrality of a "crisis of human agency" to Nietzsche's understanding of modernity, in *Nietzsche and Political Thought* (Cambridge: MIT Press, 1988), especially chapters 1–2. Rather than view this "crisis" in terms of the "natural," descensional trajectory of modernity, however, Warren attributes the "crisis" to the onset of "nihilism," a term that refers, he believes, to "*situations in which an individual's material and interpretive practices fail to provide grounds for a reflexive interpretation of agency*" (17). While this definition of "nihilism" bears a family resemblance to Nietzsche's concept of "decadence," Warren's various accounts of the "causes" of nihilism (see, e.g., 18–19) suggest a significant departure from Nietzsche's own symptomatological method. In fact, Warren's understanding of "nihilism" as a species of alienation would seem to betray the confusion of cause and effect that Nietzsche is keen to debunk.

CHAPTER 4

The Garden of Innocence?
Nietzsche's Psychology of Woman

Rochelle L. Millen

DOUBLY GUILTY

A recent article in *The New York Times* posed a peculiarly Nietzschean dilemma. The October 16, 1996 issue reported that the appointment of Ms. Agnes Grossman as the first female director of the Vienna Boys' Choir has sent "tremors" through the larger Vienna music community.

In assessing this article in our society, where the parameters of affirmative action is a more likely subject of public discussion, the Nietzschean paradox presents itself clearly: Would Nietzsche support or oppose the battle for women's right to direct the Vienna choir? Perhaps this is a good litmus test to help formulate a clear picture of Nietzsche's psychology of women. True to the nuance, ambiguity, and subtlety that pervades Nietzsche's aphoristic style, one may argue for both sides as possibilities.

The Nietzsche who wrote before 1883 and *Thus Spoke Zarathustra* would likely have publicly supported women's pursuit of musical leadership. In the three works written before *Zarathustra* (1883–85), *Human, All-Too-Human* (1878), *Daybreak* (1880), and *The Gay Science* (1882), Nietzsche often portrays women as free-spirited, dignified, and independent thinkers. Yet the well-known passage in *The Gay Science* expresses Nietzsche's ambivalence toward women—and an unorthodox theology:

> Someone took a youth to a sage and said: "Look, he is being corrupted by women." The sage shook his head and smiled. "It is men," said he, "that corrupt women and all the failings of women should be atoned by and improved in men. For it is man who creates for himself

the image of woman, and woman forms herself according to his image."

"You are too kindhearted about women," said one of those present; "you do not know them." The sage replied: "will is the manner of men; willingness that of women. That is the law of the sexes—truly, a hard law for women. All of humanity is innocent of its existence; but women are doubly innocent. Who could have oil and kindness enough for them?"

"Damn oil! Damn kindness!" someone else shouted out of the crowd; "women need to be educated better!"

"—Men need to be educated better," said the sage and beckoned the youth to follow him.—The youth, however, did not follow.[1]

In this passage, Nietzsche proposes a striking antitheses to Christian doctrine. In classic Christian theology,[2] man (the male) is guilty and woman is doubly guilty, having initiated the sin of disobedience against God in the Garden of Eden. For Nietzsche, however, in a quite marvelous reversal, "All of humanity is innocent of its existence, but women are doubly innocent." In one broad stroke, Nietzsche erases original sin, exonerates both man and woman from eternal guilt, and restores to woman her rightful dignity and autonomy. According to Nietzsche, man—not God—creates woman in "his own image." And woman—not God—gives "form" to that image. Therefore, women need to be "atoned" for by men and "improved" through them.

That is, women are not culpable for their corruption. Rather, this quality develops in response to men, who desire women to be a certain way. It is interesting to note that Nietzsche does not say how this corruption occurs or in what it consists. Woman, wanting to be desired by and desirable to men, acts in ways she perceives man wishes her to act. Thus woman's presumed "corruption" is the result not of "original sin," but of man's willing a certain perception and vision of her. Woman, in her innocence, naiveté, and submissiveness, agrees to take upon herself the not always glorious task of fulfilling the aims of man's will. In this passage men are held responsible for that which women become. Woman does not appear as a simple pleaser-of-men (almost robotic and lacking autonomy). The passage highlights the intensity and pervasiveness of the sexual—and perhaps also cultural—dynamic between the sexes.[3]

Nietzsche is obviously sensitive to the power of the dominant group, men, to influence women in ways both blatant and subtle. Perhaps he is here recognizing, in a powerful way, the impact on the female psyche of her ability to bear life. In that sense, his words become a tribute to women. Or perhaps Nietzsche, in a foreshadowing of some contemporary cognitive and moral theories,[4] does well to acknowledge the male tendency toward autonomy or willfulness and the female propensity toward cooperation and consensus decision-making. That would render this passage non-axiological, that is, a description of differences within the reality of a male-dominated social structure. Even so, the positive images of women in the above passage can also be construed as patriarchal and sexist in tone, for Nietzsche presents a caricature of women as submissive, "innocent," and as persons created in "his" image.

Nietzsche grew up in a household of five women: his mother, sister, grandmother, and two maiden aunts, all of whom were pious Christians expecting young Fritz to follow his deceased father's footsteps into the ministry, against which he rebelled. The intimate family unit clearly played a major role in his "psychology of women."

To return to our initial query; Nietzsche, it seems, would support Ms. Agnes Grossman of the Vienna Boys' Choir. We know that although it was unusual in his time for a woman to pursue a university education, he encouraged his sister, Elisabeth, to take courses at the University of Leipzig.[5] Similarly, when in 1875, the faculty at the University of Basel voted whether or not to permit women to matriculate for studies—only men could receive degrees—Nietzsche voted in favor, while Jakob Burckhardt was among those who wished to exclude women students.[6] And we know Nietzsche tended to form relationships with women who were strong, independent-minded, and intellectually astute; Cosima Wagner, Malwida von Meysenbug, and Lou Salomé fit this description.

Despite Nietzsche's positive and progressive views toward women, one cannot easily put aside the many statements throughout his writings that seem to convey the opposite picture: Nietzsche as misogynist and sexist. Nietzsche serves as a striking example of a male philosopher perpetuating patriarchal culture by arguing for the inferiority of women. Certainly one cannot convincingly argue, as Walter Kaufmann tries, that Nietzsche's varied statements about women are "philosophically irrelevant"[7] to his thinking, beside the point, or to be expected from a man in late nineteenth-century Germany. This is not to take Nietzsche seriously, nor to appreciate—despite his elliptical and aphoristic style—the meticulousness with which he wrote. Thus we must carefully confront his statements about women, scattered as they are throughout his writings, and attempt to discern if there exists a consistent attitude regarding the psychology of women.[8]

Nietzsche's comments about women before 1883 are a mix of the positive and the negative; after *Zarathustra* they become increasingly contemptuous. I believe the pre-1883 spectrum of remarks reflects more accurately the true view of Nietzsche, with the later comments mirroring a significant transition point that led to anger, bitterness, and deep unhappiness, much of it articulated in Nietzsche's antiwoman state-ments. Yet even these later statements, put in their appropriate context, seem to express Nietzsche's profound resentment and feelings of rejec-tion from the women whom he loved and trusted as a child and young man more than a degrading view of women *qua* woman. Nonetheless, it cannot be denied—if that premise is accepted—that Nietzsche fell into the all-too-human conundrum of generalizing about a group rather than focusing upon an individual experience of betrayal or unhappiness. Accomplishing the latter demands perspective, emotional distance from one's pain, high self-esteem, perhaps what we might call "a thick skin." None of these, unfortunately, were part of Nietzsche's repertoire of qualities.

The following quotation from *Zarathustra* demonstrates the anti-woman bias in Nietzsche's writing that became from this time, increas-ingly overt.

> When I went on my way today, alone, at the hour when the sun goes down, I met a little old woman who spoke thus to my soul: "Much has Zarathustra spoken to us women too; but never did he speak to us about woman . . ." And I obliged the little old woman and I spoke to her thus:
>
> "Everything about woman is a riddle. . . . Man is for woman a means: the end is always the child. But what is the woman for the man?
>
> "A real man wants two things: danger and play. Therefore he wants woman as the most dangerous plaything. Man should be edu-cated for war, and woman for the recreation of the warrior: all else is folly."[9]

In Zarathustra's words, women are clearly inferior to men.[10] They are dangerous playthings, recreational objects from which men can derive pleasure and satisfaction. Ironically, the author of these senti-ments was a sexual ascetic for most, if not all, of his life. It is generally agreed that Nietzsche's insanity was due to syphilis; however, there is speculation as to whether Nietzsche inherited the illness from his father, from visiting a brothel in his college days, or from dirty needles while a nurse in the Franco-Prussian War. It is often assumed that Nietzsche contracted syphilis when he was at Bonn because he admitted that he had visited a brothel. However, he also insisted that he "came out touching nothing but a piano."[11]

Nietzsche, in his mid-thirties, wrote that the image one has of women is derived from one's mother and determines whether one will respect, despise, or be indifferent to women.[12] Assuming this to be true in Nietzsche's case, it is quite likely that Nietzsche's misogyny was for-mulated when he was in his teens—at the latest. Nietzsche's mother resented him for challenging and questioning the Christian faith, and for not fulfilling the family's expectations. And Nietzsche resented his mother for shunning his accomplishments and his natural free-thinking spirit and for making him feel "guilty."

When returning to Nietzsche's first aphoristic work, *Human, All-Too-Human,* published in 1878—the very year Nietzsche's break with Wagner became irreparable—none of the sixty aphorisms in the section called "Women and Child" meet modern criteria of misogyny. Rather, the reverse is true. Nietzsche conveys warmth and respect, even opening the section with the statement, "The perfect woman is a higher type of human than the perfect man, and also something much more rare."[13] That perfect women are more rare might be construed as prejudicial toward women. Yet perhaps Nietzsche is acknowledging the greater social and cultural obstacles faced by a woman should she strive toward this perfection. On the whole, however, when comparing men and women as equals, Nietzsche clearly says women are of a "higher type." Elsewhere in this work, Nietzsche comments upon the early flutterings of what gradually becomes the women's liberation movement: "Those noble, free-minded women," he writes, "who set themselves the task of educating and elevating the female sex should not overlook one factor: marriage, conceived of in its higher interpretation, the spiritual friendship of two people of opposite sexes."[14]

Here Nietzsche does not consign women to marriage or insist upon some perceived lower level of female intellectual attainment. Similarly, he does not oppose the "educating and elevating" of women, although he astutely notes that the initiatives come from women themselves. Rather, he maintains that the liberation of women should not be accompanied by a denigration of marriage, for it may contain a higher level of "spiritual friendship."

Two additional aspects of this aphorism bear noting. First, Nietzsche expresses an implied disdain for physical intimacy in marriage by regarding the "spiritual friendship" as a "higher interpretation." "Higher" apparently means "higher than the physical expression of friendship in sexuality." (Disdain would not have been implied had Nietzsche suggested that sexuality was an equally elevated expression of "spiritual friendship.")[15] Second, it can be surmised that Nietzsche perceives marriage as both negative and positive for women. Thus he emphasizes the personally positive—and the socially valuable—in order that the battle for women's liberation not become the occasion for advocacy against marriage. Nietzsche understood quite readily the social, financial, and intellectual restraints under which all women—but especially married women—were forced to live. Yet he knew equally clearly that the family—and thus marriage—is the foundation of all societal structures. Women should not give up their autonomy or sacrifice their natural endowments for the abstract social good, however. Rather, despite the limitations that unfortunately still apply to women within marriage, it is in that state that true "spiritual friendship" can be attained. Perhaps this obtains because Nietzsche valued highly the creativity expressed in child-bearing and child-raising. Carrying and nurturing new life, Nietzsche implies, is the ultimate expression of human creativity. Nietzsche, then, conveys a positive view of woman as dignified, yet free-spirited, capable of great spirituality and independent intellectual accomplishment.

In his next work, *Daybreak*, Nietzsche's remarks about women refer to romantic relationships and the interchange between the loved and the beloved; they are neutral rather than polemical. An exception, however, is an aphorism entitled "Misogynists." This passage begins with a quote from a man who says: "Woman is our enemy," to which Nietzsche responds: "Out of the man who says that to other men there speaks an immoderate drive which hates not only itself but his means of satisfaction as well."[16] There can be sexism in affirming that women are a means of "satisfaction" to men, yet the wisdom of the passage is that misogyny is a form of self-hatred; men who resent half the human race are resenting half of their own humanity as well.

Finally, the work immediately preceding *Zarathustra*, *The Gay Science*, also displays sensitive attitudes toward women. Even so, as shown, Nietzsche's sensitivity is intermingled with a stereotypical image of women as malleable, docile, and *doubly innocent*.

In the autumn of 1882, Nietzsche realized his relationship with Lou Salomé was at its end. At the same time, he felt disconnected from both his mother and sister, refusing to correspond with either; Elisabeth's increasingly virulent antisemitism repelled him and his mother had accused him of desecrating the memory of his father. Nietzsche was depressed, lonely, and isolated.

The intense, even frenzied writing of *Thus Spoke Zarathustra*, shielded Nietzsche from the true depths of his despair and also distilled his imagination and intuition to the finely honed insights that abound in that work. Upon its completion, Nietzsche's growing despondence and dejection reappeared, as expressed in a letter to Franz Overbeck in February 1883: "For a short time I was completely in my element, basking in my light [i.e., while writing *Zarathustra*]. And now it's over. . . . Thus I haven't been able to forget, even for an hour, that my mother called me a disgrace to the grave of my father."[17] Here is Nietzsche, living the very dilemma he sought to describe as a crucial moment in human history; torn in two by his illnesses, isolation, and insight; haunted by guilt and resentment; a sacrifice on the altar of a new century.[18] The Nietzsche who implied in *Daybreak* that misogyny was a form of self-hatred understood clearly that his antiwoman comments expressed that very self-contempt and disdain. All those he loved had distanced themselves, angry at his free-thinking, his allegedly un-Christian thoughts and ways, his defense of Jews, his general unworthiness to be loved. In the face of this onslaught, could Nietzsche have sustained a powerful and positive self-love?

WOMAN AS SUCH

Friedrich Nietzsche was the psychologist *par excellence* of the nineteenth century. He saw with alarming clarity that to which others remained blinded. He perceived the transformation that even in his time was eroding Christian Enlightenment values, and foretold the nihilism in which Western culture was to immolate itself a mere thirty-three years after his death. When we inquire, therefore, about Nietzsche's psychology of women, we are asking a master psychologist to articulate his own theories, stratagems, observations, and methodologies. Nietzsche, however, does not accommodate us as do other great masters—Sigmund Freud, Carl G. Jung, Melanie Klein, or Helene Deutsche. The insights and descriptions scattered throughout his works compel us to reconstruct the lines of his logic, reformulate the framework of his thoughts.

Having shown how one might consider Nietzsche to be a supporter of Ms. Agnes Grossman of the Vienna Boys' Choir, an examination of opposing evidence (and it is plentiful) is now the task at hand. Yet in perusing the sections from *Beyond Good and Evil* (1886) that appear to take an antifeminist stand, one must keep in mind how Nietzsche himself described his psychologizing:

> All psychology so far has got stuck in moral prejudices and fears; it has not dared to descend into the depths. To understand it as morphology and *the doctrine of the development of the will to power*, as I do—nobody has yet come close to doing this even in thought— . . .
> A proper physio-psychology has to contend with unconscious resistance in the heart of the investigator.[19]

To be forewarned is to be forearmed; Nietzsche is cautioning us not only about the possible depths of his insights, but also about his own inner opposition to those very perceptions.

In *Beyond Good and Evil*, written several years after the first part of *Zarathustra*, Nietzsche addresses the broad issue of "woman as such" (*Weib an sich*),[20] in the context of which statements regarding specific characteristics or behaviors of woman-in-general are articulated. He comments, for example:

> We men wish that woman should not go on compromising herself through enlightenment—just as it was man's thoughtfulness and consideration for woman that found expression in the church decree: *mulier taceat in ecclesia!*[21]

> As she thus takes possession of new rights, aspires to become "master" and writes the "progress" of woman upon her standards and banners, the opposite development is taking place with terrible clarity: *woman is retrogressing.*[22]

> Almost everywhere one . . . makes her more hysterical by the day and more incapable of her first and last profession—to give birth to strong children.[23]

This is a far cry from the Nietzsche who encouraged Elisabeth to take university courses; who responded with both admiration and passion to the personality and brilliance of Lou Salomé; who supported the matriculation of women at the University of Basel in 1875; and who regarded women as doubly innocent. Did Nietzsche's bitterness and profound loneliness lead to a personal transformation of values, the development of a vision in which woman's estimate lies in her decorativeness, her being a "slave" to man-as-master, an object for male satisfaction? I think not. Despite the roughness of Nietzsche's words, which grate against modern sensibilities, the harshness of Nietzsche's post-*Zarathustra* language about women must be put in the fuller context of the philosophy Nietzsche was constructing (based upon his tearing down the foundations of the Western philosophical tradition). This is not to excuse Nietzsche's scabrous words or distasteful metaphors. It is, instead, to attempt to reach Nietzsche through his own eyes as much as possible and in the context of his total philosophy rather than exclusively with twentieth-century assumptions governing our vision.

Additional comments about "woman as such" from *Beyond Good and Evil* abound:

> To go wrong on the fundamental problem of "man and woman," to deny the most abysmal antagonism between them and the necessity of an eternally hostile tension, to dream perhaps of equal rights, equal education, equal claims and obligations—that is a *typical* sign of shallowness.[24]

> Since the French Revolution, woman's influence in Europe has *decreased* proportionately as her rights and claims have increased. . . . [W]oman must be maintained, taken care of, protected, and indulged like a more delicate, strangely wild, and often pleasant domestic animal.[25]

> Stupidity in the kitchen, woman as cook; the gruesome thoughtlessness to which the feeding of the family and of the master of the house is

abandoned! Woman does not understand what food *means*—and wants to be cook. If woman were a thinking creature, she, as cook for millennia, would surely have had to discover the greatest physiological facts.[26]

Woman has much reason for shame; so much pedantry, superficiality, schoolmarmishness, petty presumption, petty licentiousness and immodesty lies concealed in woman—one only needs to study her behavior with children!

. . . Even now female voices are heard which . . . are frightening: they threaten with medical explicitness what woman *wants* from man. . . . But she does not *want* truth: what is truth to woman? From the beginning, nothing has been more alien, repugnant, and hostile to woman than truth—her great art is the lie, her highest concern is mere appearance and beauty.[27]

Despite how Nietzsche's words might affect contemporary, feminist sensibilities, it is clear that Nietzsche is not expressing a male "chauvinism," a belief in the superiority of male traits and masculine culture. That is, if the emancipation of women means *equal* participation in the "man's world," it is this very participation that represents regression, decline, and loss of power. If the traditional masculine characteristics of rationality, seriousness, organization, productivity, and desensualization are adapted by women, then the more traditional feminine qualities of instinct, spontaneity, unpredictability, nurturing, and sensuality lose their power within society. If this were to be a woman's choice, she might in fact be exchanging strength *for* weakness.

This implication of feminine superiority relates to several threads that connect seemingly disparate concepts and comments in the body of Nietzsche's work. First, Nietzsche sees reason and instinct as integrally bound together and denies the denigration of instinct and passion by those who hold reason to be primary. For Nietzsche, reason serves and is dependent upon the life instincts. This might be stated in the more familiar Freudian terminology: libido is the human instinctual force with whose energy and drive both individual satisfaction and human culture are constructed. Second (and related to the first), knowledge remains subservient to will. This view, adapted from Schopenhauer, does not claim that knowledge lacks power or value; rather, it is of second-level significance. Will is the core of the human being. Third, Nietzsche opposed all varieties of equality, which he construed philosophically as an attempt to rid the world of differences and the tensions differences necessarily entail; to universalize that which needs to remain pluralistic; to homogenize that which demands variegation. Fourth, and following from the third, Nietzsche's stinging critique of Western culture underlies the reversal of values just described. For in European culture, nurtured by the twin breasts of Platonism and Christianity, "being" takes priority over "becoming," "spirit" over "nature." If culture is predominantly a product of male qualities expressed on the broad, societal plane, it is the very masculinity of that culture that Nietzsche is critiquing.

Another way to state this is to use the categories and terminology of *The Birth of Tragedy*, Nietzsche's first work, written in 1872. By so doing the consistent thread of Nietzsche's development can be seen. For it is in this early work that Nietzsche posits a synthesis of instinct and reason, the Dionysian and the Apollonian. The Greek deity Dionysus represents ecstasy and self-transcendence while Apollo personifies the notion of individuation. The Dionysian-Apollonian cosmic relationship, therefore, denotes an integration of flux, or becoming, with moments of individuation, or being. Thus the world-process, the world-dynamic is that of stasis within movement; of immanence within transcendence; of the fleeting present moment within the process of the always developing future.[28] For Nietzsche, to be life-affirming is to recognize the brief appearances of structure and order (the Apollonian) within the never-ending processes of instinctual power, the push toward overcoming that very structure and order (the Dionysian).

According to Nietzsche,[29] the early Greek intermingling of Dionysus and Apollo was sundered by Socrates, the very founder of the Western philosophic tradition. Socrates ascribed greater value to form than to formlessness, to unchanging "truth" beyond the realm of change and appearance. What once was a balanced and necessary interaction between reason (form) and instinct (formlessness) was severed, leading to an antagonism between the two and the constant attempt to affirm the priority of one or the other. The world in which Nietzsche proclaims the death of God and appears to denigrate woman's fight for equality is one in which Apollonian propensities have come to predominate over Dionysian forces. The culture critiqued by Nietzsche as embedded within an otherworldly Christianity mistakes form for Platonic "substance" and "truth." Form, however, is the process of creation, not the result or end-product of the processes. There is no objective truth, only the constant struggle to attain to truth-of-the-moment, the constant creation of the present.[30]

This discussion creates a different context from which to interpret Nietzsche's comments about woman's rejection of truth, the "lie," and "appearance" in the earlier citations from *Beyond Good and Evil*. For if the Apollonian-Dionysian distinction can be said to parallel masculine and feminine traits, then Nietzsche's objections to woman's emancipation (political or otherwise) can be said to mean woman's adoption of male alienation from nature, the instinctual, and Dionysian. Women's emancipation would also imply the ultimate victory of reason and science over nature and instinct, the victory of Platonic Being over the earlier Greek primordial Becoming. For Nietzsche, nature is closer to whatever truth can be found than is culture.[31] Thus woman and the Dionysian are inextricably linked and are superior to the Western emphasis on technology, reason, and knowledge, all of which remain truncated from their life-source in the Dionysian. It is this alienation from one's roots, characteristic of male-dominated culture, from which Nietzsche wishes to save woman. His aim is not only or even primarily the Nietzschean salvation of individual women, but also—and perhaps more importantly—the possible amelioration, if not actual salvation, of Western culture, which Nietzsche saw poised on the edge of an abyss. The playful unpredictability, the artistic spontaneity, the nurturance and sensuality of woman all assist the man in understanding culture as appearance rather than truth. The creative process is both masculine and feminine, necessitating the use of Apollonian and Dionysian forces. This duality must be maintained both individually and in the culture as a whole. One might claim that "Nietzsche's objections to 'equality' have their roots in his aim to preserve the conditions of creativity."[32] But this is a problematic conclusion. Can it be Nietzsche means woman must sacrifice certain kinds of equality in order to maintain the viability of the whole? This is classic and obvious patriarchalism. An alternative interpretation is possible, although perhaps not convincing.[33] It has been proposed that Nietzsche would have concurred in a tripartite feminism: recognizing the "archetypal masculine-feminine" distinction, where each element has equal significance and the feminine is given full play of its powers; recognizing the highest kind of human nature—the creator—as androgynous; understanding that not everyone can become a creator.

This explanation, while somewhat more palatable than the first, nonetheless maintains an elitism, an exclusiveness at the core of Nietzsche's formulation. Some would argue strongly against such elitism, yet necessary hierarchy is focal in Nietzsche. Nietzsche's concept of creator, as noted earlier, implies that the higher person's need for a meaningful culture overrides the needs of specific, individual human beings for a life of liberty and well-being within any culture. Yet a culture must be responsive to the needs of individuals. It is claimed by one Nietzsche commentator that Nietzsche's solution to this dilemma "is to argue that a worthy culture need only be responsive to the needs of the creator of values."[34] Thus the task of "others" is to serve and support the creator. This notion leads, in my view, precisely to the fascism it has been strongly argued Nietzsche opposed.[35]

Our final examination of Nietzsche's texts is a passage from *Twilight of the Idols*, published in 1888, the same year as four additional works.[36]

The rationality of marriage—that lay in the husband's sole juridical responsibility, which gave marriage a center of gravity, while today it limps on both legs. The rationality of marriage—that lay in its indissolubility in principle, which lent it an accent that could be heard above the accident of feeling, passion, and what is merely momentary. It also lay in the family's responsibility for the choice of a spouse. With the growing indulgence of love matches, the very foundation of marriage has been eliminated, that which alone makes an institution of it.[37]

Here the anomaly mentioned above becomes transparent. Feeling, passion, and the "momentary" are not accorded value as necessary Dionysian elements providing balance in the marriage relationship. Rather, they are "accident," incidental to the "rationality," expressed sociologically in the husband's "sole juridical responsibility" for the marriage partnership. Since love is mere feeling or accident, marriage, the most personal of all relationships, "should be founded on such impersonal (instinctual) characteristics as the sex or property drive."[38] Emotion and love in marriage must be controlled by rationality; analogously, those who represent the former (women) must be dominated by those who symbolize the latter (men).

However, given Nietzsche's powerful rebellion against the authoritarian nature of his own upbringing, is this a view he could have seriously advocated? Additionally, these notions of marriage derail Nietzsche's earlier affirmations of spontaneity and the life-giving capacity. One Nietzsche critic avers that "It must be admitted that in so unsystematic a writer as Nietzsche one cannot expect a single view on any topic, including marriage."[39] Perhaps, Nietzsche was being deliberately provocative, or putting forth this view as one of several he may have held regarding marriage. In *Twilight of the Idols*, Nietzsche opposes democracy, the equal rights of women, and the rights of workers to organize.[40] Thus he seems to develop further the arguments found in *Beyond Good and Evil*, and to be consistent with other formulations. For example, in book 5 of *The Gay Science* (added in 1886), although Nietzsche says he will make "concessions" in favor of monogamy, he quickly adds: "I will never admit the claim that man and woman have equal rights in love; these do not exist."[41] Here, however, Nietzsche is not writing directly of political rights, but of rights within the intimate love relationship, of how men and women love and ought to love based on the psychology of male and female nature.

In analyzing these various and varied texts of Nietzsche's corpus as they comment upon and explicate a psychology of woman, I am struck by how the notions of prescriptive and descriptive impact upon arriving at a conclusion on what the Nietzschean viewpoint might be. This is analogous in some ways to the history of interpretation on Genesis 1–3, which records the creation story and God's meeting with Adam and Eve in the Garden of Eden. Paul construed the transition of the Garden's innocence and the subsequent punishments from God (Genesis 3:16–19) as *prescriptive*—indeed as a curse; this is evidenced in Romans (5:12–21), where God's grace, manifested in Jesus' death, is the sole means of spiritual cleansing.

Jewish biblical commentary, however, tended to view the passages as *descriptive* of social reality; one of the principal tasks of Genesis 1–11 is to show how the world as "it is" came to be. That is, reality *demonstrates* that women bear children, and that men are usually the hunters and providers. In regard to the controversial "and he shall rule over thee" (Genesis 3:16), the Christian tradition deduces a necessary hierarchy of authority, while some rabbinic commentators, disturbed by the implied imbalance, argue that this refers solely to physiology, that is, the usual sexual position with the man on top or to the fact that sex is usually initiated by the man.[42] If the passage is interpreted as descriptive, then the corollary is that humanity's task is to restore the imbalance resulting from the sin of disobedience and reestablish the harmony of Paradise. This contrasts strongly with the prescriptive interpretation that in the nineteenth-century was used by Christian ministers to argue against anesthetics for women during childbirth; women, that is, were supposed to feel pain and suffer.

I bring in the prescriptive-descriptive axis of interpretation of these crucial verses in Genesis because this dialectic may be of aid in extrapolating a coherent, textually supported notion of Nietzsche's psychology of women from the often contradictory viewpoints expressed in his many writings. Nietzsche accepts as a given that woman is closer to nature than man. As Simone de Beauvoir states, the female is "more enslaved to the species than the male, her animality is more manifest."[43] This is compounded by her natural association with the domestic context, deriving from lactation and the as yet unsocialized nature of small children. On the other hand, as explained by Ortner, woman's other functions within this very context "show her to be a powerful agent of the cultural process, constantly transforming raw natural resources into cultural products."[44] Thus, by virtue of her social locus woman is seen as intermediate between nature and culture, implying both "middle status" and a "mediating" role;[45] the evolution of woman's secondary or inferior status in regard to culture and transcendence is therefore clear. However, if the continuum from nature to culture is viewed not vertically but in circular configuration, one can see how the intermediate or mediating position can both surround, yet be peripheral to the center. In this one image woman is polarized, representing contradictory notions: she is both all-powerful (life), yet outside of life and therefore dangerous (death).[46] Woman's intermediacy between culture and nature thus has about it an ambiguity as to value and status.

Nietzsche's psychology of women both partakes of and articulates this same ambiguity. In Nietzsche's ideal vision of woman, she represents the Dionysian, that which remains instinctual, creative, and life-affirming in a culture that claims enlightenment, but is moving toward collapse and self-destruction. But this ideal of nature transcending culture, of the Dionysian overcoming the Apollonian is precisely that: Nietzsche's ideal, predicated upon an ideal—if incomplete—psychology of woman. It is not given to Nietzsche—nor to any of us—to function in a world of pure ideals. The real world bumps against us constantly; sometimes gently, often harshly. The dissonance between pure thought and the sloppiness and slowness of reality contributes to our existential dilemma, of which Nietzsche was acutely—perhaps too acutely—aware.

Thus standing in opposition to Nietzsche's metaphysic of the purely abstract woman was the real woman, the real women in his life and in the Germany of his time. The ideal woman is therefore colored by Nietzsche's troubled upbringing by women and his various relationships/friendships: Lou Salomé, Malwida von Meysenbug, and Elisabeth. None of us is a disembodied consciousness; Nietzsche's met and unmet emotional needs in regard to women interfere with his abstract vision of the female role in history.

In addition, Nietzsche's ideal must be tempered by the slow, untidy developmental processes of history, in which movement is often agonizingly gradual; in which three steps forward may be followed by two— or four—steps backward—or the converse. And lastly, Nietzsche is writing in a post-Hegelian environment, in the context of the Bismarckian Germany that had in 1869 been united by victory in three wars and its enmity for France. The notion of individual rights is present in Germany in Nietzsche's time, but not with our American political parameters. Subsuming one's own happiness—and individual freedoms—under the umbrella of the needs of the state was a prevalent and dominant concept in Nietzsche's Germany, born out of "blood and iron" and not on the battlefield for democracy. Nietzsche cannot escape the overriding cultural views about women in his era because he cannot rise above himself. Yes, Elisabeth should take university courses and women ought to be officially admitted to the University of Basel. Yet woman—plaything of the warrior—is corrupt. All she wishes is to bring forth life, for this is the highest expression of her capacity for creativity and transcendence. Woman is "man's enemy," perhaps because she competes with him on the playing field of transcending nature. Yet she retrogresses as she becomes more self-reliant, even specifying how her sexual desires might be better satisfied. Woman, it seems, is more powerful, more true to her task in culture when she remains subservient, seeking neither enlightenment nor rights. Nietzsche is simultaneously describing the situation of his time and prescribing a view of woman divorced from his earlier ideal and set in the world of real people and human history. Thus in Nietzschean fashion, liberal Reichstag deputies

> greeted the socialists' first woman suffrage proposal in 1895 with silence. Education and employment opportunities for women won liberal favor long before woman suffrage. Liberal reluctance about the vote was compounded of general male prejudices and specific fears that women would not vote liberal.[47]

Nietzsche describes an ideal in his early works, but later prescribes a place for woman founded on anger, bitterness, and the Germanic notion of individual sacrifice for the sake of the organic whole, compounded by the political debates regarding women's employment, education, and suffrage that were part of nineteenth century German society of his time. In his own way, Nietzsche glorified and spiritualized woman. Then, almost as punishment for this high place of honor, he described her as playful property that ought to be controlled by man. Perhaps if the women who had reared him had been dominated by a loving, if patriarchal man, he would have been more whole, less fragmented and unhappy; is this, then, his unconscious wish?

NOTES

1. Friedrich Nietzsche, *The Gay Science,* trans. Walter Kaufmann (New York: Random House, 1974), 68.

2. These are Augustine's *City of God* and *On Marriage and Concupiscence.* An excellent contemporary analysis of the Augustinian perspective is found in Elaine Pagels, *Adam, Eve, and the Serpent* (New York: Random House, 1988). Other recent discussions are Lisa Sowle Cahill, *Between the Sexes* (Philadelphia: Fortress Press, 1985) and David G. Hunter, ed., *Marriage in the Early Church* (Minneapolis: Fortress Press, 1992).

3. Cf. Lynne Tirrell, "Sexual Dualism and Women's Self Creation," in *Nietzsche and the Feminine,* ed. Peter J. Burgard (Charlottesville: University Press of Virginia, 1994), 167.

4. See Carol Gilligan, *In a Different Voice* (Cambridge: Harvard University Press, 1982); Seyla Benhabib, "The Generalized and the Concrete Other: The Kohlberg-Gilligan Controversy and Oral Theory," in *Women and Moral Theory,* ed. Eva Kittay and Diana Meyers (Totowa, NJ: Rowman and Littlefield, 1987), 154–78. Also Melanie Klein, *Envy and Gratitude and Other Works,* 1946–1963 (New York: Dell, 1977).

5. Robert C. Holub, "Review Essay: Nietzsche and the Woman Question," *The German Quarterly* 68.1 (Winter 1995): 68. His source is H. F. Peters,

Zarathustra's Sister (New York: Crown, 1977), 26. Holub's review is of *Nietzsche and the Feminine*.

6. The petition was turned down by a vote of six to four. Holub, "Review Essay." See also Curt Paul Janz, *Friedrich Nietzsche: Biographie* (Munich: Hanser, 1978), I:624–25

7. Walter Kaufmann: *Nietzsche: Philosopher, Psychologist, Antichrist* (Princeton: Princeton University Press, 1974), 84.

8. For a fine discussion of Nietzsche and women, see the essays by Kathleen Higgins, Debra Bergoffen, Babette Babich, Caroline ('Kay') Picart, and Carol Diethe in the *Journal of Nietzsche Studies* 12 (Autumn 1996), published by the Friedrich Nietzsche Society of Great Britain.

9. Friedrich Nietzsche, *Thus Spoke Zarathustra*, trans. Walter Kaufmann (New York: Vintage, 1996), part I, "On Little Old and Young Women."

10. Yet, interestingly, in this passage from *Zarathustra*, the infamous phrase: "You are going to women? Do not forget the whip!" is spoken by the little old woman *to* Zarathustra.

11. Quoted in W. Santaniello, "Nietzsche's Misogyny," paper presented at the Midwest Feminist Graduate Student Conference, Northwestern University, February 1991, 1 and 6. Santaniello's sources are *Erinnerungen an Friedrich Nietzsche* (Leipzig: F. A. Brockhaus, 1901), 22ff., and Carl Pletsch, *The Young Nietzsche* (New York: Free Press, 1991), 66–67.

12. Friedrich Nietzsche, *Human, All-Too-Human*, trans. Marion Faber (Lincoln: University of Nebraska Press, 1984), 380.

13. *HU* 377. This statement recalls *Ecclesiastes* 7:28, where Koheleth's pessimism is expressed in an antiwoman comment: "one man among a thousand have I found, but a woman among all those I have not found" (my translation).

14. *HU* 424.

15. Nietzsche's strict Christian upbringing would undoubtedly have led to negative attitudes toward sexuality and one's own body.

16. *Daybreak*, trans. R. J. Hollingdale, intro. Michael Tanner (Cambridge: Cambridge University Press, 1982), 346.

17. Letter to Malwida von Meysenbug, sent from Venice, February 1883, in *Nietzsche: A Self-Portrait from His Letters*, ed. Peter Fuss and Henry Shapiro (Cambridge: Harvard University Press, 1971), 70–71.

18. Nietzsche died in 1900.

19. Friedrich Nietzsche, *Beyond Good and Evil*, in *Basic Writings of Nietzsche*, trans. and ed. Walter Kaufmann (New York: The Modern Library, 1992), 23.

20. Ibid., 232.

21. Ibid. The Latin phrases translate as "Woman should be silent in church." Thereafter in the passage (the Latin translates as): "Woman should be silent when it comes to politics," and "Woman should be silent about woman."

22. Ibid., 239.

23. Ibid.

24. Ibid., 238.

25. Ibid., 239.

26. Ibid., 234.

27. Ibid., 232.

28. See Lawrence J. Hatab, "Nietzsche on Woman," *Southern Journal of Philosophy* 19.3 (Fall 1981): 336–37. See also, Jacob Golomb, *Nietzsche's Enticing Psychology of Power* (Ames: Iowa State University Press, 1989).

29. See Hatab, "Nietzsche on Woman," 335–37.

30. Robert C. Solomon, "Nietzsche, Nihilism, and Morality" in *Nietzsche: A Collection of Critical Essays*, ed. R. Solomon (Garden City, N.Y.: Anchor, 1973).

31. Sherry B. Ortner, "Is Female to Male as Nature is to Culture," in *Woman, Culture, and Society*, ed. Michelle Rosaldo and Louise Lamphere (Stanford: Stanford University Press, 1974), 67–88.

32. Hatab, "Nietzsche on Woman," 342.

33. Ibid., 343–44.

34. Ofelia Schutte, *Beyond Nihilism: Nietzsche without Masks* (Chicago: University of Chicago Press, 1984), 179.

35. Weaver Santaniello, *Nietzsche, God, and the Jews: His Critique of Judeo-Christianity in Relation to the Nazi Myth* (Albany: State University of New York Press, 1994).

36. These are *The Antichrist, Ecce Homo, The Case of Wagner, and Nietzsche contra Wagner.* This unusually prolific output manifested Nietzsche's frenzied state prior to his breakdown.

37. Friedrich Nietzsche, *Twilight of the Idols*, "Skirmishes of an Untimely Man," in *The Portable Nietzsche*, trans. Walter Kaufmann (New York: Viking, 1954).

38. Schutte, *Beyond Nihilism*, 182.

39. Ibid., 183.

40. Ibid., 180ff.

41. *GS* 363.

42. See Rashi on Genesis 3:16. For contemporary discussions of these passages and traditions of commentary, see Phyllis Trible, *God and the Rhetoric of Sexuality* (Philadelphia: Fortress Press, 1978). Joel Rosenberg, "Biblical Narrative," in *Back to the Sources*, ed. Barry W. Holtz (New York: Summit Books, 1984), 31–82; and J. B. Soloveitchik, "The Lonely Man of Faith," in *Tradition* 8.2 (Summer 1965): 3–67.

43. Simone de Beauvoir, *The Second Sex*, trans. H. M. Parshley (New York: Bantam Books, 1961), 239.

44. Sherry B. Ortner, "Is Female to Male as Nature Is to Culture?," 80.

45. See Ibid., 184.

46. Ibid., 185–87.

47. Amy Hackett, "Feminism and Liberalism in Wilhelmine Germany, 1890–1918," in *Liberating Women's History*, ed. Berenice A. Carroll (Urbana: University of Illinois Press, 1976), 130–31.

CHAPTER 5

Nietzsche's Psychogenealogy of Religion and Racism

Weaver Santaniello

—Now they give me to understand that they are not merely better
than the mighty . . . but because God has commanded them to
obey the authorities. . . . But enough! enough! I can't take anymore. Bad air! Bad air!

—*Genealogy of Morals* I:14

—And therefore let us have fresh air! fresh air! and keep clear of
the madhouses and hospitals of culture! Or solitude, if it must be!
. . . So that we may guard ourselves, my friends, against the two
worst contagions that may be reserved just for us—

—*Genealogy of Morals* III:15

As a psychologist of religion Nietzsche's main contention is that life lives
not on morality but on metaphysical deceptions. To uncover the dynamics underlying the "psychology of convictions" Nietzsche uses psychological and genealogical methods as tools for exposing the "hideous"
errors of Western civilization.[1]

According to Nietzsche the lack of historical sense is the "family
failing" of all philosophizing.[2] Modern's believe they can psychologically analyze contemporary "man," but this approach is insufficient, for
it is limited to a narrow period of time. Consequently, throughout his
works, especially the *Genealogy of Morals*, Nietzsche seeks the *origins*
of ideas and concepts and their evolution, the "genesis of thought."[3] To
explore the origin of religion and morality Nietzsche declares that a free
spirit of solitude who has loved religion—but has outgrown it—must
employ self-analysis and historical philosophizing on the road to great
health and the "great liberation." "But," Nietzsche asks, "where today
are there psychologists?"[4]

ON THE ORIGIN OF RELIGION

In his early aphoristic works, Nietzsche lays the groundwork as a genealogist and psychologist of morality with his speculations on the origin of religion(s). He states that these metaphysical "errors" originate from a misunderstanding of dreams (in which the "second real world"—the split between soul-body, spirits-gods, initially came into being).[5] He also locates the "origin of the religious cult" in the sorcerer's misunderstanding of natural law, in which low stages of culture, believing nature to be mysterious and magical, attempted to impose laws upon it.[6] Most often, however, he cites the psychological misunderstanding of human nature and self-deception as that which initially prevailed among the founders of religions, and continues to prevail among religious believers today.[7] Fear, superstition, need, boredom, custom, the will to truth, spiritual poverty, and the desire to be released from suffering are the primary reasons we have believed—and still continue to believe in god(s).[8] Overall, Nietzsche claims, Europe's "poverty in psychological observation" is apparent because people are reluctant to dissect human actions and their own psyches; they are ashamed to expose the "nakedness of the soul" and to examine themselves.[9] To undertake such an arduous task, Nietzsche says, would impose upon an individual's happiness and peace of mind, traditionally fostered by religious and metaphysical palliatives: there is "much talk about people," Nietzsche observes, but "none at all about *man*."[10] These words resonate in the *Genealogy*, where Nietzsche embarks upon an elaborate historical evolution of morality and religion, applying physiology, psychology, sociology, etymology, and theology to his critique: "We men of knowledge" today, he warns in the opening line of the preface, "are unknown to ourselves." We don't know ourselves, we have not sought ourselves, we are strangers to ourselves, and Nietzsche claims, "we *have* to misunderstand ourselves."[11] He quotes the New Testament to stress the unfortunate fact that objective knowledge is the supreme goal today—as opposed to self-knowledge and our own personal *experience*: "Where your treasure is, there will your heart be also" (Matthew 6:21). The "beehives of knowledge" are detrimental obstacles to inner knowledge and experiencing history within ourselves.[12] Elsewhere, he uses the image of Christ on the cross to show that Jesus too was human in his uncertain quest for meaning in life. In "On the Knowledge Acquired through Suffering," Nietzsche writes that if one has been living in a "perilous world of fantasy," a sobering-up through pain is perhaps the only means of extricating him from it:

> It is possible that this is what happened to the founder of Christianity on the cross: for the bitterest of all exclamations "my God, why hast

thou forsaken me!" contains, in its ultimate significance, evidence of a general disappointment and enlightenment over the delusion of his life; at the moment of supreme agony he acquired an insight into himself.[13]

In a nutshell, Nietzsche contends that sorrow *is* knowledge and that wisdom and creativity are acquired through struggle and self-revelation: Believing in God is pacifying, yet we live in an age of knowledge—in danger of "bleeding to death" from knowing "the truth" that there is not.[14] For Nietzsche the origin of religion(s) is different than the origin of belief. Religious origins are rooted in natural instincts, the passions, and the imagination, all of which can be positive and life-enhancing. These potentially creative realms are often repressed by society's deification of reason ("Christianity is Platonism for the 'people,'" *BGE* p), or by the *acute* repression of instincts. Nietzsche thus looks to the pre-Socratics and the ancient Hebrews for positive elements of religious inclinations. He locates the negative elements of religion in dogmatism, extreme repression, and the will to "intellectual cleanliness at any price."[15]

Nietzsche can find positive aspects in the Gods of Brahminism, ancient Greece, ancient Jehovah, and in the person of Buddha, yet he rarely has anything positive to say about the Christian God (as distinct from the historical Jesus), the origins of Christianity (ascribed predominately to Paul), or about the Judaic elements that Western Christendom had "usurped" from the Jewish scholars.[16] Nietzsche is bitterly critical of antisemitism and antisemites (imputing *ressentiment* to them), and his vital critique of religion is directed against the Christian moral code in nineteenth-century Germany, especially its threefold "virtues" of pity, self-sacrifice, and self-abnegation, all of which are connected to his central psychological notion of *ressentiment*. At first glance, these three Christian virtues are clearly incompatible with Nietzsche's emphasis on individual—as distinct from communal or political—growth.

Nietzsche praises the Brahmins (the priestly caste of Hinduism) for "overthrowing their gods"; he praises the ancient Greeks for not viewing the gods "above them"; and upholds ancient Yahweh for representing the power of a people, self-confidence, and a good conscience.[17] Zarathustra's dictum: "And *they* [emphasis mine] did not know how to love their god except by crucifying man,"[18] haunted the twentieth-century Christian theologian Karl Barth throughout much of his life. Nietzsche favored polytheism, as well as Spinoza's pantheism, over Judaic and Christian monotheism, mainly because he despised the idea of God as the one and only truth, or the Christian god as "the way, the truth, and the life" (John 14:6).[19] For Nietzsche, the dogmatic believer's will to truth was inferior to that of the free-spirit's skeptical will to create:

"Even if we were mad enough to consider all of our opinions true," Nietzsche laughs, "we should still not desire that everyone believe in them." The problem of the "origin of religions," Nietzsche claims, is that when one regards one's opinion as revelation, it is made holy and thus freed from all criticism and doubt.[20] The process of elevating one's own idea above oneself and then ascribing the idea to God, is self-debasing. Clearly, Nietzsche and Zarathustra's god(s) would not be worshipped as Masters of Truth above humanity, but could only be related to humans and their own transformative powers: "I could only believe in a god who could dance," Zarathustra cries. "Now I am light, now I fly, now I see myself beneath myself, now a god dances through me."[21] Nietzsche's God works through and with the human's creative powers; the divine element of life does not resemble a judge or lawmaker, does not reward or punish, does not offer salvation in other worlds, but relates to humans in *this* one.

Psychologically considered, Nietzsche's point is that we must be sovereign over our own convictions: truth does not originate in Gods, ideals, convictions, established institutions, or in acquired moralities of duty or utility, but within ourselves. Noble creators do not seek preestablished morality in conventional tenets, they are those who are *truthful* and generate *values*: "It was ever in the desert that the truthful have dwelt, the free spirits, as masters of the desert; but in the cities dwell the well-fed, famous wise men—the beasts of burden. For, as asses, they always pull the people's cart."[22]

Nietzsche's (still) radical claim of Christian morality as barbaric, as the "religion of pity" that makes "suffering contagious," is based on the plain fact that every act of pity requires another person (or group) who suffers.[23] According to Nietzsche, the pitier acquires a feeling of superiority and power being "tender" (though slightly contemptuous) toward the other and thus continually desires a suffering agent to renew his or her *feeling* of power.[24] In this process, suffering (and the sufferer) is degraded, and pity (and the one who pities) is elevated. Thus Nietzsche, who was plagued by illness and identified strongly with the noble sufferer, emphasizes again and again that the slave morality of pity *increases* suffering: it is the practice of nihilism.[25] Nietzsche is not saying that one should not feel sympathy or compassion for another: he cites the four noble cardinal virtues as "courage, insight, sympathy, and solitude."[26] His psychological critique of pity (*Mitleid*) is not critical of one person's genuine concern for another, but of the Pitier's *intentional* desire to hurt others in order to gain a superficial sense of superiority: We must, Nietzsche says, transcend pity and achieve a "victory over ourselves."[27] This process of self-overcoming well illustrates the Nietzschean dictum that we should become masters *over* our alleged "virtues"—not slaves to them ("Of course," Nietzsche writes, "one ought to *express* pity, but one ought to guard against *having* it").[28] This assessment of slave morality—being held in bondage to any particular virtue or to one particular God—is also in keeping with Nietzsche's religious preference for the noble gods of ancient Greece versus the Christian God.[29]

Nietzsche is well aware that each of us plays the role of pitier and sufferer at different times and in different situations: yet he is concerned with *extremes*. He acknowledges Buddhism's central tenet that all humans suffer, and regards the central meaning of Christ on the cross as conveying that because we all suffer, we all are *divine*.[30] Yet Nietzsche clearly does not want us to *have* pity, for when we have pity (or any virtue) we are its *victims*.[31] Because Nietzsche regards profound or "positive suffering" as a means to wisdom, spontaneity, creativity, and spiritual power, he does not believe it can or should be abolished. Yet he keenly sees how "negative" sufferers (pitiers) enlist pity, self-contempt, and—to a greater extreme—vengeance to degrade or bring others down. In *Beyond Good and Evil* he writes:

> Where pity is preached today—and, if you listen closely, this is the only religion preached now—psychologists should keep their ears open: through all the vanity, through all the noise that characterizes these preachers (like all preachers) they will hear a hoarse, groaning, genuine sound of *self-contempt*. . . . He suffers—and his vanity wants him to suffer only with others, to feel pity.—[32]

In the passage above and elsewhere, Nietzsche clearly makes a distinction between the positive morality of "expressing pity," and the slave mentality of "having" pity, or of *wanting* others to suffer to acquire power. In contrast to that psychological dynamic which "perpetuates misery," Nietzsche insists: "The noble human being, too, helps the unfortunate, but not from pity, but by an urge begotten by an excess of power."[33]

GUILT, BAD CONSCIENCE, AND THE LIKE

In the *Genealogy*, Nietzsche expounds on how pity, suffering, self-abnegation, and self-sacrifice relate to racism, German nationalism, and *ressentiment*. In a central—but often ignored—passage, he writes: "To the psychologist who would like to study *ressentiment* close up for once, I would say: this plant blooms best today among anarchists and antisemites—where it has always bloomed."[34] According to Nietzsche, antisemites have "the will to power of the weakest!" and sanctify revenge under the (false) name of "justice."[35] Taking into consideration that the anarchist Nietzsche is referring to was Eugen Dühring, the "moral big-mouth" in Germany who thought Jews should be exterminated, and that Nietzsche's sister Elisabeth was a fierce Christian antisemite who later became Hitler's ally, it is clear that Nietzsche is embarking upon a unique psychogenealogy of racism and religion in nineteenth-century Germany.[36]

In the *Genealogy*, Nietzsche attempts to unmask the "*origin* of our moral prejudices" (preface) with his complex psychological and socio-logical exploration into the genesis of instincts and ideals. He is mainly concerned with how the "priestly-mode" of valuation (Judeo-Christian morality typified by spiritual revenge) branched off from the knightly-aristocratic mode (typified by natural noble character traits). In the first essay, Nietzsche ascertains that false ethics arose from the erroneous split between egoistic and unegoistic *actions* (emphasis mine). Briefly put, Nietzsche once again insists that the "ideals" of nobility historically arose from spontaneous self-affirmation, *not* submissive self-sacrifice—to the state, to another person, to ascetic ideals, or to any other type of external manifestation or institution. He then investigates how modern Europe's negative sufferers and pitiers (antisemites) acquired "Guilt, bad conscience, and the like."

Historically, Nietzsche says, the psychological origin of guilt arose in the economical relationships between creditor and debtor where one person first measured himself against another (*GM* II:8). Human pride and the sense of superiority *over* others also came into being. Because the "origin of justice" was initially based on equal power relationships and is a "positive attitude" (*GM* II:11), it appears that negative suffer-ers who seek the origin of justice in resentment, such as Dühring, have a "bad conscience": they are not active but reactive men who desire to injure others and make them suffer.[37] True justice, Nietzsche says, now occurs when a stronger power attempts to end the "senseless raging of *ressentiment*" among the weaker powers who employ it.[38]

Again, considering that Nietzsche, in the *Genealogy*, is addressing a racist German who loathed and sought to destroy Jews, it appears that his basic psychological thrust is as follows: racists have a bad con-science and are full of resentment; they first need to create "evil" ene-mies in order to affirm themselves. This process is contrary to nobles such as Mirabeau, who are able to shake off with a single shrug "much vermin" that eat deep into others (*GM* I:10). Comte de Mirabeau (1749–91) was a French statesman who wrote *On Moses Mendelssohn and Political Reform of the Jews*, in which he argued that all debasing distinctions against Jews should be *banished* and all avenues of liveli-hood be open to them.[39] Thus it is *especially* illuminating that Nietz-sche specifically names Mirabeau as the historical "noble," and rebukes the Jew-hating Dühring as the "apostle of revenge" consumed with *ressentiment* and a bad conscience (*GM* III:14): "For every sufferer instinctively seeks a cause for his suffering; more exactly, an agent; still more specifically, a guilty agent . . . some living thing upon which he can . . . vent his affects . . . for the venting of his affects represents the greatest attempt . . . to win relief. . . . This alone, I surmise, constitutes the actual physiological cause of *ressentiment*, vengefulness, and the like" (*GM* III:15). To clarify: the noble in Nietzsche's essay is an historical figure (Mirabeau) who upheld the Jews; the man of *ressentiment* and bad conscience (Dühring) is one who demeaned and sought vengeance against Jews. Their relation to Jews and their respective status in Nietzsche's vision of a new European hierarchy is no mere coincidence.

Prehistorically, Nietzsche says, the origin of the bad conscience arose when the human instinct for freedom and spontaneity was suppressed by external constraints, such as the state. As natural human instincts were inhibited from being discharged, they turned inward; this is what Nietzsche regards as the internalization of man: "Hostility, cruelty, joy in persecuting, in attacking, in change, in destruction—. . . : *that* is the origin of the 'bad conscience'" (*GM* II:16). Eventually, repressed instincts (rooted in self-denial) found increased pleasure in suffering by making others suffer. The so called virtues of self-denial, self-abnegation, and pity are not, Nietzsche insists, rooted in nobility that is first and foremost self-affirming; they are tied to cruelty and the will to self-maltreatment (*GM* II:18). Nietzsche further expounds that guilt and the bad conscience reached its most terrible heights through humanity's awareness of being in debt to the deity (the divine creditor, *GM* II:20), which grew as the concept of God and the feeling for divinity increased over millennia. Because humans felt guilty and fearful of God, they pushed these feelings back into themselves and their bad conscience, psychologically desiring a "final discharge"—but unable to secure it (*GM* II:21). The "stroke of genius" by Christianity was to relieve tormented humanity from a guilty conscience through atonement theories: God sacrifices himself for humanity's guilt; God (as divine creditor) makes payment (to himself) out of love for the debtor (the guilty human) (*GM* II: 21). This economic explanation that demystifies the atonement, Nietzsche claims, should put an end once and for all to the question of how the Holy God originated (*GM* II:23):

> You will have guessed *what* has really happened here, *beneath* all this: that will to self-tormenting, that repressed cruelty of the animal-man made inward and scared back into himself, the creature imprisoned in the "state" so as to be tamed, who invented the bad conscience in order to hurt himself after the more *natural vent* for this desire to hurt

had been blocked—this man of the bad conscience has seized upon the presupposition of religion so as to drive his self-torture to its most gruesome pitch of severity and rigor. Guilt before *God*: this thought becomes an instrument of torture to him. He apprehends in "God" the ultimate antitheses of his own ineluctable animal instincts; he ejects from himself all his denial of himself, of his nature, naturalness, and actuality, in the form of an affirmation, as something existent, corporeal, real, as God, as the holiness of God, as God the Judge, as God the Hangman, as the beyond, as eternity, as torment without end, as hell, as the immeasurability of punishment and guilt. (*GM* II:22)⁴⁰

Nietzsche says there are nobler uses for the invention of gods than the "self-crucifixion and self-violation of man" that has been attained in Europe over two millennia; he points to the Greek gods who warded off the bad conscience by "taking upon themselves, not the punishment, but, what is *nobler*, the guilt" (*GM* II:23). Yet elsewhere in the *Genealogy*, he does condemn the gods of Greece (along with the Christian god of Calvin and Luther) when conceived of as divine spectators in the ancient festival plays of cruelty (*GM* II: 7).⁴¹ —"Too long," Nietzsche cries, "the world has been a madhouse!" (*GM* II: 22).

Nietzsche believed that the Christian moral code of Western civilization that preached pity, self-sacrifice, and self-abnegation, was on a dangerous track leading to nihilism, the abolition of individuals, bad conscience, *ressentiment*, and the assassination of man (*GM* II:11).⁴²

In what perhaps was an attack on the Christian state, the solitary Zarathustra reiterates:

> I do not like your cold justice; and out of the eyes of your judges there always looks the executioner and his cold steel. Tell me, where is that justice which is love with open eyes? Would that you might invent for me the love that bears not only all punishment but also all guilt! . . .
>
> Finally, my brothers, beware of doing wrong to any hermit. How could a hermit forget? How could he repay? . . . Beware of insulting the hermit. But if you have done so—well, then kill him too.
>
> Thus spoke Zarathustra.⁴³

As noted, Nietzsche ascribes *ressentiment* and the morality of pity to antisemites. On the one hand, Zarathustra says that his highest hope is that "man be delivered from revenge."⁴⁴ Yet on the other, he does not adopt Christ's injunction to turn the other cheek, stating elsewhere that "a little revenge is more human than no revenge."⁴⁵ These two statements by Nietzsche/Zarathustra, that one should be delivered from revenge but that a "little" revenge is more human than none, illustrate a middle position between racist vengeance and passive Christian repression; such a position leaves ground between the nationalist psyche in

Germany and the anti-instinctual teachings of Christ. Because the Jews are not "Germans" or "Christians," Nietzsche views them as being in a superior position to become the inventors and masters of Europe: the Jews are creative and "do not take their revenge too far."[46] This line of thought also continues in the *Genealogy* where Nietzsche distinguishes between the active nobles, whose revenge is born from a (non-malicious) excess of strength, and the reactive men of *ressentiment* who are driven by pity and the desire to harm. Whereas the master's revenge exhausts itself immediately and does not poison, the slave's vengeance simmers and translates itself into the realm of ascetic ideals, such as the Kingdom of God and the Last Judgment.

Nietzsche's parable of the Lambs (Christians) and the Birds of Prey (nobles) is especially illuminating here. Lambs repress natural expressions of strength. Under the guise of forgiveness and love they find emotional outlets in leaving vengeance to God and seeing others suffer in hell fire and damnation (*GM* I:15). The Christian's repression of revenge left in God's hands, however, is most dangerous precisely *because* it is "impotent" and thus further internalizes the bad conscience that needs, Nietzsche insists, eventual release ("a final discharge").

Although Nietzsche's theory of pity in relation to racism is somewhat complex, his primary psychological insights are clear: his whole inquiry surrounds the question of *why* people would enjoy believing in a God of love who would torture others. His answer to the question is that the weak are repressed physiologically and psychologically: they either get mild satisfaction through pity (slight superiority) that is divinely sanctioned as a virtue; or—to a greater extreme—they acquire increased contempt for other religions, races, and peoples, which is also divinely sanctioned with a God perceived as One who requires rigid belief or who punishes "*His* enemies." If mild pitiers do not go as far as open hostility, they are nonetheless on the wrong road, suppressing their instincts and conceiving of a God that annihilates and destroys those without belief in a particular religious truth.

Although pity is commonly conceived as a positive sentiment directed toward powerless, unfortunate people, Nietzsche uses the term to suggest that extreme pity (or racism) is directed against artistic nobles, precisely because pitiers bear a severe, unforgiving contempt toward greatness and nonconforming inner strength: "You came close to them [the pitiers] and yet passed by," Zarathustra says, "that they will never forgive. You pass over and beyond them: but the higher you ascend, the smaller you appear to the eye of envy."[47] Nietzsche is not opposed to hierarchical relationships—quite the reverse. Yet he wants the minority "nobles" to overcome the majority of "domestic animals" who presently rule.

THE MADHOUSES OF CULTURE

Nietzsche's basic psychological tools accompany him when embarking upon almost all specific appraisals of Christendom's traditional teachings on sex, love, guilt, sin, redemption, faith, the Kingdom of God, and the Last Judgment. Most often, Nietzsche's aim is to show that these concepts are clearly not selfless—or without base egoistic motives—in the most negative sense.[48] Rather, they are usually either perverse misinterpretations of psychological states, dangerous violations against human nature, or psychological defense mechanisms by which we remain self-satisfied and content. For instance, Nietzsche claims that Christianity brought the lyrical notion of love into the world (as distinct from the heroic-epic religion of the Semites). Yet he is dissatisfied with the idea of love inasmuch as he critiques the Christian model as a heterosexual arrangement in which the lover attempts to possess and dominate the beloved at the expense of all others. This human tendency to dominate and possess—especially when sexuality is involved—is also translated into theological terms—in which the One God demands total obedience and sacrifice: "Love of *one* is a barbarism," Nietzsche contends, "the love of God too."[49] Here, Nietzsche opts again for the Greek conception of friendship as far superior to love of the neighbor or to the traditional (patriarchical) model of the nuclear family—exemplified by the Father, the Son, and the Holy Ghost.[50]

Nietzsche chides Christendom for its traditional (unnatural) teachings on sex and its (unnatural) elevation of ascetic ideals. For instance, Nietzsche finds it difficult to conceive how the natural process of sex could be considered "unholy," and the (unnatural) process of starving the body—or fasting—could be sanctified. Yet most of all, he is preoccupied with the power of Christendom's capacity to inflict ascetic "ideals" such as guilt in the minds of the masses, rendering them helpless, in bondage, and in dire need of salvation for their sins.

Nietzsche asserts that mass psychological states such as faith (which eases the psyche) and guilt (which torments the psyche) are imaginary hegemonic illusions made manifest and promoted by "vengeful priests" through social, institutional, and political spheres. That is, one must first "feel" guilty in order to be redeemed. When following Nietzsche's train of thought in the *Genealogy*, the following scenario unfolds: before Christ came, humanity felt guilty about being in debt to the deity; thus, the arrival of Christ-god (as payment) should have solved the problem of humanity's guilt. However, Nietzsche contends, this did not happen. The backwardness of Christianity is that it must now *first inflict* guilt in humanity in order to provide the necessity for salvation in Christ (which is needed to perpetuate the institution). That is, before

Christ humanity "felt" guilty (and in debt to the deity); after Christ, humanity *still* feels guilty because the "priests" need to inflict guilt upon humanity to fuel their power. This is perhaps the logic behind Nietzsche's statement: "Christianity came into existence in order to lighten the heart; but now it has to burden the heart first, in order to be able to lighten it afterward."[51] It also sheds light on why he continually praises the gods of Greece for taking upon themselves "the guilt," and why he states that Jesus, although he wanted to abolish guilt, nonetheless died for *his* guilt, not the guilt of others.[52] With the advent of the Christian God, Nietzsche says, the maximum feeling of guilty indebtedness was attained on earth. If we embark upon the reverse course, it is probable that with the decline of faith in the Christian God there will also be a decline in humanity's feeling of guilty indebtedness toward its origin: "Atheism and a kind of *second innocence* belong together—" (*GM* II:20).

From Nietzsche's perspective, faith (one illusion) needs guilt (another illusion) in order to function in perpetuating a grand delusion. As regards to guilt Nietzsche writes: "Although the shrewdest judges of the witches and even the witches themselves were convinced of the guilt of witchery, this guilt nevertheless did not exist. This applies to all guilt."[53]

Here Nietzsche is not saying that we should not be responsible human beings with a *good conscience* in our dealings with others and within society. He is rather conveying that the (false) notion of guilt has embodied itself in the bad conscience, which originates in unequal economical power relationships (between creditor and debtor), and has subsequently led to a religion of pity, resentment, and racism. Our true "original sin," Zarathustra says, is that we have felt too *much* pity and too little joy: "And learning better to feel joy, we learn best not to hurt others and to plan hurts for them."[54]

The idea of imaginary beliefs and disoriented mental states designed to pacify, soothe, or to disturb our psyches—in order to then relieve them—is what Nietzsche sees as that which characterizes much of the European Christian tradition. He reiterates that these notions, powerful though they may be in our psyches, do not really "exist": "Now the *belief* that we *love* our enemy," Nietzsche says, "even when it is not a psychological reality . . . makes us *happy* so long as it is believed."[55] Elsewhere he asks: "Is it really *necessary* that there should actually *be* a God, and a deputizing Lamb of God, if *belief* in the *existence* of these beings suffices to produce the same effects?"[56] This analysis of imaginary psychological states falsely interpreted as truths applies to his views on sin, redemption, faith, self-sacrifice, the Kingdom of God, *ad infinitum*. According to Nietzsche, Christianity is a false phenomenon of the consciousness; even the dream world is far superior for at least the latter *mirrors* reality whereas Christianity negates it.[57] For Nietzsche, consciousness evolves with humanity and has to be *acquired* through the incorporation of knowledge.[58] In this sense, Christianity is a sign of lower stages of culture, a regression against humanity's positive conscious development. This view is in stark contrast to Hegel and, of course, many Christians. Again and again, Nietzsche mocks and exposes notions such as the Kingdom of God (future fantasy) as that which is ultimately selfish. Though believers believe their adherence to such ideas are rooted in pious faith, Nietzsche believes they are actually rooted in internalized guilt and are based on a basic plebeian need for self-preservation.[59]

In the *Genealogy* and elsewhere, he also exposes the Kingdom of God as that which is not based fundamentally on love but on hate, as evidenced by its counter notion of the Last Judgment—or hell fire and damnation for nonbelievers (*GM* I:15).

THE PSYCHOGENEALOGY OF THE ANTISEMITE

Nietzsche's obvious affection for Jews and his clear disdain toward Christians and the Judeo-Christian tradition brings us to the psychological *origin* of antisemitism, which he locates within the Christian religion: "In the case of *Christ*, the rejoicing of the people appears as the cause of his execution; an anti-priestly movement from the first. Even in the case of the *anti-Semites* it is still the same artifice: to visit condemnatory judgments upon one's opponent and to reserve to oneself the role of *retributive justice*."[60] Nietzsche says that the antisemite attempts to imaginatively transform his opponent into his antithesis. He needs to believe in himself and his "good cause" and falsely misunderstands this deep hatred as pious belief in God, or in the victory of the "just God over the Godless."[61] In this manner, morality as a righteous thirst for revenge via the will to absolute truth is sanctified. Religion and racism are united, often by slogans such as: "I am the way, the truth and the life, no one comes to the Father but by me" (John 14:6). To that Zarathustra counters: "For *the* way—that does not exist."[62]

In the *Genealogy* alone, Nietzsche says he does not like the "anti-Semites who . . . today roll their eyes in a Christian-Aryan bourgeois manner" (*GM* III:26). He refers to the infamous antisemites Ernst Renan and Eugen Dühring as "moral masturbators," "moral bigmouth(s)," "historical nihilists," and describes them as the "worms of vengefulness and rancor" who swarm throughout Europe. Nietzsche insists: "They are all men of *ressentiment*" (*GM* III:14). He also states that he admires the Old (Jewish) Testament but not the New, and calls saint Luther a presumptuous peasant and a lout.[63] Moreover, he chastises Wagner—one of the most vile antisemites of all time. And, for the record, antisemites, in turn, attacked Nietzsche in nineteenth-century Germany.[64] Yet interestingly, among all this stark (and mounting) historical evidence that Nietzsche created a radical political stir within a small Wagner circle that included his sister and her antisemitic friends, most often, Nietzsche's critique of antisemitism is ignored and *one* specific quote from the entire work is often cited *out of context* to suggest that Nietzsche did not like contemporary Jews. This passage reads: "With the Jews there begins the slave revolt in morality; that revolt which has 2,000 years behind it . . . and which we no longer see because it—has been victorious" (*GM* I:7). Even a child in Sunday school could discern that Nietzsche is referring to the first-century Jews of early Christendom—as evidenced that Christian (not Jewish) morality has "2, 000 years behind it." Yet many gentiles still gravitate to that sentence, ignore Nietzsche's scathing critique of Christian antisemitism, and recite the "Jewish" slave revolt passage (actually directed against early Christian-Jews). This process conveniently serves to detract people from the overall thrust of Nietzsche's text and his actual attack against antisemites and Christians. This hermeneutical procedure, I surmise, brings us to the quintessential pathological mark of antisemites today: They desire to hurt Jews by taking texts from them and ascribing dishonest, abusive, and antihistorical modes of interpretation to the texts. They prefer myth and delusion to history and truth. And they do all this under the guise of "concern" for Jews, all the while projecting their own racist tendencies onto a guilty agent or scapegoat. One is quickly reminded of many Christian "thinkers" over the centuries who usurped Hebrew Scripture from the Jewish scholars, interpreting them in literal terms while trying to convert the "blind Jews" for "their own good." One is also reminded of Elisabeth and the Nazis desperate attempt to distort and ultimately destroy Nietzsche's texts in the 1930s and '40s "once and for all." And one is painfully reminded of the pathetic attempts of many today who, under the guise of academic scholarship, actually try to deny the holocaust and the historicity of texts themselves. Yet despite the attempts of many religious fanatics and antisemites past and present who have sought to suppress and distort Nietzsche's texts, his scathing psychological attacks against antisemitism and antisemites still remain for those who care to read them.

We learn from Nietzsche that racists harbor deep revenge and "antigenealogical" psyches: their marks are that they try to make others suffer to fuel their power; they prefer psychological delusion and myth to reality and history; they elevate themselves by humiliating others; they are self-deceived and psychologically weak; they often perform violence in the name of God; and, most often, their power is driven by the amount of vengeance or guilt they can inflict on the noble ones whom they (secretly) envy: "For this is the rub: one needs guilty men. . . . This scapegoat can be God . . . or education and training . . . or the Jews, or the nobility, or those who have turned out well in any way."[65] Genealogically, from the New Testament on, Christian history and theology has, quite unfortunately, been saturated with a history of antisemitism and a grotesque portrayal of Jews. Although recent attempts have been made to rehabilitate these gross distortions within the Christian tradition, it would be painfully naive to think that a two thousand year process of regarding Jews as "Christ killers" has miraculously vanished after the genocidal attempt to destroy all "Jewish genes." And even if Christians are not antisemites, they are often reluctant to search the roots of their tradition to expose its unbecoming origins. This, I surmise, is the *psychological* reason why Nietzsche and his texts have been grossly vilified, ignored, or distorted. Psychologically, many readers, particularly gentiles, still cannot face him.

Many thinkers—some of whom are truly sensitive Christians—have struggled with the notion that Christian theology itself "went up in smoke" after Auschwitz and that it is now hopelessly irredeemable. This question remains to be debated by those who have a serious stake in preserving the integrity and worth of religion, which is still deeply imbedded within the psyche of Western Christian culture.

CONCLUSION

All in all, Nietzsche's analysis as a psychogenealogist of religion and culture penetrates deeply into power relationships between individuals and the state, Christians and Jews, masters and slaves, men and women, friends, and our relations to the gods. His fundamental insight is that the gods we create are reflections of ourselves and our society. The origination of values has never come from above, as religion often teaches, but from humans. Once the values or gods are sanctified by powerful (and perhaps corrupt) institutions as unchangeable, those values adopted by culture cannot be challenged without dire consequences to the individual challenger. There is very little chance of overthrowing idols, but Nietzsche insists we must continue to do so and be suspicious of those who "glorify origins," and who assume that what stands "at the beginning" of all things is also what is most essential and valuable.[66] Overthrowing idols was the dangerous task Nietzsche addressed in his time: Once human beings cease to originate values, he stressed, they stop creating and cease to be human. And in order to become noble creators, we must first undergo the painful search of exploring ourselves and our inner drives, especially in relation to history, to others, to our specific culture, and the world at large.

Nietzsche continually urged that we should not consider anything true simply because it soothes our psyches or because it protects a tradition. His point is that we are afraid to accept what we know is true because it tends to disturb us: we are all afraid of truth. Over and again Nietzsche stresses that the strength of a spirit should be measured according to how much truth she can endure. This is why Nietzsche, as a psychologist of religion, states that we *have* to misunderstand ourselves—because it is often painful when we *do* understand.[67]

Though much ado is made today in contemporary philosophy over whether Nietzsche believed or did not believe in "truth," taking into account he spent much of his writing career exposing humanity's "errors"; that he spoke of "truth" as that to be gained through genealogical analysis and psychology; that he claimed Zarathustra was more "truthful" than any other living thinker (—as opposed to cowardly idealists who fled from reality); that he claimed only a few are *able* to be true;[68] and that he continually claimed many of our cherished religious ideals were based on "holy lies"—the question posed today seems to be quite analytically evasive. Nietzsche's basic thesis is that we prefer our delusions to reality ("the beast in us wants to be lied to"); morality *wants* deception, it *lives* on deception.[69] That is, Nietzsche contends that we prefer our self-deceptive screens to those sober insights we instinctively know to be true. Thus, it seems evident that it is not "truth" as such that he is calling into question, but rather, the lack of kindred spirits to address what he actually said concerning it. Succinctly put, Nietzsche is calling into question much of the entire foundation of Western Christian culture—and thus, ourselves. He made the claim that the errors of humankind were rooted in false psychology; that many of our inherited ideals (or so called monotheistic truths) were born out of cruel, perverse, narrow-minded, and pathological motives. He also stated that our religious and moral institutions had failed because they sought self-preservation and the will to (their) truth even at the destruction of its foes: the Jews. In a word, his deep and painful exploration into origins was an attempt to expose a legacy of deceptions—and destroy them—to pave the way for a new and healthier society. Thus, to dance around Nietzsche's primary issues today with rhetorical flourishes and intellectual gymnastics simply prolongs the "arduous task" of addressing ourselves *and* Nietzsche, who, as is well known, "originated" within a proto-Nazi household and environment. He was an obscure author who struggled to overcome the ethical pathos of his age typified by racism, nationalism, antisemitism, and more specifically, *Christian* antisemitism. Thus, historical philosophizing—not avoidance—is essential when evaluating his work.[70]

Nietzsche is very critical of theologians, yet he also sees that philosophers merely replace ecclesiastical dogmas with metaphysical abstractions designed to overintellectualize and avoid subjective analyses. According to Nietzsche, because philosophers have frequently philosophized within a religious tradition, or at least under the power of metaphysical need, they too have achieved hypotheses similar to Christian, Jewish, or Indian dogmas, "similar that is to say, in the way children are usually similar to their mothers."[71] This is why postmodern, analytical, and even existential readings of Nietzsche—inasmuch as they are devoid of genealogical and psychological methods—often miss their mark. "But where today," Nietzsche asks, "are there psychologists?"

NOTES

1. For discussion of the psychology of convictions, see Friedrich Nietzsche, *The Antichrist*, in *The Portable Nietzsche*, trans. Walter Kaufmann (New York: Viking Press, 1982), 55.

2. Friedrich Nietzsche, *Human, All-Too-Human*, trans. R. J. Hollingdale (Cambridge: Cambridge University Press, 1986), 2.

3. *HU* 18. Cf. *D* 44: "The *salvation* of man must depend on *insight* into the origin of things."

4. Cf. *HU*, preface, 8, and the final section in "On Higher and Lower Cultures," 292: "*Forward*—And with that, forward on the path of wisdom with a bold step and full of confidence! However you may be, serve yourself as your own source of experience! One must have loved religion . . . otherwise one cannot grow wise. But one must be able to see beyond them . . . ; if one remains under their spell, one does not understand them." See also *BGE* 218.

5. *HU* 5, 255.

6. *HU* 111.

7. *HU* 52.

8. See especially *HU* 226, "Origin of Faith," and 143. See also, "On the Origin of Religions," in Friedrich Nietzsche, *The Gay Science*, trans. Walter Kaufmann (New York: Vintage, 1974), 353; and "On the Origin of Religions," in *Daybreak*, trans. R. J. Hollingdale (Cambridge: Cambridge University Press, 1982), 62.

9. *HU*, 35, 36.

10. *HU*, 35.

11. Friedrich Nietzsche, *On the Genealogy of Morals*, trans. Walter Kaufmann (New York: Vintage, 1967), preface.

12. See also *D* 545: "Have you experienced *history* in yourselves, convulsions, earthquakes, sadness wide and protracted, happiness that strikes like lightning? . . . If so, speak of morality: but not otherwise!"

13. *D* 114. This transformation also occurs just prior to Zarathustra's insight that he needs *living* companions, not corpses or believers: "At last, however, his eyes opened: amazed, Zarathustra looked into the woods and the silence; amazed, he looked into himself. Then he rose quickly, like a seafarer who suddenly sees land, and jubilated, for he saw a new truth." See also Karl Jaspers, *Nietzsche and Christianity*, trans. E. B. Ashton (South Bend, Ind.: Gateway, 1961). I strongly disagree with Jaspers that Nietzsche's personal illness and his suffering should be separated from Nietzsche's writings in order to discern the "real truth more purely," 100.

14. *HU* 109.

15. *GS* 357; *GM* III:27. For more discussion, see Jacob Golomb's section, "From Negative to Positive Religion," in *Nietzsche's Enticing Psychology of Power* (Ames: Iowa State University Press, 1989).

16. *D* 84.

17. Cf. *D* 96, 65; *HU* 114; *AC* 25.

18. Friedrich Nietzsche, *Thus Spoke Zarathustra*, trans. Walter Kaufmann (New York: Viking Press, 1966), pt. II, "On Priests."

19. See especially *D* 91, 93; *HU* 630–35; *GS* 143, 344; and Friedrich Nietzsche, *Twilight of the Idols*, *The Portable Nietzsche*, "What the Germans Lack," sec. 5.

20. *D* 62; *AC* 9.

21. *Z* I, "On Reading and Writing."

22. *Z* II, "On the Famous Wise Men."

23. *AC* 7.

24. *GS* 13. Cf. *D* 224, 356.

25. *AC* 7. I use the term "nihilism" to denote the "pathological" and decadent transitional stage that Nietzsche links to Christian morality. For further discussion, see Richard Schacht's "Nietzsche and Nihilism," in *Nietzsche: A Collection of Critical Essays*, ed. Robert Solomon (New York: Anchor, 1973). Schacht swiftly refutes Arthur Danto's incredible claim (and the popular myth) that Nietzsche *himself* was a nihilist (promoting nihilism). Quite the contrary. Nietzsche regards nihilism as a negation of life and continually regards it as a *problem* to be overcome: "Nihilism and Christianism: that rhymes, that does not only rhyme" (*AC* 58). And again: "Some have dared to call pity a virtue. . . . To be sure—and one should always keep this in mind—this was done by a philosophy that was nihilistic and had inscribed negation of life upon its shield" (*AC* 7). Schacht perceptively notes it is difficult to discern why *anyone* would consider Nietzsche a nihilist—after an honest reading of Nietzsche's texts. However, perhaps Schacht should have sought *psychological* reasons for commonplace textual distortions (which will be discussed further below).

26. Friedrich Nietzsche, *Beyond Good and Evil*, trans. Walter Kaufmann (New York: Vintage, 1966), 284.

27. *D* 146. See also sections 133–40.

28. *HU* 50.

29. "The Greeks did not see the . . . gods above them as masters and themselves below them, as did the Jews. . . . They felt related to them, there was a reciprocal interest. . . . Christianity . . . crushed and shattered man completely,

and submerged him as if in deep mire. Then all at once, into his feeling of complete confusion, it allowed the light of divine compassion to shine, so that the surprised man, stunned by mercy, let out a cry of rapture. . . . All psychological inventions of Christianity work toward this sick excess of feeling. . . . Christianity wants to destroy, shatter, stun, intoxicate: there is only one thing it does not want: moderation, and for this reason, it is in its deepest meaning barbaric . . . ignoble, un-Greek," *HU* 114.

30. *AC* 51, 23: "Buddhism . . . is no longer confronted with the need to make suffering and the susceptibility to pain *respectable* by interpreting them in terms of sin—it simply says what it thinks: 'I suffer.' To the barbarian, however, suffering as such is not respectable: he requires an exegesis before he will admit to himself that he is suffering." For discussion on suffering and nobility, see *BGE*, 270.

31. *GS* 21. See also *BGE* 146: "Whoever fights monsters should see to it that in the process he does not become a monster. And when you look long into an abyss, the abyss also looks into you."

32. *BGE* 222.

33. *BGE* 260. Cf. *BGE* 225 on pity versus pity.

34. *GM* II:11.

35. *GM* III:14, II:11.

36. *GM* III:14.

37. For Nietzsche's views on the origin of justice, see *Human* 92; *Daybreak* 112. He refers readers in the *Genealogy* (preface, 4) to the passage in *Daybreak*, as well as other passages dealing with origins as recorded in his earlier works.

38. *GM* II:11.

39. Cf. *The Timetables of Jewish History*, ed. Judah Gribetz, Edward L. Greenstein, and Regina Stein (New York: Simon & Schuster, 1993), 238; *Encyclopedia Judaica* (Jerusalem, 1972). In the *Gay Science* 95, in a passage entitled "Chamfort," Nietzsche says that Mirabeau, as a human being, "belongs to an altogether different order of greatness than even the foremost statesmen of yesterday and today." See also *The Selected Letters of Friedrich Nietzsche*, trans. and ed. Christopher Middleton (Chicago: University of Chicago Press, 1969), no. 92, p. 180. Here Nietzsche writes of Chamfort as "a man of Mirabeau's stature in character, heart, and breadth of mind—that is how Mirabeau himself judged his friend." Chamfort collaborated with Mirabeau on the newspaper, *Mercure de France*.

40. See also, *GS* 140, 141.

41. See also *D* 18.

42. In *The Demon of Power* Nietzsche observes:

Not necessity, not desire—no, the love of power is the demon of men. . . . Luther has said it already, and better than I, in the verses: "Let them take from us our body, goods, honour, children, wife: let it all go—the kingdom [Reich] must yet remain to us!" Yes! Yes! The "*Reich*"! (*D* 262)

43. *Z* I, "On the Adder's Bite." Cf. *HU* 70, "Executions": "How is it that every execution offends us more than a murder? It is the coldness of the judges,

the painful preparations, the understanding that a man is here being used to deter others."

44. *Z* II, "On the Tarantulas." Cf. *HU* 70.

45. *Z* I, "On the Adder's Bite."

46. *D* 205.

47. *Z* I, "On the Way of the Creator." Perhaps this is why Zarathustra claims in "On the Pitying" that "Great love overcomes even forgiveness and pity."

48. *TW* "Skirmishes of an Untimely Man," sec. 33: "*The natural value of egoism.* Self-interest is worth as much as the person who has it: it can be worth a great deal, and it can be unworthy and contemptible."

49. *BGE* 67.

50. *GS* 14, 363.

51. *HU* 119.

52. *AC* 27.

53. *GS* 250; *GM* III:16; and Friedrich Nietzsche, *Assorted Opinions and Maxims*, in *Human*, trans. Hollingdale, 225.

54. *Z* II, "On the Pitying."

55. *AO* 96.

56. *AO* 225.

57. *AC* 15.

58. *GS* 11, 333, 354.

59. Cf. "Egoism against egoism," *D* 90 and *D* 456.

60. Friedrich Nietzsche, *The Will to Power*, trans. Walter Kaufmann and R. J. Hollingdale (New York: Vintage, 1967), 347. For a detailed reading of Nietzsche's *Antichrist*, see my "Nietzsche's *Antichrist*: 19th Century Christian Jews and the Real 'Big Lie,'" *Modern Judaism* 17 (1997): 163-77.

61. *GM* I:14; *WP* 348.

62. *Z* III, "On the Spirit of Gravity," sec. 2.

63. *GM* III:22, 26.

64. Letter to Paul Deussen, Nice, January 3, 1888. *Sämtliche Briefe*, 8 vols. (Berlin: Walter de Gruyter, 1975–84), 8: no. 939, p. 220.

65. *WP* 765.

66. Cf. Friedrich Nietzsche, *The Wanderer and His Shadow*, in *Human*, trans. Hollingdale, 3; Friedrich Nietzsche, *Ecce Homo*, trans. Walter Kaufmann (New York: Vintage Books, 1967), preface, 2.

67. "Through knowing ourselves, and regarding our own nature as a moving sphere of moods and opinions, and thus learning to despise ourself a little, we restore our proper equilibrium with others," *HU* 376. Cf. *BGE* 39.

68. *Z* III, "On Old and New Tablets," sec. 7.

69. *HU* 40; preface, 1.

70. See my *Nietzsche, God, and the Jews* (Albany: State University of New York Press, 1994) for a more comprehensive discussion of Nietzsche's critique of Christianity and antisemitism. For further reading on Nietzsche's relationship with Jews and Jewish culture, see the essay collection, *Nietzsche and Jewish Culture*, ed. Jacob Golomb (New York and London: Routledge, 1997).

71. *HU* 110.

CHAPTER 6

Willing Backwards: Nietzsche on Time, Pain, Joy, and Memory

Ofelia Schutte

> All joy wants eternity,
> Wants deep, wants deep eternity.
> —*Thus Spoke Zarathustra*

These key refrains from *Thus Spoke Zarathustra* offer a contrast between two perspectives, each being the product of a different kind of awareness. The contrast points to the difference between a bounded and an unbounded universe of meaning. The universe of meaning represented by the light of day is one where things are seen in the distinctness of their finitude and according to the measure of cognitive experience. In contrast to this universe of meaning there is another, represented by the twelve strokes of midnight, when time is signified not by the finite but the infinite, not by the balance of what can be summed up as positive experiences but by the language of desire for an unbounded joy, an earthly kind of eternal happiness. This "deeper" world of which Nietzsche speaks here is the world of the human psyche, at least the psyche in aspects that neither religion nor philosophy have adequately understood. The failure of both religion and philosophy to understand the deeper aspects of the self could be one reason why, in *Beyond Good and Evil*, Nietzsche prominently describes his task as that of a psychologist, at the same time acknowledging (contra the Enlightenment philosophy of self-consciousness) that the hardest thing for a man to know is his own self.

In his philosophical thinking as in these psychological observations, Nietzsche is caught between an earth-bound human, all-too-human

111

standpoint, and an agonistic desire for a higher-than-human voice. In his human stance, he is a philosopher poised between past and future, keenly aware of the finitude of his position. In his desire to reach beyond the human—at least as far as an aesthetic (not an ascetic) ideal will permit him—he regards and addresses the temporal as from a standpoint of eternity. These two sides of Nietzsche, historical and transhistorical, are joined, not without some significant tension, in his critique of European nihilism and his call for a transvaluation of all values. The positions he develops for his European contemporaries, particularly during the period between *The Gay Science* and *On the Genealogy of Morals* (1882–87), contain both a philosophy of culture and a philosophy of time, but in their dual, intersecting, and at times conflicting roles these two philosophies stand vis-à-vis one another in an unresolved tension. As a philosopher of time, Nietzsche's ideal is to affirm each and every moment of existence, cherishing the differences among all moments aesthetically. This view of life is best articulated in *The Gay Science* and in some sections of *Thus Spoke Zarathustra*. As a philosopher of culture, however, Nietzsche is committed to criticizing and negating a decadent (modern European) culture for the sake of a higher culture, a thesis for which he argues prominently in *Beyond Good and Evil* and the *Genealogy*, though also in earlier works going back to *The Birth of Tragedy*.

Through a psychological analysis of the tension experienced by the creative individual at the crossroads between past and future, Nietzsche hopes to bridge the distance between his affirmative view of time and his critical view of culture. Here I will try to articulate this tension in Nietzsche's thought and the extent to which, through his analysis of time in *Zarathustra* and the focus on freeing the individual from the psychological effects of resentment against pain and suffering, he was able to offer a way toward its resolution.

TIME, AESTHETIC TRANSFORMATION, AND SUFFERING

As early as in *The Birth of Tragedy* Nietzsche advanced the hypothesis that "it is only as an *aesthetic phenomenon* that existence and the world are eternally *justified*."[1] Nietzsche interpreted the world of Greek art as an expression of the human need to transfigure the more primitive experiences of psychic pain and suffering, such that, through Dionysian and particularly Apollonian artistic drives, a world of suffering could be transformed into a world of beauty and joy. In this sense, the pain of human experience, described in this Schopenhauerian-inspired work as the pain of individuation, could be sublimated in the joy brought about by the beauty and power of the aesthetic spectacle. Aware of the cultural forces that could subvert his aesthetic position, Nietzsche argues his standpoint against at least two separate countervoices, which he includes in the text. The first countervoice to his own is "the wisdom of Silenus," which basically regards life in time as not worth living. Silenus declares that what is best for the human race—"children of chance and misfortune"—is "not to be born, not to *be*, to be *nothing*," while what is second best is "to die soon."[2] In a different vein from the voice of Silenus, a second voice running counter to Nietzsche's is that of Socrates. Nietzsche interprets the Socratic will to truth (that is, the philosopher's rational disposition) as the spirit, or attitude, that destroys Sophoclean tragedy. In Nietzsche's view, once imagination is made wholly subordinate to reason and reason is instructed with the task of "correcting" life, as he charges Socrates with doing,[3] reason will inevitably take control over the terms that define and justify existence, displacing the vanguard role of art in this matter. If art, including artistic illusion, serves as the deepest incentive to an appreciation of (temporal) life, then whatever acts so as to deprive humanity of this redemptive effect of art betrays both life and humanity. As Nietzsche would remark in the notes to *The Will to Power*, we have art so that we do not perish from truth.[4] Art replenishes our spirits when truth leaves our capacity to love and affirm life exhausted.

In Nietzsche's view, neither reason nor religion can supply an adequate explanation regarding how to deal with irremediable pain and suffering. To use Zarathustra's metaphor, reason can only lift us up, through the language of light, of the "day," through the sense of control exerted over the anxieties produced by suffering. Reason will achieve this effect by distancing itself from suffering, at best alleviating the suffering by objectifying it in some form and attempting to eliminate its causes. Unless accompanied and redeemed by imagination, intuition, and good humor, however, in Nietzsche's view reason is ultimately utilitarian in function: it calculates the costs and benefits, leveling down the outcome of any decision so as to increase predictability, impose uniformity, and reduce all costs (including existential "costs" such as risk-taking, living with uncertainties). Although Nietzsche offers some praise for science as a highly demanding cultural endeavor,[5] ultimately the greatest challenge to reason and science are the cases of irremediable suffering that science lacks the power to heal or rectify. At the limit of such experiences, reason can only stand back, as it were, and remain silent. Such silence is reason's recognition of its limited power in relation to ordering, improving, or correcting the deeply intractable realities of human existence.

Religion, in contrast to reason, makes the experience of suffering central to its conception of human existence. But, as Nietzsche argued, it only does so in order to appropriate its meaning through the concepts of sin, guilt, and punishment. According to Nietzsche's analysis, this kind of appropriation only serves to increase the sufferer's dependence on religion's message of salvation.[6] If Silenus is an early prototype of the priestly voice for whom existence is clouded by original sin, and if Socrates represents the voice of reason wishing to narrow down the domain of pain (including emotional pain) as much as possible, then already in *The Birth of Tragedy* it may be seen that Nietzsche both speaks on behalf of acknowledging the reality of mental pain, or anguish, and seeks a nonreligious path to its healing. Such a nonreligious path is variously described in his works as aesthetic (*Birth of Tragedy, Gay Science*), transvaluative (*Zarathustra, Genealogy*), genealogical (*Genealogy*), and psychological (*Beyond Good and Evil*). In search of a contrast between his standpoint and that of Christian morality, Nietzsche insisted on being recognized as a psychologist—a diagnostician of the relationship between the values that pass under the name of "morality" and a society's overall sense of health, both physical and mental.

In order to take up the position of psychologist, it was necessary for Nietzsche not to accept the general idealist view of reason as transparent to itself. He raised the suspicion that certain widely accepted moral beliefs, such as a retributive conception of justice and an ascetic attitude toward the body, were the products of unconscious resentment rather than the expressions of a disinterested reason or of the will of God. "Who before me climbed into the caverns from which the poisonous fumes of this type of ideal—slander of the world—are rising? Who even dared to suspect that there are caverns? . . . There was no psychology at all before me."[7] Having started out in *The Birth of Tragedy* as a metaphysician who attempted to justify existence aesthetically and without the aid of Christian morality, and having passed through his own self-criticism for having been too much of a romantic when he favored such a metaphysical approach, Nietzsche gradually reinscribes his identity as that of a psychologist. His mission of providing an alternative ground of values to Christian morality, nevertheless, remained the same.

MEMORY, PAIN, AND PLEASURE

As Nietzsche embarks on an alternative path to deal with mental pain, or what we could term *suffering* (as differentiated from sheer physical pain), it is important that he address the role of memory in the (re)construction of the past, including the distant past. In the context of a person's lifetime, the past includes experiences going back to infancy and early childhood, whereas in the lifetime of a community, a culture, or civilization the recollection of the past could involve accounts of historical achievements, ancestors' legends, and other collectively held beliefs. For the sake of simplicity, I will focus here on memory as related to giving meaning to personal experience. This discussion, however, is offered in the context of two important views Nietzsche holds about the historical and cultural place of memory in the lives of individuals as social beings. One important point he raises in *Untimely Meditations* is that while the human capacity to give meaning to the past, that fabric out of which the historical sense develops, is a distinguishing feature separating the human being from sheer animal existence, to limit oneself primarily to the recollection and appreciation of the past—what he calls the antiquarian sense of history—is to fail to give sufficient attention to the full human range of creative activity. Nietzsche balances the antiquarian sense of history with the monumental and the critical senses.[8] These other two approaches liberate human beings from the weight of the past and allow them to examine the present from perspectives outside a strictly linear sense of progressive development.

Another important point regarding the relation of the present to the past is developed in the *Genealogy*. Here Nietzsche offers the well-known hypothesis that argues that the human animal acquired memory and a sense of responsibility and obligation through the infliction of pain. The experiences of pleasure, he posited, are more easily forgettable than those of pain.[9] Pleasure is not as reliable as pain if the aim is to "domesticate" humanity. In this light, Nietzsche again speaks of the importance of being able to release oneself from the effects of the capacitation and empowerment of memory as a human faculty under conditions of repeated experiences of pain. In other words, one must learn to forget, in particular, one must actively deconstruct the psychological connection between pain and memory insofar as this connection has been a crucial factor in the production and reproduction of reactive attitudes and slave moralities. This theme is developed in *Thus Spoke Zarathustra* in the chapter, "On Redemption."[10] Nietzsche conjectures, in a most important hypothesis, that if it is the case that where there is pain there is a nascent reactive desire for punishment and if the human memory is made subservient habitually to satisfying this kind of desire, the human psyche will be locked into an unhealthy reactive pattern one of whose outcomes will be a morality based on the opposition between good and evil and a retributive conception of punishment. Once these patterns of values are entrenched in the human consciousness and in social systems, Nietzsche believes they are very difficult to eradicate.[11] Such is the need for his transvaluation of all values, a program of reinterpretation of values and reconstitution of the concepts of mental and physical health that would overturn the entrenched power of the established reactive moralities. The way memory functions in giving meaning to past experiences of pain and pleasure is therefore a key determinant in the success or failure of Nietzsche's project of transvaluation.

The role played by memory in accepting the reality of pain and suffering without letting the self fall into the role of a victim is crucial in Nietzsche's thought, since a victimless account of pain is a necessary condition for both his strongly affirmative view of life and his conception of the strength of character required for the creation of a higher, non-nihilistic culture. In this sense memory must play a transfigurative role in an individual's life. Memory must point to the significance of past events and experiences that constitute crucial "markers" in a person's life, yet nevertheless allow for the self's regeneration from particularly difficult and traumatic experiences. As it happens, however, this ideal is extraordinarily difficult to put into practice because there are few models for the development of the healthy individual, of the individual free from reactive attitudes, in societies governed by the dictates of slave moralities. Zarathustra observes that one of the pivotal goals still missing in humanity is the need to put a "yoke" on the thousand necks of the "monster" that regulates the moral codes of different cultures and peoples by way of the binary opposition between good and evil.[12] Hence his (and Nietzsche's) attempt to reexamine the meaning of the basic concepts that gnaw at individuals' sense of well-being, such as pain, guilt, and punishment, always with an aim to release the meaning of these concepts from the control of a good versus evil interpretive economy.

Nietzsche developed a set of values wherein pain could be placed in a perspective other than that of binary-ruled moralities. In this way, the psychological effects of pain could ideally be freed from the customary linkage between pain and the reactive feelings (envy, guilt, resentment, and the like). One interesting document where Nietzsche makes autobiographical remarks about his approach to physical illness and the recovery from significant pain is the 1886 preface to *The Gay Science*. Here, speaking as a psychologist and a philosopher, he states: "For a psychologist there are few questions that are as attractive as that concerning the relation of health and philosophy, and if he should himself become ill, he will bring all of his scientific curiosity into his illness."[13] Furthermore, Nietzsche raises another interesting point, namely, if a philosopher writes under conditions of distress (*Notstände*), "what will become of the thought when it is subjected to the *pressure* of sickness (den *Druck der Krankheit*)?"[14] Claiming to have learned from his ill condition that a sick body longs for rest, stillness, and sunlight, Nietzsche proposes that "every philosophy that ranks peace above war," among other things, allows one to raise the question of whether it was some illness that is responsible for this type of valuation of existence.[15] Nietzsche develops the hypothesis that philosophical values may be interpreted as signs or indicators of differently constituted *bodies*. "A philosopher who has traversed many kinds of health, and keeps traversing them, has passed through an equal number of philosophies; he simply *cannot* keep from transposing his tastes every time into the most spiritual form and distance: this art of transfiguration *is* philosophy."[16]

Speaking as a philosopher, Nietzsche warns his readers that, unlike other people, philosophers "are not free to divide body from soul" or "soul from spirit." Like mothers, he states, "we have to give birth to our thoughts out of pain (Schmerz)."[17] Moreover, he adds that "only great pain, the long, slow pain that takes its time . . . compels us philosophers to descend to our ultimate depths," putting aside the "trust in life."[18] Knowing that life, including one's basic physical health, cannot be taken for granted, nevertheless, how does Nietzsche react? His response to this question, in one word, is *cheerfully.*[19] Cheerfulness (*die Heiterkeit*) before the uncertainty of his life and health, he writes, is his philosophical, as well as physical and mental, response to the experiences of illness and pain. Hence, the reader may approach the aphorisms of *The Gay Science* knowing the physical as well as emotional trajectory of the author's thoughts: "from such abysses, from such severe sickness (Siechtum), also from the sickness of severe suspicion, one returns *newborn*, having shed one's skin . . . with a second dangerous innocence in joy, more childlike and yet a hundred times subtler than one has ever been before."[20] Despising the popular pleasures of his contemporaries yet invoking his need for a "divinely untroubled . . . art," Nietzsche declares his allegiance to superficiality "*out* of profundity,"[21] aligning himself in spirit with the Greek worshipers of the Olympian gods.

The psychological contrast drawn here therefore speaks of two different kinds of "convalescence": what Nietzsche diagnoses as the usual philosophical disguising of "physiological needs under the cloak of the objective, ideal, purely spiritual," which includes the "craving for some [truth] Apart, Beyond, Outside, Above" the thinker's body,[22] and, by contrast, Nietzsche's own acknowledgment of suffering and illness together with his proposed cures—art and good humor. Does Nietzsche attempt to deceive his readers here, creating the illusion that, though physically ill, he is far healthier than most other philosophers who are unable to affirm life as cheerfully? Certainly, Nietzsche felt that in his ability to overcome some of the limitations of his physical pain and in regarding such pain even as a stimulant to attain better health, his body and mind showed a distinctly noteworthy form of resilience. Still, I would suggest that in his carefully worded preface Nietzsche remains silent about other kinds of pain and suffering whose effects he finds far more difficult to overcome. These other states of mind were revealed in more depth through his literary figure, Zarathustra.

Despite Nietzsche's attempt to represent Zarathustra as confronting various difficulties in a cheerful and even clownish manner, the periods and moods of deep depression and existential anxiety undergone by Zarathustra cannot be erased from his character. Moreover, at the time when Zarathustra's story is first announced (in *GS* 342, the last section of the first edition) we see the title Nietzsche gave to this aphorism was "Incipit tragoedia" (the tragedy begins). In *Thus Spoke Zarathustra,* Nietzsche presents Zarathustra as knowing that cheerfulness cannot be sustained indefinitely as a posture against suffering and pain. For example, Zarathustra recognizes that the worst enemy that can attack his creative spirit lies deeply within himself. "The time will come when that which seems high to you will no longer be in sight, and that which seems low will be all-too-near. . . . And you will cry, 'All is false!'"[23] In the face of such deep pessimism about the loss of all values, Nietzsche's Zarathustra must find a kind of joy other than the surface-prone satisfaction Nietzsche would describe in his 1886 preface to *The Gay Science.* This deeper joy is linked to the existential psychological project of healing the reactive (unhealthy) state of the will that finds itself in impasse over obstacles it appears unable to overcome (along with a memory-state that has lost sight of a person's healthy objectives). In addressing the issue of "the revenge of the will against the passing of time," Nietzsche will unveil a new role for the human memory at the same time that he will liberate the imagination from the burden of the inescapability of linear thinking.

THE PROBLEM OF THE REVENGE AGAINST TIME

In *Zarathustra,* Nietzsche faces the challenge of continuing to uphold a view of the individual who can rise above pain and suffering and live cheerfully and joyfully, all the while facing those challenges and intensifying those issues already raised in *The Gay Science.* While the topics of the death of God, the collapse of established values, and the hypothesis of the eternal recurrence are introduced in *The Gay Science,* they are only developed at length in *Thus Spoke Zarathustra.* Moreover, it is only in *Zarathustra* that the ultimate state of the human being's sense of powerlessness is explored. This is the sense of being powerless to reverse the effects of the past, or the inability to change one's life in a direction contrary to linear time. In "On Redemption," Nietzsche appeals to the notion of the will as will to power—in contradistinction to the Schopenhauerian notion of the will in perpetual need of being redeemed from itself—as he attempts to deal with what he characterizes as the deepest of human frustrations: the sense of the irreversibility of time and the corresponding inability to will "backwards."

In this chapter Zarathustra contrasts two distinct ways of dealing with the past in one's personal experience. The past is represented as the "it was" (*es war*), that is, the moments, conditions, and events that, due to their past nature, are perceived as lying outside the compass of the present exercise of willing. The main contrast or tension shown is that between a will that becomes disempowered and vindictive as it perceives itself limited in its functioning by the irreversibility of the past (the "it was" is the "stone" it cannot move) and a will that can take a course other than this vindictive reaction, keeping its energy and focus fully directed on projects of self-overcoming and creativity.[24] Insofar as Zarathustra describes himself as a cripple at this bridge between past and future where either continued disempowerment or a momentous act of self-overcoming takes place, it is suggested that, even for him, the struggle between the vindictive (reactive) tendency of the will and the life-affirming movement of self-overcoming of the creative will that is the will to power is not fully resolved. That is to say, Zarathustra is shown as understanding the way to a higher, healthier state of being, but he does not always feel strong enough to move in this direction as energetically and forcefully as he would like. While Nietzsche represents Zarathustra's will in a state of tension, for the sake of clarification this discussion will highlight the distinction between these two possible kinds of willing in terms of their differentiated characteristics. In Nietzsche's text, the psychological contrast between the person who succumbs to an attitude of resentment and the one who opts for overcoming such an attitude, though central to the exposition, may not be as easily discernible, given Nietzsche's punctuation of this passage with enigmatic comments and self-imposed moments of silence.

Zarathustra describes himself as someone at a bridge overlooking the past and attempting to foresee the future of humanity. He declares that he feels crippled by what the present and past show about human beings, a feeling that can only be overridden when he positions himself as a seer of what must come. For such a future to be possible, however, humanity has to be able to will something higher than its present existential state, and for humanity to be able to will something higher without any significant psychologically impeding blockages, its will to such self-overcoming (its will to power) must be capacitated to pursue this challenging aim. The problem Nietzsche perceives is that the will is not capacitated to do this yet; indeed, the will seems trapped in a losing relationship with the past where, no matter how strong the will may take itself to be, it will always turn out that the force of the past is more powerful than it. Without power against that which has already been done, Zarathustra observes, the will is an angry onlooker of all that has passed—all the moments and experiences that from its present position, it cannot reverse, since it cannot will backwards. Anger over this limitation develops into a deadly rage or revenge (*Rache*).[25] Once subject to such rage, in Zarathustra's account the will compulsively vents its revenge, derived from its sense of impotence over the past, on anything at all that is able to suffer. The ultimate metaphysical doctrine that emerges from this state of rage is that life itself is nothing but punishment and suffering, the doctrine Nietzsche thought he saw exemplified in Schopenhauer's philosophy of the will. My intention here is not to pursue the metaphysical implications of Nietzsche's thinking on willing and time,[26] but to detain the clock, as it were, at the point where Nietzsche thinks he can offer an alternative to the emergence of the reaction of anger in the frustrated will, and to study the details of Nietzsche's alternative description insofar as it has something to tell us psychologically.

In Zarathustra's proposed will-to-power picture—the picture Nietzsche develops in contradistinction to that of the will consumed by rage,—the "it was" presents itself to the will as an accident (*Zufall*) or an enigma (*Rätsel*).[27] The "it was," as it were, is something that awaits being given a place and a meaning in the life of an individual. If the individual is able to exercise the will to power creatively, Nietzsche believes she or he can and must respond to the enigma of the "it was" by placing it in the perspective of the commanding voice that declares, with respect to it, "Thus I willed it."[28] In this interpretation, rather than view the will as lacking in power because it is impotent to change the past, I look at the past as lacking in relevance or meaning in the absence of the imposition of my will on it. The "it was" is a riddle in need of being given its place in the course of things. The will to power, the creative will, is what ties together these seeming fragments and riddles (past moments), giving them a direction that can then be subsumed in the creative will's vision of the future (a higher future). Whether the direction which Nietzsche gives to the interpretation of the will to power, linking it to the ideas of the *Übermensch* and the eternal recurrence, is a direction we are bound to accept is not at issue here. My concern rather is to understand the psychological operation Nietzsche is asking us to perform. This operation consists of a movement that throws the concept of lack back on the past and places on the "it was" the burden of seeking redemption in our (present) creative action. The opposite movement, that of the will operating in a modality of rage or revenge, then characterizes the debilitating psychological state in which any present creative action will be incapacitated because of the purported inability of our will to run counter to the force of time.

But, all this being said, there has to be more to Nietzsche's position than the mere giving meaning to the past through a strong imposition of our will on it. It seems he is also arguing at least two additional points. Clearly he is also saying that, whatever happened in the past, it is not for me to blame others for it or take recourse in extreme views in which life is seen as a punishment. I must not assume the role of the avenger or the victim. Moreover, he seems to be conveying the view that there must be something especially empowering about reclaiming that past (the "it was") as mine regardless of the pain or discomfort this may engender. One could raise the point differently, asking: of the two movements Nietzsche seems to articulate with respect to the past throughout his works, namely, learning to forget it (constructively) and claiming it all back under the auspices of the "Thus I willed it," what is it about the latter approach that appears to be so empowering for him? Why not simply forget the pain, or the disability, and move on with one's life— cheerfully?[29] To elucidate why returning to the memory of the past and claiming its significance for one's creative life appears to carry such empowering effects in Nietzsche's teaching it is useful to consider yet more extensively what is at stake in "willing backwards."

THE RETURN TO JOY AND THE
UNCHAINING OF THE CREATIVE MEMORY

It was mentioned earlier that in addressing the issue of the revenge of the will against the passing of time, Nietzsche is striving to show an alternative role for the memory and imagination. In this role, activities of remembering and imagining are released from the narrative of linear thinking and its assumption of the irreversibility of time. In Nietzsche's alternative conception, the primary focus affecting the role of imagination and memory are of an entirely different nature. Specifically, in recalling the past our main concern would shift from the sense of impotence suffered at past (irreversible) losses to the unexpected recovery of past moments of joy. The certainty of past limitations is traded in for the riddle of whether past moments of joy can be reexperienced. Nietzsche assumes that there are some intense experiences of joy in a person's past (at least one such experience) and that if we are able to release ourselves from the present moment to let the joyful moment recur so as to energize our memory and imagination, then such a past moment is not altogether irretrievable.[30] "Willing backwards" would then be shorthand for the psychological operation that allows us to get to the experience of joy regardless of the time (linearly conceived) of its occurrence. One would be redeemed from the revenge against "the passing of time" insofar as the moments of joy, which are those that one would most likely not want to let go of, can be simultaneously thought of as both passing away and returning in their significance to our lives. The intervals of time marking the disappearance of those moments from our consciousness would be conceived as productive rather than destructive, insofar as the memory of the experience produces further effects of joy in our current lives. But if we were also to become aware of the losses we have experienced in the interim—the loss of our youth, of some of our earlier ideals, of our earlier optimisms—there is a fall-back position to sustain us, if we are attentive to Nietzsche's text. The fall-back position is that we can take some pride and perhaps even a great deal of delight in the long and tenacious process of our "self-overcoming," which is another name for the creative work of the will to power.[31]

Now to expand on the above there are several more aspects of Nietzsche's teachings that demand clarification. With regard to his conception of time, Nietzsche represents time not as an undifferentiated succession of moments but as moments differentiated among themselves by a movement of parting and coming together. A parting moment may be conceived as being met, or encountered, by an arriving moment in a spatiotemporal rather than merely temporal-sequential configuration of events. Moreover, since whatever parts and arrives in this way is a moment, the "arriving" moment may also be conceived at a different level of abstraction as a "returning" moment. If a moment can be thought of having an end, under "willing backwards" the end would become its beginning while its beginning as conceived according to linear time would become its end, and so on. But if we are right in holding that Nietzsche wants to liberate our memory and imagination from the burden of linear time, then "willing backwards" could not be limited to a mere (linear) inversion or reversal of the accepted way of conceiving time; it would need to involve a willing backwards as against the concept of linear time as such. Otherwise the will might still be stuck in a feeling of revenge against the passing of time, only in this second, hypothetical case, the revenge would hold against the passing of time from future to past in an irreversible direction, something that is counterintuitive to our usual experience of time but nevertheless conceivable. This is one reason why, speaking of the flow of time, Nietzsche shifts from the standpoint of the passing of time to the metaphor of the eternal return of every moment. When he does this he is engaging in a Gestalt shift from an emotional economy of lack to one of overabundance, a theme Nietzsche was fond of pursuing in his mature philosophy.

In Nietzsche's view, for the revenge of the will against the passing of time to be redeemed, the linear interpretation of the "it was" must be released altogether. The referent that would bind the sense of all the moments as they fit together in a person's life and memory would not be linearity (a telos) but something altogether different, namely, the power of joy. With this shift, there would also be a corresponding shift from the religious or moral metanarrative of the struggle of good and evil as expressed in the teleological development of humanity (down to the concept of the Last Judgment) to the aesthetic/psychological narrative where the referent that binds all moments of a person's life together is the joyful moment, the joyful experience. As with the healthy individual, so would it be with a healthy culture. Its art, morality, and politics would not be constructed out of the reactive emotions governed by the need to retaliate loss for loss, pain for pain, but rather out of the sense that in spite of the losses one endures in life, there is also in humanity a healing capacity for creative action and gift-giving. Such is the positive message of Nietzsche's attempt at a transvaluation of all nihilistic and reactive values, eminently narrated in *Thus Spoke Zarathustra*.[32]

In Nietzsche's alternative narrative on the relationship between willing, time, and the creation of a higher culture, there are two principal existential moments: the moment of questioning and the moment of joy. The moment of questioning is that in which we reach awareness that joy is the primary signifier of the will to power in its modality of life affirmation. The moment of joy propels us into an unconscious domain represented as an abyss where an inexhaustible and always replenishable chain of meaning linked to the experience of joy (the "ring of recurrence") affirms itself eternally. Nietzsche uses many metaphors to describe this concept and process: falling in the well of eternity, being part of a ring of recurrence, letting humanity's "polluted stream" be washed unto the sea.[33] If all moments are "baptized" in the chain of significations that go back to an experienced moment of joy, then the "parting" and "return" of moments can be seen as overflowing occasions for the dissemination of such joy. This is in part what Nietzsche means by "gift-giving"; the ultimate gift-giver is life as it shares its bounty toward all living things from moment to moment. The strength of Nietzsche's interpretation lies in unchaining the memory from its restricted, reactively oriented, course (a product of a decadent or nihilistic culture) and allowing the self to forcefully break the chains by connecting its conscious awareness to the powerful life-affirming processes of the unconscious.[34]

Having noted the strengths of Nietzsche's position, the question also arises as to its possible limitations. Assuming that the account I have given preserves a substantial part of the spirit of Nietzsche's teaching regarding the healing of the will from the revenge against time, it makes sense to ask, does his account work? It may be that his solution may not work for everyone. In Nietzsche's account, a great deal of burden is placed on the healing power of joy and on the assumption that the demand for joy is the most powerful demand springing from the unconscious. Yet Nietzsche himself held that large portions of humanity would not only ignore but might be repelled by his teaching, just as he was repelled by the petty as well as grandiose manifestations of humanity's resentment. Whom would Nietzsche's teachings reach and what effects could they be expected to have on our culture? At a minimum, Nietzsche's account shifts the attention from a resentment-oriented economy of desires to a joy-oriented "surplus" type of emotional state of being. I would argue that if a person is able not only to conceive this type of shift but to practice it to some extent in her or his own life, this actually involves an emotional performance whose healing effects on the psyche cannot be underestimated. Nevertheless, in shifting to the gift-giving, joy-oriented perspective, one must be careful not to erase the significance of real experiences of loss and deprivation—experiences whose meaning cannot simply be swept under such metaphysical concepts as the eternal return of all moments or the wheel of becoming. There is something important about the specificity of all the different moments in one's life that seems to be lost if the limitations they indicate must always be seen in the light of the moments of surplus energy invoked by Nietzsche. There is also something about the specificity of certain kinds of setbacks, injuries, and losses in one's life whose meaning would be utterly lost (as well as the appropriate action to take with regard to them) if one simply baptized their occurrence symbolically within the innocence of becoming or reacted to them via the emotional attitude "even this loss won't hurt me because my spirit is overrich with life." In times of great loss, like the death of a loved one, such an attitude appears misguided, inappropriate, and unrealistic. If one is to use Nietzsche's ideas in a constructive manner, it is imperative to respect the specificity of such experiences of loss and displacement prior to incorporating such experiences in narratives that emphasize other conceptions, such as "willing backwards" or eternal return. Neither a reference to a surplus of moments in the inexhaustible well of life nor to a surplus of joy at some (other) point in our past experience is an adequate counterpart to hold down the grief one might feel at moments of irretrievable loss. In other words, Nietzsche is right to focus on joy to displace resentment, but it may be misguided of him to think that if one is to overcome all traces of resentment in oneself, every experience of pain or loss must be filtered through an unbreakable chain of significations leading back to an experience of joy. It is quite possible that a more modest approach—a more human and less godlike approach—will show us that a breakable (but fixable) chain of significations letting joy enter into our memories and hearts from time to time is sufficient to resist resentment when we are faced with experiences of deep pain and truly irrecoverable human losses. Still, Nietzsche seems on target to hold that the revenge of the will against the passing of time and against the sense of impotence before the "it was" should be fought at all costs. In this regard, not only Nietzsche's position as articulated in his works but our position as readers of Nietzsche cannot help but have significant psychological as well as political consequences.

NOTES

1. Friedrich Nietzsche, *The Birth of Tragedy*, trans. Walter Kaufmann (New York: Vintage, 1967), 5, p. 52.

2. *BT* 3, p. 42.

3. *BT* 15, pp. 95–96.

4. Friedrich Nietzsche, *The Will to Power*, trans. Walter Kaufmann and R. J. Hollingdale (New York: Vintage, 1967), 822.

5. Friedrich Nietzsche, *The Gay Science*, trans. Walter Kaufmann (New York: Vintage, 1974), 293.

6. *GS* 326.

7. Friedrich Nietzsche, *Ecce Homo*, trans. Walter Kaufmann (New York: Vintage, 1967), "Why I Am a Destiny," sec. 6.

8. Friedrich Nietzsche, "On the Uses and Disadvantages of History for Life," in *Untimely Meditations*, trans. R. J. Hollingdale (Cambridge: Cambridge University Press, 1983), 2–3, pp. 67–77.

9. Friedrich Nietzsche, *On the Genealogy of Morals*, trans. Walter Kaufmann (New York: Vintage, 1967), II:1–3.

10. "*The spirit of revenge*, my friends, has so far been the subject of man's best reflection; and where there was suffering, one always wanted punishment too," Z II, "On Redemption."

11. Nietzsche speaks of the social creation of memory as implemented by a device he calls "mnemotechnics." "'Only that which never ceases to hurt stays in the memory . . . ,'" he says, "is a main clause of the oldest (unhappily also the most enduring) psychology on earth," *GM* II:3.

12. Z I, "On the Thousand and One Goals."

13. *GS*, preface, 2.

14. Ibid.

15. Ibid.

16. Ibid., 3.

17. Ibid.

18. Ibid.

19. Ibid., 4.

20. Ibid.

21. Ibid.

22. Ibid., 2.

23. Z I, "On the Way of the Creator."

24. Z II, "On Redemption."

25. Ibid.

26. For such an analysis, see Joan Stambaugh, *The Problem of Time in Nietzsche* (Lewisburg, Pa.: Bucknell University Press, 1987).

27. Nietzsche does not clarify whether the "it was" refers primarily to the moment in time or to the experiences "contained" in it; presumably it refers to both.

28. Z II, "On Redemption."

29. As mentioned above, Nietzsche believed that forgetting the past should be construed as an artful endeavor. He distinguishes between sheer forgetting and active forgetting; the point of the latter is complementary to the exercise of reclaiming the past without succumbing to resentment.

30. Against the religions that teach pity for the suffering Nietzsche advocates to share "*not suffering but joy*" (GS 338). See also GS 341 and Z III, "The Other Dancing Song."

31. Z II, "The Tomb Song."

32. In particular, part I of *Zarathustra* begins and ends with images of gift-giving.

33. Z IV, "At Noon"; Z III, "The Seven Seals"; Z, Prologue, sec. 3.

34. The dreamlike scene where a shepherd is transformed from someone overwhelmed by pain to someone moved to ecstatic laughter is a case in point (Z III, "The Vision and the Riddle"). The shepherd's "biting" of the head of the snake and spitting it out symbolizes, among other things, the liberation from resentment.

CHAPTER 7

Nietzsche and the Emotions

Robert C. Solomon

Nietzsche is well known for his passionate writings. He also wrote and thought deeply, if not always consistently or systematically, about the passions, about emotion, about the less rational and reflective aspects of human behavior. There are long-standing objections against him, his celebration of the irrational, his rejection of reason, his emphasis on the "Dionysian" at the expense of "Apollonian," philosophical frenzy instead of calm contemplation. There is some truth to these charges, of course, and considerable if scattered textual support to back them up. Nevertheless, I believe that they are deeply flawed and reflect a profound misunderstanding not only of Nietzsche but of the emotions and, I would suggest, of the nature of philosophy. Nietzsche was not an "irrationalist," whatever that is supposed to mean, much less irrational. And emotions are not, as such, irrational either, a point that Nietzsche explicitly made on a number of occasions and in a number of very different ways. And for all of the emphasis that has been placed upon "reason" in the history of philosophy, even the greatest rationalists, for example, Plato, Descartes, Spinoza, and Kant, have insisted (in various ways) on the importance of passion and its ineliminable role in philosophy. It was Plato, after all, who defended philosophy as the product of *eros*, and Kant, before Hegel, who said that "nothing great is ever done without passion."

I would not go so far as to suggest that Nietzsche had a "theory" of the emotions. Indeed, whether Nietzsche had any theories at all (and whether the purpose of philosophy is to produce theories) is a matter I do not want to explore here. But it is clear that Nietzsche had some fascinating and insightful things to say about the emotions, both as a generic category and, more importantly and in much more detail, as particular phenomena in human life. Consider, as a small initial sampling, his many comments on pity, on resentment, on love and relationships, on the various kinds of suffering, on vengeance. Much of what Nietzsche had to say anticipated Freud and other psychoanalysts, particularly Adler and Jung, but so much of what he said went so far beyond them as well. Since those relationships, no doubt, make up much of this volume, I will say very little about them here. But what I would like to do is to begin by questioning the very metaphor under which these discussions proceed, namely, the "depth" metaphor, and ask whether, indeed, the human psyche is or is capable of being "deep" (where "profound" and "profundity" are just high-class terms for much the same image) or whether the truth about passions, despite those Freudian subterranean images, is rather on the surface. Nietzsche once said of the romantics, "they muddy the waters to make them look deep." I want to ask how much we mystify the emotions, perhaps in order to make them appear more mysterious and less comprehensible and, consequently, more overpowering and less our responsibility. Indeed, perhaps Nietzsche's greatest single contribution to a philosophy of the emotions is to get us to stop looking "below" the surface and appreciate, what we philosophers have so easily forgotten, the richness and complexity of the "face."[1]

NIETZSCHE ON THE EMOTIONS

In the long history of philosophy, emotions have often been ostracized. Philosophy is the history of reason, and emotions are alien, if not enemies of reason. Thus we find the Greeks and Romans sometimes equating various emotions with possession and madness. Socrates warned Crito against them and the Stoics thought all emotions irrational, not in the usual sense that they were bestial and "blind" but rather in the more sophisticated sense that they were mistaken judgments about oneself and one's place in the world. Horace thought anger was madness, as did Ovid of love. Many emotions were sinful in the eyes of medieval Christians, and Gregory the Great declared pride, envy, and anger—not to mention lust and the others—to be "deadly." Kant declared the "inclinations" (including the emotions) to be irrelevant to morals, and many modern philosophers follow him in this. There is a countercurrent in this history, Aristotle notably, Hume, of course, "romantics" of various generations, but the unmistakable mainstream of Western philosophy (not to let off the East) is a profound prejudice against the passions, the emotions, even the kinder, gentler moral sentiments. "*Il faut tuer les passions*" [One must kill the passions] screams Nietzsche (in italics as well as in French) in his *Twilight of the Idols*, "all the old moral monsters are agreed on this."[2] He goes on to chastise the New Testament in particular, but it is by no means Christianity alone that is guilty of this war on the emotions. In an earlier section of the same book, Nietzsche had set the blame squarely on Socrates, who had made reason a "tyrant." He often rips into Kant, whom he once called "the Chinese of Kønigsberg," presumably a racist reference to the apparent affectlessness of a people whom he had rarely encountered. Indeed, "the East" shares some of the blame as well, although what Nietzsche knew of Asian philosophy was more or less limited to India and the "Near" East. Buddhism, which he knew from Schopenhauer, is no friend of the passions either. The "Noble Truths" of Buddhism declare that life is suffering suffering comes from passion (desire), which is eliminable. One cannot imagine a view more opposed to Nietzsche's, except that the combined forces of philosophy and religion seem to converge in the same position. To appreciate Nietzsche's view of the emotions—and to also appreciate his flamboyant style and his sense of morals—one must begin by acknowledging (whether or not accepting) the fact that he saw much of the history of humanity in terms of this unending war on the passions and the passionate life.

In this light, it would make sense to note that reason, and with it philosophy, has often been called "deep." Interesting or even unintelligible thoughts are readily declared "profound." Indeed, in quite a few (more or less) contemporary cases, one is tempted to suggest that the more unintelligible or murky (even ungrammatical) a philosophical position is, the more profound it seems. Reason may be presented in metaphors of light and clarity, but in philosophy it is very often the opposite that is the case. Profundity suggests darkness. (Thus the "dark sayings" of Heraclitus.) Hegel is often thought to be most profound when he is clearly in over his head. Heidegger seems to be deepest when he makes no sense at all. Reason, in its analytic mode, may be all clarity and entailment (in other words, about as superficial—in the sense of "all on the table"—as one can get) but in its Continental odyssey, it seems to be the very opposite, despite Husserl's bold promises of "apodictic evidence" and Heidegger's much-touted promise of a "clearing."

Regarding the emotions, there has long been a popular thesis that "deep down, we are all the same." This is, of course, the ruling metaphor of depth psychology. It remains a secondary matter whether what is "down there" are libidinal urges or universal archetypes, a "will to power" or the need for salvation. So, too, it is secondary whether the deep, dark cellar of the soul is ruled by instinct or controlled by culture-bound forces of repression. The first question, and the one that Nietzsche was asking, was whether such "depth" metaphors make sense in the first place. Despite the fact that he is considered by his fans as the "deepest" of philosophers and that he clearly inspired the seemingly bottomless use of such metaphors in the psychology and philosophy that followed him, I think that Nietzsche intended no such topography. To be sure, he uses the adjectives "deep" and "profound" when referring to any number of things (including some of his own ideas), but these have taken on the meaning of high praise, and I am certainly not denying that Nietzsche uses the terms in this innocent sense. But he anticipates, I think, Heidegger's rather profound (in the high-praise sense) attack on Cartesian dualism and on the very idea that emotions (or anything else) can be "in" the mind. What twentieth-century depth psychology adds to such container metaphors is a literal twist, the suggestion that the mind includes an up-down dimension as well as its thought-balloon shape. Think of Freud's famous "topographical" drawings in his early works, although he sometimes uses the architectural and sexually suggestive metaphor of an "anteroom."

Such container metaphors dominated early modern philosophy of mind (e.g., Locke's closet metaphor, the empiricist use of "introspection" more generally, Leibniz's oddly postmodern conception of monads) despite the fact that Descartes defined the mind as "unextended [nonspatial] substance." Kant challenged both dualism and the spatial metaphor but arguably remained an "internalist" (which at least implies externality) in his concept of the *phenomenon*. Nietzsche argues against all such models, perhaps most famously in his "How the 'True World' Finally Became a Fable" (Kant only reaches stage 3) but much more pointedly in his various attacks on the "subject" and his scattered comments on the nature of mind. He applauds the medievals (I take it ironically): "Neither antiquity nor our own age has such extensive breadth of soul: its spaciousness was never greater."[3]

The mind, Nietzsche says, is a convergence of forces (in Deleuze's overly abstract terminology), "a mass of passions flowing off in different directions" in Nietzsche's own "fluvial" imagery.[4] It is not a peculiar "place." It is not "inside" of anything. It has no properties that are not ultimately biological (but without taking this term in the reductionist fashion in which it is used so often today). The emotions, according to this picture, are interpreted not as "inner feelings" pressing to "get out," the "internal enemy" of *Twilight* (5:3), but as natural, biological phenomena, part and parcel of the makeup of a value-seeking organism. An emotion is nothing more than its expression, but this is not to say that there is only an expression. So, too, an emotion is no more than its "physiology" (again, in a nonreductionist sense), but this is not to say that there is only physiology. An emotion is a strategy, the strategy of a biological creature with an inbuilt need to exert and express itself. Accordingly, emotions are not deep but, if one wishes to maintain the opposition, superficial. An emotion is a look, a gesture, an activity, a plot, a plan, a passion. It is a way of life, a way of "being tuned" (in Heidegger's happy phrase) to the world. One does not get a "glimpse" of an otherwise hidden emotion, when one catches another person's eye. What one sees, if one looks (and that, of course, includes a whole history, a context and a culture) is the other person, in toto. Any further division into "cause" and "effect" is almost certain to fall into one of Nietzsche's "four errors" (*TW*, 6). An emotion is not a cause nor is its expression a mere effect. One might say (as Nietzsche more usually says of *Triebe*, "drives") that an emotion is nothing less than a person, and a person just *is* his or her emotions. Of course, Nietzsche does not pursue this thesis systematically or consistently, but it is a "deep" set of insights that I want to pursue here. The neutral language between activity and passivity, the process (fluvial) metaphor instead of the static "state" and "trait" images of contemporary psychology, the insistence on biological life rather than "inner life," are all rich suggestions in the direction of a theory—or several theories of emotion.

Nietzsche does not have a theory of emotions, but piecing together various general comments (in particular, from section 5 of *Twilight of the Idols*), one can make at least the following suggestions: talk about emotions is not separable from talk about ethics as well as theories (no matter how merely tacit or inchoate) about "human nature." Emotion and reason are neither opposed nor separate. Emotions are not transparent (and are therefore prone to self-deception and misdescription). Emotions are, all-in-all, good, desirable as a category rather than suspicious or sinful, but positive and negative, not all good, not unqualified. Emotions have structures and strategies (archetypes, resentment as a clue, love) personification.

The emotions, according to Nietzsche (in several different sources), might be divided into two categories. In *Twilight*, he famously refers to these as the "life-enhancing" and the "life-stultifying" passions. There are, of course, any number of other divisions that might be made (and Nietzsche, despite his reputation with the postmodern crowd, seemed to thrill in divisive polarities). And one might well object to the oversimplification involved in this particular scheme, as if all emotions had a single ethical dimension and had value quite independent of their context. But the point to be made here is that emotions have value, and different values, and that the very idea that emotions as such are either good or bad, healthy or unhealthy, moral or immoral, is—simpleminded. This is not a new point, of course. The Greeks were quite clear about the complex role of emotions in ethics, and the medieval philosophers spent considerable effort distinguishing them (by way of accounts of sin and virtue). Even Kant says compassion is beautiful.[5]

One predictable aspect of Nietzsche's conception of the passions is his use of master-slave metaphors. In itself, this isn't very interesting, in part because "master-slave" is so pervasive an image in Nietzsche. But we might note that it is also a pervasive metaphor in the entire history of the passions in philosophy. One of the most enduring metaphors of reason and emotion has been the image of master and slave, with the wisdom of reason firmly in control and the dangerous impulses of emotion safely suppressed, channeled or, ideally, in harmony with reason. The master-slave metaphor has traditionally displayed at least two features that still determine much of the philosophical view of emotion today, the inferior role of emotion—the idea that emotion is as such more primitive, less intelligent, more bestial, less dependable, more dangerous and thus to be controlled by reason, and more profoundly, the reason-emotion distinction itself, as if we were dealing with two different natural kinds, two conflicting and antagonistic aspects of the soul. Even those philosophers who sought to integrate them and reduce one to the other (typically reducing emotion to an inferior genus of reason, a "confused perception" or "distorted judgment") maintained the distinction and continued to insist on the superiority of reason. It was thus a mark of his considerable iconoclasm that the Scottish skeptic David Hume, in the eighteenth century, famously declared that "reason is, and ought to be, the slave of the passions," but even Hume, despite an ingenious analysis of the structure of emotions, ultimately fell back on the old models and metaphors. It is in this long-standing context that we should both appreciate the historicality of Nietzsche's use of "mastery of the passions" language and can also appreciate his attempts to get beyond that. Thus the radical force of Nietzsche's quick claim, "As if every passion didn't contain its own quantum of reason" and, in general, his defense of the passions.[6]

Nevertheless, Nietzsche's frequent treatment of emotions in the metaphor of streams and torrents conveys the strong sense that emotions are forces of nature barely within our control and separate from the self. In the second volume of *Human, All-Too-Human*, Nietzsche tells us, "A man who refuses to become master over his wrath, his choler and revengefulness, and his lusts, and attempts to become a master in anything else, is as stupid as the farmer who stakes out his field beside a torrential stream without protecting himself against it."[7] That looks suspiciously like a metaphor from Plato's *Republic*, including his rejection of the pleasures of the body and a defense of a rationalism that Nietzsche clearly despises.[8] In *Twilight*, he writes that "All passions have a phase when they are merely disastrous, when they drag down their victim with the weight of stupidity—and a later, very much later phase when they wed the spirit, when they 'spiritualize' themselves."[9]

Again, the dangerous torrent metaphor, only slightly animated by "stupidity." But then there is "the later phase" when they "wed the spirit" or "'spiritualize' themselves." I think what Nietzsche, with his too many mixed metaphors, is getting at is a thesis more insightful and more personal than the usual "mastering the passions" patter. It fits into his much larger "dialectic of the self" (or what Parkes calls "composing the soul") in which the self and what belongs to the self is negotiable, always in question, always "in play." The tradition, before and following Nietzsche, that takes the emotions to be strictly "other," the agitations of the body infecting the soul or the "it" from below, fails to appreciate the extent to which the self includes and embraces (not yet to say "chooses") its emotions, the extent to which it is constructed of them and motivated to compose itself according to their own ideas. Malebranche (often quoted by Adam Smith) says that "every passion creates its own justification."[10] In a similar vein, we might say that every passion *is* its own justification, in the sense that each passion both has its own autonomy and distinctness and contributes to the overall blend of the soul, "the grand arc of a total passion."[11]

The emotions, like our own body as infants, at first strike us as something "other," as beyond our control. Gradually—sometimes suddenly—we learn control, mastery, we make them our own. With cultivation and practice, we can become quite skillful, graceful, elegant, "completely in control." And yet, any great artist will tell you (they are often anxious to do so) that their relation to their "daemon" or "muse" or simply "passion" is still one of intimate otherness. Thus Parkes points out that "it is a maxim of depth psychology that when something of one's own is constantly denied it becomes alien, other, and thereby disturbing—if not terrifying" and Nietzsche responds by insisting that we "deprive the passions of their terrifying character and thereby prevent their becoming devastating torrents."[12] (Freud certainly picked up the maxim here, declaring that "where there is id, there shall ego be.") The passions both define the self and are not of the self, as, in infancy, the body both escapes the self and yet defines the self. To understand the shadow role of the passions as both self and not self, as in control and beyond control is an essential part of Nietzsche's distinctive romanticism and, I would argue, his inchoate theory of the emotions.

Like Freud after him, or, rather, anticipating Freud who may or may not have imitated him, Nietzsche defends an "economic" model of the emotions. Why he defends such a model, I have only partial answers. I myself have often suggested that the emotions are "investments," investments of the self, and so, needless to say, I am sympathetic with the model and its explanatory advantages. But then I, like Freud, am a good *bourgeois*, accustomed to capitalism and quite taken in—often against my better judgment—by economic ways of thinking. Such is surely not the case with Nietzsche, who quite rightly claims to be far more spiritual and whose materialism was for the most part confined to his enthusiasm for Democritus, Epicurus, Lucretius, and ancient atomism. In England, intellectual life had been thoroughly taken over by the (relatively) new economic vocabulary, notably in the philosophy of political economist John Stuart Mill and his updated version of "utilitarianism." But Nietzsche despised Mill and his movement and considered them vulgar (as he surely would have American pragmatism with its emphasis on the "cash value" of ideas). Parkes suggests that Nietzsche means to suggest the root of "economics" in the Greek *oikos* (household, where *oekinomicus* meant, for Aristotle notably, something like household management),[13] indicating the domestication of the emotions. But I doubt that Nietzsche would use "domestication" in such a positive light, especially when discussing the power of the passions. One domesticates a dog or a cat, not a lion. And becoming a lion, in one of Nietzsche's favorite metaphors, is certainly not to be identified with becoming domesticated.

Nevertheless, the economic metaphor certainly makes sense in the context of Nietzsche's many fluvial metaphors, of emotions and passions as streams and torrents, but I would suggest that engineering models might work more efficiently than economic images. The ideas of channeling (sublimation) and flow pervade Nietzsche's discussions of the emotions, and the dominant ideal here is self-control, self-mastery, but emphatically without the suppression of the emotions, much less their destruction. (From Nietzsche's notes: "The most short-sighted and pernicious way of thinking wants to make the great sources of energy, those wild torrents of the soul that often stream forth so dangerously and overwhelmingly, *dry up* altogether, instead of taking their power into service and economizing it."[14]) Freud, too, adopts this "hydraulic" model of emotions, understanding "the psychic apparatus" in terms of volume and pressure, damming (not damning) and flow, channeling and sublimation. The model has its virtues, as does the investment model that, I have suggested, is inappropriate here despite Nietzsche's use of economic terminology. In particular, it suggests an ineliminable force that must be dealt with, coped with, and cannot simply be suppressed. One can dam up or rechannel a river but one cannot (except over time, with population explosion and environmental stupidity) get rid of one. So, too, as Nietzsche often tells us, only fools and hypocrites want to eliminate the emotions.

Nevertheless, one must wonder how such a model, how such a metaphor, could have taken such a firm hold on our language. To be sure, it "feels as if" emotions "flow" through us, "rise up" in us, are "about to explode" in us. But this only pushes the question one step back: Why does it feel that way? Why does the language of flow seem to fit "the stream of consciousness" so well? Or is it the other way around, that we cannot think of our psychic life in any other terms because we have now no other terms? (Cf. "We are not rid of God because we still have faith in grammar," *TW* 3:5.) But, to make a fast suggestion, suppose having an emotion were more like "having something to say." No spatial metaphors there, and insofar as the "flow" imagery is the least bit applicable, it applies only to the results of saying—the flow of *parole*—rather than as a model for what is going on "in a person's mind." Or, consider some of Nietzsche's own scattered suggestions about "harmonizing" the mind,[15] aimed at Plato, derived from his own love of music and no doubt inherited from Schopenhauer and Buddhism (although more akin to Taoism). That, too, is a truly non-spatial model for emotions, and though one might talk of "flow" in the rather minimalist sense of "the flow of the music" [i.e., the flow of time] this model certainly doesn't recommend either an engineer or an economist. It requires a musician, or, following Parkes, a composer. But Nietzsche's model of emotions, despite his more semioticist and musical inclinations, remains firmly tied to physics and physical imagery. This might be argued to belie even his still naturalistic biological intentions, betraying a reductionist impulse that even the greatest of thinkers find all-too-tempting.

NIETZSCHE ON PITY AND RESENTMENT

Nietzsche talks much more about particular emotions than he does about emotions in general, and so, piecing together what Nietzsche has to say about this or that passion is probably more productive in the long run for formulating a "theory" that makes some sense in terms of his texts. This has advantages that transcend the nature of Nietzsche's texts. Too much of emotions theory begins rather naively, with the view that emotions are a distinctive class of phenomena, with defining characteristics and if not an essence then at least "family resemblances." Nietzsche would have been the first to appreciate, if he had focused in on the matter, that the various words in various languages that [to varying degrees] circumscribe the emotions do not define a "natural kind." The language of emotions is a historical language, strongly affected by the cultural and, especially, the moral context. While some emotions are almost always included (anger, for instance), others are not (the varieties of love, a notorious example). If we were to try to corral the emotions that are of special concern to Nietzsche in a single category, we would find it extremely awkward. Much of what he has to say about particular emotions is sharply critical and negative. He famously campaigns against pity (*Mitleid*) and he has surprisingly vitriolic comments about love. He wages war against resentment, or, tellingly, against *ressentiment*, where the French term is not to be taken as equivalent to the English or the German terms. Both terms are revealing in what they exclude as well as what gets said. Nietzsche only grudgingly considers the virtues of resentment when it is put to the service of the will to power (the "genius" of the Jewish people). He does not consider those kindred emotions that fuel resistance to oppression, and his attack on *ressentiment* makes no allowances for what we would call "sensitivity." In his attack on pity, he seems to be oblivious to the virtues that his mentor Schopenhauer defended so elegantly in the same emotion (tellingly translated into English as "compassion" not "pity"). But then he sometimes argues on both sides of an emotion, bringing out critical ambiguities that confuse our understanding. Notably, following dozens of sarcastic comments about the limpness of Christian love, Nietzsche writes in *Twilight:* "The spirituality of sensuosity . . . called *love* . . . represents a great triumph over Christianity."[16] It becomes clear that while Nietzsche saw great virtue in passionate love, he had nothing but contempt for that meek sentiment that shares (or has usurped) the same name. But making such distinctions is by no means simple or straightforward. The types of love (as well as many other emotions) flow and transform themselves into one another. In particular, the triangular relation between love, pity, and resentment occupies a great deal of Nietzsche's attention.

Nevertheless, to describe Nietzsche's view primarily in terms of a concerted campaign *against* the emotions would obviously be completely wrong-headed. True, he attacks certain emotions, notably pity and resentment, but the thrust of his philosophy is ardently pro-passion, a defense of emotions in the exemplary life. The problem is, there is no particular positive passion that exemplifies this role. Love might serve, as it certainly did for some of Nietzsche's romantic predecessors, but the very idea of love had become so corrupted, in Nietzsche's eyes, that it fails to serve as a singular example. Some of his more striking examples, hatred and "the need for enemies," for instance, seem intended more to shock the reader than to defend the passionate life as such.[17] (One must distinguish well here between hatred and resentment, and the differences are essential.) Some of the more violent passions come out on both sides of the ledger, the various emotions of revenge, for instance, and justice, by contrast, turns out not to be much of a passion at all.[18] I would argue that what really holds the place of positive passion in general for Nietzsche is his famous phrase, "will to power," which refers not to power as such (nor to will) but to the centrality of the passions in human life.

("What is good?—All that heightens the feeling of power, the will to power, power itself in man."[19])

It is in place of any particular positive passion that Nietzsche celebrates the "torrents" of the psyche metaphorically. What he obviously admires and defends is the strength of the emotions, the passions experienced as raw physical (as well as psychic) energy. So considered, the primary division among the various emotions, corresponding (or replacing) the distinction between life-enhancing and life-stultifying passions, would be those that are based on strength, on the one hand, and those that are based on weakness, on the other. With that in mind, I want to briefly focus attention on those two emotions that best exemplify the "weakness" side of the story, at least in Nietzsche's rendition.

Nietzsche had a substantial variety of views on *pity,* by no means all forming a single perspective, but, among his various attacks, he argued that pity was nothing but a false front for an insecure sense of superiority. As such, it was a hypocritical form of contempt rather than care and consideration. But, sometimes, it is those who are pitied who are the target of Nietzsche's attack, for example, at least they still *have* one *power,* in spite of all their weakness: "the *power to hurt.*"[20] Sometimes the attack on pity is just an attack on weakness, the grounds being predominantly aesthetic:

> Today that is called virtue itself among the little people—pity. They have no respect for great misfortune, for great ugliness, for great failure.
>
> From pity, a great cloud approaches; beware![21]

Elsewhere, pity itself is a weakness, or rather causes weakness, or both, as the following problematic quote suggests:

> Pity [*Mitleiden*], insofar as it really induces suffering [*Leiden*] . . . is a weakness like every losing of oneself through a *harmful* affect.[22]

Often Nietzsche is just a bit enigmatic, for example:

> *Why beggars go on living.*—If alms were bestowed only out of pity all the beggars would have starved to death.
>
> *Why beggars go on living.*—The greatest bestower of alms is cowardice.[23]

One can guess (and find it in his letters) that Nietzsche was one of those sensitive souls who simply couldn't bear the sight of the very poor or the guilt that accompanied the encounter with beggars. In this light, we might interpret much more literally than he intended Nietzsche's comment in *The Gay Science* where he suggests that "there is no trick which enables us to turn a poor virtue into a rich and overflowing one; but we can reinterpret its poverty into a necessity so that it no longer offends us when we see it and we no longer sulk on its account."[24] It is worth noting again that the German word *Mitleid* can be translated either as "compassion" or as "pity," and it is usually translated the first way in Schopenhauer, who praised it, and the second way in Nietzsche, who excoriates it. (In *The Gay Science*, Nietzsche unceremoniously refers to "the nonsense about pity" in Schopenhauer.[25])

In one sense, it is true that almost every case of *Mitleid* involves a sense of superiority, namely, by virtue of the fact that the person suffering has an unwanted affliction that the person feeling compassion does not have. I am "superior" to the beggar to whom I give money because I have money and he does not. So too I am "superior" to (in this case, just "luckier" than) my friend because he had the heart attack and I did not. But it is clear that this limited sense of superiority—namely, the superiority of good fortune by virtue of which one person suffers a tragedy which the other does not—is not enough to make the harsh case that Nietzsche wants to prosecute. In the second case, in particular, it is not because I am a superior *person* that my friend had the heart attack and I did not. It may be true that I take better care of myself than he does, but the very opposite could also be true. Even in the first case, one cannot simply argue that I am superior to the beggar because I have money and he does not: he may very likely be a hard-working family man caught in hard times while I am a prodigal (even if generous) heir. In an instance of pure chance—you are shot in the leg by the terrorist's stray bullet rather than I—it is quite clear that the built-in sense of superiority here does not take us any distance at all; it means only that you are suffering and I am not. And it certainly does not follow from this that I am feeling compassionate *in order to* feel superior. Quite the contrary, in all three cases I will mostly likely feel embarrassed (if not worse) about my comparative well being.

And yet, we can all think of those cases in which a grand display of compassion is self-serving and apparently designed precisely in order to demonstrate as well as feel one's own superiority. One manufactures pity as a means to appear and feel oneself to be not only a good person but a person with great merit. One is virtuous, first of all, for feeling this grand emotion and recognizing the plight of this poor unfortunate, and one is virtuous, second but even more, because one is not the sort of person who is prone to such misfortune. One might note that this sometimes obnoxious but often quite ordinary display of supposedly selfless emotion is the professional liability of liberals, for whom the self-aggrandizement of pity is always a temptation. Indeed, one can (or should) easily understand that conservative criticism and the accompanying accusations of hypocrisy when millionaire liberals and well-heeled liberal professors make their careers out of compassion but make no sacrifices and accuse those who would pay for their plans (usually the working middle-class) of selfishness and lack of public spiritedness. So, too, one can understand the usual reaction to extreme acts of charity and self-sacrifice, when such acts impoverish and do not ennoble the giver (which, when generalized, gives rise to a fraudulent notion of "altruism" [or pity] as self-sacrifice, for instance, in the works of Ayn Rand). But, as always, one must be cautious about taking such examples as illustrative instead of cautionary, and what they show about pity and compassion is not necessarily the self-serving nature of these sentiments.

What lies at the heart of Nietzsche's inconsistent attacks, I think, is a mixture of contempt and helplessness in the face of both poverty and compassion. The philosopher whose last fully conscious action was embracing a dumb animal to keep it from being beaten was deeply troubled both by the weakness of others and his own weakness. Of course, the weaknesses are not the same. In the case of the former, poverty and the penalties of bad luck and bad upbringing have always had ambiguous existential status, perhaps nowhere more so than in contemporary America. On the one hand, there is the unavoidable recognition of misfortune and inherited disadvantage. And, on the other side of misfortune, anyone with any sense, "self-made" or not, must recognize that success in life is always (at least in part) an accident, a gift, the product of contingencies over which one had no conceivable control. Both fortune and misfortune fall under the rubric of "*amor fati*" (love of fate) and perhaps in his moments of abstraction Nietzsche could wholly accept both of them, but it should not be surprising that most people hesitate both to give up credit to their own achievements and would be equally hesitant to accept the blame if or when misfortune fell on them. The latter hesitation leads us into the familiar ambiguity of fortune, namely, the "existential" suspicion that, no matter how terrible a person's circumstances (with certain minimal limits, perhaps) he or she could "do something about it if he/she tried." Thus the weakness of poverty becomes weakness of will, weakness of the spirit becomes unwillingness. This obviously taps into some pervasive concerns of Nietzsche's, namely the whole question of "will," of "self-improvement," of trying to become what you are not or could not be as opposed to "becoming what one is." The point here concerning pity is that Nietzsche sees pity as a multiple embodiment of weaknesses, on a number of different fronts and in a number of different dimensions.

In all of these, pity is not merely a "feeling" or an "expression" or even a "reaction" so much as it is a *strategy*. Both on the part of the supposedly compassionate and on the part of the pitied, pity is (or can be) manipulative, contemptuous, and self-justifying.[26] The contempt and self-justification are not confined to the person with pity. The pitied are often in a position to feel "upward contempt" and ideological justification in confronting their benefactors, and it is this, no doubt, that so deeply and personally troubled Nietzsche. Thus there is a suggestion that the attack on pity is really an attempt at the "self-containment" and invulnerability to the misfortunes of life (on one's own part and for others) defended by the Stoics.[27] I think this pulls some important threads out of Nietzsche's philological inheritance but nevertheless misses the point of his texts. Pity is a way of seeing the world, a way of "being tuned," but by way of pathos and impoverishment rather than exuberance and strength, and this is what Nietzsche holds against it:

> With difficulty I escaped the throng of the pitying, to find the only one today who teaches "pity is obtrusive"—you, O Zarathustra. Whether it be God's pity or man's—pity offends the sense of shame. To be unwilling to help can be nobler than that virtue which jumps to help.[28]

I will end this discussion of pity by saying that I do not at all agree with Nietzsche's condemnation of *Mitleid* as such, but I do see the point of his attack. Here, as elsewhere, Nietzsche gives us "only a perspective." One would be callous to accept it as the whole story about pity, but one would be foolish as well to dismiss it as nothing but "heartless."

There is much more to say about *resentment* (and *ressentiment*), but for the purposes of this essay I will keep my comments short.[29] It remains to be seen whether we live for pleasure or, as Nietzsche quipped, only the English utilitarian does, but it is by no means an unreasonable hypothesis that we live for power rather than pleasure and ultimately prefer a sense of self-importance to mere satisfaction. Indeed, experience seems to bear that out, even if one then adds that self-importance is one of our most successful sources of pleasure. The pleasure is not the end to which self-importance is the means. Power may be a means, of course, and often it is defined that way ("the power to . . ."). But what Nietzsche sees so clearly is that power is rarely only a means, and resentment is, above all, an emotion concerned with power.

Resentment begins with both an awareness of power and an awareness of one's own lack of power, although this may, of course, be merely perceived (and faulty) rather than a reflection of actual abilities or status. Lack of power is not the *cause* but the *content* of resentment, and resentment in turn is not merely the cause but the content of morality, as Nietzsche envisions it. It is not the soil from which morality springs (one of Nietzsche's routine metaphors) but rather the structure of morals as such. In the famous "master-slave" analysis of morality in *Genealogy of Morals*, Nietzsche's emphasis on nobility and resentment is an attempt to stress character and virtue above all else in ethics, and thus he deserves credit as one of the modern founders of what is now called "virtue ethics." A "master morality" of nobility is an expression of good, strong character. An ethics of resentment is an expression of bad character—whatever its principles and their rationalizations.

> [The man of *ressentiment*] loves hiding places, secret paths and back doors, everything covert entices him as his world, his security, his refreshment; he understands how to keep silent, how not to forget, how to wait, how to be provisionally self-deprecating and humble. A race of such men of *ressentiment* is bound to become eventually cleverer than any noble race; it will also honor cleverness to a far greater degree.[30]

> [W]ith noble men cleverness can easily acquire a subtle flavor of luxury and subtlety—for here it is far less essential than the perfect functioning of the regulating unconscious instincts or even a certain imprudence, perhaps a bold recklessness . . . or that enthusiastic impulsiveness in anger, love, reverence, gratitude and revenge.[31]

There is considerable confusion about what exactly resentment is for Nietzsche, and more troublesome, why he attacks it so. Again, I think the answer must be put in terms of weakness, the impoverishment of a worldview. "This *need* to direct one's view outward instead of back to oneself—is of the essence of *ressentiment*: in order to exist, slave morality always first needs a hostile external world; it needs, physiologically speaking, external stimuli in order to act at all—its action is fundamentally reaction. The reverse is the case with the noble mode of valuation: it acts and grows spontaneously."[32] Resentment is a bitter emotion, typically a reaction to an injury or slight (whether intended or not) and it is often linked up with frustrated fantasies of revenge ("that falsification perpetrated on its opponent—*in effigie* of course—by the submerged hatred, the vengefulness of the impotent" [*GM* I:10] and again, "the submerged, darkly glowering emotions of vengefulness and hatred" [*GM* I:13]). But here, I think, the nature of resentment becomes clear not just as a vengeful outlook on the world but, more importantly, an impotent, frustrated vengeful outlook on the world. The frustration of fantasies further feeds the resentment, which stimulates increasingly drastic fantasies, and thus resentment *poisons* and overwhelms. By way of contrast, "should [*ressentiment*] appear in the noble man, [it] consummates and exhausts itself in an immediate reaction, and therefore does not *poison*."[33] Thus the resentful man has "deep" feelings; the noble man acts. But what "depth" refers to here is neither profundity nor repression but pervasiveness, obsessiveness, frustration. Frustration lies at the heart of resentment, and this is what distinguishes it from effective anger.

Does resentment lie behind morality as such, as its underlying motive and definitive characteristic? Is what we call "morality" in fact a "slave" morality, based on and an expression of weakness? This is much the same defensive question asked by Max Scheler, and my answer is much the same too: Nietzsche had a series of powerful psychological insights but overstated and oversimplified them. There are aspects (and uses) of morality (and Christianity) that do indeed invite a diagnosis of resentment, but it is wrong to think that the condemnation is therefore global, much less "the definitive refutation." There are indeed "herd" and servile aspects of morality, and the motivation of morality may indeed (in part) be based on *ressentiment*—but even *ressentiment* has its virtues.

Accordingly, Nietzsche has mixed feelings about resentment. If creativity is one of the highest virtues—and it certainly seems to be for him—then resentment would seem to be one of the most virtuous emotions, for it is certainly among the most creative, perhaps even more so than inspirational love. (Compare the schemes of Iago and Richard the Third with the witless reactions of Othello and Orlando, for example.) Insofar as language and insight, ruthless criticism and mastery of irony are skills worth praising, then resentment would seem to be one of the most accomplished emotions as well, more articulate than even the most righteous anger, more clever than the most covetous envy, more critical than the indifferent spirit of reason would ever care to be. Not surprisingly, our greatest critics and commentators are men and women of resentment. Nietzsche is surely right, that our most vocal and influential moralists are men and women of deep resentment—whether or not this is true of morality as such. Our revolutionaries are men and women of resentment. In an age deprived of passion—if Kierkegaard is to be believed—they alone have the one dependable emotional motive, constant and obsessive, slow-burning but totally dependable and durable. Through resentment, they get things done. Whatever else it may be, resentment is not ineffectual.

Nietzsche famously tells us in *Twilight* that certain emotions "drag us down with their stupidity"—but resentment is surely not one of them. There is no emotion more clever, more powerful, more life-preserving if not life-"enhancing," no emotion more conducive to the grand act of revenge that Nietzsche himself wishes to perpetrate on modernity and the Christian world. Resentment creates its own power, which displaces its own targets and (even despite itself) satisfies its desire for revenge. Thus the victory of the slave over the master in Hegel's *Phenomenology*. Thus the victory, writ large, of slave morality. The felt impotence of resentment should not be confused with its expression, which is a kind of arrogance, or with the practical results of resentment, which sometimes tend to be powerful and effective indeed. ("A race of such men of *ressentiment* is bound to become eventually cleverer than any noble race."[34])

CONCLUSION: NIETZSCHE, THE "WILL TO POWER," AND THE PASSIONATE LIFE

I have not tried to suggest that Nietzsche had anything like a "theory" of emotions, but I think that he did clearly present us with something much more important. That is a celebration and defense of the passionate life, something that has been woefully rare in philosophy. Reason has indeed remained a "tyrant" since the days of Socrates, several generations of romantics notwithstanding. Emotions have too long been disdained and dismissed, and it is Nietzsche, I want to suggest, who gets a lion's share of the credit for reinstating them. Granted, he focused much more keenly on the negative emotions—the emotions of weakness—than he did on the positive, "affirmative" emotions. But this, I have suggested, is not a fair indication of his motives. The celebratory spirit that pervades Nietzsche's writings—not to be reduced to mere "style"—is itself definitive of the passionate life, and if the most powerful emotions are more often described in terms of metaphors and euphoria (*"amor fati!"*, "the will to power") that in itself says something profound about Nietzsche's view of life. Excessive focus—excessive rationality if you like—suggests defensiveness, narrowness, *ressentiment*. What constitutes the good life is rather a generalized joy of living, the virtues that come from enthusiasm rather than from mere good breeding. This is why I want to take Nietzsche, not Aristotle, as my ultimate mentor in the area of virtue ethics and the champion of the passionate life. There is also much to be learned from him, even if too often only in the form of hints, on the important subject of emotions, not least of all, those that he inspires, just reading him.

NOTES

1. Nietzsche often celebrates his own insights in psychology. What he fails to appreciate are his related talents in the field once called *physiognomy*. Many of his most cutting descriptions are not depictions of what is deep in the mind at all, but portraits of postures and tell-all facial expressions. For example, consider this brilliant line from the *Genealogy*: "While the noble man lives in trust and openness with himself (*gennaios* "of noble descent" underlines the nuance "upright" and probably also "naive"), the man of *ressentiment* is neither upright nor naive nor honest and straightforward with himself. His soul *squints*."

Friedrich Nietzsche, *On the Genealogy of Morals*, trans. Walter Kaufmann (New York: Random House, 1967), I:10.

2. Friedrich Nietzsche, *Twilight of the Idols*, in *The Portable Nietzsche*, trans. Walter Kaufmann (New York: Viking Press, 1982), "Morality as Anti-Nature," 1.

3. Friedrich Nietzsche, *The Wanderer and his Shadow*, in *Human, All-Too-Human*, 2 vols., trans. R. J. Hollingdale (Cambridge: Cambridge University Press, 1986), 222.

4. For more on this, see Graham Parkes' wonderful book, *Composing the Soul: Reaches of Nietzsche's Psychology* (Chicago: University of Chicago Press, 1994), 145ff.

5. In his essay, "Observations on Feeling of the Beautiful and Sublime," of 1764.

6. Friedrich Nietzsche, *The Will to Power*, trans. Walter Kaufmann and R. J. Hollingdale (New York: Random House, 1968), 387.

7. *WS* 65.

8. This connection is pointed out by Parkes, *Composing the Soul*, 146–47. One might note that Plato, who is talking about *eros* and "flowing toward learning" is not anything like the calculative rationalist that Nietzsche so despised in his own times. Indeed, Plato's conception of the passions is still a field, however overmined, with unsuspected riches.

9. *TW*, "Morality," 1.

10. I was reminded by this by Smith scholar Charles Griswold, in correspondence.

11. *WS* 65.

12. Parkes, *Composing the Soul*, 147; Nietzsche, *WS*, 37.

13. *Oekinomicus* as opposed to *Chrematisike*, which would characterize the field of economics today—profit-crazy and purely financial.

14. *Will to Power*, trans. Walter Kaufmann and R. J. Hollingdale (New York: Random House, 1967), 381.

15. For example, in his early essay, "On Moods" (1864) discussed by Parkes, *Composing the Soul*, 42ff.

16. *TW*, "Morality," 3.

17. "Not contentment but more power: not peace at all, but war; not virtue but proficiency" Friedrich Nietzsche, *The Antichrist*, trans. R. J. Hollingdale (New York: Penguin, 1968), 2.

18. *GM* II. One might argue, of course, that justice isn't an emotion anyway, so Nietzsche's denial treatment of justice as a rather benign and nonconfrontational emotion may seem rather obvious. But what Nietzsche is addressing here is not the contemporary view of "justice as fairness," but the classical view of justice advocated by Socrates, Plato, and Aristotle. For them, justice was a personal virtue and was designed explicitly to contrast with the more ancient Homeric conception of justice as vengeance. I have discussed this in detail in my book, *A Passion for Justice* (Lanham: Rowman and Littlefield, 1994).

19. *AC* 2.

20. *HU* 50.

21. Friedrich Nietzsche, *Thus Spoke Zarathustra*, trans. Walter Kaufmann (New York: Viking Press, 1966), part IV, "The Ugliest Man."

22. *Daybreak*, trans. R. J. Hollingdale (Cambridge: Cambridge University Press, 1982), 134.

23. WS 239, 240.

24. Friedrich Nietzsche, *The Gay Science*, trans. Walter Kaufmann (New York: Random House, 1974), 17.

25. GS 127. Schopenhauer's argument is in his small book, *On the Basis of Morality*, trans. E. F. Payne (Indianapolis: Bobbs-Merrill, 1965).

26. The phrase "upward contempt" comes from William Miller, "Upward Contempt" (unpublished ms.) and his *Humiliation* (Ithaca, N.Y.: Cornell University Press, 1993).

27. Martha Nussbaum, "Pity and Mercy: Nietzsche's Stoicism," *Nietzsche, Genealogy, Morality*, ed. Richard Schacht (Berkeley: University of California Press, 1994), 139–67.

28. Z IV, "The Ugliest Man."

29. I have discussed these issues at much greater length in my "One Hundred Years of Ressentiment," in *Nietzsche, Genealogy, Morality*, ed. Schacht, 95–126. What follows is adapted, in part, from that essay.

30. GM I:11.

31. GM I:10.

32. GM I:10.

33. GM I:10.

34. GM I:10.

PART 2

Nietzsche and Psychology

CHAPTER 8

The Birth of Psychoanalysis
from the Spirit of Enmity:
Nietzsche, Rée, and Psychology
in the Nineteenth Century

Robert C. Holub

At the very beginning of Graham Parkes' *Composing the Soul: Reaches
of Nietzsche's Psychology* (1994), the author points to the dearth of
studies on Nietzsche as a psychologist.[1] Citing Nietzsche's hyperbolic
assertions that he is a psychologist without equal, Parkes finds it strange
that his labors in disclosing the workings of the human mind have gone
largely undiscussed. "Perhaps what has disconcerted," Parkes speculates, "is the gross immodesty of his claims to psychological acumen; at
any rate the secondary literature, now burgeoning more than ever, has
generally ignored the psychological dimensions of Nietzsche's
thought."[2] Parkes contention may strike readers familiar with Nietzsche
criticism as somewhat unusual. He himself implicitly concedes in a footnote that there has been a steady stream of commentary that has explicitly mentioned the psychological implications of Nietzsche's philosophy,
from Ludwig Klages' *The Psychological Accomplishments of Nietzsche*
[*Die psychologischen Errungenschaften Nietzsches*] (1926)[3] to Jacob
Golomb's *Nietzsche's Enticing Psychology of Power* (1987).[4] Indeed,
perhaps the most important study in American Nietzsche research, Walter Kaufmann's *Nietzsche: Philosopher, Psychologist, Antichrist* (1950)[5]
elevates Nietzsche's psychology to an equal footing with his philosophical and antitheological achievements. One suspects that part of the reason that Parkes bemoans the lack of work on Nietzschean psychology
has to do with his disagreements with previous studies. In his carefully

documented monograph, which deals with both Nietzsche's biography and writings, Parkes argues that Nietzsche validated a divided or multiple personality: for Nietzsche "great health" involves "souls burgeoning on many levels with various parts in the psyche shaping, forming, commanding, exercising protracted discipline on other parts until ultimately control is relaxed so as to allow spontaneous activity from awareness of a full range of perspectives."[6] Works that reach a different conclusion have not necessarily neglected psychology as a key element in Nietzschean thought; they have merely propagated a different view of the psyche, its development, and its potentials according to a divergent reading of Nietzsche's texts.

Parkes' remarks are significant, nonetheless, because they point obliquely to a problem, or a series of questions, one encounters in writing about Nietzsche and psychology; namely, what do we understand when we speak of psychology? What did Nietzsche understand by psychology? How did he relate to psychological developments of his own time? And how did his writings contribute to developments in psychology after his time? We know more about the last of these questions, which deals with reception and influence, than we do about the more historically oriented queries. In general Nietzsche's name is absent, or at best marginal, in the vast literature that recounts the history of psychology.[7] To a certain extent this absence is not unexpected since Nietzsche was not a psychologist in any traditional sense. He certainly did not write systematically about what scientists in the nineteenth-century would have considered the human mind and its functioning, and he was therefore recognized in his own time and in succeeding generations as neither an experimental nor a speculative psychologist.[8] Even in a volume dedicated to the more philosophical aspects of psychology, such as Daniel N. Robinson's *An Intellectual History of Psychology*,[9] Nietzsche does not receive extensive treatment. Although Robinson is aware of Nietzsche's own claims to be a psychologist, he maintains that he promised more than he delivered. Indeed, Robinson suggests that Nietzsche's notions of psychology were actually rather superficial. Had he been a superior psychologist, Robinson asserts, he "might have found in the universality of religious inclinations a vein of interests running deeper than the will to power."[10] Like most histories of psychology, therefore, Robinson's relegates Nietzschean influence to little more than a footnote.

The situation changes rather drastically, however, if one considers Nietzsche's impact on the particular branch of psychological speculation and research known as psychoanalysis. Although Freud himself and some of his more devoted followers have denied Nietzschean influence, most recent literature on the topic has confirmed Nietzsche's importance

for the development of psychoanalytic theory, as well as for the application of psychoanalysis to more general cultural occurrences. There is
good reason to assume that Freud himself was well acquainted with
Nietzsche's thought. Despite his public disavowals, Freud probably read
Nietzsche's works as a young man (he quotes him as early as 1875), and,
quite probably, throughout his life.[11] But Freud could also have learned
a great deal about Nietzsche from the Viennese circles he frequented in
the 1880s. For a time Nietzsche was in active correspondence with both
Siegfried Lipiner and Josef Paneth, both of whom Freud had also met.
Lipiner appears to have been responsible for introducing Nietzsche's
writings to Viennese student reading groups in the 1870s; indeed,
William McGrath has demonstrated how important Nietzsche was for
precisely the social milieu Freud frequented.[12] Paneth was a physiologist
and a close friend of Freud's during their university studies; like Freud,
Paneth was first attracted to more traditional scientific procedures, and
it was he who replaced Freud in the laboratory of Ernst Brücke in the
early 1880s. At the very least Freud imbibed Nietzschean thought
through the ambiance of the intellectual circles to which he, Lipiner, and
Paneth belonged.[13] It is certainly possible that psychoanalysis would not
have required Nietzsche as a precursor; but it is unlikely that Nietzsche's
thought did not have a seminal influence on Freud's thinking during his
formative intellectual years.[14]

If Nietzsche does have a lasting significance for psychological
thought, then it must be sought in connection with Freud and the beginnings of psychoanalysis. But Nietzsche's relationship to psychoanalysis
is clearly one of forerunner and intellectual source, not colleague and
direct collaborator. Unlike Freud, who broke away from established
medical practices, but, on account of his educational background and
theoretical self-understanding, continued to claim membership status in
the scientific community, Nietzsche stood on the outside of the scientific
and psychological establishment of his own times. Indeed, the only academic circles to which he truly belonged were those connected with classical philology, the discipline in which he received his training and university appointment. It is clear that he was interested in other areas of
knowledge, especially after 1870, but it is sometimes difficult to piece
together what he actually knew about the foremost developments in the
natural sciences of his era.[15] In the area of psychology, which was just
becoming established as a science, we are confronted only with clues
from which we can make general approximations about what he knew.
Since we are certain that Nietzsche read and appreciated Friedrich
Albert Lange's *History of Materialism* [*Geschichte des Materialismus*],
we can assume with some confidence that Nietzsche was acquainted
with at least the major psychological developments in the early and mid

nineteenth-century, and that he knew something of Lange's views on nineteenth-century psychology.[16] Lange's discussion is shaped by his endeavor to distinguish a truly scientific psychology from a speculative or metaphysical variety, and he laments the perseverance of the latter even in the writings of the mathematical psychology of a Johann Friedrich Herbart. The problem Lange portrays is one that Nietzsche very likely took to heart: unless we are going to validate a metaphysical notion of the soul, all psychic phenomena are ultimately reducible to physiological processes. We cannot speak of something occurring in our minds, whether it is a sense impression or a thought, without imagining that there are concrete transfers of energy or movements within the nervous system. On the other hand, Lange argues, psychological observations can have scientific validity even if they investigate the realm of the nonphysiological. The reason for this is simply that psychological observations exist on a different level; just as the investigation of physiology is not unscientific because it does not look at atomic particles within the actual nerves, so too psychological procedures cannot be disqualified as science because they do not take up their investigation at the level of the nervous system. Method is thus more important than the level of investigation, and Lange bolsters his claim that we can achieve exacting results in research on human action and speech by citing studies in animal psychology, developmental psychology, linguistics, and anthropology. Lange therefore validates psychology as a science when it discards its metaphysical trappings and adopts empirical procedures, although he suggests that physiology and neurology hold the ultimate key to many psychological questions.[17]

Nietzsche's reflections on psychology occasionally take up the kind of issues that Lange outlines and that were important for the burgeoning psychological movement in the late nineteenth-century. Although Nietzsche rarely mentions the actual individuals involved with psychological and psychophysiological research, and although he virtually ignores the pioneering efforts of Wilhelm Wundt, who in 1879 established the first laboratory for psychological research at Leipzig,[18] the university Nietzsche had attended a little over a decade earlier, he does appear to be familiar with at least the "philosophical" issues informing developments in psychological research. In a lengthy passage in *Beyond Good and Evil* Nietzsche discusses a scientific psychology in connection with other demystifying developments in the history of natural science. He begins by citing two Polish scientists, emphasizing their nationality perhaps because of his own misguided self-identification as a Pole. Copernicus and Boscovich, he writes, have been the most triumphant opponents of ocular evidence to date. Copernicus, of course, argued against the view that the earth was a fixed point around which the heavens revolved and thus destroyed the geocentric universe of the medieval church. Ruggero Giuseppe Boscovich, a Jesuit monk known today primarily for his pioneering work in geodesy, is cited by Nietzsche for his refutation of materialistic atomism. Boscovich called into question the substantiality of atomic particles by arguing against the notion that particles collide; instead he attributed the apparent collision of atoms to repulsive forces. Nietzsche claims that he therefore "taught us to abjure belief in the last thing on earth that 'stood firm,' belief in 'substance,' in 'matter,' in the earth-residuum and particle atom: it was the greatest triumph over the senses hitherto achieved on earth" (*BGE* 12). The reference to substance, as advocated by materialistic atomism, is today "an abbreviated means of expression" in which no one believes any longer. These sentiments about the centrality of Boscovich's views, like much in Nietzsche that pertains to the natural sciences, is drawn directly or indirectly from Lange,[19] who credits Boscovich with anticipating physical theories of the nineteenth-century and of reducing small particles to an "empty heritage."[20]

Nietzsche could have profitably pursued the direction that Lange follows in his brief discussion of Boscovich: Lange observes that the atom has become a bearer, rather than the origin of forces (*Kräfte*), and that all effects, "even the effect on our senses," are mediated through something that is not material, something constituted in empty space.[21] It is quite possible, of course, that such a thought had an impact on Nietzsche's later formulations placing power (*Macht*), another immaterial notion, at the very center of his philosophical concerns. But in this passage from *Beyond Good and Evil* Nietzsche chooses a different path of reasoning. Just as Boscovich eliminated materialistic atomism, so too we must now proceed to eradicate the "soul atomism" that is an inheritance of Christianity. Nietzsche explains that this expression designates "that belief which regards the soul as being something indestructible, eternal, indivisible, as a monad, as an *atomon*." Nietzsche makes it clear, however, that he, unlike "clumsy naturalists," does not advocate the elimination of the soul, "one of the oldest and most venerable of hypotheses," from scientific consideration. Rather, he envisions a more exacting and perhaps even empirical realm for what he terms "new psychology": "The road to new forms and refinements of the soul-hypothesis stands open: and such conceptions as 'mortal soul' and 'soul as multiplicity of the subject' and 'soul as social structure of the drives and emotions' want henceforth to possess civic rights in science" (*BGE* 12). Similar in reasoning to Lange, Nietzsche appears here to deprecate an older tradition of psychological thought based on metaphysical and idealist assumptions, and to validate simultaneously investigations based on a new conception of psychic phenomena that are empirically observable, but not simply attributable to a microlevel of neurological activity.

Although, as this passage suggests, Nietzsche occasionally identifies psychology with scientific or quasi-scientific procedures, he more often employs the term "physiology" when he refers to issues that resemble those discussed in psychological circles of his time.[22] Indeed, psychology and physiology are two notions that frequently appear in his later writings and notes, and it is occasionally difficult to tell where one science ends and the other begins. In *Twilight of the Idols*, for example, he writes about "we psychologists" in one section, and in a later section changes the phrase to "we physiologists:"[23] in *Beyond Good and Evil* he begins to write about physiology and physiologists directly after the passage cited above in which he refers to the new psychology. The terms were not interchangeable in his writings, but it is evident that Nietzsche strongly identified with the activities of both psychology and physiology—although he had no formal or practical training in either. Physiology appears to be the term that Nietzsche usually reserves for more scientific or materialist considerations. It is used frequently in conjunction with "doctors" and "illness," often in a metaphorical sense, and is usually opposed to the priest and especially to the moral poisons of the Christian religion. In his notebooks Nietzsche experiments with phrases such as "physiology of power" and "physiology of art." But, like the psychology of Nietzsche's era, physiology also has to do with the nervous system and with sensory impressions that are recorded by the human mind, for example in certain sections of *Beyond Good and Evil*.[24] From his use of the term it appears that Nietzsche believed that a more scientific or material procedure may have clarified human behavior, consciousness, and the unknown realm of mental processes. In *On the Genealogy of Morality* he equates the physiologist with the vivisectionist of mind (*GM* III:4). These occasional uses of physiology indicate that in Nietzsche's thought it was probably proximate to certain branches of psychology as they were practiced in the late nineteenth-century.[25]

When Nietzsche referred specifically to psychology, by contrast, he usually meant something slightly different. Although in his notebooks we can discern a notion of psychology that relates to any process internal to the human being,[26] whether it is connected with cognition, ethics, or sensory impressions, throughout most of his writings we can discern two dominant, and ultimately related, fields of meaning. The first is an older, commonsense designation of psychology as the art of knowing other people, of understanding what motivates and moves people to behave in the way they do. Nietzsche uses psychology in this fashion, for example, when he refers to Stendhal as a great psychologist, admiring him for his ability to discern the internal workings of the human mind.

Most of all, however, Nietzsche believes that he himself is a superior psychologist in this sense of the word. He fancies himself an instinctive and accurate "reader of the souls" of other human beings, and he ascribes to himself and to other profound students of human psychology special and significant characteristics, especially when they encounter special cases of human beings. The born psychologist, for example, must avoid compassion. Furthermore,

> he *needs* hardness and cheerfulness more than other men. For the corruption, the ruination of higher human beings, of more strangely constituted souls, is the rule: it is dreadful to have such a rule always before one's eyes. The manifold torment of the psychologist who has discovered this ruination, who discovers this whole inner "wretchedness" of the higher human being, this eternal "too late!" in every sense, first once and then *almost* always throughout the whole of history—may perhaps one day make him turn against his whole lot and drive him to attempt self-destruction—to his own "ruination." (*BGE* 187–88)

Nietzsche is especially fond of flaunting his prowess as a psychologist when he dissects the artist or, more specifically, Richard Wagner, who is for Nietzsche in his late works the prototypical artist. In this usage psychology is an instrument not only for analyzing individuals and the complex workings of their mind, but also a means to disclose the secret mechanisms of humankind in general. In various passages in his later works the psychologist is elevated from a mere scientist to an almost omniscient sage able to read into the depth of the human soul. It is no coincidence, therefore, that in the megalomaniacal *Ecce Homo*, Nietzsche can write bluntly: "before me there was no psychology at all" (*EH* "Destiny," 6).

The other recurrent field of association for psychology is ethics, in particular the proscriptions stemming from the Christian tradition. At one point Nietzsche employs the phrase "moral psychologist" (*Moral-Psycholog* [*BGE* 100]), indicating how closely he identifies psychological and moral issues.[27] At another point he refers to Zarathustra as "the first psychologist of the good" (*EH*, "Destiny," 5). In this context the word "psychology" assumes multiple meanings. It refers at times to the mentality of those people who adhere to a system of moral values informed by a Christian ethical system, and at other moments to the mental mechanisms of individuals identified with that system,[28] or to certain abstract principles, such as in the phrases the "psychology of belief," or the "psychology of conviction." But Nietzsche also uses the term to designate a type of observation that remains tied to that ethical system; he writes in this case about "previous psychology" or "older psychology" to distinguish it from his own more penetrating psychological observations. Finally psychology relates to morality in that a true psychology will be able to penetrate through the obfuscation of Judeo-Christian values and discern what is really involved in the propagation of moral systems. Generally these manifold connections between morality and psychology are not difficult to understand. If psychology entails all internal processes, then it ought to be able to explain the mechanisms by which human beings adopt principles that determine their behavior patterns. Since Nietzsche in his later years believed that morality and religion held the key to understanding the deplorable state of humankind in modernity, it is not surprising to find repeated references to the psychology of specific modern, moral, and religious types. Indeed, in his notebooks dating from 1885 until 1888 psychology is one of the most frequently encountered words in both the general sense of a mentality or mental composition, and in the sense of an analytical approach to understanding this mentality.

If we believe Nietzsche, therefore, it is difficult not to view him as a psychologist. Although he remained largely on the outskirts of the developing academic discipline of psychology, he was an ardent advocate of psychology in its more commonplace sense, and, as we have seen, a central contributor to that branch of psychological theory known as psychoanalysis. Nietzsche's first years as a writer would not have indicated that he was destined to place such an emphasis on psychology in any of its various connotations. As a member of the extended Wagner cult and a professor of classical philology at Basel, his focus in his early years was German culture and its potential for greatness under the auspices of Wagnerian opera. His significant concentration on educational reform and a critique of the educational system in Germany must also be understood in the context of these general cultural aspirations, as well as his own personal experiences and involvements.[29] In none of these early writings, neither in the published texts nor in the unpublished lectures and notebooks, does psychology in any of the senses described above play a major role. There are perhaps passages that anticipate later insights into the human psyche, but the focus is cultural and pedagogical. Even the term psychology is almost completely absent from his writings during these years. Nietzsche the psychologist is manifestly a product of his post-Wagnerian development, and this aspect of Nietzsche does not emerge until the mid-1870s.

The most significant inspiration, interlocutor, and eventual adversary Nietzsche encountered along his path toward psychological prowess was Paul Rée.[30] Previously, studies of the relationship between these two men have rarely concentrated on the contribution Rée made to Nietzsche's development. Instead, it has been framed in most commentary in one of two ways. Either it has been filtered through their entanglement with Lou Salomé,[31] or it has been discussed as a rather one-sided affair in which the "genial and original" Nietzsche was responsible for just about anything worthwhile that the putatively less talented Rée had to say.[32] But the actual situation was somewhat different. Unlike Nietzsche, whose studies were confined largely to classical philology, Rée had been a student of philosophy at Leipzig who also had gained some expertise in natural sciences during a semester in Berlin. When he arrived in Basel in May of 1873 and was introduced to the circle around Nietzsche by their mutual friend Heinrich Romundt, he had already entered on a different intellectual career path. To be sure he attended courses given by Nietzsche and was thus in some sense his student. But the seminars and lectures that Nietzsche offered during Rée's Basel years were the traditional fare of classical philology. Rée's passion—and increasingly Nietzsche's as well—was consumed by what Nietzsche was to call "moral psychology," and it was Rée who took the lead in developing ideas and in publishing books related to this topic. In 1875 Rée's dissertation, "On the Concept of Beauty in the Moral Philosophy of Aristotle," was accepted at the University of Halle. In the same year he published an anonymous volume of aphorisms modeled on the *Refléxions* of La Rochefoucauld entitled *Psychological Observations*.[33] And two years later, before anything aphoristic or overtly psychological had appeared from Nietzsche's pen, Rée brought out a book *The Origin of Moral Sentiments*.[34] Quite obviously Rée developed his thoughts during the mid-1870s in connection with Nietzsche. Especially important for their relationship and intellectual proximity was the winter they spent in Sorrento as guests of Malwida von Meysenbug. From reports we possess it is evident that there was a free and productive exchange of ideas among all parties. But we should not forget that during their initial years of acquaintance, while both were in Basel, Nietzsche was preoccupied with the cultural issues around the *Untimely Meditations*, and that only in 1876 do we find evidence that he was involved with the same sort of issues that had concerned Rée for many years. At the beginning of their relationship, Nietzsche was very definitely following Rée's intellectual lead, if not in the precise nature of thought, then at least in the topics that he chose to pursue.[35]

Rée's dominating influence in the mid-1870s is evident if we compare Nietzsche's initial foray into "moral psychology," the two volumes of *Human, All-Too-Human*, with Rée's early publications. The similarities are unmistakable, and even if we grant that Nietzsche might have been moving independently toward conclusions similar to Rée's, it is undeniable that Rée's publications preceded Nietzsche's, and that he is therefore more likely to have served as a point of reference for his friend's development. The correspondence in their thought and writings can be discerned in three areas.[36]

1. In the most general terms, both men opposed idealist ethics and embraced some variety of materialism. Rée's "psychology" was consistently informed by developments in the natural sciences, in particular Darwinism, and although Nietzsche was less enthusiastic about Darwin,[37] he too rejected metaphysical and religious explanations for moral feelings. Indeed, both Rée and Nietzsche advanced arguments that claim a logical and historical priority for actual actions or events that later become enshrined in a principle. Idealist commentators mistakenly believe in the primacy of the principle or abstract thought, while Rée and Nietzsche claim that the relationship must be reversed. According to Rée, for example, a sense of justice results from punishment, rather than causing it. Similarly, Nietzsche views abstract notions of morality as outcomes of a more original, economic relationship between individuals. Along these same lines, both writers maintain that the conscious motivations for actions—often idealist principles— are often masks for reasons of which we are not, or are no longer, aware.

2. Rée and Nietzsche both recognized that morality is relative temporally and geographically. Although Rée defines morality in terms of egotism and altruism, he believes that such a notion represents the latest in a series of stages of moral development. Originally actions were regarded as good because of their social utility; today actions and motives have been severed from their origin in social utility and are judged independent of their results according to their purported altruism. Nietzsche's relativism is likewise manifested in his analysis of the "principle stages in the history of the sensations of virtue" in *Human, All-Too-Human*. At issue in this aphorism is the dubious claim that virtue and vice must exist because we have feelings of pleasure and displeasure after performing virtuous or vicious acts. Not only does Nietzsche argue that virtue is a relative notion changing as human societies develop; he also claims, as Rée does, that the site of virtue alters with time. The reason for ascribing virtue to an individual as well as the entity to which virtue is assigned are not constants in the course of human history.

> First of all, one calls individual actions good or bad quite irrespective of their motives but solely on account of their useful or harmful consequences. Soon, however, one forgets the origin of these designations and believes that the quality "good" and "evil" is inherent in the actions themselves, irrespective of their consequences. . . . Then one consigns the being good or being evil to the motives and regards the deeds in themselves as morally ambiguous. One goes further and accords the predicate good and evil no longer to the individual motive but to the whole nature of the man out of whom the motive grows as

the plant does from the soil. Thus one successively makes men accountable for the effects they produce, then for their actions, then for their
motives, and finally for their nature. (*HU* 34)

This historical chain of ascriptions demonstrates, according to Nietzsche, a fundamental confusion about moral virtue. In the switch from
the results of actions, to actions themselves, to motives, and to human
nature, morality is not explained, but simply defined differently.

3. Finally, both Nietzsche and Rée in the 1870s adhered to a rigid
notion of determinism. For both men freedom of will is an illusion. Our
actions, Rée intimates, are necessary; the sentiments that accompany
those actions, by contrast, are subject to change. We are deceived into
believing we possess freedom of will because of certain superfluous emotions. In most people, pangs of conscience, for example, accompany egoistic actions, making us believe that we could have acted otherwise, even
though, according to Rée, the performance of those actions was beyond
our control. Pangs of conscience would seem to function only as metaphysical comfort for human beings, persuading us that we have choices,
and that a realm of freedom actually exists. But they have nothing to do
with egotistical or altruistic actions, since Rée argues that if we were
accustomed to considering altruistic actions reprehensible, then pangs of
conscience would accompany them.[38] Nietzsche advances a similar claim
in *Human, All-Too-Human*, when he discusses the feeling of displeasure
that results from the performance of a deed. Arguing against Schopenhauer, he maintains that a feeling of displeasure is not rational "since it
rests precisely on the erroneous presupposition that the deed need *not*
have taken place of necessity." As further proof of the irrationality of
pangs of conscience Nietzsche points to its variability in different individuals, and to the fact that one can disaccustom oneself to them (*HU*
39). Ultimately both Nietzsche and Rée would appear to subscribe to the
dictum: "No one is accountable for his deeds, no one for his nature"
(*HU* 39).[39]

The joint psychological project to which Nietzsche and Rée contributed in the 1870s was never one of perfect harmony. Nietzsche often
displayed a predilection for less utilitarian explanations; Rée relied more
heavily on what he understood as scientific evidence from evolutionary
biology or anthropology.[40] But although these differences existed and
perhaps grew larger in the early 1880s, only after the estrangement of
the two men as a result of their involvement with Lou Salomé does
Nietzsche's position become privately and publicly antagonistic to Rée's.
Rée had evidently considered dedicating his next book, *The Genesis of
Conscience* (1885),[41] to his friend, but in the aftermath of their triangular relationship with Lou Salomé, Nietzsche "liberates" himself from all

association with his former friend. In March of 1883 he wrote to Overbeck: "I just want to mention another liberation to you: I have refused to allow Rée's main book, 'History of Conscience,' to be dedicated to me—and thus ended a relationship out of which many insalubrious confusions originated" (*SB* 6:339). Six weeks later he wrote in a similar vein to Köselitz: "I've 'finished' with Rée: i.e. I *forbade* him to dedicate his chief work to me.—I don't want to be confused with anyone anymore" (*SB* 6:360). Nietzsche was obviously still sensitive to the common (and probably accurate) perception, especially among Wagnerians, that Rée had influenced his change of intellectual course during the 1870s. By the time Rée's book appeared in 1885, Nietzsche was predisposed to detest it. Although at one point he speaks in a complimentary fashion about the "simple, clear, and almost antique form" of the book (*SB* 7:100), he leaves little doubt that its content is distasteful to him. "Yesterday I saw Rée's book on conscience: —how empty, how boring, how false! One shouldn't talk about things that one hasn't experienced" (*SB* 7:99). And in another letter: "Yesterday I found Rée's *Genesis of Conscience*, sent by the book dealer, and after a quick perusal I thanked my destiny, which saw to it that two or three years ago the dedication to this work to me would be prohibited. Impoverished, incomprehensible, 'senile'" (*SB* 7:102).

Publicly Nietzsche breaks with Rée in the introduction to *On the Genealogy of Morality* (1887). Nietzsche mentions only Rée's *The Origin of Moral Sentiments*, neglecting his other writings on moral psychology, and referring consistently to both Rée and his books in the most condescending fashion. He admits that he was given "the initial stimulation" to write about the emergence of morality by Rée's "clear, honest and clever, even too-clever little book," but immediately criticizes it for its "back-to-front and perverse kind of genealogical hypotheses." He then reinterprets the history of their relationship to make it appear that Rée had never had an impact, save perhaps a negative one, on his own thought:

> I have, perhaps, never read anything to which I said "no," sentence by sentence and deduction by deduction, as I did to this book: but completely without annoyance or impatience. In the work already mentioned which I was working on at the time, I referred to passages from this book more or less at random, not in order to refute them—what business is it of mine to refute!—but, as befits a positive mind, to replace the improbabilities with the more probable and in some circumstances to replace one error with another.[42]

Nietzsche admits error in himself to the extent to which he was inhibited in his earlier works because he formulated his ideas clumsily, and because he lacked at that time an adequate vocabulary to express his thoughts. He continues a few pages later by stating his conviction at the time that Rée would adopt a more sensible method since he was at least posing the right questions. "Was I mistaken?" he asks rhetorically. The answer is clear. Rée, Nietzsche observes, is too beholden to Darwin and the English tradition of moral speculation; he is unable to discern, therefore, "the whole, long, hard-to-decipher hieroglyphic script of man's moral past" (*GM* preface:7). With these comments in his introduction he thus seeks to persuade his readers that he has left Rée and his thought behind, proceeding instead to more profound and historically reliable theorizing on the origins of moral systems.

Even a superficial examination, however, reveals that Nietzsche has much in common with Rée, even in his later moral-psychological writings. Like Nietzsche, Rée too cites etymology as a clue to the hidden meaning of ethical terms, speaking of the origin of good as noble [*vornehm*], as Nietzsche later did in *On the Genealogy of Morality* (1887); and Rée also discusses the origins of conscience in the context of revenge and an equivalence paid to an injured party. At the same time Nietzsche is at pains to distance himself from Rée by providing explanations that are more profound with regard to the human psyche. Indeed, one could argue with good reason that Nietzsche's depth psychology, his contribution to the unborn tradition of psychoanalysis, a contribution later denied by Freud, results directly from his endeavor to provide his reader with a profundity lacking in Rée's explanations. Rée's basic framework did not alter much from the 1870s to the 1880s; much of what he includes in *The Genesis of Conscience* is an elaboration of what he had sketched in his *Origin of Moral Sentiments*.[43] To a large extent he remains true to the tradition Nietzsche associates with "English psychologists" in the initial chapter of *On the Genealogy of Morality*: punishment is viewed in terms of its social utility; conscience arises through education and traditions, reinforcing values that are socially useful as well. Nietzsche, by contrast, stresses two elements in his explanations that depart from Rée's thought and contribute to at least the illusion of greater depth. The first of these is the connection between memory and conscience. Nietzsche begins his second essay in *On the Genealogy of Morality*, which can be read as an answer to Rée's *Genesis of Conscience*, by explaining how the process of civilization, which he casts in a rather dubious light, is dependent on instilling in humankind a consciousness of the past. The production of conscience, part of this civilizing process, is a long, arduous, and extremely violent procedure: "there is nothing more terrible and strange in man's pre-history than his *technique of mnemotechnics*" (*GM* II:3). Rée's notion of an original social utility is here converted into a disciplining and repressive activity at the very dawn of civilization. Even more suggestive for psychoanalytic theory is Nietzsche's explanation for bad conscience. In contrast to Rée, who considered bad conscience (pangs of conscience, consciousness of guilt, punishing conscience [*strafendes Gewissen*])[44] the result of a social process, Nietzsche, in a grand psychologizing and mythologizing gesture, contends that bad conscience results from a momentous transformation in the very essence of early man, when instincts are internalized or interiorized. This interiorization marks simultaneously the transition from semi-animals, "happily adapted to the wilderness, war, the wandering life and adventure" (*GM* II:16), from a "pack of blond beasts of prey, a conqueror race, which, organized on a war footing, and with the power to organize, unscrupulously lays its dreadful paws on a populace which, though it might be vastly greater in number, is still shapeless and shifting" (*GM* II:17), to the human being, "imprisoned within the confines of society and peace" (*GM* II:16). This abrupt metamorphosis of the human being, or perhaps more accurately, *to* the human being, marks the decisive psychological and historical event for our species. From this time forth humankind acquires depth; as the analyst of this profound transformation in the species Nietzsche claims that he, as opposed to the superficially scientific Rée, has discovered the key, not only to human civilization, but to the human "soul."

Nietzsche's journey along the road of psychology is thus an interesting and somewhat circuitous one. For mainstream psychology of the nineteenth and twentieth century his impact is virtually nonexistent. His knowledge of psychological developments in his own era appears to have been scant; he knew some of the scientifically oriented literature at first or second hand, but most of his knowledge of psychology appears to have been drawn from books that were more philosophical in orientation. When he himself used the word "psychology," he drew on a nonscientific tradition introduced to him, or reinforced in him, by Paul Rée, and related to ethics. Indeed, most of Nietzsche's psychology would be most properly termed "moral psychology." And although Rée himself gravitated toward scientific studies, and Nietzsche was initially attracted to natural scientific explanations, the latter was obviously more comfortable with more speculative modes of thought. Nietzsche's only genuine contribution to psychology, his anticipation of some of the historical and psychic mechanisms associated with psychoanalysis, results from his endeavor to reach a more profound level of understanding than he found in previous moral psychologists, in particular in the writings of Rée. There are hints of concepts and motifs associated with depth psychology in his writings from the 1870s; even before *Zarathustra* one could argue that Nietzsche had "discovered" the unconscious as a force in human psychic life.[45] But only when Nietzsche ceased to work with Rée on a common intellectual project, only after he breaks with him on a personal basis, only when he begins to counter his theories directly in the mid-1880s, does he assume a perspective that qualifies him as a seminal contributor to the psychoanalytic wing of psychology. It is perhaps an irony of history that Nietzsche's most seminal contribution to what Freud considered the "science" of the human mind,[46] occurs only after he had broken with the more scientific proclivities of his friend Rée and became reliant on the less empirical evidence derived from his private historical mythology, philological speculation, and simple intuition.

NOTES

I would like to thank here Austin Cattermole for his assistance in helping me research this essay.

1. In this essay Nietzsche's works will be cited from the following sources and abbreviated in the text as follows:

BGE = *Beyond Good and Evil*, trans. by R. J. Hollingdale (London: Penguin, 1972).

BW = *Nietzsches Briefwechsel*, ed. Giorgio Colli and Mazzino Montinari (Berlin: de Gruyter, 1975–84).

EH = *Ecce Homo*, trans. by R. J. Hollingdale (London: Penguin, 1979).

GS = *The Gay Science*, trans. by Walter Kaufmann (New York: Vintage, 1974).

GM = *On the Genealogy of Morality*, trans. by Carol Diethe (Cambridge: Cambridge University Press, 1994).

HU = *Human, All-Too-Human*, trans. R. J. Hollingdale (Cambridge: Cambridge University Press, 1986).

SB = *Sämtliche Briefe*, ed. Giorgio Colli and Mazzino Montinari (Munich and Berlin: Deutscher Taschenbuch Verlag and de Gruyter, 1975–84).

SW = *Sämtliche Werke*. Kritische Studienausgabe, ed. Giorgio Colli and Mazzino Montinari (Munich and Berlin: Deutscher Taschenbuch Verlag and de Gruyter, 1967–77).

Occasionally I have altered these translations slightly. Translations from the German texts are my own. References from English translations refer to section numbers unless otherwise specified.

2. Graham Parkes, *Composing the Soul: Reaches of Nietzsche's Psychology* (Chicago: University of Chicago Press, 1994), 2.

3. Ludwig Klages, *The Psychological Accomplishments of Nietzsche* (Leipzig: Barth, 1926).

4. Jacob Golomb, *Nietzsche's Enticing Psychology of Power* (Ames: Iowa State University Press, 1989).

5. Walter Kaufmann, *Nietzsche: Philosopher, Psychologist, Antichrist*, 4th ed. (Princeton: Princeton University Press, 1974).

6. Parkes, *Composing the Soul*, 363.

7. To establish Nietzsche's virtual absence from the canonical history of psychology, I consulted widely among available texts. See, for example, J. C. Flugel, *A Hundred Years of Psychology 1833–1933*, with an additional part: 1933–1963 by Donald J. West (New York: Basic Books, 1964); Robert Thomson, *The Pelican History of Psychology* (Baltimore: Penguin, 1968); Richard Lowry, *The Evolution of Psychological Theory: A Critical History of Concepts and Presuppositions* (New York: Aldine, 1971); Raymond E. Fancher, *Pioneers of Psychology* (New York: Norton, 1979); Daniel N. Robinson, *Toward a Science of Human Nature: Essays on the Psychologies of Mill, Hegel, Wundt, and James* (New York: Columbia University Press, 1982); and J. D. Keehn, *Master Buildings of Modern Psychology* (New York: New York University Press, 1996). In all of these volumes Nietzsche is either not mentioned or mentioned only in a cursory fashion.

8. It is not the case that Nietzsche has gradually been removed from the history of psychology, or simply forgotten in English-language histories. The following books also include scant or no mention of him in their sweep of the field: Th. Ribot, *German Psychology of To-Day: The Empirical School*, trans. by James Mark Baldwin (New York: Charles Scribner's Sons, 1886); Otto Klemm, *Geschichte der Psychologie* (Leipzig: B. G. Teubner, 1911); Max Dessoir, *Outlines of the History of Psychology* (New York: Macmillan, 1912); Edna Heidbreder, *Seven Psychologies* (New York: Century, 1933). While I have undertaken significantly less than a complete survey of psychological histories, the results in the works I consulted were so uniform that I believe I am justified in concluding that Nietzsche, despite his own claims to preeminence, does not play any significant role in the mainstream histories of psychology.

9. Daniel N. Robinson, *An Intellectual History of Psychology*, 3rd ed. (Madison: University of Wisconsin Press, 1995).

10. Ibid., 291.

11. Freud, like Nietzsche, had the tendency to hide contemporary influences in order to highlight more effectively his own originality.

12. William J. McGrath, *Dionysian Art and Populist Politics in Austria* (New Haven: Yale University Press, 1974).

13. Even if Freud did not learn about Nietzschean ideas from his own readings or in conversations with his closest associates, then he certainly was acquainted with some of the same sources that informed Nietzsche's writings. Both men shared an interest in the classics, in cultural history, and in anthropology; although Freud was a more serious student of science, Nietzsche was often concerned with the natural sciences, in particular biology.

14. See Ronald Lehrer, *Nietzsche's Presence in Freud's Life and Thought: On the Origins of a Psychology of Dynamic Unconscious Mental Functioning* (Albany: State University of New York Press, 1995).

15. Although there has been considerable study of aspects of Nietzsche's knowledge of natural science and individual natural scientists, there is still no comprehensive study that surpasses the information in Alwin Mittasch's

Friedrich Nietzsche als Naturphilosoph (Stuttgart: Kröner, 1952).

16. For a comprehensive study of Lange's influence on Nietzsche see George Stack's *Lange and Nietzsche* (Berlin: de Gruyter, 1983). In 1989 (volume 21.2) *International Studies in Philosophy* devoted several articles to a discussion of this book.

17. Lange's discussion can be found in volume two of his *Geschichte des Materialismus* (Leipzig: Verlag von J. Baedeker, 1908), 375–408.

18. Nietzsche mentions Wundt once in his notebooks in the late 1870s ("Wundt 'Superstition in Science'" [Aberglaube in der Wissenschaft] [8:620]), but he does ask his publisher, Constantin Georg Naumann, to send him a copy of *On the Genealogy of Morality* in November of 1887 (8:186). He also requests that a copy be sent to Hermann Helmholtz (Nietzsche wrote "Helmholz"), another important figure in physiological psychology, and someone Nietzsche otherwise never refers to in his works. In 1870 Nietzsche had mentioned Helmholtz in passing in connection with chromatics (3:161); records from the Basel library indicate that he had taken out Helmholtz's book *The Doctrine of Tonal Sensations as Physiological Basis for the Theory of Music* [*Die Lehre von den Tonempfindungen als Grundlage für die Theorie der Musik*]. And in 1877 he writes in a letter to Paul Rée that Wundt is publishing an essay on philosophy in Germany in the journal *Mind*. Otherwise, there is no trace of the most important names in psychology in Nietzsche's writings. His library does contain several works that relate to psychology and that discuss recent developments. But among the books he owned, or at least among the books that he owned and that remained in his library after his death, we do not find the most important volumes of psychological writings from the nineteenth-century. See Max Oehler, *Nietzsches Bibliothek* (Weimar: Gesellschaft der Freunde des Nietzsche-Archivs, 1942).

19. It is possible, of course, that Nietzsche had independent knowledge about Boscovich, who was actually a Croatian, not a Pole. Probably under the influence of Lange, Nietzsche borrowed Boscovich's two-volume *Philosophiae naturalis theoria redacta ad unicam legem virium in natura existentium* from the Basel library in March and October of 1873, and again in April and November of 1874. Boscovich is mentioned only in this one instance in Nietzsche's works, although he does appear also in the notebooks from the 1880s, obviously in sketches and drafts related to this aphorism. In a letter to Heinrich Köselitz from march of 1882, Nietzsche uses a formulation similar to the one found in the aphorism from *Beyond Good and Evil*: "If anything is ever really refuted, then it is the prejudice about 'material': to be sure not by an idealist, but by a mathematician—by Boscovich. He and Copernicus are the two greatest opponents of appearances. After him there is no material any longer, except perhaps as a popular abbreviation. He thought atomistic theory to its conclusion" (*SB* 6:183). In a later letter to Köselitz from August of 1883, Nietzsche mentions that his study of Boscovich had taken place earlier, at the time that he was studying the atomistic theories of the ancients (*SB* 6:442).

20. Lange, *Geschichte des Materialismus*, 192.

21. Ibid.

22. For a discussion of Nietzsche's relationship to the physiological literature of his time and his readings in physiology, see Hubert Treiber, "Zur Genealogie

einer 'science positive de la morale en allemagne': Die Geburt der 'r(é)ealistischen Moralwissenschaft' aus der Idee einer monistischen Naturkonzeption," *Nietzsche-Studien* 22 (1993): 164–221.

23. *SW*, pp. 471, 546.

24. In aphorism 15 Nietzsche employs physiology in the sense of the science that studies the way in which the human body receives and transmits external stimuli, but the implications of physiology are drawn out to an absurd conclusion: "If one is to pursue physiology with a good conscience one is compelled to insist that the organs of sense are *not* phenomena in the sense of idealist philosophy: for if they were they could not be causes! Sensualism therefore at least as a regulative hypothesis, certainly a heuristic principle.—What? and others even go so far as to say that the external world is the work of our organs? But then our body, as a piece of this external world, would be the work of our organs! But then our organs themselves would be—the work of our organs!" (*BGE* 15).

25. Nietzsche's interest in physiology starts early in the 1870s. We have records from the Basel library that indicate he withdrew Otto Funke's two-volume *Textbook of Physiology* [*Lehrbuch der Physiology*] (1855–57) in 1870. For complete information on Nietzsche's borrowings from the Basel library, see Luca Crescenzi, "Verzeichnis der von Nietzsche aus der Universitätsbibliothek in Basel entliehenen Bücher (1869–79)," *Nietzsche-Studien* 23 (1994): 388–442.

26. See, for example, the entries in volume 11, pages 64 and 99. The latter entry, for example, reads as follows:

To Psychology

1. Every "ethical" feeling that comes to consciousness in us is *simplified*, the more it becomes conscious, i.e. it approximates a concept. In itself it is multiple, a sounding together of many tones.

2. The "inner" word is incomprehensible as is the outer: the simultaneous sounding [*Miterklingen*] of many harmonic tones makes clear by means of music that produces an image [*Abbild*].

3. In order that something can be known in a mechanical world order, there must be a perspectival apparatus [*Perspectiv-Apparat*] that makes possible (1) a certain impression of the stationary, (2) a simplification, (3) a selection and elimination. The *organic is a contrivance on which consciousness can develop because it itself* necessitates *the same presuppositions for its preservation.*

4. The internal world must be transformed into appearance in order to become conscious: many stimuli perceived as a unity etc. On account of what force do we hear a chord as a unity and in addition the type of sounding of the instrument, its intensity, its relationship to what was just heard, etc.?? The same force brings every image of the eye *together*.

5. Our continuous practice in *forms*, inventing, multiplying, repeating: *forms* of seeing, hearing, touching.

6. *All these forms, which we see, hear, feel* etc. are *not present in the external world*, which we determine mathematically and mechanically.

7. My presumption that all features of the organic are *therefore* not derivable for us out of mechanical causes, because we ourselves have *read into them* anti-mechanical processes: we have put in them the underivable.

8. Caution: not to treat the very complicated as something *new*. (*SW* 11:99–100)

27. See also Nietzsche's series of reference to "moral psychology" (*Moral-Psychologie*) in his notebooks from 1885 and 1886 in the context of sketches for *Beyond Good and Evil* (12:82, 83, 86).

28. Nietzsche mentions in various contexts the psychology of the priest, the redeemer, father-confessor psychology, and puritan psychology.

29. See chapters 2 and 3 of my *Friedrich Nietzsche* (New York: Twayne, 1995), 14–54.

30. There is not much biographical information on Rée, who evidently led a rather reserved and quiet life. See K. Kolle, "Notizen über Paul Rée," *Zeitschrift für Menschenkunde* 3 (1927/28): 168–74; Hubert Treiber, "Paul Rée—ein Freund Nietzsches," *Bündner Jahrbuch* (1987): 35–58; and the discussions in Curt Paul Janz, *Friedrich Nietzsche: Biographie*, 3 vols., 2nd revised ed. (Munich: Hanser, 1993), especially 1:640–44, 741–52. The chapter on Paul Rée in Theodor Lessing's *Der jüdische Selbsthaß* (Berlin: Jüdischer Verlag, 1930), 55–79, is somewhat unreliable in terms of facts and interpretation.

31. For a documentation of this triangular relationship, see *Friedrich Nietzsche Paul Rée Lou von Salomé: Die Dokumente ihrer Begegnung* (Frankfurt: Insel Verlag, 1970).

32. Kaufmann is typical in this regard. Most of his discussion involving Rée focusses on the complex relationship the two men had with Lou Salomé. With regard to influence he writes that "Rée was conscious mainly of his debt to Nietzsche" (48). Kaufmann, like many commentators, confuses Rée's deferential attitude and his politeness with intellectual dependancy. Nietzsche strove for originality and often neglects to mention influences in an endeavor to appear more original. But it would be a mistake to take him at his own word about his own originality.

33. *Psychologische Beobachtungen* (Berlin: Duncker, 1875).

34. *Der Ursprung der moralischen Empfindungen* (Chemnitz: Schmeitzner, 1877).

35. Nietzsche tried to downplay his indebtedness to Rée, just as he covered most of his borrowings from contemporaries and contemporary sources. In a letter to their mutual friend Erwin Rohde in June of 1878 he cautions Rohde to "look for only *me* in my book [*Human, All-Too-Human*] and not friend Rée. I am proud to have discovered his magnificent qualities and aims, but he *did not have even the slightest* influence on the conception of my 'Philosophy in nuce': this was *complete* and to a large extent down on paper as I became more closely acquainted with him in the fall of 1876" (*SB* 5:333). Nietzsche's notebooks belie this claim; there is little evidence of his "positivistic turn" before late 1876, when he was already living with Rée in Sorrento, and scant concern for topics related to moral psychology. We know from an earlier letter, written in October of

1875, that Nietzsche was at least acquainted with Rée's *Psychological Observations*, which appeared anonymously: "In looking through a number of new books I found recently your work and immediately recognized a few of those thoughts as your property" (*SB* 5:122), and thus it seems likely that the topics broached in this book were influential for Nietzsche even if we believe he had completed parts of *Human, All-Too-Human* before traveling to Sorrento. With regard to the Nietzsche-Rée relationship in Sorrento, Malwida von Meysenbug confirms the influence of Rée on Nietzsche in her *Memoirs of an Idealist*, 2 vols. (Berlin: Schuster & Loeffler, 1916): "Rée had a special predilection for the French moralists and told this to Nietzsche, who perhaps had already read them earlier, but whose close acquaintance with them certainly did not remain without influence on his later development and brought him to the expression of his thoughts in aphorisms, as I had the opportunity to note later. He was also obviously influenced by the strict scientific, realist perspective of Dr. Rée, which was nearly something new compared to his previous works, which were always permeated by a inherent poetic and musical element, and which caused him almost a childlike pleasure and astonishment" (2:245). Only in *Ecce Homo* did Nietzsche concede that Rée had had a significant influence on his thought during the 1870s (*EH*, "Human," sec. 5).

36. The most insightful and complete study of Rée's influence on Nietzsche is Brendan Donnellan's "Friedrich Nietzsche and Paul Rée: Cooperation and Conflict," *Journal of the History of Ideas* 43 (1982): 595–612. An older work that deals less with influence than with simple explication and comparison is Samuel Danzig, "Drei Genealogien der Moral: Bernard de Mandeville, Paul Rée und Friedrich Nietzsche" (Ph.D. diss., University of Bern, 1904).

37. Although there are occasional remarks on Darwin and evolution scattered throughout his works, the most direct and concentrated passages are found in *Twilight of the Idols* ("Anti-Darwin") and in his notebooks from the years 1887 and 1888. He was certainly not an opponent of evolution, but he had misgivings about Darwin's explanations. Two aspects of what Nietzsche understood as Darwinism are particularly problematic for him: the explanation for the mechanisms by which species evolve and separate from one another, and the notion of progress or perfection of forms. With regard to the first of these issues Nietzsche obviously believed that Darwin had generalized from a limited situation. The notion of a "struggle for existence," the most popular slogan in the popularized German reception of Darwinism, was inadequate to explain the development of a species or the evolution from one species to another. Instead Nietzsche, following the lead of other contemporary critics of Darwin, postulates an internal force that accounts for adaptive changes and ultimately the evolution of the species. Nietzsche's most serious objection to Darwinism involves what he takes to be an implicit claim concerning the progress and perfection of the species. His views are based almost entirely on observations concerning the human species, which, we should note, was mentioned in Darwin's *Origin of the Species* just a single time. According to Nietzsche, if there is a struggle for existence, then it is not the strongest, the most beautiful, and the most genial who prevail, but the most base and common.

38. Rée, *Ursprung*, 40.

39. There are, of course, many other areas in which Rée's and Nietzsche's thought coincides in their writings of the 1870s. And there are also some fairly significant differences, even in these early years. For a more detailed comparison, see Donnellan.

40. Rée's own explanation of the differences between his views and Nietzsche's, expressed to Siegfried Lipiner, shows Rée's usual deference to his friend in intellectual matters, but may also indicate some ambiguous feelings about Nietzsche's views: "I told him that you have all the views that I have, but in addition you have a great many views to which I have no relationship" (*NB* 2:6/1: 583).

41. *Die Entstehung des Gewissens* (Berlin: Duncker, 1885).

42. *Genealogy of Morals*, Preface, 4.

43. For a discussion of Rée's views on conscience, see Hermann Bertele, "Paul Rées Lehre vom Gewissen und die Kritik derselben bei Theodor Elsenhans und H. G. Stoker" (Ph.D. diss., University of Munich, 1927). It is somewhat strange that Bertele never mentions Nietzsche in connection with Rée or the concept of conscience.

44. Rée, *The Genesis of Conscience*, 212.

45. Obviously Nietzsche is only one in a line of writers who discovers the unconscious, and certainly one of the later "discoverers." See Lancelot Law Whyte, *The Unconscious before Freud* (New York: Basic Books, 1960); and Henri F. Ellenberger, *The Discovery of the Unconscious: The History and Evolution of Dynamic Psychiatry* (New York: Basic Books, 1970). It is interesting to note that alongside a notion of the unconscious as a repository of repressed or forgotten thoughts and experiences, there is also a tradition of the unconscious in the more scientifically oriented psychological tradition. In this tradition, the unconscious refers to stimuli or sensory impressions that are not recorded as, or recognized in, conscious mental activity.

46. Like many recent commentators, I am skeptical about the scientific validity of Freud's work. For one of the most recent volumes in a long line of criticism, see Richard Webster, *Why Freud Was Wrong: Sin, Science, and Psychoanalysis* (New York: Basic Books, 1995). At the very least it is certainly significant that Freud's theories have almost completely vanished from the curriculum of psychology departments and now exist only in their textually attenuated form in circles of cultural critics.

CHAPTER 9

Nietzsche and Freud, or: How to Be within Philosophy While Criticizing It from Without

Eric Blondel

Both Nietzsche and Freud would have felt offended if their work had been described and dealt with without further ado as "philosophy." They did protest most vigorously when they were considered simply as philosophers—at least when the word and concept referred to the classical tradition or some of the contemporary achievements in this field: Plato, Descartes, Kant, Schopenhauer, for instance, or Hartmann, Dühring or—quite ironically as regards Freud—Nietzsche himself! Both were indeed very suspicious and touchy on that point. How could we blame them, knowing what they blamed philosophy for?

It still remains both dealt with philosophical problems, and in spite of their often wild and contemptuous attitude toward philosophy, they can nonetheless be regarded, if not as philosophers in the traditional acceptation of the word, at least as philosophical critics (or enemies) of philosophy, and *therefore,* shall I say, as practitioners of philosophical thinking and questioning.

I shall strictly limit myself to conceptual discourse, and do not by any means pretend here to be original or radically new. In fact it seems to me that during the sixties and the seventies too much (and often intellectual nonsense) was written about the metaphorical similarities between Nietzsche and Freud (particularly around the question of the subject), a method that was exciting for the mind but failed to define precise philosophical issues. The French philosopher and Freud specialist Yvon Brès, especially in his book *Critique des raisons psychanalytiques,* disproved that kind of approximative method and broke down the pseudo-theories of similarities that resulted from them. However trite, traditional, and disappointing it may appear, in order to avoid that sort of intellectual small talk, I shall stick to a simple purely philosophical problem. I shall try in the following paragraphs to show how Nietzsche and Freud felt concerned with philosophy, how they may be said to have "practiced" (and criticized) it and in what different though strangely common ways they both contributed something radically new to philosophical thinking. But as I intend to be concise and simple, I shall only stress some of the main conceptual features of this comparison, that is to say, the main questions and problems they share.

Though Nietzsche and Freud ask some similar questions, they differ considerably in their ways and styles of questioning. —My first remark, to introduce the question of their different styles of thought is intentionally provocative. At any rate I do not remember having read anything of the sort anywhere. It relates to the style, or rather the "mood" in which they proceed, or, still more precisely, in which they approach problems. To put it bluntly (and I shall develop and qualify this assumption hereafter), Nietzsche has no sense of humor, in the sense of showing an ability to look at oneself critically, tongue-in-cheek, or more simply to be able to laugh at oneself in the most serious contexts or dangerous situations. Nietzsche has indeed a sense of tragedy, a sense of serious cases and tasks (*düstere Sache*), a sense of high and supreme responsibility (*über die Massen verantwortliche Sache*)[1] to which he reacts by another similar way of taking things and himself in earnest— waging war, fighting, through aggressive attitudes and words, in short, rhethorical hyperbole, pamphlets, and all kinds of polemical means (*Streitschrift*, i.e. "pamphlet" is the subtitle of the *Genealogy of Morals*). But I repeat: Nietzsche has no sense of humor.

This introductory and derogatory remark needs of course to be explained and justified. I do not mean it simply psychologically, as a personal insult or only to take revenge on Nietzsche for the three or four decades I spent reading his works and trying to understand what he meant exactly, which as a matter might well have developed in me a kind of fatigue or *ressentiment*! . . . I do not mean either that Nietzsche's books are only serious or boring: it is true indeed that Nietzsche's reader often laughs at his ironical remarks, attacks, puns, and plays on words (to be honest, I am also told that young German readers today cannot read *Thus Spoke Zarathustra* without laughing, but at Nietzsche's expense in this case). My assumption that Nietzsche has no sense of humor must be understood in two senses: on the one hand Nietzsche is certainly endowed with a brilliant sense of irony, but on the other hand as a person and in his writings, he never mocks himself or laughs at his own self, never looks at himself with this particular critical and humorous detachment that characterizes properly humor. I assume Freud's definition of humor as self-mockery, derision against the unhappy, desperate, or frightened ego, which creates a moment of indulgent attitude of the superego toward the ego: "Don't be so despondent, things are not so serious, don't complain, you'd better laugh at yourself and the threatening disaster." Nietzsche only laughs at others, never at himself. Just have another look at the way he makes his own self-satisfied portrait in *Ecce Homo*: at first the reader tries to persuade oneself that this bragging is not in earnest, but one soon realizes that Nietzsche is talking seriously: this kind of excess might be construed as pride or megalomania, but its main purpose is to fight bad conscience and to pave the way for *Heiterkeit*, the antimoral exaltation of the self. "*Le moi n'est pas haïssable*": such is the motto that Nietzsche opposes to Pascal's famous sentence, since morality consists in self-denial. Everybody knows that this kind of idiosyncrasy is not precisely that of Freud, who is famous for his (Jewish and Austrian) sense of humor, and also for his scientific, objective, and clinically neutral tone, even when bitingly criticizing morality or civilization. Only on one point do they share a common taste and reference, namely tragedy, in particular Greek and Shakespearean tragedy. But before I go any further into the latter point, I wish to suggest that in Nietzsche's case, aggressiveness is explicitly considered as a kind of psychological remedy, recreation, cure, or relaxation—which means that the aim or end of the effort is also psychological, that is to say, emphasis is no longer laid on the speculative problems as such, but is shifted onto something deeper, more important, and more vital—the affects, life, the feeling of life, and the will to power, and above all *Heiterkeit*, alacrity, cheerfulness, gleefulness, or light-heartedness (as I would like to translate it in English, or as I translated it in French: *belle humeur*). The aim of Nietzsche's philosophical striving, under the name of *Heiterkeit*, is the heightening of the will to power, the strengthening of affirmation, in short the exaltation of the self. Will to power is by essence linked with a "self," that is to say a drive or a complex of drives—*Triebe*—submitting, subjecting, subduing, or making slaves of other drives and thus erecting themselves as commanding, subjecting powers—subjects. This affirmation should be contrived by all means, and especially through the elimination of all attitudes liable to sound, look, or feel like bad conscience. But precisely what is humor if not a kind of bad conscience, inasmuch it consists in criticizing oneself, that is to say mocking, lowering, abasing, and even humiliating oneself, however gently or leniently? Nietzsche's philosophical remedy against despair, tragedy, despondency, and all negative affects of that sort, even *ressentiment* is extraversion and *Selbstüberwindung*, heroic attitude, attacks, polemic, and self-satisfaction—certainly not humor as we defined it before, which, along

Nietzschean terms cannot be construed otherwise as a kind of weakness: a confession that one is in fault with oneself, with self-confidence, self-affirmation, and with the increasing of the will to power and with *Heiterkeit*.

And this leads to a second remark in this connection—writing, thinking, philosophical writing and thinking are no longer simply speculative activities, but the author, the writer, the thinker also expresses their will to power. This means that author and reader get involved in a psychological situation, a situation where power and affects are at stake. This leads me to a third correlative remark, that in spite of the opposition between a therapist who keeps "benevolent neutrality" in the face of the raving but secret violence of the unconscious, of the id or of the superego, and a philosopher who claims he "prefers to be a satyr rather than a saint"[2] and who constantly uses and abuses violent rhetoric, polemics, pamphlets, or hyperboles, Nietzsche can nonetheless be considered as a psychologist, in the same way as Freud, insofar as he tries to treat his reader not only as a reader, as an intellect, but as a living person, as a psychological human being, whose feelings, violence, affects, values, will to power can be aroused, stimulated, transformed by the act of reading—which is also an expression of the will to power, not a simple act of the mind, but a movement of the muscles, of the drives and of the affects, of the will, that is to say: an interpretation. Nietzsche prides himself on being a mischievous ear (*böses Ohr*), somebody with "ears behind his ears," an "old psychologist and Pied Piper before whom . . . that which would remain silent must become outspoken."[3] And this is confirmed by the famous assertion in the preface of the *Genealogy of Morals*: "I will never let anybody pride himself on being a good judge (of my *Zarathustra*), who has not been one time or other deeply hurt or deeply charmed by each and every word of it."[4]

Now the second feature that brings us to compare the similarities of Nietzsche's and Freud's philosophical points of view is that both are interested in and concerned with disease, pathological states, morbid traits, and all kinds of illnesses in individuals, groups, and civilizations (religion, art, morality, and even—philosophy!). They are on the Magic Mountain, in the neurotic "hospital" described by Dostoyevsky (Nietzsche hints at the latter in section 31 of the *Antichrist*,[5] and it is noteworthy that a psychologist-writer like Stefan Zweig, was a friend of Freud's and an enthusiastic reader of Nietzsche and Dostoyevsky). And this is also linked with what I said before about their sense and love of tragedy. Thomas Mann called Nietzsche (as well as Dostoyevsky) an "insane criminal" ("Dostojewski—mit Massen," in *Adel des Geistes*), whereas Freud was an admirer of such Shakespearean characters as Hamlet and King Lear, whom he used as symbols to define and describe the human condition. Incidentally, Hamlet often plays in Nietzsche's mind and thoughts the same role as Oedipus in Freud's work. Tragedy means that the fate of humanity is doomed to contradictions that cannot be solved by reason since they are related to the passions (i.e., affects, feelings, desires, and will to power). The tragedy of Oedipus for instance means that humanity cannot help desiring what is forbidden in itself (love of the mother and hate of the father are per se forbidden desires), that every individual's sex life is in itself dominated by the impossibility of such desires and, "last but not least," that the truth about ourselves is fated to be unconscious. Tragedy, therefore, very adequately defines the condition human beings are subject to—they have to suffer a destiny that they are not free to choose, that on the contrary is imposed on them; that is to say, they are victims, preys of uncontrollable forces and are literally duped by them. Still more to the point, the fact that they are creatures of affects, feelings, desires, and so on, means that human beings are tragic creatures inasmuch as they are passive. Humans suffer, in the various meanings of that word—they endure pain, cruelty, "the pangs of despised love" (as Hamlet magnificently puts it), but they are more passive than active, they have to expose themselves to what hurts or strikes them, that is, affects them. Creatures of *affects* like human beings are creatures who are *affected.*

This brings us to a further, closer determination of Freud's and Nietzsche's approach to humans within the framework of their antiphilosophical anthropology—a determination that they most certainly inherited from Schopenhauer's theory of the will, which does not mean that they did not modify his metaphysical theory. As the French philosopher Michel Henry, an outstanding phenomenologist, said in his *Généalogie de la psychanalyse,*[6] Schopenhauer's invention, under the concept of will, is that of affect as a nonrepresentation, of desire as life that is felt, the reality of humanity consisting of "life being felt," in other words being *affected* without necessarily being conscious, that is to say rational, conceptual, liable to representation, to conscious thought and reason. The reality of humanity as creatures of affects implies another "logic" than that of reason (which Nietzsche calls "dialectic"), so that one could venture to say that humans are psycho-il-logical creatures. This accounts for the fact that Nietzsche rejected philosophy and morality, insisting on the superficial character of conscious reason and, conversely, on the theory of drives and psychology of the "body" and "instincts" (or on physiology), whereas Freud, in the *Traumdeutung,* reconstructs the rules of this "other logic" that is called the *"Entstellungsprozesse."* Dreams prove that life expresses itself (as drives, will, desires, affects, feelings) in a quite different way from that of conscious reason. This duality can be expressed in different terms—for instance the

Schopenhauerian antithesis of will and representation, or Freud's opposition of manifest and latent contents of dreams, or Nietzsche's constant opposition between reason, consciousness, on the one hand, and instincts and affects on the other. But this antithesis might also be traced back to the (partly specifically German) conflict of Enlightenment and Romanticism, which can be illustrated, among other works, by Thomas Mann's *Magic Mountain* and Musil's *Man without Qualities.*

After Schopenhauer, Nietzsche and Freud left us this idea that we have to manage and struggle with the fact that humans are creatures whose real natures are unknown to themselves or at least opaque, obscure, and only accessible to fumbling interpretation (a kind of conjectural, second-rate, even second-hand knowledge). But as a result of this condition, one is only a subject, no longer the master in one's private kingdom; no longer what Freud derisively calls "his Majesty the Baby," or, to put it otherwise, one is like the character Freud mentions, who is asked: "Where are you going, Itzig?" and answers: "Ask my horse." The same conception is expressed by Nietzsche in the first sentence of the preface to the *Genealogy of Morals:* "We do not know ourselves, we men of knowledge, and we ourselves are unknown to ourselves."[7] And this condition of slavery—a condition symbolized by tyranny—due to the latency and the unknown quality of the forces that direct us, a latency and ignorance that fly in the face of the Socratic principle "Know thyself," can be defined by the word *illusion.* The word means deception and delusion: we don't "know" what we are up to, what we are thinking, and we are like Hamlet who protests and is outraged when he feels that others are "playing on him like a flute." Illusion, from the Latin verb *"ludere,"* means that we are played with, we are just toys in the hands of some "fate," or deity (instincts, will, desire . . .) who, as Gloucester says in *King Lear,* treats us "as flies": "As flies to wanton boys are we to the gods—They kill us for their sport."[8] And it is quite likely that Schopenhauer, Nietzsche, and Freud derived this common idea, inherited from Shakespeare, the French moralists, the Greek tragedies, and the Bible—that the condition of humanity is the miserable condition of a deluded and suffering slave laboring under the illusions imposed by the will, instincts, drives and unconscious desires, Destiny (*Fatum*), and even God—of whom Freud wrote to Pfister that he (Freud) would have more faults to reproach Him with than God would with what *he* had done to Him.

This conception of humanity's submission to illusion, indeed, is not new. And it is true that Schopenhauer and Nietzsche both acknowledged they were partly indebted not only to Shakespeare, the Bible and the Greek tragedies, but also to Spinoza, who wrote in his *Ethics* that man should not believe "he (was) an empire in an empire."[9] It should be noted here that Nietzsche and Freud belong to a tradition that could be called tragic, according to which the condition of humanity is primarily that of subjects deprived of "natural" liberty, which means that freedom is not something we are endowed with from the beginning, but something that we must contrive to obtain, something we have to strive for, and force our way to.

But here arises a blunt, difficult, and serious question: How are we to get out of slavery, how are we to attain to reason and consciousness if reason, consciousness, and freedom are something we can only hit upon at the end of such a long struggle? One must confess that it is difficult to become—and particularly to make oneself—free; in this philosophical context, since freedom is needed, but is not close at hand or naturally given, striving for freedom encloses us in a vicious circle. In that case one need only substantiate the view that it is only "thanks" to the contradictions and the unbearable sufferings undergone by the subject because of one's illusions, that one is *prompted* to escape one's miserable and submitted plight. Marx and the Marxists reckoned exclusively with the inner contradictions of capitalism to lead it to its collapse. Freud does not explain why and how a neurotic patient could be led or decide to begin a cure that would free him from his difficulties (and especially how the resistance can be worn down). As for Nietzsche, the violence of his polemical attacks on the reader and the passionate, that is to say, poetical, affective, and psychological quality of his addresses to the reader's affects, seem to preserve him from the total inefficiency of his philosophical discourse on decadence, morality, Christianity, and nihilism.

But what about the method, precisely? Both Nietzsche and Freud can be considered, philosophically speaking, as physicians. Their aim and concern is indeed to cure people who are patients, that is, suffering and diseased persons. The disease is neurosis or decadence. "Man is the sick animal par excellence," Nietzsche writes in the *Genealogy of Morals*[10] and in the *Antichrist*. A doctor tries to cure diseases and to relieve pains: as far as Nietzsche is concerned, his main cure can be called medical only in a metaphorical sense (for no one seems to have ever recovered from asthma, sexual troubles, or conjugal problems thanks to a good reading-cure based on *Thus Spoke Zarathustra*, *The Birth of Tragedy*, or even *Genealogy of Morals*!) and the only prescription (a psychological, psychosomatic, and philosophical one indeed rather than a medical one) he gave and recommended is *Heiterkeit,* cheerfulness, "belle humeur," as he wrote to Jean Bourdeau around December 17, 1888: "I reckon *Heiterkeit* among the proofs of my philosophy."[11]

But a doctor is also someone who detects diseases and gives his diagnosis, a science that is called in Nietzsche's German *Semiotik*, the science of the signs (*semeia*) of diseases, in other terms a "symptomatology."[12] In this respect, there is a close analogy between Nietzsche and Freud: both are therapists who use language, in what Freud called (in English when he lectured in the United States) a "talking-cure." And both of them needed a "third ear" or what Nietzsche called "Ohren noch hinter den Ohren," a second pair of ears. Genealogy is the method attempting to guess and interpret from outside, from visible appearances, what is wrong inside. Because of the duality between manifest and latent significations, between reason and instinct, between will and representation, the thing in itself and phenomenon, Nietzsche, as is for instance patent in the preface of *Twilight of the Idols*, substitutes hearing and smelling for sight. Instead of intuition, vision, theory, evidence (the latter being canceled by latency), genealogy as a method of diagnosis uses and promotes the senses that can "feel" at a distance, that can seize what is hidden or indirectly manifested.[13] Although space does not permit details here, I will just mention the fact that Nietzsche's "philosophizing with a hammer" (the subtitle of *Twilight of the Idols*) means that the said hammer is more like a "*Stimmgabel*," a tuning-fork, or the hammer of the "*Hammerklavier*"—than a sledge-hammer, as is generally admitted.

Two final remarks here about Nietzsche and Freud. It is striking how little sex or eros plays a part in Nietzsche's genealogy, or, to use his favorite word, in his physiology. He writes in *Ecce Homo* that all prejudices come from the bowels,[14] and he often expresses what he believes to be cynical and coarse theories about the relationship between ideals and physiology. His most daring(?!) expression about sex is one in *Ecce Homo*, where he pretends to be "medicynical" (his own coinage, a crisis of *medizinisch* and *medi-zynisch*) when saying that there is something wrong in the physiology of noble-souled women.[15] But his physiology, which is extremely eloquent about digestion, remains almost completely silent about sex. If we remark that Nietzsche in this respect remains far behind Schopenhauer's views about sex (the sexual organs being according to the latter the materialization, "objectivation," that is, the material expression of the will), we can only conclude, either that Nietzsche simply considered sex and eros as just a particular case of the will to power, or still more simply that the son of the Lutheran minister in Röcken, though a compulsive reader of Luther, Rabelais, Montaigne, and Swift, still had some progress to make to free himself from repression and Christian morality.

Has one noticed—but it would require another, much longer philosophical essay—that the main concern of Nietzsche and important interest of Freud is not only the individual, but civilization as a whole, that is to say the decadence, the "*Krankheit der Menschheit*," the disease of humankind , that is, morality—or, to put it in Freudian terms, the *Unbe-*

hagen in der Kultur, Die Zukunft einer Illusion, the discontent in civilization, the future of an illusion? This enlargement of the scope in comparison with the individual point of view could suggest that the two "therapists" or doctors, as *Ärzte der Kultur,* doctors of civilization, naturally tend to go further than the psychological, specifically individual, and individually affective point of view, in order to show that what is challenged is the foundation of the rational and universal values defining a human, a doctrine, a system of values as morbid, abnormal, pathological, destructive, or absurd. And if this latter judgment implies that some criteria are required outside the purely descriptive and objective field of science or psychology, on what ground can the validity of the concepts of decadence, force, normality, and health be founded?

On philosophy, if one is willing to assume that such is the name of what Freud calls science and interpretation and of what Nietzsche calls genealogy, or psychology—the new name of what was already practiced by the French moralists, such as La Rochefoucauld, Chamfort, Montaigne, Pascal, and the old classical tradition, from the Bible to Shakespeare. Although Nietzsche and Freud had excellent reasons to distrust philosophy as a merely conscious and superficial discourse generating illusions and inefficient against suffering and sickness, even as generating disease and morbidity, they could not avoid asking and dealing with questions that must be considered as philosophical problems. Only, they both gave back to philosophy its interpretative quality and method which it had lost or forgotten. "Where is the wisdom we have lost in knowledge?"

NOTES

1. Friedrich Nietzsche, *Twilight of the Idols,* in *The Portable Nietzsche,* trans. Walter Kaufmann (New York: Viking Press, 1968), preface.

2. Friedrich Nietzsche, *Ecce Homo,* trans. Walter Kaufmann (New York: Random House, 1967), preface, 2.

3. *TW,* preface.

4. Friedrich Nietzsche, *On the Genealogy of Morals,* trans. Walter Kaufmann (New York: Random House, 1967), preface, 8.

5. See also a wonderful posthumous fragment on this subject in the Colli-Montinari edition, *KSA,* vol. 12, section 10(50); *Will to Power,* trans. Walter Kaufmann and R. J. Hollingdale (New York: Random House, 1967), 740.

6. Paris, 1985

7. *GM,* preface, 1.

8. *King Lear,* act 4, scene 1—a remembrance of a similar expression which was already to be found in Montaigne's *Essays.*

9. Spinoza, *Ethics,* III, preface.

10. *GM* III:13; *AC* 14.

11. *KSA*, vol. 8, n. 1196, p. 534.

12. *TW*, "The Improvers of Mankind," 1.

13. For want of space, I take the liberty of referring the reader to chapter 7, "Nietzsche and Genealogical Philosophy," in my *Nietzsche, the Body and Culture* (Stanford and London, 1991). Here I expound on the consequences of this metaphorical shift from the philosophical theoretical intuition to the genealogical senses, that is, smelling and above all hearing.

14. *EH*, "Why I Am So Clever," 1.

15. *EH*, "Why I Write Such Good Books," 5.

CHAPTER 10

Freud and Nietzsche, 1892–1895

Ronald Lehrer

In *The Discovery of the Unconscious*, Henri Ellenberger places Nietzsche in a central position regarding the ideas that would inform Freud's development of psychoanalysis. He writes of Nietzsche's ideas that they "pervade psychoanalysis," and of Nietzsche's influence that it "is obvious, even in Freud's literary style."[1] Ellenberger comments on "the truly fantastic success that Nietzsche's ideas enjoyed in Europe in the 1890's," and asserts that "an entire generation was permeated with Nietzschean thinking . . . in the same way as the former generation had been under the spell of Darwinism."[2] He goes on to state that "for those acquainted with both Nietzsche and Freud, the similarity of their thought is so obvious that there can be no question about the former's influence over the latter."[3] It is important to bear in mind that Ellenberger arrived at such conclusions in the context of a comprehensive examination of the various scientific and medical influences on the development of Freud's thought.[4]

Although the areas that Ellenberger opened for exploration in his great work have, for the most part, received a great deal of attention in the past twenty-five years, his ideas on the centrality of Nietzsche's role in the development of a psychology of dynamic unconscious mental functioning have not, at least in the English-speaking world, received the degree of serious attention and investigation one might have expected.[5] And while a growing number of scholars might be willing to agree that from the early 1900s, or even the late 1890s, Nietzsche's influence appears evident in Freud's work, there has been relatively little commentary in the English-speaking world on the possible influence of Nietzsche on Freud from the 1880s through 1895.

Is there evidence that Freud's ideas as expressed in published writings of the period 1892–1895[6] are similar to some of Nietzsche's psychological concepts? Is there evidence of Freud's possible exposure to Nietzsche during this period or earlier? Is there evidence of the possibility of Nietzsche's influence on Freud's published writings of this period?[7]

THE 1870s AND 1880s

In examining the matter of similarity of thought in Freud and Nietzsche, one should consider the possibility, even the likelihood, that parallels found may be due in large part to related influences on both thinkers. In addition to broad intellectual forces of the period that influenced both men,[8] they were also specifically influenced by some of the same psychological ideas that were current. For example, Nietzsche acknowledged Schopenhauer's great influence on him, and it has appeared to a number of scholars that Schopenhauer anticipated, and may have significantly influenced, Freud as well.[9] Nietzsche was in all likelihood influenced by other thinkers who had an impact on Freud. Nietzsche carefully read Hartmann (influenced by Schopenhauer) on the nature of unconscious mental functioning, and through his reading of F. A. Lange as well as Hartmann he was exposed to the psychological concepts of such figures as Herbart, Fechner, Wundt, and others (Fechner's *Zend-Avesta*[10] and Nietzsche's *Thus Spoke Zarathustra* both look back to ancient Iranian Zoroastrians). In addition, Ian Hacking has emphasized that we should not think of Nietzsche as operating in a different intellectual world from the psychological explorations of such French figures as Ribot and Janet; that in fact he probably read Ribot and, toward the end of his productive life, possibly even read Janet.[11] (He was also aware of other figures who may have influenced him, such as Mill [and the "English psychologists"], Helmholz, and Taine.) It is important to keep such shared influences in mind when considering the more specific influences of Nietzsche upon Freud.

On the other hand, it is also important to recognize Nietzsche's great prominence in Freud's circle of friends and acquaintances from the 1870s through the 1890s. William McGrath[12] has made us aware of Nietzsche's powerful intellectual presence for young Viennese intellectuals in the 1870s. Despite the relatively few copies sold, Nietzsche's early writings, such as *The Birth of Tragedy*[13] and essays later included in the volume *Untimely Meditations*,[14] were greatly admired and intensely discussed by Freud's friends and acquaintances at the university. Among these friends and acquaintances were Siegfried Lipiner, an early interpreter and populizer of Nietzsche; Heinrich Braun, later a prominent socialist intellectual; Viktor Adler, who would later unite

Austria's socialist movements; and Joseph Paneth, Freud's close friend who, with Adler, co-led a formal discussion at the university on Nietzsche's work, in particular the 1874 essay "On the Uses and Disadvantages of History for Life," the second of the *Untimely Meditations*.[15] This essay contains important passages on individual and collective memory and forgetting. Regarding Adler, Steven Beller writes of "the book which had the greatest influence on Adler and his friends, Nietzsche's *The Birth of Tragedy*."[16] Berggasse 19, which was Viktor Adler's residence before Freud moved there in 1891, was a place where many people gathered for discussion and debate. It appears that Nietzsche was often a topic of discussion.[17]

Joseph Paneth was a close friend of Freud's at the university, and the two men remained friends after leaving the university. Freud respected Paneth, who figures (along, I believe, with Nietzsche) in Freud's "Non Vixit" dream.[18] Freud and Paneth studied philosophy together at the university and took a number of philosophy courses with Franz Brentano. In 1875 Freud wrote to his friend Silberstein that since the demise of a journal with which he, Paneth, and Lipiner had been involved, "From now on I shall have to keep my philosophical ideas purely to myself or pass them on unrefined to Paneth."[19] Regarding Freud's relationships with friends during this period, Peter Newton suggests that "Joseph Paneth was perhaps closest to him in aspiration and interests."[20]

Paneth was an avid reader of Nietzsche and retained an interest in him (and in philosophy more generally) after leaving the university. From late December of 1883 through March of 1884, he spent time near Nice where Nietzsche was staying. During this time Paneth was able to speak with Nietzsche on a number of occasions. He wrote much to Freud about these meetings.[21] It appears that Freud destroyed Paneth's letters, but letters of Paneth to his fiancée written during the same period do survive and offer us an idea of some of what he may have conveyed to Freud.[22] Elsewhere,[23] I have explored Freud's relationship to Paneth, including Paneth as a direct link between Freud and Nietzsche. I will only note here that antisemitism, science, philosophy, Schopenhauer, Meynert, and the importance of unconscious mental processes were among the matters discussed by Paneth and Nietzsche. In addition to his letters to Freud, Paneth surely discussed Nietzsche with him upon his return to Vienna. This link of Freud to Nietzsche through Paneth was strong enough for Gunter Godde to describe Paneth as the person who interpreted Nietzsche for Freud.[24] When late in life Freud recalled this time, he wrote, regarding Nietzsche, that "in my youth he was a remote and noble figure to me," or, more accurately, that in his youth Nietzsche signified an unattainable or inaccessible nobility.[25]

NIETZSCHE'S EARLY WRITINGS

Without going into detail regarding the content of the early writings of Nietzsche with which Freud's friends were involved, I will note that in his writings of the early to mid-1870s Nietzsche recognized important functions of dreams, the instinctual substratum beneath individuated form, the importance of incest in the Oedipus myth as portrayed by Sophocles, how scholarly inquiries are influenced by the needs of the scholar, and how even the quest for truth can be prompted by the "drives." (Freud follows Nietzsche's use of "*Trieb*," but Nietzsche refers to many drives in addition to the sexual and aggressive drives. Nietzsche also uses the term "instinct" [*Instinkt*] in a variety of ways.) During this period Nietzsche also wrote of the intellectual hero, idealization of a group leader, a kind of psychological resistance, the importance of creatively integrating the more primitive aspects of our nature, the importance of integrating our past and making it our own, and the importance of active forgetting.[26]

As to Freud's familiarity with Nietzsche's writings during the mid-1870s, although we do not know exactly what he actually read, it appears, as one would expect, that he was familiar with notions of the Apollonian and Dionysian as they had recently been presented in *The Birth of Tragedy*. In May of 1875, as Nietzsche is being discussed all around him, Freud refers to a female acquaintance of Silberstein's as a "Dionysian" tormentress (or maenad).[27] Also, the brilliant young classical scholar, Wilamowitz, had directed a well-known attack on *The Birth of Tragedy*, and it is quite likely that Freud knew about this attack.[28] In March of the same year, Freud's interest in philosophy was strong, and he was reading his much-admired Feuerbach. It appears that he had also been reading Nietzsche, as in his letter to Silberstein he refers to a specific passage in Nietzsche's 1873 essay "David Strauss, the Confessor and the Writer," the first of the *Untimely Meditations*. Nietzsche was clearly well enough known to both Freud and Silberstein for Freud to have to mention nothing about Nietzsche. A phrase is quoted and Nietzsche's criticism of Strauss is noted without any further elaboration deemed necessary.[29]

Once we arrive at the year 1878 and the publication of the first volume of *Human, All-Too-Human* (with two other works to follow in the next two years, later to be included as volume 2), and then in 1881 and 1882 the publication of *Daybreak* and *The Gay Science*, Nietzsche offers psychological insights that are remarkably close to (although certainly not restricted to) Freudian ideas that would later serve as foundation principles for psychoanalysis. Regarding the psychological insights in these works, one can note that Nietzsche discusses the nature of instincts and drives, the relationship between conscious and unconscious mental processes, dynamic psychic conflict, sublimation, the development of conscience, the nature of dreams, and that multiple motives, including those related to gratification, defense, and assuaging of conscience, influence our beliefs and actions.[30]

Is it possible that by 1892 some of Nietzsche's (and Schopenhauer's) ideas found their way into Freud's (and Breuer's) early work? At the very least, do certain Nietzschean currents move along lines not unrelated to Freud's (and Breuer's) explorations during this period?

CATHARSIS

It is worth noting that in addition to being Freud's friend, Paneth also knew Breuer. He may even have been the person who introduced Freud to Breuer. Breuer, like Paneth, was steeped in philosophy and probably had at least some general knowledge of aspects of Nietzsche's philosophy and psychology. (He certainly appears to have been familiar, as was Paneth, with Schopenhauer.[31]) This is of some significance when we consider the importance of catharsis for Breuer and Freud, and that the great influential figure in late-nineteenth-century discussions on catharsis, Jacob Bernays (1824–81), was linked to Nietzsche. (Freud was linked to Bernays through his marriage to Bernays' niece, Martha Bernays.) Bernays' influential and much discussed work on catharsis, *Grundzüge der verlorenen Abhandlung des Aristoteles über Wirkung der Tragödie*,[32] was published in 1857 and appeared in a second edition, with great interest in intellectual circles, in 1880, about the time Breuer began working with Bertha Pappenheim ("Anna O.").[33]

This recognition of Bernays' relationship to Breuer and Freud is not a recent phenomenon. Robin Mitchell-Boyask points out (as has Hirschmüller[34]) that Alfred Freiherrn von Berger's 1897 essay on Aristotle's theory of catharsis (in a volume that was in Freud's library) links Freud to nineteenth-century philology, psychology, and medicine by connecting Bernays' work to the writings on hysteria by Breuer and Freud.[35]

Nietzsche was familiar with and valued Bernays' work. He drew on Bernays' conception of catharsis in tragedy and possibly other ideas for *The Birth of Tragedy*.[36] In *The Birth of Tragedy*, Nietzsche writes of "the pathological discharge, the catharsis of Aristotle, of which philologists are not sure whether it should be included among medical or moral phenomena."[37] Bernays was one of the few philologists to defend this work.[38] Also, as we will see, Nietzsche was quite concerned with the fate of a quantum of emotionally charged energy or force pressing for discharge.

A linking of Bernays with both Nietzsche and Freud is made by Arnaldo Momigliano, who writes:

> What was really new in Bernays was the development of the implications of the medical interpretation for the understanding of Greek tragedy. Bernays connected the cathartic process with the ecstatic practices of the Dionysiac rites. The way was open for Nietzsche. . . . [Bernays] was certainly entitled to see in this book [*The Birth of Tragedy*] an extreme development of his interpretation of *Katharsis*. The link between Bernays and Nietzsche—both, as we know, pupils of Ritschl—is obvious, but to us Bernays' analysis of *Katharsis* suggests the name of Freud even more than the name of Nietzsche.[39]

Hirschmüller indicates that Bernays' concept of discharge pointed toward a commonly accepted physicophysiological conceptual model entailing the law of conservation of force developed by Julius Robert Mayer and elaborated upon by Helmholtz and Joule between 1842 and 1860. This concept of physical energy was later extended to other fields, such as in psychology by Fechner, who may have influenced Nietzsche as well as Freud.[40] It appears that Nietzsche was influenced by the concepts of force or energy developed by Mayer.[41]

When Freud was bringing the idea of a quota of affect into his explanation of symptom formation in 1893, he may also have drawn on the work of Hughlings Jackson. According to Macmillan, it was after absorbing Jackson's ideas that Freud began to consider the purpose of the nervous system as "maintaining its quantity of excitation at a fixed level; that it achieved its aim by disposing of surplus excitation, especially increases brought about by emotion; and that symptoms were a consequence of abnormalities in the disposal of the excess."[42]

In the fourth part of his paper "Some Points for a Comparative Study of Organic and Hysterical Motor Paralyses," Freud alerts the reader that he is passing over into the field of psychology. He writes of psychic impressions being

> provided with a certain quota [or simply, sum or amount] of affect (*Affektbetrag*), of which the ego divests itself either by means of a motor reaction or by associative psychical activity. If the subject is unable or unwilling to get rid of this surplus, the memory of the impression attains the importance of a trauma and becomes the cause of the permanent hysterical symptoms. The impossibility of elimination becomes evident when the impression remains in the subconscious. We have called this theory "*Das Abreagieren der Reizzuwächse*" [The Abreaction of Accretions of Stimulus].[43]

In his important paper of 1894, "The Neuro-Psychoses of Defense," Freud writes, regarding psychic functioning, of "a quota [sum, amount] of affect or sum of excitation—which possesses all the characteristics of a quantity . . . which is capable of increase, diminution, displacement and discharge."[44] In an appendix to the paper, the editor, Strachey, singles out this particular passage for its importance.[45]

In the additional book 5 to the second edition of *The Gay Science*, Nietzsche writes:

> I have learned to distinguish the cause of acting from the cause of acting in a particular way. . . . The first kind of cause is a quantum of dammed-up energy [or force] that is waiting to be used up somehow . . . while the second kind is . . . for the most part a little accident in which this quantum "discharges" [or releases] itself in one particular way . . . the tremendous quantum of energy that presses . . . to be used up somehow.[46]

Although Freud writes of a quota of affect or sum of excitation and Nietzsche of a quantum of dammed-up or pent-up force or energy, both write of the need for such psychic excitation or energy to find avenues for discharge. They both agree that problems arise when adequate discharge or release is not possible. (As we will see, both thinkers also have an important place for the ability *not* to react.)

Nietzsche writes of the fate of the discharge of drives, even positing that dreams express, among other things, attempts at compensation for drives aroused but ungratified during the day.[47] Nietzsche writes of both inherent, internal drives pressing for release (which Freud will increasingly emphasize in the late 1890s) and aroused drives or feelings in need of adequate reaction or release (which Freud emphasizes earlier in the 1890s). Nietzsche emphasizes that drives not allowed outward expression may turn inward against the self, thus initiating the process leading to the formation and symptomatology of bad conscience. The social situation of civilized society prevents adequate reaction to drives and feelings pressing for expression, leading to the consequent turning of the drives against the self. We will see that in 1892, for Freud too the social situation is of importance in the development of symptomatology.

Also, as in the passage from *The Gay Science* quoted above, Nietzsche distinguishes between the aim (relief through discharge or release of dammed-up energy) and the particular ways in which the force or energy may be discharged (which may vary), a kind of conceptualization often thought to be one of Freud's important and original formulations. Strachey was not the only one to regard such a formulation (in Freud) as of great importance. Whatever the influences of Mayer and others, Nietzsche recognized his own formulation as "one of my most essential steps and advances."[48]

Nietzsche does not, however, think in terms of a constancy principle operative in the functioning of the nervous system and mind in quite the same manner as Freud, who ultimately takes such notions to the extreme of a self-destructive or death instinct. As Young and Brook point out, for Schopenhauer and Freud pleasure is typically characterized in negative terms: "For Schopenhauer, pleasure is the momentary cessation of the will's striving, for Freud the discharge or at the very least the achievement of constancy in the flow of stimuli from the drives."[49] On a related matter, perhaps with Schopenhauer in mind, Nietzsche writes: "Every ethic with a negative definition of happiness, every metaphysics and physics that knows some *finale,* some final state of some sort . . . permits the question whether it was not sickness that inspired the philosopher."[50]

In 1895 Freud writes: "Everything depends on reinforcing the patient's nervous system in its capacity to resist . . . the existence of a hysterical symptom means a weakening of the resistance of that nervous system. . . . To get rid of symptoms . . . is to give back to patients the whole amount of their capacity for resistance."[51] In *Twilight of the Idols*, Nietzsche writes of Dionysian frenzy in which "the whole affective system is excited and enhanced: so that it discharges all its means of expression at once."[52] But the "*first* preliminary schooling for spirituality" is "not to react at once to a stimulus, but to gain control of all the inhibiting, excluding instincts . . . the inability to resist a stimulus. . . . In many cases, such a compulsion is already pathology, decline, a symptom of exhaustion . . . this physiological inability *not* to react."[53] Nietzsche writes of individuals with such symptomatology that they are "similar to certain hysterical types who also, upon any suggestion, enter into *any* role."[54] Nietzsche was concerned throughout his productive life with matters pertaining to the ways in which the multiplicity of our psychic selves can function in healthy, creative ways rather than in pathological ways that lead to exhaustion and breakdown. He was aware of literature on hysterical patients and was aware, as was Schopenhauer, of Mesmerism, magnetism, and somnambulism.[55] In *The Case of Wagner*, Nietzsche writes that "Wagner est une névrose" and that his heroes and heroines present the "problems of hysterics."[56]

For Nietzsche, *not* reacting does not have to lead to *ressentiment* or bad conscience. Drives and affects press for release or discharge, but immediate release or discharge is not always optimal. (Recall that for Freud associative psychical activity can serve in place of motor reaction for the ego's divesting itself of a quota of affect.) Nietzsche would agree with findings of contemporary psychology to the effect that inhibition is a fundamental process in the nervous system: "Without such inhibitory processes, our mental lives would be unbearably chaotic."[57] Nineteenth-century psychology was also concerned with this matter. For Nietzsche there is always the possibility of creative sublimation. The first step toward spirituality, the ability not to react to a stimulus with immediate discharge of the drives or affects, can be seen as an essential step in the process of sublimation.

INCOMPATIBLE IDEAS AND REPRESSION OR INHIBITION

It is not, however, only on the matter of psychic excitations or energy pressing for discharge that the ideas of Nietzsche and Freud move along somewhat related paths. In the "Neuro-Psychoses of Defense," Freud writes of (intentional) forgetting that takes place as a result of an inability "to resolve the incompatibility between the unbearable idea and his ego." On the same page Freud writes of patients recollecting, in relation to these (especially sexual) ideas, "their efforts at defense, their intention of 'pushing the thing away,' of not thinking of it, of suppressing it."[58] (Freud does not regard these processes as entirely unconscious.) In *Human, All-Too-Human,* Nietzsche writes:

> Man is very well defended [*gegen*] against himself . . . he is usually able to perceive of himself only his outer walls. The actual fortress is inaccessible, even invisible to him, unless his friends and enemies play the traitor and conduct him in by a secret path.[59] [Young and Brook quote Schopenhauer on the "secret decisions" of the will, and how the intellect "can only get to know them . . . by spying out and taking unawares."[60]]

Nietzsche writes of attempts to ward off ideas that are incompatible with the I or ego. He suggests that we forget a great deal of our past and banish it from our minds because "we want the image of ourself that shines upon us out of the past to deceive us and flatter our self-conceit— we are engaged continually on this self-deception."[61]

In *Ecce Homo* (completed in 1888, but published in 1908), which Freud would read in preparation for a discussion of it at a 1908 meeting of the Vienna Psychoanalytic Society, Nietzsche writes:

> An instinct of self-preservation . . . gains its most unambiguous expression as an instinct of *self-defense* [*Selbstvertheidigung*]. Not to see many things, not to hear many things, not to permit many things to come close . . . [and, significantly, Nietzsche continues] . . . when defensive expenditures . . . become the rule and a habit, they entail an extraordinary and entirely superfluous impoverishment. . . . Warding off, not letting things come close, involves an expenditure . . . through the constant need to ward off, one can become weak enough to be unable to defend oneself any longer.[62]

In *Studies on Hysteria*, Freud writes:

> It has indeed been generally admitted by psychologists that the accep-
> tance of a new idea . . . is dependent on the nature and trend of the
> ideas already united in the ego, and they have invented special techni-
> cal names for this process of censorship to which the new arrival must
> submit. The patient's ego had been approached by an idea which
> proved to be incompatible, which provoked on the part of the ego a
> repelling force of which the purpose was defence against this incom-
> patible idea.[63]

Nietzsche is one psychologist who writes of an active, positive faculty
of, apparatus of, repression or inhibition "which is like a doorkeeper, a
preserver of psychic order."[64] (In *The Interpretation of Dreams*, Freud
will write of the censorship as the watchman or guardian of mental
health.[65]) Breuer writes of distressing ideas that in normal people may be
"successfully suppressed, in which case they vanish completely."[66] He
distinguishes between defense resulting "merely in single converted ideas
being made into unconscious ones" and "a genuine splitting of the
mind."[67] Repression (or suppression, inhibition, defense, or censorship)
may, under certain circumstances, lead to pathology, but it is also a necessary mental operation for the maintenance of normal, healthy psychic
functioning.

Nietzsche writes of aroused feelings and drives that are denied discharge or release finding alternative outlets, such as in dreams[68] or in
turning drives against the self in the formation of bad conscience. As will
be shortly seen, he also links trauma and memory. But he does not write
in the manner of Freud of a banished incompatible memory being
loaded with a quantity of undischarged affect that causes psychic
trauma and the symptomatology of hysteria. He also does not write of
a cure for pathology along the lines of Breuer and Freud.[69] Nietzsche is
concerned with the operations and functions of memory and forgetting,
the ways in which we construct and preserve our selves by reworking
memories, the enduring impact of traumatic memories, the ways in
which dreams take us back to our own and humankind's past, and the
importance of integrating our past. But memory as the path to self-
knowledge does not have the kind of centrality in his thought that is the
case with Freud.[70]

We can also note that Freud writes of the phenomenon of resistance.
Regarding the overcoming of resistance, Freud writes of "the unlocking
of a locked door."[71] At one point he writes of a "motive for resistance"
and a few sentences later that "we may investigate a psychical genealogy of a symptom."[72] He uses the same German words as does Nietzsche: "Genealogie" and "Widerstände." Further on he writes of a

motive for "resistance" (Widerstände) that remains "unconscious" (*unbewußt*).[73] In *Beyond Good and Evil*, Nietzsche writes not of the unconscious resistance of patients, but that "a proper physio-psychology has to contend with 'unconscious resistance' [*unbewussten Widerständen*] in the heart of the investigator."[74]

Nietzsche also writes in *The Antichrist* (completed in 1888, published in 1895) of "this wishing-*not*-to-see what one does see, this wishing-not-to-see *as* one sees."[75] In 1895 Freud writes in *Studies on Hysteria*, of the hysterical patient's "'not knowing'" as "in fact a 'not wanting to know'—a not wanting which might be to a greater or less extent conscious."[76] We see that even where direct influence is unlikely or impossible regarding specific passages and works, at times the ideas of Nietzsche and Freud move along quite similar paths.

We can also note, regarding the use by Freud (and, following him, Breuer) of the concept of overdetermination (*überdeterminiert*), Strachey's comment that it is "unlikely that the notion of multiple causation should never have been expressed earlier by other writers in similar terminology."[77] Nietzsche is one of the thinkers who expresses such an idea. In *Daybreak*, he offers an analysis of pity in which he writes that "we are, to be sure, not consciously thinking of ourself but are doing so strongly unconsciously." He goes on to suggest that "we never do anything of this kind out of *one* motive,"[78] and he suggests unconscious motives that may be involved in reactions of pity. In the *Genealogy*, Nietzsche writes that the meaning of punishment (or the ends to which it is adapted), is overdetermined or overloaded (*überladen*) "by utilities of all kinds."[79]

"PRELIMINARY COMMUNICATION" AND *STUDIES ON HYSTERIA*

An important intellectual event occurred in the German-speaking world in 1892 with the publication of the first edition of Nietzsche's collected works.[80] In 1894 Lou Salomé's study of Nietzsche was published in Vienna.[81] In 1895 Nietzsche's sister, Elisabeth Förster-Nietzsche, published the first volume of her biography of Nietzsche.[82] It was also in 1895 that *The Antichrist* and *Nietzsche Contra Wagner* were first published. These events could only have greatly enhanced Nietzsche's renown and influence. Could that influence have extended to Freud?

Nietzsche's well-known man of *ressentiment* is precisely the man who cannot express his will, desire, and natural reactions outward upon the world and, instead, festers with subterranean envy and desires for revenge. If one were to read of injury and humiliation, desires for revenge, the incapacity to freely react, and the development of pathology, in the writings of Freud during this period (1892–95), one might raise the possibility of a Nietzschean current being one of those currents affecting Freud at this time.[83]

In fact one does find such matters discussed in the "Preliminary Communication,"[84] which was completed at the end of 1892 (published in 1893) and later (1895) included as the first chapter in Studies on Hysteria. I believe that there is a shift in tone at the beginning of section 2 of the "Preliminary Communication," and that a Nietzschean current may well be directly evident.

For Nietzsche, there is a connection between trauma and memory. Certain kinds of trauma prevent the normal wearing away of memories, normal forgetting. This is exactly a major concern of Breuer and Freud. Normal forgetting occurs with ideas "that are no longer affectively operative."[85] But if a reaction to an event, a trauma, that provokes an affect (accompanying a presentation, an idea [Vorstellung]) is prevented adequate reaction through action or language (which allows the "memory of such a trauma, even if it has not been abreacted [to enter] the great complex of associations"), then "the memories which have become the determinants of hysterical phenomena persist for a long time with astonishing freshness and with the whole of their affective colouring . . . however . . . these memories . . . are not at the patient's disposal."[86] One reason why an adequate reaction to a psychical trauma may not have taken place is "because social circumstances made a reaction impossible."[87]

Breuer and Freud write of the distressing affects (such as fright, anxiety, shame, or physical pain) that may operate as trauma and precipitating causes for hysterical symptoms. (In common hysteria, as opposed to "traumatic" hysteria, "instead of a single, major trauma, we ['not infrequently'] find a number of partial traumas forming a group of provoking causes."[88]) The memory of the trauma "acts like a foreign body which long after its entry must continue to be regarded as an agent that is still at work."[89] Breuer and Freud write that the individual hysterical symptoms permanently disappeared when the memory of the provoking event was revealed along with the arousal of its accompanying affect, and the patient was able to put the affect into words along with a detailed description of the event.

However, after opening section 2 with a statement about the failure of certain memories to succumb to the typical wearing away process and the importance for that process of "an energetic reaction to the event that provokes an affect," Breuer and Freud immediately include in their reactions "acts of revenge . . . in which affects are discharged."[90] They also refer to the consequences of "an injury that has been repaid,"[91] in implicit contrast to one that has not been repaid. They refer to how "a person's memory of a humiliation" may be helped by a "process of association" through which affectively operative ideas are worn away.[92] In addition to bringing ideas into a process of association, language can, as in confession, help in abreacting an affect. In considering that it is in these very pages that the terms "catharsis" and "abreaction" make their first published appearance (Freud had used the latter term about six months earlier in a letter), it is worth noting again Nietzsche's strong link to Bernays. It is also in this section, immediately after writing of the social circumstances that make a reaction impossible, that Breuer and Freud make their early use of the term "*verdrängt*" (repressed) and also use the word "*hemmte*" (inhibited). Nietzsche typically used words such as "*Hemmung*" (inhibition) and "*Zerückgetretene*" (repressed).

In *Studies on Hysteria*, Breuer writes:

> We pointed out in our "Preliminary Communication" to what a varying extent the affect of anger at an insult, for instance, is called up by a recollection, according to whether the insult has been repaid or endured in silence. If the psychical reflex was fully achieved on the original occasion, the recollection of it releases a far smaller quantity of excitation. If not, the recollection is perpetually forcing on to the subject's lips the abusive words which were originally suppressed.[93]

In a footnote Breuer adds:

> The instinct for revenge which is so powerful in the natural man and is disguised rather than repressed by civilization, is nothing whatever but the excitation of a reflex that has not been released. To defend oneself against injury in a fight and, in doing so, to injure one's opponent is the adequate and preformed psychical reflex. If it has been carried out insufficiently or not at all, it is constantly released again by recollection, and the "instinct of revenge" [and the hateful man of *ressentiment*] comes into being.[94]

Among many passages in Nietzsche that resonate with such ideas is one from the *Genealogy* in which he writes of "the *ressentiment* of natures that are denied the true reaction, that of deeds, and compensate themselves with an imaginary revenge . . . the submerged hatred, the vengefulness of the impotent."[95] Furthermore, for Nietzsche, "pain is the most powerful aid to mnemonics"; "'if something is to stay in the memory it must be burned in: only that which never ceases to *hurt* stays in the memory'—this is a main cause of the oldest (unhappily also the most enduring) psychology on earth."[96] (The child psychiatrist Lenore Terr has stated that after experiencing a traumatic event, children retain "'burned in' visual impressions."[97]) For Nietzsche, one important cause of intensification (and potential transformation) of psychic pain, is thwarting of adequate reaction. As Claudia Crawford points out, for Nietzsche "the slave [in contrast to the master] who is not able to act is also not able to forget."[98] Nietzsche states that the man of *ressentiment* understands "how not to forget."[99] The slave does not banish the memory of a trauma to an unconscious realm from which is derived the impetus for hysterical symptomatology. This does not entail that the slave may not be unconscious of many matters pertinent to his view of himself, others, and his situation that, for example, accompany the development of *ressentiment*. But Nietzsche does not write of the relationship between a quota of undischarged excessive affect connected to a forgotten or repressed memory and the formation of hysterical symptomatology. Nietzsche does not posit a transformation, through channeling along certain nervous pathways, of the energy aroused by a forgotten or repressed memory of a psychological trauma such that the conversion of this energy, not allowed more direct discharge, results in bodily symptoms specifically related to, even specifically symbolizing, the trauma.[100]

It may prove impossible to determine whether or not certain facets of the thinking of Freud (and Breuer) at this time were specifically influenced by Nietzsche. But Nietzsche's psychological explorations were serious, and he identified himself as a psychologist on many occasions for good reason. His explorations frequently move along paths quite related to the explorations of Freud during this period as well as in years to come. I suggest, given the links between Freud and Nietzsche in the 1870s and 1880s, and the prevalence and influence of Nietzsche in the German-speaking world in the 1890s, that the similarity of some of the themes and the use of language in the "Preliminary Communication" (and at a few other points in *Studies on Hysteria* as well as in other writings of Freud of this period) may very well be due in part to the direct and indirect influence of Nietzsche. When we consider Freud's relationship to Nietzsche after this period, we can, at the very least, recognize that Freud's concerns and areas of exploration resonated with Nietzschean ideas from the period of his earliest psychological writings. And we can note that as Freud would come to apply his psychological findings in the field of psychopathology to people generally, Nietzsche too emphasized that the same basic processes operated in both sick and healthy individuals. This is particularly well articulated in a note that was unpublished at the time:

> It is the value of all morbid states that they show us under a magnifying glass certain states that are normal—but not easily visible when normal.—
> Health and sickness are not essentially different . . . there are only differences in degree between these two kinds of existence: the exaggeration, the disproportion, the nonharmony of the normal phenomena constitute the pathological state.[101]

CONCLUSION

Although many commentators have remarked on Nietzsche's anticipation of and possible influence on Freud, there has been, particularly in the English-speaking world, limited exploration of the specific details of such anticipation and influence. Also, commentators who have explored these matters often refer to Freud's work from 1900 on. In particular, there has been relatively little exploration of the relationship of Nietzsche's ideas to Freud's thought during the early and mid-1890s.

Nietzsche was a very strong intellectual and emotional presence for the circle of friends and acquaintances within which Freud traveled in the 1870s and 1880s. Through his own reading of Nietzsche and through the influence of these friends and acquaintances, there can be no doubt that Freud was exposed to at least some of Nietzsche's ideas. Although we do not yet have very much in the way of studies on the influence of Nietzsche on those around Freud in the 1890s, Nietzsche's influence was great enough for an authority on the period like Ellenberger to compare Nietzsche's influence during the 1890s to Darwin's influence on the previous generation. I have also remarked on the link from Bernays to Breuer and Freud as well as to Nietzsche, and I have noted that 1892 was the year of publication of the first edition of Nietzsche's collected writings. There is also the fact of Nietzsche's frequent references to himself as a psychologist and his high regard for the discipline of psychology. He writes that "psychology shall be recognized again as the queen of the sciences, for whose service and preparation the other sciences exist. For psychology is now again the path to the fundamental problems."[102] Like Freud, Nietzsche regarded himself as a groundbreaking explorer of this path toward the fundamental problems.[103]

Nietzsche wrote, as did Freud from 1892 through 1895, of the relationship between painful psychic trauma and memory, the need for aroused drives and affects to find adequate reaction or discharge, the pathological consequences of humiliations and injuries to which one is unable to react adequately with repayment or acts of revenge, consequences of the conflict between the ego and unbearable ideas, and of repression or inhibition. Freud's early patients were not able to forget in the normal way, a necessity for sanity and life that was stressed by Nietzsche from early in his career. As noted, Nietzsche and Freud also emphasized the importance of the inability *not* to react, and related such inability to certain hysterical types. Nietzsche was concerned throughout his productive life with matters pertaining to the ways in which the multiplicity of our psychic selves can function in healthy, creative ways rather than in ways that lead to exhaustion and breakdown. Of great importance, Nietzsche was one of the thinkers who extended nineteenth-century explorations of the cerebral unconscious and unconscious inference into the realm of the dynamic unconscious.

Throughout his career, Freud absorbed, integrated, and transformed a remarkable range of influences. Nietzsche may have been among the most important influences, and his influence may have begun earlier than has been generally recognized. At the very least, we can appreciate that in important respects Freud's early psychological explorations moved in directions related to trends and directions followed by (and to some extent created by) Nietzsche. Regarding matters on which the two thinkers differed, it is by no means clear that Freud's conceptualizations were improvements. In fact, we have just begun to explore the nature, implications, and ramifications of Nietzsche's actual and potential contributions to psychology and psychiatry.[104]

NOTES

1. Henri Ellenberger, *The Discovery of the Unconscious* (New York: Basic Books, 1970), 542.

2. Ibid., 276.

3. Ibid., 276–77.

4. See the central role of Nietzsche for Ellenberger in Mark S. Micale, introduction to *Beyond the Unconscious: Essays of Henri F. Ellenberger in the History of Psychiatry*, intro. and ed. M. S. Micale, trans. F. Dubor and M. S. Micale (Princeton: Princeton University Press, 1993), 25–26.

5. But see the bibliography I have compiled at the end of this volume.

6 On Freud's development during this period, see Ola Anderson, *Studies in the Prehistory of Psychoanalysis* (Stockholm: Norstedt, 1962). On Freud's development as a psychotherapist during 1892–1893, see Lewis Aron, "From Hypnotic Suggestion to Free Association: Freud as a Psychotherapist, circa 1892–1893," *Contemporary Psychoanalysis* 32.1 (1996): 99–114. See also Mikkel Borch-Jacobsen, "Neurotica: Freud and the Seduction Theory, " *October* 76 (Spring 1996): 15–43.

7. Since it is not as relevant as other material to the more purely psychological concerns of this paper, I do not deal with Freud's *Project for a Scientific Psychology, The Standard Edition of the Complete Psychological Works of Sigmund Freud*, 24 vols., trans. and ed. James Strachey (London: Hogarth Press, 1953–1974 [1950 (1895)]), 1:295–391. I'll note here that I deal with what Freud and Breuer wrote, not what they actually did with their patients. On the work with, and writing about Bertha Pappenheim see Mikkel Borch-Jacobsen, *Remembering Anna O.: A Century of Mystification*, trans. Kirby Olson in collaboration with Xavier Callahan and Mikkel Borch-Jacobsen (New York: Routledge, 1996).

8. On some general shared influences, see Lehrer, *Nietzsche's Presence in Freud's Life and Thought: On the Origins of a Psychology of Dynamic*

Unconscious Mental Functioning (Albany: State University of New York Press, 1995), 7–9.

9. See W. Bischler, "Schopenhauer and Freud: A Comparison," *Psychoanalytic Quarterly* 8 (1939): 88–97; R. K. Gupta, "Freud and Schopenhauer," *Journal of the History of Ideas* 36.4 (Oct.–Dec. 1975): 721–28; Christopher Young and Andrew Brook, "Schopenhauer and Freud," *International Journal of Psycho-Analysis* 75 (1994): 75–101.

10. Gustav Theodor Fechner, *Zend-Avesta, oder über die Dinge des Himmels und des Jenseits*, 2 vols. (Leipzig: Voss, 1851).

11. Ian Hacking, *Rewriting the Soul: Multiple Personality and the Sciences of Memory* (Princeton: Princeton University Press, 1995), 197. For some relevant quotes of Ribot by Hacking, see *Rewriting the Soul*, 205–9. See also H. E. Lampl, *Flair du Livre. Friedrich Nietzsche und Théodule Ribot, eine travaille Hundert Jahre "Zur Genealogie der Moral"* (Zurich: am Abgrund, 1988).

12. William J. McGrath, *Dionysian Art and Populist Politics in Austria* (New Haven: Yale University Press, 1974).

13. Friedrich Nietzsche, *The Birth of Tragedy out of the Spirit of Music* in *Basic Writings of Nietzsche*, ed. and trans. Walter Kaufmann (New York: Random House, 1968 [1872]).

14. Nietzsche, *Untimely Meditations*, trans. R. J. Hollingdale, intro. J. P. Stern (New York: Cambridge University Press, 1983 [1873–76]).

15. See McGrath, *Dionysian Art*, 62.

16. Steven Beller, *Vienna and the Jews, 1867–1938* (Cambridge: Cambridge University Press, 1989), 157.

17. See Aldo Venturelli, "Nietzsche in der Berggasse 19. Über die erste Nietzsche-Rezeption in Wien," *Nietzsche-Studien* 17 (1984): 448–80.

18. See Lehrer, *Nietzsche's Presence*, 90–99.

19. Walter Boehlich, ed. *Letters of Sigmund Freud to Eduard Silberstein, 1871–1881*, trans. A. J. Pomerans (Cambridge: The Belknap Press of Harvard University Press, 1990), 86.

20. Peter Newton, *Freud: From Youthful Dream to Mid-Life Crisis* (New York: Guilford Press, 1995), 63.

21. See Ernst L. Freud, ed., *The Letters of Sigmund Freud and Arnold Zweig*, trans. Elaine and William Robson-Scott (New York: New York University Press, 1970), 78.

22. See Richard Frank Krummel, "Dokumentation: Joseph Paneth über seine Begegnung mit Nietzsche in der Zarathustra-Zeit," *Nietzsche-Studien* 17 (1988): 478–95.

23. See Lehrer, *Nietzsche's Presence*, 19–33.

24. Gunter Godde, "Freuds philosophische Diskussionskreise in der Studentenzeit," *Jarbuch der Psychoanalyse* 27 (1991): 73–113. See also W. W. Hemecker, *Vor Freud. Philosophiegeschichtliche Voraussetzungen der Psychoanalyse* (Munich: Philosophia Verlag, 1991).

25. E. Freud, *Letters of Freud and Zweig*, 78; Ernest Jones, *The Life and Work of Sigmund Freud*, vol. 3 (New York: Basic Books, 1957), 460; Freud and Zweig *Briefwechsel*, ed. E. Freud (Frankfurt am Main: S. Fischer, 1986), 89. On the correct translation, see Peter Heller, "Freud in His Relation to Nietzsche,"

in *Nietzsche and Jewish Culture*, ed. Jacob Golomb (New York: Routledge, 1997), 212n1. On Nietzsche's place in the Freud–Zweig correspondence and Nietzsche's possible presence in *Moses and Monotheism*, see Lehrer, *Nietzsche's Presence*, 231–56. See Deborah Hayden (this volume) on Nietzsche's letter to Paneth in which he looks fifty years ahead to being understood by a few individuals. It is quite possible that through Paneth or the letter itself, if Paneth showed it to him, Freud learned of Nietzsche's hopes. According to Peter Swales (personal communication), there is an unpublished letter of Freud's indicating that during this period Freud was already much taken with the work of Georg Brandes, who in a few years would be one of the early literary scholars to hold Nietzsche's work in very high regard. Brandes also corresponded with Nietzsche in the late 1880s. In March of 1900, Freud attended a lecture by Brandes and sent a copy of his dream book to him at his hotel. See Jeffrey Moussaieff Masson, *The Complete Letters of Sigmund Freud to Wilhelm Fliess, 1887–1904*, trans. and ed. Jeffrey Moussaieff Masson (Cambridge: The Belknap Press of Harvard University Press, 1985), 406–7.

26. See Lehrer, *Nietzsche's Presence*, 44–48, 90–99.

27. See Boehlich, *Letters of Freud to Silberstein*, 115.

28. See Robin N. Mitchell-Boyask, "Freud's Reading of Classical Literature and Classical Philology," in *Reading Freud's Reading*, ed. Sander L. Gilman, Jutta Birmele, Jay Geller, and Valerie D. Greenberg (New York: New York University Press, 1994), 40.

29. See Boehlich, *Letters of Freud to Silberstein*, 102.

30. See Lehrer, *Nietzsche's Presence*, 34–51.

31. See Albrecht Hirschmüller, *The Life and Work of Joseph Breuer* (New York: New York University Press, 1989 [1978]), 41, 49. Peter Swales (personal communication) has pointed out that Dr. Otto von Fleischl-Marxow, brother of Freud's colleague Ernst von Fleischl-Marxow (who figures, along with Paneth and, I believe, Nietzsche in Freud's "Non Vixit" dream), had, from 1873, a home in Rome that became a meeting place for many German-speaking celebrities, including Liszt, Wagner, Brahms, and many others. He was personally acquainted with Nietzsche, who visited him in Rome, and also maintained a friendship with Breuer. It would seem likely that Breuer heard some Nietzsche stories that he passed on to Freud.

32. Jacob Bernays, *Grundzüge der verlorenen Abhandlung des Aristoteles über Wirkung der Tragödie* (New York: Georg Olms, 1970 [1857, 1880]).

33. In Bernays' concept of catharsis, psychological relief is derived from discharge of aroused emotion. Macmillan points out that Bernays' conception of Aristotle's idea of catharsis in tragedy entailed "the process by which the audience watching a tragedy were purged of the emotions of fear and pity. . . . Bernays' thesis was in a very long line of medical and quasi-medical interpretations construing catharsis as removing fear and pity from the soul, much as a suitable medicine might purge the body of a disease. . . . What was novel about Bernays' argument was how he envisaged the mechanism of purgation. . . . For Bernays . . . purging came about not because of a *reduction* of the emotions but because of their *discharge*." Malcolm Macmillan, *Freud Evaluated: The Completed Arc* (Amsterdam: North-Holland, 1991), 21, 22.

34. Hirschmüller, *Breuer*, 156–58.

35. See Mitchell-Boyask, "Freud's Reading," 28–29.

36. See M. S. Silk and J. P. Stern, *Nietzsche on Tragedy* (New York: Cambridge University Press, 1981), 207, 217, 415.

37. Nietzsche, *BT* 22.

38. See Mitchell-Boyask, "Freud's Reading," 28.

39. Arnaldo Momigliano, *Jacob Bernays* (Amsterdam: North-Holland, 1969), 17.

40. See Hirschmüller, *Breuer*, 159.

41. See Ellenberger, *Discovery*, 273. On Mayer see Kenneth L. Caneva, *Robert Mayer and the Conservation of Energy* (Princeton: Princeton University Press, 1993).

42. Macmillan, *Freud Evaluated*, 100. Anne Harrington suggests that in addition to such influence, Jackson may have influenced Freud's conclusion that psychic processes, internal thought processes, are able to become perceptions, able to be perceived by consciousness, through the verbal mode, the word, or symbol. *Medicine, Mind, and the Double Brain: A Study in Nineteenth-Century Thought* (Princeton: Princeton University Press, 1987), 240–47. Nietzsche writes that "man, like every living being, thinks continually without knowing it; the thinking that rises to consciousness . . . *takes the form of words, which is to say signs of communication.*" *The Gay Science*, ed. and trans. Walter Kaufmann (New York: Vintage Books, 1974 [1882; 1887]), 354.

43. Freud, "Some Points for a Comparative Study of Organic and Hysterical Motor Paralyses," *SE* 1:171–72 (1893). See discussion below on trauma and memory.

44. Freud, "The Neuro-Psychoses of Defense," *SE* 3:60 (1894).

45. See Strachey, appendix to "The Neuro-Psychoses of Defense," *SE* 3:62–68 (1962 [1894]).

46. Nietzsche, *GS* 360.

47. See Lehrer, "Freud's Relationship to Nietzsche," 379–89.

48. Nietzsche, *GS* 360.

49. Young and Brook, "Schopenhauer and Freud," 108.

50. Nietzsche, "Preface for the Second Edition," *Gay Science*, sec. 2.

51. Joseph Breuer and Sigmund Freud, *Studies on Hysteria* (1895), *SE* 2:264.

52. Friedrich Nietzsche, *Twilight of the Idols* in *The Portable Nietzsche*, ed. and trans. Walter Kaufmann (New York: The Viking Press, 1954 [1888]), "Skirmishes of an Untimely Man," sec. 10.

53. Ibid., 511–12.

54. Ibid., 519.

55. See Graham Parkes, *Composing the Soul: Reaches of Nietzsche's Psychology* (Chicago: University of Chicago Press, 1994), 61–62, 255–56, 441n19.

56. Friedrich Nietzsche, *The Case of Wagner* in *Basic Writings of Nietzsche*, trans. and ed. Walter Kaufmann (New York: Random House, 1968), 5.

57. Daniel L. Schacter, *Searching for Memory: The Brain, the Mind, and the Past* (New York: Basic Books, 1996), 234. In keeping with his views on perception and his perspectivism, Nietzsche also anticipates contemporary accounts

of seeing that suggest that "for ordinary seeing . . . we need to be continuously blind in order to see . . . blindnesses are . . . the very condition of seeing itself." James Elkins, *The Object Stares Back: On the Nature of Seeing* (New York: Basic Books, 1996), 13. Nietzschean (and Freudian) themes also appear in writings that fall under the heading of cognitive science. For example, on the Nietzschean themes of the self as a multiply authored fictional construction, that mind does not require consciousness, that much mental activity and decision-making is unconscious, that conscious awareness often reflects, rather than an executive in charge, an endpoint reached after unconscious dynamic conflict and the emergence of a "winner," that consciousness is like a regent ignorant of the actions of its subjects, see Owen Flanagan, *The Science of the Mind* (Cambridge: The MIT Press, 1991), 208, 309, 311, 344, 358. At the beginning of his chapter on Freud, Flanagan writes that "Freud revolutionized as much as Nietzsche—and in part because of Nietzsche—our philosophical conception of human nature" (*Science of the Mind*, 55).

58. Freud, "Neuro-Psychoses," *SE* 3:47. The context of this discussion includes the idea that this kind of "forgetting" did not succeed, but gave rise to pathological reactions such as hysteria, obsessions, or even hallucinatory psychosis, all of which were associated with splitting of consciousness.

59. Nietzsche, *Human, All-Too-Human: A Book for Free Spirits*, trans. R. J. Hollingdale (New York: Cambridge University Press, 1986 [1878–80]), 491.

60. Schopenhauer quoted in Young and Brook, "Schopenhauer and Freud," 109.

61. Friedrich Nietzsche, *Assorted Opinions and Maxims*, in *Human*, 37.

62. Nietzsche, *Ecce Homo* in *Basic Writings of Nietzsche*, trans. and ed. Walter Kaufmann (New York: Random House, 1968), "Why I am So Clever," 8.

63. Breuer and Freud, *Studies on Hysteria*, *SE* 2:269.

64. Friedrich Nietzsche, *On the Genealogy of Morals [1887]* in *Basic Writings of Nietzsche*, trans. and ed. Walter Kaufmann (New York: Random House, 1968 [1887]), II:1. Nietzsche is perhaps influenced here by, among others, Ribot.

65. Freud, *Interpretation of Dreams*, *SE* 5:567.

66. Breuer and Freud, *Studies on Hysteria*, *SE* 2:235.

67. Ibid., *SE* 2:236.

68. See, for example, Nietzsche, *Daybreak: Thoughts on the Prejudices of Morality*, trans. R. J. Hollingdale (New York: Cambridge University Press, 1982 [1881]), 119.

69. Young and Brook point out that Schopenhauer does link unbearably painful memories not exactly with repression but with a destruction of the thread of memory as a desperate seeking of refuge from the memories in madness. Young and Brook, "Schopenhauer and Freud," 112.

70. Regarding memory and self-knowledge, with, I will add, possible implications for understanding certain differences between Nietzsche and Freud, Ian Hacking writes of how

we have come to think of ourselves . . . as very much formed by our past. Hence, in our times, false consciousness will often involve some deceptive memories. It need not do so. The Delphic injunction "Know thyself!" did not refer to memory. It required that we know our character, our limits, our needs, our propensities for self-deception. It required that we know our souls. Only with the advent of memoro-politics did memory become a surrogate for the soul. (Hacking, *Rewriting the Soul*, 5, 95, 260).

71. Breuer and Freud, *Studies on Hysteria*, SE 2:283.

72. Ibid., 2:281.

73. Ibid., 2:302.

74. Nietzsche, *Beyond Good and Evil*, 23.

75. Nietzsche, *The Antichrist* in *The Portable Nietzsche* trans. and ed. Walter Kaufmann (New York: The Viking Press, 1954 [1895 (1888)], 55.

76. Breuer and Freud, *Studies on Hysteria*, SE 2:270.

77. Strachey in ibid., 2:212n1.

78. Nietzsche, *D* 133.

79. Nietzsche, *GM* II:14.

80. Nietzsche, *Gesamtausgabe*, ed. Peter Gast (Leipzig: Naumann, 1892).

81. Lou Salomé, *Friedrich Nietzsche in seinen Werken* (Vienna: Carl Konegen, 1894).

82. Elisabeth Förster-Nietzsche, *Das Leben Friedrich Nietzsche*, 2 vols. (Leipzig: Nauman, 1895–1904).

83. Clement Rosset writes that for Nietzsche

the hateful person . . . finds . . . it is impossible to give to his hatred some expression. . . . In a . . . comparable manner, . . . [in] the *Studies on Hysteria* . . . Freud defines repression as the effect . . . of an absence of reaction (or of an "abreaction"). (Rosset, *Joyful Cruelty*, trans. and ed. David F. Bell [New York: Oxford University Press, 1993], 59)

84. Breuer and Freud, "On the Psychical Mechanism of Hysterical Phenomena: Preliminary Communication" (1893), SE 2:3–17. On the respective contributions of Breuer and Freud to the "Preliminary Communication," see Hirschmüller, "The Genesis of the *Preliminary Communication* of Breuer and Freud," trans. Christine Trollope. In *100 Years of Psychoanalysis: Contributions to the History of Psychoanalysis*, ed. André Haynal and Ernst Falzeder (London: H. Karnac, 1994), 17–30.

85. Breuer and Freud, "Preliminary Communication," SE 2:9.

86. Ibid.

87. Ibid., SE 2:10. For Schopenhauer, soundness of mind requires that "a new adverse event must be assimilated by the intellect." If this is prevented by "resistance and opposition of the will to the assimilation . . . and . . . if the resultant gaps are arbitrarily filled up for the sake of the necessary connection; we then have madness." Schopenhauer quoted in Young and Brook, "Schopenhauer and Freud," 113. On the term "abreaction," see Jean Starobinski, "On the Word 'Abreaction,'" trans. Annabel McQuillan. In *100 Years of Psychoanalysis*, 31–39.

88. Breuer and Freud, "Preliminary Communication," SE 2:6.

89. Ibid.

90. Ibid.

91. Ibid.

92. Ibid.

93. Breuer and Freud, *Studies on Hysteria*, SE 2:205–6.

94. Ibid.

95. Nietzsche, *GM* I:10.

96. Ibid.

97. Leonore Terr quoted in Schacter, *Searching for Memory*, 202.

98. Claudia Crawford, "Nietzsche's Mnemotechnics, The Theory of Ressentiment, and Freud's Topographies of the Psychic Apparatus," *Nietzsche-Studien* 14 (1985): 288.

99. Nietzsche, *GM* I:10.

100. On Freud's errors here (and the influence on him here of Charcot), and their consequences, see Richard Webster, *Why Freud Was Wrong* (New York: Basic Books, 1995), 71–258. Nietzsche and Breuer also share a concern regarding the abuse of metaphors, reification, and notions of underlying entities, substances, and subjects. See Nietzsche, *Daybreak*, 119 and *Beyond Good and Evil*, 17; Breuer, *Studies*, 227–28. They both also write of unconscious sexuality or sensuality and its disguised expression in adolescent girls. See Breuer, *Studies*, 245–46; Nietzsche, *Genealogy*, III:8.

101. Nietzsche, *The Will To Power*, trans. Walter Kaufmann and R. J. Hollingdale, ed. Walter Kaufmann (New York: Random House, 1967 [1883–88]), 47. Nietzsche continues: "The error in treatment: one does not want to fight weakness with a *systéme fortifiant* [a method that strengthens], but rather with a kind of justification and *moralization*; i.e., with an *interpretation.*"

102. Nietzsche, *Beyond Good and Evil*, 23.

103. Here one might consider the significance of Freud's slip of the pen when, on October 6, 1910 he wrote to Ferenczi that "I am also that psychoanalytic [the sign for "psychoanalytic" is used] superman [*Übermensch*] whom we have constructed." *The Correspondence of Sigmund Freud and Sándor Ferenczi, Volume I, 1908–1914*, ed. Eva Brabant, Ernst Falzeder, and Patrizia Giampieri-Deutsch under the supervision of André Haynal, transcribed by Ingeborg Meyer-Palmedo, trans. Peter T. Hoffer, intro. André Haynal (Cambridge: The Belknap Press of Harvard University Press, 1993), 221 (letter no. 171). Freud meant to write that he was *not* that psychoanalytic superman. The German edition of the letter does not have a note or commentary on the slip, but it does have the "nicht" (not) in brackets to indicate that it was not Freud's word. Sigmund Freud, Sándor Ferenczi, *Briefwechsel, Band I/1, 1908–1911*, ed. Eva Brabant, Ernst Falzeder, and Patrizia Giampieri-Deutsch, under the supervision of André Haynal, transcribed by Ingeborg Meyer-Palmedo, (Vienna, Cologne, Weimar: Böhlau Verlag, 1993), 310. The edition of the English translation has not only no note or commentary, but includes the "not" without any brackets at all, conveying the impression that it was written by Freud. Peter Hoffer, the English translator, elsewhere has written, "Can there be any doubt that, when Freud wrote to Ferenczi on October 6, 1910, 'I am not that [psychoanalytic] superman whom we have constructed' . . . , he had Nietzsche on his mind?"

Peter T. Hoffer, review of *Nietzsche's Presence in Freud's Life and Thought,* by Ronald Lehrer, *Psychoanalytic Books: A Quarterly Journal of Reviews* 7.4 (Winter 1996): 622. If Hoffer is right, can there be any doubt that it is all the more significant that Freud omitted the "not," and that Hoffer included it in the English edition and elsewhere without any indication of what Freud actually wrote?

104. I will note here André Haynal's comment, representative of a certain psychoanalytic line of thinking, that while poets, such as Sophocles and Shakespeare, and philosophers, such as Schopenhauer and Nietzsche (whose insights, however brilliant, emerged from the realm of poetic and artistic intuition), had grasped the irrational, it was "the Freudian revolution [that] discovered that the irrational . . . has a *structure* that we can try to *understand*" (*Psychoanalysis and the Sciences,* trans. Elizabeth Holder [Berkeley: University of California Press, 1993], 237). Haynal gives the example of how criminal acts against "the enemy" can be understood as "justified by the projection inherent in fanaticism through the scapegoat mechanism and under the pretext of extirpating evil." However, there is nothing in this explanation, no mechanism that Haynal may have in mind, of which Nietzsche was not aware. And Haynal, who is well aware of the great importance of Nietzsche for Freud, even goes on to demonstrate that Nietzsche was quite aware of the irrational having a structure that we can try to understand by noting that "Nietzsche observed that *people who are dissatisfied with themselves are always ready to avenge themselves; we others become their victims.*" (Haynal refers to the passage as presented in Herman Feifel, *The Meaning of Death* [New York: McGraw-Hill, 1965]. Nietzsche writes that every complaint [*Klagen*], in the sense of lamenting one's lot, is also accusation [*Anklagen*].) And, speaking of the structure of the irrational in criminal acts, there is the remarkably rich exploration by Nietzsche in "On the Pale Criminal" (*Thus Spoke Zarathustra,* trans. Walter Kaufmann [New York: The Viking Press, 1954], I, sec. 6). (See Freud's reference to Nietzsche's discussion of what Freud refers to as "Criminality from a Sense of Guilt," *SE* 14:333.) There can be no doubt that Freud attempted to systematically explore the structure of the irrational of the individual person to a far greater extent than did such predecessors as Nietzsche, but he did not discover that the irrational has a structure that we can attempt to understand. We shouldn't minimize Nietzsche's intuitive and artistic genius, but we also shouldn't minimize his rigorous eduction as a classical philologist, his interest in psychological science as well as the psychology he learned from poets and novelists, and his serious, although clearly limited, interest in science more generally, all of which had great impact on the development of his psychological concepts.

CHAPTER 11

Nietzsche and Jung: Ambivalent Appreciation

Graham Parkes

> Nietzsche's mind was one of the first spiritual influences I experienced. It was all brand new then, and it was the closest thing to me.
>
> —C. G. Jung (1938)

As recounted in his *Memories, Dreams, Reflections*, Carl Gustav Jung went to the University of Basel in 1895, some sixteen years after Nietzsche had resigned from his professorship there.[1] The stories about him told by people who had known Nietzsche personally were generally unflattering, since he had never quite been accepted by that ultraconservative population; but for the young Jung this was all the more reason to want to read his books.

> Nietzsche had been on my program for some time, but I hesitated to begin reading him because I felt I was insufficiently prepared. . . . I was held back [also] by a secret fear that I might perhaps be like him, at least in regard to the "secret" which had isolated him from his environment. Perhaps—who knows?—he had had inner experiences, insights, which he had unfortunately attempted to talk about, and had found that no one understood him. . . . I feared I might be forced to recognize that I too was another such strange bird.[2]

Some years earlier Jung had undergone a number of numinous fantasy experiences, about which he had maintained a diplomatic silence, mentioning them to no one. This prompted the realization that he was "actually two different persons": one a schoolboy of no more than average talents, the other an old man from the eighteenth century, who was close to "nature," "the night," and "dreams."[3] Jung later came to think that interplay between two such personalities, the ego and a figure personi-

205

fying the unconscious, "is played out in every individual" (albeit unconsciously for the most part); but as a student he feared the condition could be pathological—hence the anxiety over the "strange bird."

> Of course, [Nietzsche] was a professor, had written whole long books and so had attained unimaginable heights, but, like me, he was a clergyman's son. . . . He spoke a polished High German, knew Latin and Greek, possibly French, Italian, and Spanish as well, whereas the only language I commanded with any certainty was the Waggis-Basel dialect. He, possessed of all these splendors, could well afford to be something of an eccentric, but I must not let myself find out how far I might be like him.[4]

By the time he wrote these words in the late fifties, Jung had himself written many long books—more and longer than Nietzsche's—but what is significant is the ambivalence: the feeling that while Nietzsche is different from him they are nevertheless alike. Jung mentions the "clergyman's son," but further things in common are the youthful love of solitude and a feeling of oneness with the natural world; and he must have sensed many more to be so anxious about finding himself too like Nietzsche.

> In spite of these trepidations I was curious, and finally resolved to read him. *Thoughts Out of Season* was the first volume that fell into my hands. I was carried away by enthusiasm, and soon afterward read *Thus Spoke Zarathustra*. This, like Goethe's *Faust*, was a tremendous experience for me. *Zarathustra* was Nietzsche's *Faust*, his No. 2 [personality], and my No. 2 now corresponded to *Zarathustra*—though this was rather like comparing a molehill with Mount Blanc. And *Zarathustra*—there could be no doubt about that—was morbid. Was my No. 2 also morbid? This possibility filled me with a terror which for a long time I refused to admit.[5]

Since the understanding reader of *Zarathustra* is unlikely to find the book "morbid," one suspects an element of projection in this judgment. But just as Nietzsche was tormented by the prospect of suffering a fate similar to his father's, who succumbed to brain disease, Jung's fear that he might be all-too-similar to Nietzsche with respect to morbidity prompts him to distance himself from the mad philosopher and blinds him to ways in which Nietzsche's psychology prefigured his own.

I

There are several hundred references to Nietzsche in Jung's published works, but only a few extended discussions. He appears to have read all Nietzsche's books, though many of his pronouncements about the ideas suggest a less than careful reading. Nevertheless, the positive remarks he makes about Nietzsche indicate a substantial influence on the development of his own psychological ideas.

In an early essay (from 1905) Jung suggests that the account of Zarathustra's journey to the underworld in *Thus Spoke Zarathustra*[6] is a case of "cryptomnesia," insofar as Nietzsche was unconsciously recalling a passage he had read as a young boy in a collection of stories about the supernatural. Such phenomenal recall takes place in "an abnormal mental state," as evidence for which Jung cites Nietzsche's own account of the "inspiration" behind the writing of *Zarathustra*.[7] Under such circumstances, Jung writes,

> consciousness only plays the role of slave to the daemon of the unconscious, which tyrannizes over it and inundates it with alien ideas. No one has described the state of consciousness when under the influence of an automatic complex better than Nietzsche himself.[8]

Jung is referring here to his idea of the "feeling-toned complex," an autonomous configuration of unconscious forces and images that is capable of some kind of perception, of association with other complexes, and of motivating certain actions "from its invisible seat in the unconscious."[9] Our unconscious must harbour an immense number of psychic complexes which would astonish us by their "strangeness."[10] Jung cites the first part of Nietzsche's characterization of inspiration in *Ecce Homo*:

> Has anyone at the end of the nineteenth-century a clear idea of what poets of strong ages called "inspiration"? If not, I shall describe it. — As long as the slightest vestige of superstition persists, one can hardly dismiss the idea that one is merely the incarnation, mouthpiece, or medium of more powerful forces. The concept of revelation—in the sense that suddenly and with indescribable certainty and subtlety something becomes *visible*, and audible, something that convulses one to the depths and bowls one over—describes the simple fact. One hears, one does not seek; one takes, one does not ask who gives; a thought flashes up like lightning, with necessity, formed without hesitation—I never had any choice in the matter.

Jung comments: "There could scarcely be a better description of the impotence of consciousness in face of the tremendous automatism driving up from the unconscious." He twice praises Nietzsche's *description* of inspiration, which tends to suggest that he has little to offer in the area of *understanding* the phenomenon. But in fact Nietzsche presents a number of ideas about the potent activities of the deeper psyche, and he develops them in terms of autonomous, personified complexes. But let us first consider the archaic background to these phenomena.

Shortly before Nietzsche's death Freud wrote in *The Interpretation of Dreams*:[11]

> We can guess how much to the point is Nietzsche's assertion that in dreams "some primeval relic of humanity is at work which we can now scarcely reach any longer by a direct path"; and we may expect that the analysis of dreams will lead us to a knowledge of man's archaic heritage, of what is psychologically innate in him.

This is a significant reference with respect to an important feature of psychoanalysis. Jung too cites Nietzsche with approval, quoting at length from the aphorism in *Human, All-Too-Human* to which Freud was referring and which deals with the relation between dreams and archaic, "primitive" ways of thinking. In elaborating a distinction between "directed thinking" and "dreaming or fantasy-thinking," Jung proposes "[drawing] a parallel between the mythological thinking of ancient man and the similar thinking found in children, primitives, and in dreams."[12] He then introduces a long quotation with the apposite remark that "in this regard Nietzsche takes up an attitude well worth noting":

> In sleep and dream we recapitulate the entire curriculum of earlier humanity. . . . In my opinion, just as nowadays people still infer in dreams, so human beings used to infer *in waking too* for thousands of years. . . . In the dream this primordial piece of humanity continues to operate in us, for it is the basis on which higher reason developed and continues to develop in every human being. The dream takes us back to remote conditions of human culture and gives us a means of understanding them better. Dream-thinking is so easy for us now because we have been so well drilled over vast stretches of human development in precisely this form of fantastic and easy explanation in terms of the first thing that strikes us.

This idea of "dream-thinking" prefigures what Jung calls "fantasy-thinking," a process he discusses in later works too. Indeed one of the main things that distinguishes his psychology from Freud's is its bolder epistemological stance: while Freud retained, in spite of his appreciation of the prevalence of projection and introjection, the traditional realist's suspicion of fantasy, Jung followed Nietzsche in assigning a crucial role to the imagination in the constitution of experience. In a part of the aphorism omitted by Jung in his citation, Nietzsche discusses a process related to dream-thinking that takes place while we are awake.

> When we close our eyes the brain produces a host of light-impressions and colors. . . . Now the understanding, in concert with fantasy, immediately works this in itself formless play of colors into definite figures, shapes, landscapes, lively groups. . . . Here, then, fantasy continuously

presents images [to the mind], depending on the visual impressions of the day for their production, and dream-phantasy operates in just the same way.[13]

Although it is prefigured in Kant's idea of the productive (transcendental) imagination, without which even perception would be impossible, Nietzsche's notion of a deep-level fantasy activity that conditions all experience has been given remarkably little attention. Jung's most pregnant formulation of the idea is to be found in the first chapter of *Psychological Types* (1921):

> The autonomous activity of the psyche . . . is, like every vital process, a continually creative act. The psyche creates reality every day. The only expression I can use for this activity is *fantasy*. . . . [Fantasy is] the mother of all possibilities, where . . . the inner and outer worlds are joined together in living union. . . . But here comes the great difficulty: fantasy is for the most part a product of the unconscious . . . [and] essentially involuntary. . . . It has these qualities in common with the dream.

The prototype of this process, though Jung doesn't mention it, is the synthesis effected by the schematism in Kant ("a blind though indispensable function of the soul . . . of which we are seldom even conscious"). Nietzsche's contribution consists in his explicit elaboration of the archaic dimension of the phenomenon—his discovery that "ancient humanity and animality, in fact the entire primeval period and past of all sentient being continues in me to invent, love, hate, infer."[14] The idea this remark invites us to entertain, the experience to experiment with, is that in being here now we are always potentially "there then" too—where "there" is any time between now and our ancestors' beginnings, in human or animal form, in plant or even mineral figuration.

In general, Jung's remarks about Nietzsche show that he values him more as a poet than as a philosopher, as evidenced in his concern with *Zarathustra* and in his frequent discussion of the poetry. In *Symbols of Transformation*, for example, he amplifies the mythical background to the imagery of four of Nietzsche's mature poems. But it is less the poetic language that appeals to Jung than the archetypal images and symbols:

> What seems like a poetic figure of speech in Nietzsche is really an age-old myth. It is as if the poet could still sense, beneath the words of contemporary speech and in the images that crowd in upon his imagination, the ghostly presence of bygone spiritual worlds, and possessed the capacity to make them come alive again.[15]

Nietzsche would say that he possesses this capacity through inhabiting "bygone spiritual worlds" in imagination. Jung too spent a fair part of his life in bygone worlds—*ausser sich*, as Nietzsche puts it[16]—which explains the appeal for him of this conception of fantasy activity. In an aphorism entitled "Estranged from the present" Nietzsche writes: "There are great advantages to estranging oneself from one's time to a great extent and being driven away from its shores, as it were, back onto the ocean of past worldviews."[17] While the motivation for such wandering is the new perspective it affords for a better understanding of one's own age, Nietzsche also thinks that an existential engagement with history, which allows one to benefit from various cultures as from different climates, is salutary in itself.

II

There are three extended discussions of Nietzsche's ideas in Jung's works: in the essay "On the Psychology of the Unconscious" (1917), in a chapter of *Psychological Types* (1921) entitled "Apollinian and Dionysian," and in the *Zarathustra Seminars* (1934–39).

In the early essay, Jung discusses Freud's psychoanalysis and the "eros theory" and then turns briefly to "the other point of view: the will to power."[18] He contends that "a yea-saying to instinct . . . was what Nietzsche desired and taught," and characterizes "the Superman" as "the man who through obedience to instinct transcends himself."[19] But when we look at the life of the teacher of this doctrine, Jung claims,

> we are bound to admit that Nietzsche lived beyond instinct, in the lofty heights of heroic sublimity . . . until the tension shattered his brain. He talked of yea-saying and lived the nay. His loathing for man, for the human animal that lived by instinct, was too great. . . . Hence his life does not convince us of his teaching.

This is hopelessly muddled. Nietzsche did look down on "the human animal that lived by instinct"—but that's because he believed that to become fully human it is necessary to practice rigorous and protracted self-discipline, to the point where one can relax the regime and let the chastened instincts, or drives, play themselves out spontaneously.

On the simplistic assumption that "living the life of instinct" necessarily means acting it out, Jung asserts that while Nietzsche obviously didn't discharge his eros ("the instinct for the preservation of the species") through intercourse with his fellow human beings, he was driven rather by "the instinct of *self*-preservation."[20] He then equates this latter instinct with "the *will to power*"—a spectacular equation in light of the numerous passages in Nietzsche's works where he specifically denies the primacy of that "instinct" and claims that will to power is a manifestation of life that is willing to *sacrifice* rather than preserve itself "for the sake of power." Jung seems to forget Schopenhauer's cosmic notion of will, which Nietzsche adopts (and adapts), insofar as he misunderstands will to power as merely "the power of the ego,"[21] as one pathetically narrow drive rather than all drives. His subsequent remarks about will to power, all the way through the *Zarathustra* seminars, show that Jung continues to misunderstand it reductively, and to ignore Nietzsche's recommendations that we understand *all* life—"the living" *simpliciter,* "the will of life," "our entire drive-life," and even "the world" as a whole—as "will to power and nothing else."

In the second chapter of *Psychological Types* Jung discusses Schiller's ideas about the roles played in the psyche by the various drives (*Triebe*) and by fantasy (*Phantasie*), especially as articulated in *On the Aesthetic Education of Man* (1795). He acknowledges the influence of Schopenhauer on Nietzsche's early work but overlooks the latter's own interest in Asian thought: "For Nietzsche this pull toward the East stopped in Greece." In introducing the ideas of Apollinian and Dionysian, Jung says that he will present a number of quotations from *The Birth of Tragedy* so that the reader may criticize his interpretation of them.[22] Such criticism has to begin almost immediately, where Jung, after having introduced Nietzsche's idea of the Dionysian drive, criticizes him for failing to make clear a crucial point.

> If it is permissible to conceive the natural creature as a "work of art," then of course man in the Dionysian state has become a natural work of art too; but in so far as the natural creature is decidedly not a work of art in the ordinary sense of the word, he is nothing but sheer Nature.[23]

Jung is missing the point here: quite in the spirit of Goethe and Schiller, Nietzsche emphasizes that the Apollinian and Dionysian drives are "artistic powers that burst forth from nature itself *without mediation by the human artist,* and in which nature's art-drives [*Kunsttriebe*] find immediate and direct satisfaction," and goes on to talk at some length about these "art-drives of Nature."[24] Jung appears to be unaware that Schopenhauer uses the term *Kunsttriebe* to refer to the "art-drives" by virtue of which animals build nests, spin webs, and so forth. Indeed there is a venerable tradition in German *Naturphilosophie* of ascribing artistic powers to nature as a whole—thereby maintaining a continuity between nature and human culture—that culminates in Nietzsche's later ideas about the natural world as will to power. If Jung wants to refute the notion of a natural *Kunsttrieb* he is of course free to do so; but it is fruitless to criticize Nietzsche's thought without reading his writings with due care. If the Dionysian human being is a work of art it is because she or he is shaped by "the true creator" and "artist of worlds," Dionysus[25]—and is thus by no means "nothing but sheer Nature" as Jung maintains.

Jung's failure to appreciate the philosophical basis for Nietzsche's staging of the interplay between the Apollinian and Dionysian leads him to throw out another misdirected criticism. He accuses Nietzsche of forgetting that the problem of Apollo and Dionysus was an "essentially religious" one for the Greeks.[26] He goes on to inveigh against "aestheticism," claiming that "with Nietzsche as with Schiller the religious viewpoint is entirely overlooked and is replaced by the aesthetic." But Nietzsche's book is concerned with the birth of tragedy in ancient Greece (as well as the rebirth of culture in modern Germany) out of the spirit of music, and not with Greek religion per se. Nietzsche was in any case well informed in this area; and if his account of the Apollinian and Dionysian had been lacking, his close friend Erwin Rohde (who was on his way to fame as a scholar of Greek religion) would certainly have remarked the failing.

The basis of Jung's misunderstanding of Nietzsche's position as an aestheticism is no doubt the repeated pronouncement: "It is only as *aesthetic phenomenon* that existence and the world are eternally *justified.*" But since Jung fails to see that the Apollinian drive for beautiful *Schein* (shining/seeming) is originally "an art-drive of nature" that produces the entire phenomenal world in reaction to the "eternal suffering and contradiction" of the "primal One" at the core of the cosmos (*BT* 4), he misses the metaphysical dimension to Nietzsche's talk of aesthetic projection, which anticipates his own idea that all reality is conditioned by archetypal fantasy. But for all his criticisms Jung does concede, in his final paragraph, that Nietzsche "gained deep insight into the Dionysian qualities of his unconscious."

This is the extent more or less of Jung's estimation of Nietzsche's contributions to depth psychology: he excels in the description of autonomous phenomena of the unconscious such as inspiration; he realizes the extent to which dreams can take us back to archaic phases of human development; and his openness to archetypal imagery allows him to convey a vivid sense of "bygone spiritual worlds." Jung also has great, though by no means unqualified, admiration for *Zarathustra*, which he associates with illustrious traditions. He speaks of "the records of all ages, from the Holy Scriptures down to Nietzsche's *Zarathustra*," and again of "the *Aurea Catena* [Golden Chain] which has existed from the beginnings of philosophical alchemy and Gnosticism [and passes through Goethe's *Faust*] down to Nietzsche's *Zarathustra*."

Beyond this, Jung's assessment is basically negative. The autobiographical account quoted earlier continues as follows:

Nietzsche had discovered his No. 2 only late in life, when he was already past middle age, whereas I had known mine since boyhood. Nietzsche had spoken naïvely and incautiously about this *arrheton*, this thing not to be named, as though it were quite in order. His morbid misunderstanding [was] that he fearlessly and unsuspectingly let his No. 2 loose on upon a world that knew and understood nothing about such things. . . . But he found only educated Philistines—tragicomically, he was one himself. Like the rest of them, he did not understand himself when he fell head first into the unutterable mystery and wanted to sing its praises to the dull, godforsaken masses.[27]

The tone of these dismissive remarks is different since Jung is now talking about the man rather than the ideas. And indeed the bulk of his negative judgment of Nietzsche's psychology stems from a disparagement of his psychology in the sense of his personal makeup and dynamics. The crowning consideration concerns the effects of this morbidity on others: "Among my friends and acquaintances I knew of only two who openly declared themselves adherents of Nietzsche. Both were homosexual; one of them ended by committing suicide, the other ran to seed as a misunderstood genius."[28]

It may be that many Nietzsche enthusiasts are failures (what he calls *Missratenen*), but it is by no means clear that Nietzsche's works are responsible. As a psychologist, Jung does not shrink from psychologizing Nietzsche, but his assessment is flawed by his not having bothered to "take the history" by informing himself sufficiently of the circumstances of Nietzsche's life. Adducing his own case, as one who confronted the forces of the unconscious psyche more successfully, he writes:

I was not a blank page whirling about in the winds of the spirit, like Nietzsche. Nietzsche had lost the ground under his feet because he possessed nothing more than the inner world of his thoughts—which incidentally possessed him more than he it. He was uprooted and hovered above the earth, and therefore he succumbed to exaggeration and irreality. For me, such irreality was the quintessence of horror, for I aimed, after all, at *this* world and *this* life. . . . Thus my family and my profession always remained a joyful reality and a guarantee that I also had a normal existence.[29]

Jung is surely right in suggesting that a lack of customary ties to the everyday world (such as wife and children and a job provide) encouraged a solitude that was a factor in Nietzsche's mental collapse. And since he is convinced that Nietzsche had a syphilitic infection, that would be another, more important factor. But the implication that Nietzsche was unaware of what was happening to him is absurd. His letters from the period show a conscious decision to renounce human contacts and give up seeing his friends in order to fulfill his task of writing the books he had to write—in the full knowledge that they would not be appreciated for decades and the effort would destroy his health. Under trying family circumstances, and then obliged by ill health to retire from teaching, Nietzsche nevertheless aimed at *this* world and *this* life while renouncing all forms of metaphysical solace. He was admittedly "uprooted" by comparison with Jung's parochial *Bodenständigkeit*, but he shared with Zarathustra a love of the earth (in several different countries) that was quite incompatible with a desire for "hovering."

III

Between 1934 and 1939, Jung conducted a series of seminars at the Zurich Psychological Club on the topic of Nietzsche's *Zarathustra*. Before being curtailed by the outbreak of the war, the seminar had worked through most of the first three parts of the book, up to the chapter "On Old and New Tablets."[30] The break-off is tantalizing for the reader since it comes just at the culmination of part 3 and the book as a whole—though some of the participants no doubt took it as a blessing. Transcripts of the sessions were made, and though they were not intended for publication an edition of them appeared in 1988. While not as Herculean as the labor of editing must have been, the reading of this text, which runs to 1,544 pages, is a daunting undertaking. For appreciators of *Zarathustra* it is also highly exasperating: less than half the text has to do with Nietzsche's book, the rest being expositions of Jung's own psychological ideas. And of the portion that does treat *Zarathustra*, much consists of free association by other members of the seminar with little understanding of the history of philosophy or Nietzsche's place in it, and minimal acquaintance with the rest of his oeuvre.

Though better equipped than the other participants, Jung's understanding of Nietzsche's thought as a whole is patchy and his sense of the life somewhat nebulous. One does not expect from him closely argued readings of texts—vatic amplification is more Jung's style—but it is sad, given the time and energy so many intelligent people expended in the seminar, that he didn't try to set aside his prejudices and apply his exegetical talents to the rich and complex text of *Zarathustra*. The reader interested in Nietzsche's philosophy should know not only that Jung approaches the text primarily as a psychological document, which is a valid if somewhat restricted way to read it, but also that he does not consider it a philosophical text at all, which betrays a woefully restricted understanding of what constitutes philosophy. On one occasion Jung even goes so far as to say—flying in the face of the dictum that "it takes one to know one"—that Nietzsche is *not really a philosopher*. Still, the seminar transcripts can enhance our understanding of *Zarathustra* through the numerous amplifications of the mythical symbolism and archetypal imagery. (Since only the indefatigable reader will be able to extract this benefit, it would be a great contribution if someone produced an appropriately edited version that weighed in at around 10 percent of the current bulk.)

The ambivalence manifested by Jung in his other remarks about Nietzsche informs these pages too. There are, on one hand, a few highly positive evaluations of Nietzsche's contributions to psychology, as in this passage from the first term of the seminars:

> Nietzsche is really a modern psychologist. In our days, he would have made a famous analyst, for he had an ingenious flare [flair?] for the dark background and the secret motivations; he has anticipated a great deal of Freud and Adler. . . . [In his encounter with the shadow] Nietzsche came more truly and more specifically to grips with the psychology of man; therefore, his critical work was chiefly psychological.[31]

Of course the name "Jung" belongs there with "Freud and Adler," in spite of the former's reluctance to admit the extent to which his own ideas mirror Nietzsche's. This similarity is one of the reasons for the appearance of a negative tone in Jung's praise of Nietzsche's psychological acumen. For example, the remark that "Nietzsche at his mental best was really a discriminating psychologist" is tempered by the comment that "Nietzsche, being exceedingly psychological and discriminating in his other writings, when it comes to himself is not critical."[32] Yet, in spite of the numerous criticisms throughout the seminar, Jung is still able to say toward the end: "[Nietzsche] is one of the greatest psychologists that ever lived."[33]

Jung also compliments Nietzsche on the prophetic nature of his thought:

> [Nietzsche] anticipated, through his sensitivity, a great deal of the subsequent mental development [in modern culture]; he was assailed by the collective unconscious to such an extent that quite involuntarily he became aware of the collective unconscious that was characteristic of his time and the time that followed. Therefore, he is called a prophet, and in a way he is a prophet.[34]

And it is further to Jung's credit that he sees through one of the chronic stereotypes and appreciates Nietzsche's negative attitude toward individualism:

> Nietzsche is supposed to be the arch-individualist and the forefather of all individualists; he is ranked with Marx and such people, which is a

tremendous mistake. He is not at all an individualist in that sense, because his conception of the self is a perfectly decent idea which really links him up with the whole of mankind. . . . But you still hear wherever you go that he preaches individualism, because people cannot make a difference between the self and the ordinary ego.[35]

Jung is distinguishing here between the personal ego and "the Self" (a term of art referring to the totality of the psyche including the impersonal, collective unconscious), with the implication that Nietzsche appreciates this distinction too—at least some of the time. Nietzsche's use of the term *das Selbst* in the chapter in *Zarathustra* entitled "On the Despisers of the Body"[36] definitely anticipates Jung's usage, insofar as it exemplifies a general distinction between the complex of drives (or will to power) that constitutes the "I" and the larger configuration of drives that constitutes the body—which is in turn embedded in the even larger matrix of drives that is the totality of life. Calling the body, most of the activity of which proceeds unconsciously, "the Self" also serves to remind us that the drives animating the human organism come from an archaic source that predates by far the birth of the individual.

A few minutes later, however, Jung is suggesting that Nietzsche's conception of the self may be flawed after all.

I don't know why Nietzsche was not able to realize this quite simple thought of the self's being the total and himself only a part. . . . I got that formula from the East. Nietzsche unfortunately had not studied Eastern philosophy; that would have been a tremendous help to him there.[37]

Jung gives frequent voice to his prejudice concerning Nietzsche's ignorance of Eastern thought, though sometimes less categorically, as when he says: "Nietzsche had very little knowledge of the East. The only knowledge available to him was Schopenhauer's philosophy, and that is not the right vehicle for Indian philosophy."[38] He then admits that Nietzsche might have found some Buddhist ideas in Schopenhauer's philosophy, but he totally ignores the fact that the man who became the most prominent figure in Indian philosophy during Nietzsche's lifetime, Paul Deussen, was a classmate at Schulpforta and remained a friend to the end. And though Nietzsche was eventually put off by Deussen's admiration for Schopenhauer's thought, this did not prevent him from learning a few things about Indian philosophy from him. But whatever the extent of the influence of Asian ideas, there is no doubt that Nietzsche's idea of the world as will to power involves a distinction between the I and a greater, transpersonal self.

In spite of the occasional moments of high praise, Jung's attitude toward Nietzsche in the seminars as a whole is preponderantly negative.

The most common refrain—and this is his main criticism—is that Nietzsche lacked the psychological discrimination to realize that the ego (himself) and the self (as represented by Zarathustra) are different. Jung reiterates this objection so often that it becomes a veritable *Leier-Lied*, a hurdy-gurdy song whose repetitions might hold some aesthetic appeal if the content weren't so absurd. Jung gives forceful voice to the criticism in the seminar's very first session.

> The way in which [Nietzsche] wrote [*Zarathustra*] is most remarkable. He himself made a verse about it. He said: "Da wurde eins zu zwei und Zarathustra ging an mir vorbei," which means: "Then one became two and Zarathustra passed by me," meaning that Zarathustra then became manifest as a second personality in himself. That would show that he had himself a pretty clear notion that he was not identical with Zarathustra.[39]

This is right on the mark—and confirmed by a remark Nietzsche makes in *Ecce Homo* just a page-and-a-half before the account of "inspiration" that we saw Jung quote earlier: "On these two routes [which he used to hike, near Rapallo] the whole of the first part of *Zarathustra* came to me, and above all Zarathustra himself, as a type: or more precisely, he *overcame* me."[40] To say that Zarathustra "overcame" him doesn't mean that the archetypal figure obliterated his own personality and went on to write its autobiography, *Thus Spoke Zarathustra*: Nietzsche is simply expressing the extent to which Zarathustra presented himself as an autonomous person.

But then Jung goes on to ask, puzzlingly:

> But how could [Nietzsche] help assuming an identity [between him and Zarathustra] in those days when there was no psychology? Nobody would then have dared to take the idea of a personification seriously, or even of an independent, autonomous spiritual agency. Eighteen eighty-three was the time of the blooming of materialistic philosophy. So he had to identify with Zarathustra in spite of the fact that he felt, as this verse proves, a definite difference between himself and the old wise man.

How could Nietzsche help assuming such an identity? Simply by virtue of being "a *psychologist* without equal,"[41] as Jung himself acknowledges on occasion. Jung's psychology is richer for his having taken personification more seriously than Freud did, but he failed—perhaps refused—to see that Nietzsche precisely "dared to take the idea of a personification seriously," and that this is an important dimension along which his psychology "dares to descend into depth" and open up the way for subsequent depth psychology.[42] Jung's frequent claims that Nietzsche "[fell] into the materialist mistake" confirm his misunderstanding of the idea of will to power. Body and soul for Nietzsche are composed of drives, which as will to power are "forces" rather than "stuff,"[43] so that his experimental philosophy undercuts the distinction between materialism and idealism.

Jung appears to have forgotten that he once cited with approval[44] Nietzsche's account of the inspiration thanks to which he wrote *Zarathustra*: "One hears, one does not seek; one takes, one does not ask who gives; a thought flashes up like lightning, with necessity, formed without hesitation—I never had any choice in the matter." Such remarks clearly reflect an encounter with "an independent, autonomous spiritual agency." The consequences of this forgetting for Jung's reading of *Zarathustra* are dire, since the *idée fixe* concerning Nietzsche's lack of psychological discrimination prevents him from understanding the roles played by the wide variety of figures (personifications) that populate this most poetic of philosophical texts.

The source of Nietzsche's problems, according to Jung, is that he (Nietzsche, the flesh-and-blood thinker) identifies with Zarathustra (an archetypal figure). In a discussion of "Zarathustra's Prologue" Jung presents what he calls a *soreites syllogismos*, in which he purports to demonstrate the identities between Nietzsche and the rope-dancer and Zarathustra and the jester and the *daimonion* and Zarathustra's shadows.[45] The conclusion he draws from this amazing display of pseudological legerdemain is that "Nietzsche the man is equal to Zarathustra. . . . This whole complication starts from the fact that Nietzsche is identical with Zarathustra."[46] Well, *Jung's* whole complication starts here—since these identifications (perhaps because they're the fruits of such a large investment of reasoning power on Jung's part) bring in their train a series of others: Zarathustra with the anima (!), Zarathustra with "the Superman," the ego with the self, the superman with a god, and so forth. As anyone who approaches the text with due respect for its literary and philosophical merits knows, the imagery of *Zarathustra* is not only complex but above all precise—just as the images the psyche produces spontaneously in fantasy and dream are precise. So when Jung simply (or complexly) lumps together a number of figures that Nietzsche has taken care to distinguish, all hope for an illuminating reading of the text is lost. To take just one example: in "Zarathustra's Prologue" (sec. 3) the protagonist appears as one who is going to *teach* the doctrine of the *Übermensch*, and there is no textual justification for asserting that he *is*, or even becomes, the *Übermensch*. Jung's assumption of the identity of Nietzsche with Zarathustra and Zarathustra with the *Übermensch* as axiomatic premises for his "syllogism," taken in conjunction with his repeated citation of the verse in which Nietzsche describes how Zarathustra "became manifest as a second personality in himself," must count as one of the most perverse hermeneutic gestures in the history of textual interpretation.

IV

Jung, at least, is convinced by his own reasoning, since the next time he quotes the "one became two and Zarathustra passed by me" he claims that Nietzsche did *not* "realize" that Zarathustra was a figure distinct from himself: "He was identical."⁴⁷ What apparently leads Nietzsche not to understand what he himself writes about Zarathustra as "other" is his uncritical acceptance of the concept of the "I":

> He says "I," the ego consciousness, without clearly examining that concept of the "I." He never asks what the "I" is really, he has no psychological criticism. The moment he began to criticize it psychologically, he would see that the statement "I," or the expression "ego consciousness," is too limited, it is a mistaken concept: it is wrong.⁴⁸

It is true that in 1935 Nietzsche was not widely recognized as a consummate deflator of the importance of consciousness and destructor of the notion of the "I"; but one has to wonder where Jung's mind was wandering when he encountered those numerous passages in the published works where Nietzsche denigrates consciousness and argues that the "I" is a restrictive fiction, put together for the purpose of coping with practical life. All the way from his first book (in which "the 'I' of the lyric poet resounds from the abyss of Being" since his "I-ness is not the same as that of the waking, empirically real human being" [*BT* 5], and the Dionysian phenomenon involves "a giving up of the individual by entering into an other being" [*BT* 8]) to *Twilight of the Idols* (where he excoriates the Socratic ideal of "life [as] bright, cold, circumspect, conscious" [*TW* 2:5], mocks the "crude fetishism" of "reason" that "*projects* its faith in the I-substance onto all things" [*TW* 3:5], and claims with delight that the I has "become a fable, a fiction, a play on words" [*TW* 6:3]), Nietzsche argues for the preponderance of unconscious drives over the "surface" that is consciousness, and for analyses of the "synthetic concept" of the "I" into its component drives. It would be hard to think of anyone who accomplished a more deft critique of just how "limited" and "mistaken [a] concept" the "I" really is.

Jung sometimes expresses his criticisms of Nietzsche's psychological naivete in the same terms that Nietzsche himself used (to express the opposite):

> The Alpha and Omega of all the trouble with Nietzsche is of course that he is all the time identical with his figures, never separated from them. He has no psychological critique whatever and so he cannot give them their true value; he cannot conceive of a psychological existence that is not himself, not his consciousness.⁴⁹

In *The Birth of Tragedy* Nietzsche wrote:

> The poet is a poet only insofar as he sees himself surrounded by figures who live and act before him and into whose innermost being he sees. . . . If one is able constantly to be viewing a living play and to live surrounded by hosts of spirits, one will be a poet.[50]

Since Nietzsche was a poet as well as a philosopher, and knew himself to be one, it is difficult to doubt that he could "conceive of a psychological existence that is not himself"—especially when he explicitly characterizes the epic poet as one that is protected "by the mirror of seeming [*Schein*]" against "becoming one with and fused with his figures" (*BT 5*). It may well be that Nietzsche's eventual *Umnachtung*, in which he became "every name in history," consisted in a fusion with the figures of the archetypal imagination prompted by mental exhaustion: but Jung's claim that Nietzsche's psychology is vitiated by his inability to give his figures "their true value" is totally groundless.

At other times Jung accuses Nietzsche of being subject to "the materialistic and rationalistic attitude of his time, which naturally assumed that one's thoughts were oneself."[51] Again the texts of the antimaterialist and irrationalist Nietzsche say the opposite. As one of the more reflective thinkers in the Western tradition Nietzsche thought deeply about thoughts, and the fruits of this thinking are expressed in an aphorism from 1879 that begins:

> Nothing is more difficult for the human being than to apprehend a thing impersonally: I mean to see in it just a thing and *not a person*. One may well ask whether it is possible at all for a human being to suspend the clockwork of his drive to imagine and create persons for even a moment. For he deals with *thoughts*—even the most abstract ones— as if they were individuals with whom one has to struggle or make friends, whom one has to tend, care for, and nourish.

Nietzsche was consistently impressed by the autonomy of thoughts and expressed this often in his writings, most notably in the famous dictum (which is said to have impressed Freud): "A thought comes when 'it' wants, and not when 'I' want. . . . It thinks [*Es denkt*]."[52] We see here, too, that Nietzsche "[took] the idea of a personification seriously" enough to doubt whether "the drive to imagine and create persons" can ever be suspended—let alone shut down altogether.

Since his schooldays at Pforta intellectual inquiry was worthwhile for Nietzsche only if it was infused with *personality*: it was the characters of his teachers, their presence as human beings, that animated for him the subjects they taught. And when he wrote about the first philosophers he came to admire he again emphasized the personal element: in the preface to *Philosophy in the Tragic Age of the Greeks* he proclaims his concern "to set into relief that part of each [philosophical] system that is a piece of *personality*," so as to bring to light "the great human being" behind the philosophy. One of the reasons Nietzsche's personality comes through so forcefully in his writings is precisely that they derive from his engaging his thoughts as persons. In an aphorism addressed to "those who are solitary" he writes: "If we do not respect the honor of other persons in our conversations with ourselves just as much as we do in public, we are not decent human beings." And how did he respect the honor of these persons he encountered in his solitude? Just the way Jung did in his relations with the personified complexes: by listening to what they had to say. In a letter written from the Engadine in 1883, while he was working on *Zarathustra*, Nietzsche wrote: "Oh, how much still lies hidden within me and wants to become word and form! It cannot possibly be sufficiently still and high and lonely around me, so that I can hear my innermost voices!"

Jung frequently criticizes Nietzsche for lapsing into a defeatist and pathological withdrawal from the real world. But he fails to appreciate that Nietzsche withdrew because he needed solitude in order to write, and that he needed to write rather than talk because he had learned that his contemporaries were not ready for what he had to say—which therefore had to be addressed through the written word to future generations. And Jung's *idée fixe* about Nietzsche's lack of self-awareness, together with his often reiterated prejudice to the effect that Nietzsche failed to face up to the "shadow" side of existence in its mundanest aspects, further confounds his understanding of Nietzsche's personal psychology as well as his reading of *Zarathustra*. Let one example stand for the numerous instances of this syndrome throughout the seminars. In a discussion of the "The Return Home"[53] Jung talks about Zarathustra's saying that one should live on mountains in order to escape the bad vapors of the marshes.

> Again [Nietzsche] makes the attempt to lift himself up out of the marsh of other people. He says,
> "With blessed nostrils do I again breathe mountain-freedom. Freed at last is my nose from the smell of all human hubbub!"
> That is his extraordinary illusion. He thinks when he is climbing up to the Engadine, filling his lungs with the wonderful mountain air, that he has gotten rid of himself. But he carries all the collective hubbub with him up to the mountains, because he himself is the ordinary man.[54]

Jung here follows his usual practice of substituting "Nietzsche" for "Zarathustra," which in this case is more misleading than ever. This is not to deny that it can be illuminating to consider the autobiographical background to *Zarathustra*; but to identify the author with the protagonist *tout court* vitiates the interpretation of any text with a dramatic element to it.

But even Zarathustra is aware of the "collective hubbub" within him, as is clear from the briefest reflection on a major theme in the text concerning the connections between contempt for the rabble and self-love. In the chapter "On the Rabble" Zarathustra says that the deepest source of his nausea and disgust—"the mouthful on which I choked the most"—is the knowledge that life *requires* even the rabble.[55] The necessity of the meanest and basest features of existence is the hardest thing for Zarathustra to swallow—and affirm as desirable. But although Jung discusses this chapter as well as the intimation of the idea of eternal recurrence in "On the Vision and the Enigma,"[56] where the themes of nausea and choking mouthfuls recur in the image of the shepherd into whose throat the black snake has crawled, he fails to connect them and thus completely misinterprets the shepherd passage. The same imagery is echoed in "The Convalescent" when Zarathustra explains to his animals that what had crawled into his throat and choked him was "the great disgust with the human," the thought of "the eternal recurrence of even the smallest."[57] And the major way Zarathustra comes to terms with this thought, in such a way that he can affirm life in its totality, is through learning how to *love himself*. This the most difficult of tasks because it involves self-knowledge; and since the self comprises much that is worthy of contempt, loving oneself entails despising oneself as well as knowing oneself—"loving with great love and with great contempt!"

And if Zarathustra is cognizant of the despicable features of the human soul, Nietzsche is equally aware of their presence within himself. In an unpublished note that begins with the exclamation "Our relationship to ourselves!" Nietzsche writes:

> We have transposed "society" into ourselves, in miniature, and to retreat into oneself is thus no kind of flight from society, but an often painful dreaming-on and interpreting of our experiences. . . . We take into ourselves not only God but all beings that we recognize, even without the names. . . . Olives and stones have become a part of us: the stock exchange and the newspaper as well. . . . People who live alone, as long as they do not go under, develop themselves into societies.

Nietzsche was by no means under the illusion that up in the mountains of the Engadine he had "gotten rid of himself": indeed it's hard to think of any finer emblems for "the collective hubbub" than the stock exchange and the newspaper.

V

One of the first identifications Jung made between the major figures in *Zarathustra* was that between Zarathustra and the anima,[58] which refers to the image of the feminine in a man's psyche, and to the image of the soul in the human being more generally. Jung's prejudice that Nietzsche didn't have much of a relation to the feminine gives him the idea that the anima won't figure significantly in the text of *Zarathustra*.

> It all comes from the fact that we have no anima in *Zarathustra*. Only very near the end anima figures appear in the erotic poem "Unter Töchtern der Wüste." . . . It takes the whole development of *Zarathustra* to call Nietzsche's attention to the fact that there is an anima.[59]

This assertion will strike the reader familiar with *Zarathustra* as strange, in view of the importance of several feminine figures in the text aside from the Daughters of the Desert.

It seems stranger still when, on the appearance of the first group of feminine figures, in "The Dancing Song" (Z II:10), Jung immediately characterizes them as "a multiplicity of animae."[60] And when Zarathustra sings his song about his relations with Life, Jung appropriately identifies that as an anima figure too.[61] But though he sees that Zarathustra's "wild Wisdom" is another anima figure, his tendency to collapse all interesting multiplicities into unities leads him to say that Zarathustra is now *simply calling life "his wild wisdom"*[62]—when the song makes it perfectly clear that Zarathustra is dealing with two separate feminine figures. And to compound the confusion Jung takes the line "For thus do things stand with us three" to be referring to "Zarathustra, Nietzsche, and the anima"[63] rather than Zarathustra, Life, and his Wisdom. Finally, on "The Stillest Hour" (Z II:22), Jung says of that enigmatic figure—appropriately, again—"That is the anima, of course."[64] So it would seem, contrary to Jung's initial assertion, that by the end of the first half of *Zarathustra* its author is quite aware of "the fact that there is an anima."

On the credit side of this issue, Jung does recognize the prefiguration of Zarathustra's wild wisdom, in the form of the lioness that appears at the end of "The Child with the Mirror" (Z II:1), as "a symbol of the anima because it is nature."[65] And he also perceptively associates the lioness with the lion of the "Three Transformations" (Z I:1) and the figure of Dionysus: "He is the spirit of the lion, and out of that spirit the child is born—for the time being only a lion cub, something absolutely undefined which needs development and care."[66]

Lastly, let us turn briefly to the idea of eternal recurrence. Although Nietzsche regarded it as the central idea of *Zarathustra* and his "most affirmative" thought, it receives scant treatment in Jung's seminars. In the discussion of the chapter "On Redemption" (Z II:20), where Zarathustra says that will to power has to learn *das Zurückwollen*—willing backward and wanting things back again—there is no indication that anyone in the seminar sees that the issue is the will to eternal recurrence as the most affirmative (manifestation of) will to power.[67] And when they arrive at "The Vision and the Enigma" Jung ignores the dramatic narrative completely and misinterprets the vision as a memory of a prior ascent, a memory that comes to Zarathustra while he is still in the abyss alluded to in the previous chapter.[68] And although Jung acknowledges that the dwarf (who he fails to mention is also "half-mole") represents "the spirit of gravity," he ignores what this spirit stands for in the text up to that point: the rationalist and Christian traditions from Plato to Schopenhauer. So when the dwarf contemptuously mutters, "All that is straight is a lie. All truth is crooked, time itself is a circle" (Z III:2 §2), Jung fails to hear the echoes of earlier theological allusions, and—with breathtaking disregard of one of *Zarathustra's* major themes—he misinterprets the dwarf as "Zarathustra's higher mind" and "the originator of the idea" of eternal return.[69] This is to reduce—*ad absurdum*—the great thought that Nietzsche proposes in place of traditional Western metaphysics to a mere modification of traditional ontotheology.

Apparently unaware of the relation of this presentation of the idea of eternal recurrence to its initial intimation in the aphorism entitled "The Greatest Weight,"[70] Jung misreads Nietzsche as saying that the moment, *der Augenblick*, is ordinary—"an ordinary day, an ordinary hour, so why bother about it?"—and accuses him of failing and "fearing" to realize "what might be contained in the unique moment . . . and why it is unique."[71] But the whole point of the prospect of eternal recurrence is that it places the greatest weight on our every choice and action, in such a way that the moment is far from ordinary but rather a locus of crucial decision, since whatever I choose I'll be doing eternities of times again, the same way—so it had better be the right way, and a choice coming from my true self (rather than from a socially conformed "I") for once, if possible. So even if the seminars hadn't been interrupted it is doubtful whether anything interesting would have been said about eternal recurrence—especially since Jung fails to realize the need to read *Zarathustra* in the context of Nietzsche's other works from that period.

For an admirer of Nietzsche's thought who respects Jung for the breadth of his learning and his contributions to psychology, the latter's treatment of Nietzsche overall is bound to engender puzzlement. The misinterpretations of the philosophical ideas one can explain by recalling that Jung wasn't a philosopher, but the misconceptions concerning

Nietzsche's life and character are a different matter. It is simply presumptuous of Jung to pronounce on Nietzsche's character on the basis of gossip gleaned during his time in Basel rather than the biographical information available by the time of the *Zarathustra* seminars. At first it may seem that condemnations such as the following are merely occasional off-the-cuff remarks: "If you say [Nietzsche] was just a poor lunatic, that his brain was rotting away and decayed, you are right, that is perfectly true."[72] But such aspersions become more frequent as the seminar progresses and Jung's irritation increases:

> [Nietzsche was in reality] a neurotic, a poor devil who suffered from migraine and a bad digestion, and had such bad eyes that he could read very little and was forced to give up his academic career. . . . All that contributed to the most beautiful inferiority complex you can imagine.[73]

Jung frequently mentions, in both the seminar transcripts and his other writings, that irritation is a prime indication that some kind of projection is taking place. In fact he talks of the connection between uncontrolled emotion and projection just before declaring himself to be profoundly irritated by Nietzsche's psychological obtuseness.

> It is awfully curious that Nietzsche, a highly intelligent man, had not a scientific mind. . . . That is the most unspeakably foolish and irritating way in which he screws himself into his madness, an awful fatality. . . . And the fatality does not consist of anything tragic or great; it consists of a lack of intelligence, the lack of a scientific and philosophical attitude.[74]

It is hard to imagine reading the texts of Nietzsche that Jung read, and not seeing that it was precisely his "scientific" mind that allowed him to accomplish such a trenchant critique of Western culture. But it is easier if one recalls Jung's own complex with regard to the scientific status of his own psychological theories. And perhaps similar considerations apply to Jung's characterization of Nietzsche as "a man who received a sort of revelation, yet in a mind that was clouded, an understanding which was not quite competent, so he was unable to realize the meaning of his own words."[75] A telling contrast with Freud's high estimation of Nietzsche's degree of self-understanding.

Jung's dismissal of Nietzsche's ideas on the basis of his defective personality would be less interesting if it weren't for the irony that it's precisely on those topics where Jung sees the worst failings (the acknowledgment of autonomous personal agencies in the psyche other than the I) that Nietzsche most importantly anticipates Jung's own ideas. This is not to suggest that Jung appropriated these ideas from Nietzsche in a surreptitious manner, but rather that he was a careless reader of Nietzsche's works—so that his idea that Nietzsche suffered from bouts of cryptomnesia may be better applied (like many of his criticisms) to his own case.

NOTES

References to Nietzsche's works correspond to the abbreviations cited at the outset of this book. References to Jung will be to the volume and paragraph number of the *The Collected Works of C. G. Jung* (Princeton, 1970–77), and to the page numbers of *Memories, Dreams, Reflections* (New York, 1961) and the volume and page numbers of *Nietzsche's Zarathustra*, 2 vols. (Princeton, 1988)—abbreviated C, *MDR*, and *NZ* respectively.

1. *MDR* 95.
2. *MDR* 101–2.
3. *MDR* 33–34, 44–45.
4. *MDR* 102.
5. *MDR* 102.
6. *Z* II:18.
7. *EH* 3, "Z" 3.
8. *C* 1:184.
9. *C* 1:170.
10. *C* 1:172.
11. Chapter VII B.
12. *C* 5:26.
13. *HU* 13.
14. *GS* 54.
15. *C* 5:460.
16. *HU* P5.
17. *HU* 616.
18. *C* 7:35.
19. *C* 7:36.
20. *C* 7:38.
21. *C* 7:42.
22. *C* 6:225.
23. *C* 6:227.
24. *BT* 2.
25. *BT* 5.
26. *C* 6:231.
27. *MDR* 102–3.
28. *MDR* 103.
29. *MDR* 189.
30. *Z* III:12.
31. *NZ* 1:120.
32. *NZ* 1:745.

33. *NZ* 2:1347.
34. *NZ* 2:1300.
35. *NZ* 1:713.
36. *Z* I:4.
37. *NZ* 1:715.
38. *NZ* 2:1382.
39. *NZ* 1:9–10.
40. *EH* 3, "Z" 1.
41. *EH* 3.5.
42. *BGE* 23.
43. *BGE* 36.
44. *C* 1:184.
45. *NZ* 1:129–30.
46. *NZ* 1:131.
47. *NZ* 1:295.
48. *NZ* 1:350.
49. *NZ* 1:534.
50. *BT* 8.
51. *NZ* 1:543.
52. *BGE* 17.
53. *Z* III:9.
54. *NZ* 1:1422–3.
55. *Z* II:6.
56. *Z* III:2.
57. *Z* III:13, sec. 2.
58. *NZ* 1:31.
59. *NZ* 1:533.
60. *NZ* 2:1152.
61. *NZ* 2:1163.
62. *NZ* 2:1167.
63. *NZ* 2:1165.
64. *NZ* 2:1244.
65. *NZ* 2:871.
66. *NZ* 2:898.
67. *NZ* 1240–41.
68. *NZ* 2:1257.
69. *NZ* 2:1271–73.
70. *GS* 341.
71. *NZ* 2:1289.
72. *NZ* 1:696.
73. *NZ* 2:1213.
74. *NZ* 2:1237.
75. *NZ* 2:1489.

CHAPTER 12

Adler and Nietzsche

Ronald Lehrer

Alfred Adler (1870–1937) had his own ideas on matters of a medical, psychological, and psychosocial nature before he met Freud in 1902. As expressed, for example, in his thirty-one page monograph *Health Book for the Tailor Trade* (1898),[1] Adler was interested in the impact of working conditions on physical and mental health as well as other matters that pertained to public health issues. From early in his career he developed policy recommendations for preventive measures as well as for treatment. The thinker who had the greatest influence upon Adler in these early years was Marx.

There is no indication in this early period of Adler's life of anything like the depth of involvement with Nietzsche that characterizes the young adult years of Jung and Rank, or, for that matter, even Freud. Late in life Freud looked back to his young adulthood (to around the time of his mid-twenties), and reflected that "in my youth he [Nietzsche] signified a nobility to which I could not attain."[2] As a child, Jung heard talk of Nietzsche on the streets of Basel (where Nietzsche had taught). He was familiar with Nietzsche's writings by his early twenties, and he later wrote that he had approached the neuroses "from the side of psychiatry, prepared for modern psychology by Nietzsche."[3] He appeared to identify with Nietzsche even in his own personal descent into the unconscious, archetypal, and possible madness.[4] His fear of a fate like Nietzsche's led him to avoid Nietzsche for a while, but he also acknowledged the great stimulation he received from Nietzsche.[5] For Rank, Nietzsche was "his first inspiring teacher, 'a model, guide, and leader.'"[6] As was the case with Jung, Rank would refer to Nietzsche on many occasions in his writings, and Nietzsche's influence is evident throughout his work. Later in his life, Rank wrote to George Wilbur, who would become editor of *American Imago*: "Your discovery of Nietzsche's influence is quite correct, particularly in earlier days."[7] Although Adler was Rank's family physician and introduced him to Freud's *The Interpretation of Dreams* (lending him his own copy) during a period in which Rank was deeply involved with Nietzsche, there is no evidence of which I am aware indicating that Rank's passion for Nietzsche was picked up by Adler at the time.

NIETZSCHE AND THE EARLY ANALYSTS

We do, however, learn of Adler's great enthusiasm for Nietzsche's *On the Genealogy of Morals* at an April 1, 1908 meeting of the Vienna Psychoanalytic Society. According to the minutes, generally taken by Rank (who was first brought to the meetings by Adler in 1905), Adler mentioned that he had "once tried to establish a direct line from Schopenhauer, through Marx and Mach, to Freud." He stated that at that time he had omitted Nietzsche in his attempt, which probably reflected his limited involvement with Nietzsche earlier in his life.[8] At this meeting, Adler enthusiastically declared that "among all great philosophers . . . Nietzsche is closest to our way of thinking."[9] He also commented on Nietzsche's self-knowledge, as did Freud, and stated that "in Nietzsche's work, one finds almost on every page observations reminiscent of those we make in therapy, when the patient has come rather a long way and is capable of analyzing the undercurrents in his mind."[10] Regarding Nietzsche's achievement in the *Genealogy,* Adler suggested that "it was given to him to discover in all the manifold expressions of culture just that primal drive which has undergone a transformation in civilization, and which is then, in the mind of the philosopher, condensed as the ascetic ideal."[11]

Additional evidence that Adler had Nietzsche on his mind at this time is reflected in his presentation of a paper on April 26, 1908 in Salzburg at the first psychoanalytic congress and at a June 3 meeting of the society.[12] That paper was "The Aggression Drive in Life and in Neurosis" ("Der Aggressionstrieb im Leben und in der Neurose").[13] At the June presentation, Freud stated that "Adler's description of the instinctual life contains many valuable and correct remarks and observations," but he believed that "what Adler calls aggressive drive is our libido."[14] He further criticized Adler for confounding two things: "He lumps together the aggressive drive and sadism (sadism is a specific form of the aggressive drive which involves inflicting pain)."[15] Freud also noted that "for Adler, anxiety is a phase in which the transformed aggressive drive is turned against the subject."[16] Adler replied that "sadism and masochism are already complex phenomena in which sexuality and aggression are combined. Aggression need not always be cruel."[17] According to the minutes, the meeting concluded with "a long debate . . . on the identity of or difference between Adler's aggressive drive and our libido."[18]

In his published paper on the aggression drive,[19] Adler referred to an aggressive drive that can enter consciousness in more primitive or more sublimated forms. He wrote of aggression that can be displaced onto an alternate object or goal, and he raised the idea of transformation of instincts into their opposite. He also suggested that the aggressive drive may be turned against the subject.[20] Ellenberger pointed out that "these concepts . . . originated with Nietzsche."[21] Adler's aggressive drive, how- ever, was not merely a blind destructive drive pressing for discharge, but a superordinate drive that entailed a "confluence" of drives. In his study of Adler's life and thought, Edward Hoffman suggests that with this concept Adler was groping toward what we now might regard as a human propensity toward assertiveness. And according to Josef Rattner, this aggression drive was anchored in the total activity of the organism and existed in confluence with other drives to which it contributed energy for their activity.[22] Freud's disagreements with Adler over what he believed to be Adler's positing of an autonomous aggressive drive and minimizing of libidinal drives were among the factors that led to the split between the two men in 1911. At a later point, Jung would look back to this period and write:

> I saw Freud's psychology as, so to speak, an adroit move on the part of intellectual history, compensating for Nietzsche's deification of the power principle. The problem had obviously to be rephrased not as "Freud versus Adler" but "Freud versus Nietzsche." It was therefore, I thought, more than a domestic quarrel in the domain of psy- chopathology.[23]

At the October 28, 1908 meeting of the society, Nietzsche's *Ecce Homo* was discussed. There was talk of Nietzsche as a case, whether or not he should be considered to have been neurotic, and the possible impact on his mental makeup and writing of paresis, generally thought to be the cause of his mental collapse. Mention was again made of the fact that Nietzsche "anticipated a great deal" of Freud's teachings while Freud insisted that Nietzsche was not an influence on him. Freud also stated that "the indication that this work of Nietzsche is fully valid and to be taken seriously is the preservation of the mastery of form."[24]

There was discussion of Nietzsche's introspective capacities, and Freud suggested that "the degree of introspection achieved by Nietzsche had never been achieved by anyone, nor is it likely ever to be reached again."[25] Mention was made of Adler, at the previous meeting on Nietzsche, having stressed the fact that in paretics "psychic processes that had previously been masked become evident; what had been under the pressure of the censor emerges."[26] Adler did not reduce Nietzsche's great capacity for introspection to paresis. (To some extent, at this meeting Freud may have pathologized Nietzsche's introspective achievement, but he, too, did not reduce Nietzsche's capacity for introspection to paresis.) Rather, Adler suggested that the censorship in Nietzsche was different than it typically is in others; that is, it was weaker, and this weaker or less vigilant censorship allowed for his "considerable (capacity for) introspection."[27] The paresis then further weakened the censorship, allowing additional psychic processes to become evident. Adler also concluded, regarding this work, that "intelligence is preserved on Nietzsche's level."[28]

In attempting to understand the extent of Nietzsche's impact on Adler and other analysts during the next few years, one should keep in mind that Nietzsche's name and ideas would come up numerous times at meetings, lectures, and in analytic journal articles. The following instances include some of what Golomb[29] has found in this regard, as well as additional material, and indicates the involvement of the early analysts with Nietzsche. Additional instances could also have been noted.

At a November 1908 meeting, Wittels quotes Nietzsche. (We can note that it is in 1908 that Nietzsche is brought up by Freud's patient, the "Rat Man," who quoted Nietzsche to Freud: "'I did this,' says my Memory. 'I cannot have done this,' says my Pride and remains inexorable. In the end—Memory yields." Freud seems to have responded enthusiastically to the quotation. Adler would also refer to this aphorism in *The Neurotic Constitution* [1912].[30]) At a March 1909 meeting, Rank, while discussing the history of ethics, refers to the "hard, cruel Nietzsche." At meetings in January, April, and November 1910, Tausk, Oppenheim, and Hitschmann refer to Nietzsche. At a meeting in January 1911, there is a reading from *Daybreak* on the role of the instincts in dreamlife. In February 1912 Tausk gives a lecture, "Nietzsche as Psychoanalyst," to the Medical Society of Vienna (and it was reported in the *Zentralblatt*, an official journal of the analytic movement). (In 1926, Freud made the remarkable comment to an interviewer that "Nietzsche was one of the first psychoanalysts," and then went on to quote Zarathustra on pleasure wanting deep eternity.[31]) At a society meeting in March 1912, Gaston Rosenstein, discussing the necessity of including the battle of the instincts in understanding civilization, states that "Nietzsche postulates a hierarchy of the instincts for the individual who is to be considered a whole personality." In 1913 Nietzsche is mentioned by Winterstein in a paper published in *Imago* on psychoanalytic observations on the history of philosophy. (Winterstein had discussed the topic at a society meeting in December of 1912.)

Other early analysts, such as Otto Gross and Sabina Spielrein, can be mentioned. Gross was a brilliant and flamboyant figure who preached his own brand of extreme "Nietzschean" psychoanalysis to Jung and anyone else who would listen. Spielrein, in November of 1911, read part of her paper, "Destruction as the Cause of Coming into Being," at a society meeting.[32] (Adler was not present at the meeting.) During the discussion, Nietzsche's name was raised in connection with Fechner, and it was suggested that Nietzsche drew on Fechner in his development of the idea of the superman. The paper would be published the following year in the *Jahrbuch*. In this paper Spielrein explored the ramifications of a destruction drive (even referring to a death instinct in her talk) that is inherent in the sexual instinct, and its relationship to, among other things, creation, procreation, and the instability and potential dissolution of the ego. She applied such understanding to a diagnosis of Nietzsche.[33] These indications of the involvement of early analysts with Nietzsche, could be greatly expanded upon.

Lou Andreas-Salomé was another link between the early analysts, including Adler, and Nietzsche. Andreas-Salomé may have had her interest in things psychological stimulated along psychoanalytic lines by her friend, Poul Bjerre, a Swedish doctor who had been to a society meeting in January of 1911 and who would later write *The History and Practice of Psychanalysis*.[34] Apparently she spent a good deal of time with him in conversation in August and September of 1911, and then traveled with him to the third psychoanalytic congress held in Weimar.[35] It was at this congress that Andreas-Salomé met Freud and made her request to study psychoanalysis with him. (It was during this congress that Ernest Jones and Hanns Sachs called on Elisabeth Förster-Nietzsche and discussed with her the similarity of psychoanalytic ideas and certain ideas of her brother.[36])

It may be that at first Freud did not take Andreas-Salomé very seriously; toward the end of her life, she recalled that Freud "laughed at my impetuous request to study psychoanalysis with him."[37] In January of 1912 Freud and Jung wrote to one another regarding Andreas-Salomé, and Jung, perhaps reflecting her impact at the congress, referred to her as "Frau Lou Andreas-Salomé, of Weimar fame."[38] It is worth noting that she wanted to send Jung a paper on the topic of sublimation, a topic explored and developed by Nietzsche.

Andreas-Salomé did six months of preliminary study on her own and then visited Freud in Vienna. She recalled that he laughed even more heartily than at Weimar when she told him that she also wanted to work with Adler[39] (to whom she would write during the coming summer).

Apparently Freud agreed to this "on the condition that I wouldn't talk about him in the other camp or mention them in his presence."[40] In April of 1912 Freud would hear very positive things about Andreas-Salomé from no less respected a figure than Karl Abraham, who wrote that "I have come to know her very well and must admit that I have never before met with such deep and subtle understanding of analysis. She will visit Vienna this winter and would like to attend your meetings."[41] A few months later, Andreas-Salomé would be welcomed to the Vienna Society meetings and quickly develop a very close and enduring relationship with Freud.

When she came to Vienna in the fall of 1912, Andreas-Salomé did at first meet with Adler's group as well as Freud's. It is difficult to imagine this situation without wondering about Andreas-Salomé's role as the longed-for mother-wife who would bestow, upon the man who wins her, legitimacy as Nietzsche's son and true heir, or of the rivalry over who would displace Nietzsche as a father of the modern world who brings the new tablets of self-understanding. But it was no contest. Within a couple of months Andreas-Salomé knew she would eventually leave Adler and his group. Many months later, on August 12, 1913, she wrote to Adler regarding her reasons for doing so. In that letter she mentions Adler's ideas of a drive for power and male protest, and that Adler regards them as being based on a feeling of inferiority. She also notes that Adler looks for an organic basis for the feeling of inferiority. She appears to have two major objections to such ideas. First, that psychology follows its own course, with its own methods and means, so that "the organic as such neither explains nor determines the psychical for us; instead, the former portrays, so to speak, the latter (and vice versa)." And second, that she does not agree that "the feeling of inferiority, stemming from the organic, is a basic feeling in the psyche."[42] She acknowledges that one may strive for power for reasons of powerlessness, "but only because we understand the drive for power (or whatever we want to call it for the moment) as a synonym for life itself, which prevails everywhere, directly and indirectly, as the eternally-same."[43] (But see the 1910 statement of Adler's below on an initial assertive expansion of instinct before there is a sense of powerlessness.)

According to Adler's 1907 book, in its English translation known as *The Study of Organ Inferiority and Its Psychical Compensation: A Contribution to Clinical Medicine*,[44] organ inferiority, that is a weakened, less functional organ of an individual, can lead to physiological forms of compensation. Adler spoke of this and related ideas a number of times at society meetings. However, he increasingly emphasized that organ inferiority also leads to psychological reactions and that the origins of neurosis are found in these feelings and psychological processes that become enduring components of mental development. He found that feelings of inferiority can also be caused by purely psychosocial factors and that it is such feelings and psychological reactions that are most important even when organ inferiority is present. By 1910 and 1911 he was recognizing the importance of the subjective feelings of inferiority.[45] As Hoffman[46] has pointed out, Adler would later anticipate recent developments in the study of stress in his emphasis on the subjective reaction to stressful events: "It is not our *objective* experiences which bring us from the straight path of development, but our personal *attitude* and *evaluation* of events, and the *manner* in which we evaluate and weigh occurrences."[47]

We can, however, also consider that to the extent that Adler regarded organ inferiority, a sense of inferiority, and the attempt at compensation as fundamental aspects of the human condition, we can find Nietzsche among Adler's possible mentors. In *Human, All-Too-Human* we read that "in the case of the individual . . . rarely is a degeneration, a mutilation, even a vice and physical or moral damage in general without an advantage in some other direction." A few pages later, and even more to the point, Nietzsche writes that "it has already been remarked that . . . a serious deficiency in an organ offers the occasion for an uncommonly successful development of another organ, the reason being that it has to discharge not only its own function but another as well." In a note from *The Will to Power* Nietzsche writes that "a *deficiency*, a *degeneration*, can be of the highest utility in so far as it acts as a stimulant to other organs."[48] For Adler, the inferior organ itself may also eventually become strengthened as it becomes involved in attempts at compensation. As Rattner has pointed out, for Nietzsche as for Adler "organ inferiority . . . is not just a handicap; it may also be an opportunity, since the organism is equipped with possibilities for compensation and overcompensation."[49]

THE NEUROTIC CONSTITUTION

In 1911 a book appeared that greatly influenced Adler and helped provide him with a new conceptual framework that he utilized in his book, *The Neurotic Constitution*. The book was *The Philosophy of 'As if'* by Hans Vaihinger.[50] Vaihinger elaborated upon the idea of conceptual fictions (a concept that Andreas-Salomé believed Adler did not properly understand[51]). He pointed out that the idea of legal fictions had long existed, and that Bentham had pointed to fictions in other fields as well. While Vaihinger devotes a great deal of space to the ways in which Kant's thought is compatible with his orientation, he concludes the book with a section on Nietzsche, whom he clearly regards as an important influence.[52] (The names of Kant and Nietzsche are included in the full title of the German edition of the book. Preceding the chapter on Nietzsche is a section on F. A. Lange, who had a great impact on Nietzsche. While Andreas-Salomé discusses Adler and Vaihinger in her journal, she does not discuss Vaihinger's relationship to Nietzsche.)

Vaihinger's chapter on Nietzsche looks to that side of Nietzsche's thought that emphasizes that our beliefs and basic categories of understanding, such as our categories of logical thinking, are more or less useful fictions, necessary for survival and growth, but not to be regarded, in any traditional sense, as true representations of the real world. This is not meant to devalue regulative fictions, such as the fictions of logic, but to enable us to appreciate them for what they are, that is, fictional syntheses and unities. With such an appreciation of our condition, we may be able to recognize the necessity of illusion and avoid the damage that is caused when the character of truth or reality is erroneously ascribed to regulative fictions. In recognizing the necessity of such fictions as fictions, we may come to appreciate that this is not a condition about which to be in despair (which Nietzsche recognizes as a very real possibility), but a condition one can recognize as inherently creative and inventive. It is possible then to develop a will to illusion, a "will to seem," that takes joy in illusion. It is in this light that Vaihinger sees Nietzsche's perspectivism; that is, perspectives are formed through the capacity (and necessity) of our thought for narrowing, simplifying, inventing, and falsifying. Functioning from such perspectives is a basic condition of life and even, paradoxical as it may seem, of knowledge.

Adler utilizes such ideas in his suggestion that the neurotic person lives in a world of fictions. While utilizing fictions in various areas of life and functioning is necessary and provides us with the very means to solve what are for us very real problems, such as being able to take steps in the chaos of the world, the neurotic person comes to believe too literally in his or her fictions.

Adler, like Nietzsche, also emphasizes the importance of the future and goals for optimal growth, development, and functioning. The neurotic person's guiding goal or fictional final goal supports an attempt to provide overly limiting security and escape from life's challenges rather than the attempt to face and confront life's challenges and compensate in whatever ways may be possible. Setting such processes in motion is a sense of inferiority and powerlessness. A dangerous point is reached when a guiding fiction and related goals are confronted with a reality that does not, so to speak, correspond to them or fit with them or work with them. While the normal person is not bound to his fiction, is ready to dispense with it as an aid when it is no longer useful, and the psychotic person dogmatizes the fictional goal and asserts its actual completed realization, the neurotic person, as if "under the hypnotic influence of an imaginary life plan," clings to and attempts to realize or bring about the fictional goal and is "nailed to the cross of his fiction."[53]

It is also of interest that Nietzsche is known for his critique of traditional conceptual and moral polarities or binary oppositions, such as of pleasure-unpleasure, good-evil, reason-instinct, egoistic-unegoistic, true-false, and the like, and that Adler suggests that the neurotic's fictitious world is structured around pairs of opposing concepts, such as feelings of inferiority-exaltation, defeat-triumph, and masculine-feminine. For the neurotic individual, any indication of the feared side of the polarity acquires powerful potential to injure, as any indication of the desired side of the polarity acquires powerful potential to exalt. The neurotic person is, among other things, one who has become hypersensitive and overly reactive to such potential indications.

A type of perspectivist approach is utilized by Adler in his notions of guiding fictions, fictional final goals, life-plans, and the selectivity and even distortions (from an acceptable norm) of perception, memory, and logic that conform to the particular life-plan or strategy. Adler would later write of the ways in which early in life we develop "conceptions, perceptions, feelings, actions, and thoughts," and that "each of these belongs to the style of life created by the child." (Adler would also stress the importance for the person acting in a therapeutic capacity of entering into an individual's perspective, of being able to "see with his eyes, hear with his ears, and feel with his heart." He would have the therapist or educator "put yourself in his place.") The life-plan is also related to self-image and self-ideals and the ways in which we use memory to support such self-images and maintain self-consistency (or self-unity) and self-esteem.[54] Adler would have appreciated Nietzsche's comment in *Human, All-Too-Human*: "we want the image of ourself that shines upon us out of the past to deceive us and flatter our self-conceit—we are engaged continually on this self-deception." Rattner suggests that for Nietzsche and Adler "repression is a continuous refurbishing of the psyche, in order for it better to correspond to the 'guiding idea.'" Adler adds (in agreement with Nietzsche) that memory is utilized "for the purpose of constructing a bridge into the future where reside greatness, power, and satisfactions of all sorts."[55] It is such ideas of Adler that led J. H. Van den Berg to suggest that Adler was "the first to argue that the neurotic is not suffering from his past, he is creating it."[56]

Adler also makes use of the concept of fictions for his own system and explanations derived from it. As with Vaihinger, one's own system, theory, and explanations may be useful and help solve problems, but they are not to be regarded as objectively true and valid representations of the real world. One makes sense of the neurotic person's behavior by regarding him "as if" he were trying to reach or achieve a (fictional) goal. Adler appears to be somewhat ambivalent about the place of truth and reality in this scheme, and later he would be willing to regard well-supported findings as valid in a more traditional sense of the term.

Perhaps the most well-known link between Nietzsche and Adler's book of 1912 is Adler's introduction of Nietzsche's term, "will to power." Ansbacher[57] points out that in successive editions of this work, Adler adjusted his use of this term. In the first edition, Adler related the term to his idea of "masculine protest," that is, a striving to assert one's "masculine," active nature in the face of feelings of inferiority that are linked to (feared) "feminine" components of one's psyche. He appeared quite pleased to use Nietzsche's term as he stated that "Nietzsche's 'will to power' includes much of our understanding."[58] Also at about this time, in 1913, Adler described Nietzsche as "one of the soaring pillars of our art" of psychotherapy.[59] But when Adler was interpreted as endorsing the idea that the fundamental human drive is a drive for power, particularly power over others, he had second thoughts about the use of the term. When the second edition of the book appeared seven years after the first edition, Adler wrote of a life task that entails "the reduction of the striving for personal power and . . . the education toward the community."[60] Three years later, in the third edition of the book, Adler wrote that "the views of Individual Psychology demand the unconditional reduction of the striving for power and the development of social interest" (or, more correctly, "community feeling" [Gemein-schaftsgefühl]).[61] Certain Nietzschean members of Adler's group, such as Froeschel and Schrecker, would reject Adler's shift of emphasis and leave the group.[62]

Adler did not, however, reject Nietzsche; he only altered his emphasis. The striving for power was rooted in human nature but awakened by a sense of inferiority and inadequacy beginning in infancy as reflected in the desire for recognition and attempts to compel attention. Later in life, Adler would subsume the striving for power under the more basic striving toward overcoming. At one point toward the end of his life, he would write of two basic powers "in the structure of life" and "in the process of evolution." One of the powers pertained to social-relatedness and community feeling, but the other, probably older, power was "the striving to overcome" that was originally developed "for the victorious overcoming contact with the outside world."[63] However, Adler had proposed related ideas early in his career, such as at the meeting of November 2, 1910, when, speaking of an aggressive or assertive drive, he stated that "initially, the child shows a boundless expansion of instinct, which is useful insofar as the child learns in this way to 'feel out' the world."

However, "the initial, boundless expansion of instinct becomes obstructed by two factors: by the awakening of the sense of guilt, and by the fear of humiliation and disgrace."[64]

For Adler, as for Nietzsche, man was in essence not merely a reactive creature, an outcome of an algorithmically determined adaptation to his environment, but an active, creative being capable of modifying his environment. The striving for superiority that Adler wrote of had its foundation in a striving for overcoming that characterized even primordial life; a striving that entailed a "coercion to carry out a better adaptation" to the surrounding world. In addition, man, as an active and creative being, formed the stand he took on life and his lifestyle in Nietzschean fashion as "an artistic creation."[65]

Adler suggested that certain more extreme forms of exerting power over others may have their origins in a lack of adequate social feeling or a lack of more productive and constructive forms of power and mastery. Nietzsche did not suggest that one exercises more primitive forms of power over others due to weak social or community feeling, but he did recognize that one exercises power over others in benefiting them or hurting them, and that one may exercise power in the form of hurting others because of a lack of a more fundamental sense of power: "Benefiting and hurting others are ways of exercising one's power upon others . . . the state in which we hurt others . . . is a sign that we are still lacking power, or it shows a sense of frustration in the face of this poverty."[66] Adler drew on Nietzsche for his understanding of the many manifestations of striving for power, including ways in which weak and masochistic individuals utilize their helplessness and self-hatred in the service of glorifying themselves and infecting and subjugating others.

This striving to overcome is also related to Adler's Nietzschean concept of the "counterfoil" (*Gegenspieler*), that is, the person who is in some sense an obstacle, but as such is the person in relation to whom one exercises and measures one's strength. A person functioning in such a capacity in relation to us, is a needed resistance for the experience and feeling of increase of power to be possible.[67] Adler follows Nietzsche here, including, it would seem, Nietzsche's teachings about the potential value of enemies.

Needless to say, Adler's sympathies for socialism and democracy, his ideal of the "fellowman, whose law of movement is prescribed by the welfare and perfection of mankind," and his belief that "every individual is seized by this striving for perfection. . . . It is not at all necessary first to innoculate man with the desire to develop into superman, as the daring attempt of Nietzsche has maintained,"[68] move in directions that in important ways run contrary to traditional interpretations of what Nietzsche was getting at.[69] But while Adler regarded community feeling and its "action line" of social interest as helping basic needs and strivings, he eventually placed such strivings alongside of the even more primordial striving for overcoming. And even in regard to the power and value of community or social feeling, one finds ideas somewhat related to Adler's in Nietzsche:

> To feel sensations of pleasure on the basis of human relations on the whole makes men better; joy, pleasure, is enhanced when it is enjoyed together with others, it gives the individual security, makes him good-natured, banishes distrust and envy. . . . *Similar expressions of pleasure* awaken the fantasy of empathy, the feeling of being like something else: the same effect is produced by common sufferings, by experiencing . . . dangers, enemies in common. It is no doubt upon this that the oldest form of alliance is based: the sense of which is that to act together to ward off and dispose of a threatening displeasure is of utility to each individual. And thus the social instinct grows out of the feeling of pleasure.[70]

That a social "instinct" grows out of feelings of pleasure is not the same as social relatedness and feeling that are primary and are accompanied by pleasure. In addition, Nietzsche is known for having written of the necessity of a certain degree and kind of solitude for the strong, healthy, creative individual, and the dangers of the union-seeking herd for such individuals. Nevertheless, here Nietzsche demonstrates a keen awareness of the power, satisfactions, and benefits of the social instinct in terms related to ideas developed by Adler.[71] He also has a central place in his psychology for the value of sublimated forms of expression of our more primitive drives and affects, forms of expression that are typically social and cultural achievements. Adler raises important issues that continue to call for our attention pertaining to what may be optimal kinds of relationship between strivings toward overcoming (including in the forms of power and mastery) and social relatedness and community feeling.

CONCLUSION

In the late 1920s and 1930s, Adler had achieved great success, even popularity, in the United States and parts of Europe. But in recent decades his importance and influence have to a great extent been unacknowledged. One can consider his focus on the positive dimensions of strivings for power and mastery; his impetus to ego psychology (at an analytic society meeting, Freud criticized Adler with the judgment that "this is ego psychology, deepened by the knowledge of the psychology of the unconscious"[72]); his emphasis on systematically helping children develop confidence in their abilities to find effective solutions in the face of problems;

his groundbreaking work in schools (few educators are aware that many of our most recent developments in teaching, for example, the emphasis on cooperative learning and peer tutoring, were utilized by Adler and his colleagues); his explorations of the impact on development of birth order; his understanding of earliest memories not as screen memories but as reflections of and clues to our ongoing and less than fully conscious concerns in life; and much more that has found its way into more recent theory and practice. And while Nietzsche is generally acknowledged as an important source and resource of the existential psychotherapy tradition, there does not appear to be general awareness of Adler's influence on such figures as Rollo May and Viktor Frankl (as well as Carl Rogers and Abraham Maslow, whose work shares much with this tradition). Nor do many people seem to be aware that Adler's ideas on such matters as the importance of action as well as insight during the course of psychotherapy, the centrality to the therapeutic process of uncovering a person's fundamental life project, with the attending self-deceptions and security measures, and the necessity of guarding against the danger of any system or theory obscuring the unique individual ("general rules . . . should be regarded as nothing more than an aid to a preliminary illumination of the field of view in which the single individual can be found—or missed. Thus we . . . lay strong emphasis on flexibility and on empathy into nuances"[73]) were the likely source of some of the foundational principles of the existential tradition.

In conclusion, and to return to the early decades of modern depth psychology, Nietzsche was a prominent presence for a number of analysts who were associated with Freud. (As Golomb points out,[74] a number of analysts, and Adler would be included, appear to have utilized Nietzsche in their attempts to liberate themselves from Freud.) While some analysts and scholars loyal to Freud minimized the debt of psychoanalysis to thinkers such as Schopenhauer and Nietzsche, even as they documented the psychological insights of these thinkers,[75] there is another side of this story that to a great extent has been overlooked in recent years. It can, in fact, sometimes appear that Freud and his wayward "disciples," such as Adler, Jung, and Rank (and their respective followers), actually vied for the place of legitimate descendent and heir to Nietzsche. (There may also have been something going on along these lines between Freud and Thomas Mann.) One can catch what for many of us today may be a surprising glimpse of this state of affairs in the 1933 pamphlet by Crookshank, *Individual Psychology and Nietzsche*, in which the author early on wants his readers to be quite clear that "in spite of what the Freudians may say. . . . Adler is infinitely closer to Nietzsche than is Freud";[76] perhaps reminding us that Adler had been quite clear in 1908 that "Nietzsche is closest to our way of thinking."

NOTES

1. Alfred Adler, *Gesundheitsbuch für das Schneidergewerbe*, No. 5 of the series: *Wegeiser der Gewerbehygiene*, ed. G. Golebiewski (Berlin: Carl Henmanns, 1898).

2. Freud quoted in Ernst Jones *The Life and Work of Sigmund Freud*, 3 vols. (New York: Basic Books, 1953–57), 3:460.

3. Carl Jung, *Two Essays on Analytical Psychology. Collected Works of C. G. Jung*, ed. Herbert Read, Michael Fordham, and Gerhard Adler, trans. R. F. C. Hull (Princeton: Princeton University Press, 1966), 7:117–18. Jung added that in addition to Freud's views, "I also had before my eyes the growth of the views of Adler" (118).

4. See Herbert Lehman, "Jung Contra Freud/Nietzsche Contra Wagner." *International Review of Psychoanalysis* 13 (1986): 201–9.

5. See Henri F. Ellenberger, *The Discovery of the Unconscious: The History and Evolution of Dynamic Psychiatry* (New York: Basic Books, 1970), 278.

6. Dennis B. Klein, *Jewish Origins of the Psychoanalytic Movement* (New York: Praeger, 1981), 114.

7. Otto Rank quoted in Walter Kaufmann, *Freud, Adler, and Jung: Discovering the Mind, vol. 3* (New Brunswick, N.J.: Transaction Publishers, 1992 [1980]), 269.

8. Herman Nunberg and Ernst Federn (eds.), *Minutes of the Vienna Psychoanalytic Society*, vols. 1–4, trans. M. Nunberg (New York: International Universities Press, 1962–75), 1:358.

9. Ibid.

10. Ibid.

11. Ibid.

12. See ibid., 1:390, 1:406–10.

13. Adler, "Der Aggressionstrieb im Leben und in der Neurose." *Fortschritte der Medizin* 226 (1908): 577–84.

14. Nunberg and Federn, *Minutes*, 1: 408.

15. Ibid.

16. Ibid.

17. Ibid., 1: 409.

18. Ibid., 1: 410.

19. "Der Aggressionstrieb."

20. See Adler in *The Individual Psychology of Alfred Adler: A Systematic Presentation in Selections from His Writings*, ed. and annotated Heinz L. Ansbacher and Rowena R. Ansbacher (New York: Basic Books, 1956), 34–37.

21. Ellenberger, *Discovery*, 638.

22. See Edward Hoffman, *The Drive for Self: Alfred Adler and the Founding of Individual Psychology* (Reading, Mass.: Addison-Wesley, 1994), 61; Josef Rattner, "Alfred Adler und Friedrich Nietzsche," *Alfred Adler zu Ehren. Zu Seinem 50 Todesjahr (1937). Jahrbuch für Verstehende Tiefenpsychologie und Kulturanalyse* 6/7 (1986/87): 22–38. Dr. Rattner provided me with an English translation of the paper by John Burns.

23. Jung, *Memories, Dreams, Reflections,* recorded and ed. Aniela Jaffé, trans. Richard and Clara Winston, revised edition (New York: Vintage Books, 1965), 152.

24. Nunberg and Federn, *Minutes,* 2:30.

25. Ibid., 2:31–32.

26. Ibid., 2:33.

27. Ibid.

28. Ibid..

29. See Jacob Golomb, "Freudian Uses and Misuses of Nietzsche," *American Imago* 37.4 (Winter 1980): 371–85. The noted comments made at society meetings are found in Nunberg and Federn, *Minutes,* 2:176, 411, 491; 3:54; 4:84, 133–37. Tausk's lecture was reported in *Zentralblatt* 2 (1912): 546. Winterstein's paper, "Psychoanalytic Observations on the History of Philosophy," was published in *Imago* 2 (1913): 175–237.

30. Freud, "Notes upon a Case of Obsessional Neurosis" (1909), *The Standard Edition of the Complete Psychological Works of Sigmund Freud,* 24 vols., trans. and ed. James Strachey (London: Hogarth Press, 1953–74), 10:184. Adler, *The Neurotic Constitution,* trans. Bernard Glueck and John E. Lind (Freeport, N.Y.: Books for Libraries Press, 1972 [1926]), 61. First German edition: *Über den Nervösen Charakter: Grundzüge einer vergleichenden Individual-Psychologie und Psychotherapie* (Wiesbaden: Bergmann, 1912). The quote is from *Beyond Good and Evil,* sec. 68.

31. Freud, in George Sylvester Viereck, *Glimpses of the Great* (New York: The Macaulay Company, 1930), 35. See *SE* 21:168–69.

32. See Nunberg and Federn, *Minutes,* 3: 329–35.

33. Sabina Spielrein, "Die Destruktion als Urasche des Werdens," *Jarbuch für psychoanalytische and psychopoathologische Forschungen* 4 (1912): 465–503. In 1917 Jung would write to Spielrein that the drive orientation (Freud) and ego or "I" orientation (Adler) inhibit or repress each other. He suggests that the emphasis of the ego orientation on self-preservation has severed it from the real will to power, and he tells Spielrein that "you must read Adler or Nietzsche" (Sabina Spielrein, *Tagebuch einer heimlichen Symmetrie. Sabina Spielrein zwischen Jung und Freud,* ed. Aldo Carotenuto (Freiburg: Kore, Verlag Traute Hensch, 1986), 215. One might wonder if Jung meant to write "you must read Adler *on* Nietzsche." Jung wrote the word "oder" ("or") but could conceivably have meant to write "über," with the meaning of "on" or "concerning."

34. Poul Bjerre, *The History and Practice of Psychanalysis,* trans. Elizabeth N. Barrow (Boston: Richard G. Badger, 1916).

35. Ernst Pfeiffer, Notes to *Looking Back: Memoirs,* by Lou Andreas-Salomé, ed. Ernst Pfeiffer, trans. Breon Mitchell (New York: Paragon House, 1990 [1973, 1967, 1951]), 206.

36. See Ernest Jones, *The Life and Work of Sigmund Freud,* 3 vols. (New York: Basic Books, 1953–57), 2:86.

37. Andreas-Salomé, *Looking Back,* 103.

38. Jung in William McGuire (ed.), *The Freud/Jung Letters,* trans. Ralph Manheim and R. F. C. Hull (Princeton: Princeton University Press, 1974), 477.

39. Andreas-Salomé, *Looking Back*, 103.

40. Ibid.

41. Karl Abraham in Hilda C. Abraham and Ernst L. Freud (eds.), *A Psycho-Analytic Dialogue: The Letters of Sigmund Freud and Karl Abraham, 1907–1926*, trans. Bernard Marsh and Hilda C. Abraham (New York: Basic Books, 1965), 114.

42. Andreas-Salomé, Letter to Alfred Adler, August 12, 1913, in *Looking Back*, 208.

43. Ibid.

44. Adler, *Study of Organ Inferiority and Its Psychicial Compensation: A Contribution to Clinical Medicine*, trans. Smith Ely Jelliffe (New York: The Nervous and Mental Disease Publishing Company, 1917 [1907]); *Studie über Minderwertigkeit von Organen* (Vienna: Urban und Schwarzenberg, 1907).

45. See *The Individual Psychology of Alfred Adler*, 44.

46. See Hoffman, *The Drive for Self*, 199.

47. Adler, *Understanding Human Nature*, trans. Walter B. Wolfe (New York: Greenberg, 1927), 245.

48. Nietzsche, *Human, All Too Human*, trans. R. J. Hollingdale (New York: Cambridge University Press, 1986), 224, 231; *The Will to Power*, ed. Walter Kaufmann, trans. Walter Kaufmann and R. J. Hollingdale (New York: Random House, 1967), 647.

49. Rattner, "Adler und Nietzsche," 33.

50. Hans Vaihinger, *The Philosophy of 'As if': A System of the Theoretical, Practical and Religious Fictions of Mankindd*, trans. C. K. Ogden (New York: Harcourt, Brace and Co., 1925). First German edition: *Die Philosophie Des Als Ob. System der theoretischen, praktischen und religiösen Fiktionen der Menschheit auf Grund eines idealistischen Positivsmus. Mit einem Anhang über Kant und Nietzsche* (Berlin: Verlag von Reuther & Reichard, 1911).

51. Andreas-Salomé, *The Freud Journal of Lou Andreas-Salomé*, trans. Stanley A. Leavy (New York: Basic Books, 1964), 128.

52. Vaihinger, *Philosophy of 'As if,'* 328–40.

53. Adler, *The Neurotic Constitution*, 66–67.

54. Adler quoted in Hoffman, *The Drive for Self*, 261, 243.

55. Nietzsche, *Human*, 2 part 1, sec. 37; Rattner, "Adler und Nietzsche," 26; Adler, *The Individual Psychology of Alfred Adler*, 98.

56. J. H. Van den Berg, "Neurosis or Sociosis," in Harold Bloom, (ed.), *Sigmund Freud* (New York: Chelsea House, 1985), 57. Adler wrote that "the neurotic does not suffer from reminiscenses, he makes them" (*The Individual Psychology of Alfred Adler*, 292).

57. Heinz L. Ansbacher, "Adler's 'Striving for Power' in Relation to Nietzsche," *Journal of Individual Psychology* 28.1 (1972): 12–24.

58. Adler quoted in ibid., 12.

59. Adler quoted in ibid., 14.

60. Adler quoted in ibid., 13.

61. Adler quoted in Ansbacher, "Adler's 'Striving for Power,'" 13. That the term "Gemeinschaftsgefüehl" is better translated as "community feeling" rather than "social interest," was suggested to me by Heinz Ansbacher (personal

communication, August 25, 1997). Hoffman suggests that Adler's experience as an army physician during World War I and his response to the violence that continued in the aftermath of the war may have been important factors in his shift toward an emphasis on social or community feeling (see *Drive for Self*, 92–123).

62. See Hoffman, *The Drive for Self*, 101–2.

63. Adler, *The Individual Psychology of Alfred Adler*, 240.

64. Nunberg and Federn, *Minutes*, 3:45.

65. Adler, *Superiority and Social Interest: A Collection of Later Writings*, ed. Heinz L. Ansbacher and Rowena R. Ansbacher, 3rd revised edition (New York: W.W. Norton, 1979), 32; Adler, *Superiority and Social Interest*, 52.

66. Nietzsche, *The Gay Science*, trans. Walter Kaufmann (New York: Vintage Books, 1972 [1882; 2nd ed. 1887]), 13.

67. See Ellenberger, *Discovery of the Unconscious*, 576.

68. Adler, *Superiority and Social Interest*, 53, 31.

69. But see Lawrence J. Hatab, *A Nietzschean Defence of Democracy: An Experiment in Postmodern Politics* (Chicago: Open Court, 1995).

70. Nietzsche, *Human, All Too Human*, part 1, sec. 98.

71. See Josef Rattner, *Alfred Adler*, trans. Harry Zohn (New York: Frederick Ungar, 1983), 43–49.

72. Nunberg and Federn, *Minutes*, 3:147.

73. Adler, *The Individual Psychology of Alfred Adler*, 194–95. Such a point of view can allow that we can and should utilize general principles, but that we should attempt to carefully determine their most appropriate and unique application with each individual person.

74. See Golomb, "Freudian Uses and Misuses of Nietzsche."

75. See Israel Levine, *The Unconscious: An Introduction to Freudian Psychology* (New York: Macmillan, 1923), 11–45.

76. F. G. Crookshank, *Individual Psychology and Nietzsche*. Individual Psychology Pamphlets, No. 10 (London: The C.W. Daniel Company, 1933), 9. Many Freudian oriented analysts and scholars have minimized Freud's relationship to Nietzsche, but Walter Kaufmann, who held Freud in the highest regard, vociferously insisted that "in important ways Freud was closer to Nietzsche [than Adler]"; "Adler was less close to Nietzsche than Freud was" (*Freud, Adler, and Jung*, 226, 261). One wonders what the history of psychoanalysis might have been if Freudian oriented analysts, psychotherapists, and scholars had acknowledged Nietzsche as the "prompter" of psychoanalysis (see Erich Heller, "Observations about Psychoanalysis and Modern Literature,"in *In the Age of Prose* [New York: Cambridge University Press, 1984], 177–91).

CHAPTER 13

Reversing the Crease: Nietzsche's Influence on Otto Rank's Concept of Creative Will and the Birth of Individuality

Claude Barbre

> If I am simply on a walk, the rock face is an obstacle; if I am a painter, it is not.
>
> —Adam Phillips

In a recent conversation, a colleague told me that her son, a distinguished research biologist, had said, "since my mentor was the scientific son of Theodosius Dobzhansky, that must make me the grandson of Dobzhansky." Such a statement illustrates the profound influence a person can have on another to the extent that he or she feels intimately connected with that individual as part of a family of kindred spirits. But more importantly, the remark illustrates quite vividly what Heinz Kohut called the "selfobject" experience, that is, an intrapsychic phenomenon in which the presence or activity of an object, often another person, an idea, or a cause, helps to bring forth, guide, and sustain a person's sense of self. In our example, the ideas of Dobzhansky, twinned with the historical presence of a mentor, form a particular relationship in which the biologist feels nourished and supported by the object of his attachment and affection. Esther Menaker describes this relationship well when she notes that "through processes of internalization of the 'other' (object), the self grows; it forms its own structure out of the building blocks of the goals, ambitions, and ideals of the other, its chosen selfobject, by adding them to its original inherent self. This process goes on throughout life, changing in context and character according to the needs of given developmental phases."[1] Our biologist, then, underscores an important aspect of the growing and developing self—namely, just as we burgeon from a family tree rooted in our particular biological ground, we are also living members of a selfobject tree that is our psychological heritage and home.

The biologist's insight leads us to a particular selfobject tree, that of the philosopher-psychologist Otto Rank. For though this brilliant theorist was born into poverty and illness, exacerbated by social and family traumas, he was able to find vital nourishment and support from the ideas and presence of others who ultimately sustained and helped make possible the growth of his singular, creative genius. Two of the most nourishing selfobject experiences for Otto Rank were the ideas and writings of Friedrich Nietzsche, and a personal relationship with Sigmund Freud. His selfobject tree branches strongly from these two sources. In fact, if Freud—Rank's historical mentor—can be viewed as a surrogate father to him, as many have suggested,[2] we must not forget the impact of Friedrich Nietzsche's writings on Rank's life and work, almost equally paternal. In fact, we can say that as a part of Rank's selfobject tree Nietzsche grew and was grafted. As we shall see, especially in the light of Nietzsche's writing on will and creativity, Otto Rank indeed became the grandson of this great philosopher-poet, who was his Dobzhansky—and like a grandson who internalizes and idealizes the elder, he added his own special vision and theoretical differences to the ideas of Nietzsche whom Rank would call his "model, leader, and guide."[3]

Even before Rank discovered Nietzsche's work, his life evinced a striving toward self-becoming. Rank was born in 1884 into a poor family and a background deprived "economically, emotionally, culturally, and intellectually."[4] From an early age, Rank used his diary, his daybooks, much in the way that Rousseau did his *Confessions*, as an instrument for discerning and structuring a self. Rank's youthful diaries became his constant act of discernment, a creation of being through ecriture.[5] The first daybook entry, dated January 1, 1903, highlights his direct use of language as self-cure,[6] and betrays a Nietzschean indebtedness in regard to a desire for "self-observation" and "overcoming" the self:

> I begin this book for my own enlightenment. Before everything, I want to make progress in psychology. By that I understand not the professional definition and explanation of certain technical terms established by a few professors, but the comprehensive knowledge of mankind that explains the riddles of our thinking, acting, and speaking, and leads back to certain basic characteristics. For an approach to this idealistic goal, which only a few souls have tried to reach, self-observation is a prime essential and to that end I am making these notes. I am

attempting in them to fix passing moods, impressions, and feelings, to preserve the stripped-off layers that I have outgrown and in this way to keep a picture of my abandoned way of life, whereby if, in reading these notes later on I want to trace the inner connections and external incidents of my development, I shall have the material for it, namely, my overcome attitudes and viewpoints displayed in order before me.

From Rank's early daybook writings we can see the large influence of Nietzsche on his emotional and intellectual development. At the most desperate time in his life, working at a machine shop, he notes: "For a long time I had serious thoughts of suicide which, as Nietzsche says, helped me get past many a night and many a day. Then in reaction came a tremendous love of life and creative joy, which swept me into activity."[7] Indeed, Rank exclaims in a 1903 entry that there was a period "whose goal and climax was Friedrich Nietzsche," and he concludes that "to him I will set up a special memorial, for he was to me at once ideal leader and guide. . . . I virtually bathed in Nietzsche's genius, and got a charmed weather-tight and bullet-proof skin that should protect me against attacks from without as go along my way."[8] He makes a point of ending the last of his daybooks with a remark that reveals the philosopher's perspectives: "How much limitation still lies in the word 'Freedom.' The goal of humankind lies neither in their end nor in the highest specimens but in strife, struggle, excelling, overcoming," and concludes: "Whence would I have had my practical psychological knowledge if I had not been guided to by J.F.N. (Nietzsche)."[9] It is clear from these daybook entries that Rank consistently viewed his many experiences through a keen Nietzschean lens.

It was at this time he discovered Freud during one of his many excursions to the library, and with the help of Alfred Adler, who presented a monograph of Rank's writings on the artist to Freud. In October 1904, a quotation from Freud, in conjunction with a thematic reference from Nietzsche, appears without comment in some writing on the concept of time and death: "To represent time as a serpent is a contribution of genius, for first through it comes the ideas of time, together with that of end and death in the world. Serpent-paradise-Nietzsche."[10] Here we see Rank employing Freud's dream association method. Indeed, Rank was moved by psychoanalytic theories because he thought they explained the creativity of the artist with impressive insights; it was an area of study that was to occupy him throughout his life. Inspired by Nietzsche's focus on self-creation, the aesthetic dimension of the daybooks, especially his calligraphy, attests to Rank's early preoccupation with the psychology of creative activity and the personality of the artist. The artist would later symbolize for Rank a clear example of human striving for self-expression, growth, and change. He would reject "explanations" of the artist and his or her work in terms of causal psychological terms, and instead apply his perception of the operation of the creative process to the understanding of human psychology in general and to life overall. Rank would say explicitly: "Creativeness lies equally at the root of artistic production and of life experience."[11]

Rank's initial appointments of himself as artist widened into his first written work, Der Kunstler (The Artist), which eventually brought him to Freud's attention. Freud recognized in this twenty-one-year-old a creative will that prevailed over the cultural and emotional poverty of his background. Rank saw in Freud a mentoring positive paternal presence and kindred spirit. Yet, Rank's explorative mind often seemed to find new material in the increasingly mapped terrain of psychoanalysis. Exemplifying a typical trait of Rank's, he sought to bring his readings of psychoanalysis into his own language and idiom when writing Der Kunstler, using the new-found theories to explore the creative forces of the artistic personality by employing the word "artist" much as Freud did with the word "sexuality."[12] The burgeoning emphasis on the spontaneous growth of the self, and the undetermined potentialities of the psyche became for Rank the expression of will in theory and in life.

Reading Der Kunstler, Freud was so impressed with the twenty-one-year-old writer, that he sent for Rank and encouraged him to complete his education at the university, ensuring his financial ability to do so by making him the secretary of the Psychoanalytic Society, the first paid position in the movement. From his relationship to Freud, as in effect a foster son, Rank began to work with Freud in many ways. Der Kunstler, the first psychoanalytic work not written by Freud, was followed by The Myth of the Birth of the Hero, which included a section on family romance written by Freud. As Robert Kramer notes, "For every edition of The Interpretation of Dreams since 1911, Rank helped Freud revise, word by word, every line of his case celebre of self-analysis."[13] In 1914, Freud asked Rank to contribute two chapters on literature and myth to The Interpretation of Dreams, resulting in Rank's name appearing just below Freud's on the title page. Kramer captures well the close emotional relationship with Freud when he notes:

> He dined Wednesdays with Professor and his family at Berggasse 19 before meetings of the Vienna Psychoanalytic Society, over which Rank, now vice-president, presided in Freud's frequent absences. The youngest and freshest of the Committee members, he held a unique position in the nucleus of the secret ring: Freud cosigned Rank's circular letters to the Committee, giving them an imprimatur the others did not enjoy. . . . Summing up Rank's vital role during these years, Hanns Sachs described him, simply as Freud's Doppelganger, his shadow: "Lord Everything Else."[14]

During Rank's deep involvement with the psychoanalytic movement, Nietzsche's influence is often cited and developed by him. In the
minutes of 1908–9, for example, the development can be traced through
a number of references to Nietzsche, often culminating in gentle challenges to Freud, suggesting the growth of a new self-reliance. Despite
Rank's remark at one gathering, that "the sadistic instinct (masochistic)
and its suppression play the chief role in Nietzsche's life"—a clear
attempt to fit his thoughts into psychoanalytic terminology—he concludes by saying about the philosopher "that he explored not the external world, as did other philosophers, but himself reveals a development
reversing the earlier transfer from within onto the external world."[15] In
this remark is Rank's thinking that human knowledge is the product of
subjective understanding, which eventually led him to challenge a deter-
ministic point of view in psychology.

As much as Rank admired Freud's work and company, growing differences between the two were evident in their view of human growth
and development. Since the time of *Der Kunstler*, Rank, influenced by
Nietzsche's writing on the "new psychologist," had thought of the ego
not as a derivative of the drives or a byproduct of frustration and failed
gratification as understood by Freud, but as a given primary self that
strives to acquire and accomplish the building blocks necessary for its
own growth and development. He also realized that the expression of
this striving, the creative will, is accompanied by anxiety since it involves
a separation of that self from the oneness with which life began. An ego
theory of motivation was advanced. In addition, with Ferenczi in *The
Development of Psychoanalysis* (1923) Rank championed the living and
reliving of affective experience in the therapeutic session, rejecting the
criticism of the Berlin school that maintained that repetition is predominately a form of resistance. Both men emphasized not only the experiential phenomenon of the therapeutic experience but also the viability of
action and repetition over verbal memory.

The Development of Psychoanalysis anticipates Rank's lifelong
emphasis on the curative effect of emotional experience (*Erlebnis*) over
intellectual understanding (*Einsicht*). Robert Kramer puts it well: "It is
not the infantile past but the living present—the *Erlebnis* of one's own
difference, the consciousness of living, with all its painful feeling, thinking, and acting—that the patient denies, forgets, or wishes to escape. For
Rank, difference is the *Erlebnis* that the patient has never before been
willing to accept, fully and consciously, without feeling overwhelmed by
Angst or guilt."[16] As Kramer intimates here, Rank believed that neurosis
is the result of an individual's inability to affirm his own difference, his
or her own unique idiom given from birth, and thus evinces a failure in
creativity rather than in sexuality, as Freud saw it. Indeed, as Menaker

points out, "Otto Rank has sometimes been called a philosophical psychologist for his theories did not grow initially or primarily out of a concern with therapy, but rather out of a preoccupation with the meaning of life."[17]

Intrigued with his realization that willing leads to guilt, Rank began to search for the origins of anxiety, which he thought he found in the experience of birth. An attempt to conform his original thoughts to Freud's biological determinism influenced the work that is usually immediately associated with his name, *The Trauma of Birth*. In it he considered the initial physiological separation from the mother as creating an anxiety-producing experience that becomes the prototype of future anxiety. Rank would later depart from this literal interpretation, suggesting that the birth experience is a metaphor for the struggle for psychological separation and self-discovery. Although Freud was at first pleased with Rank's efforts, the emphasis on the mother-child interaction as primary clashed with Freud's theory of the Oedipus complex and castration anxiety, for "by claiming that the ambivalent pre-Oedipal relationship between mother and child is the heart of transference, he thereby relegated fear and love of the Oedipal father to a secondary place."[18] Up to this time psychoanalytic understanding of human psychology had been predominantly patrocentric, and the theory of anxiety focused for the most part on the idea of castration anxiety. Rank's creative act of writing *The Trauma of Birth* was construed as a challenge to the libido theory itself. Eventually, Rank's modification of theory and therapeutic procedure (later developed in *Will Therapy, Truth and Reality, Art and Artist, Beyond Psychology*) contributed to his break with Freud, which came in 1926, and to his dismissal from the American Psychoanalytic Association in 1930. By the time of his death in New York in 1939, Rank had contributed extensively to the study of the role of creativity, the meaning of birth and separation, the fear of mortality and the wish for immortality, and the nature of the will.[19]

Nietzsche's writing on will and self-creation demonstrates the philosophical roots of Rank's many theories, especially in light of his "will therapy." Rank no doubt had Nietzsche in mind when he remarked that "psychotherapy does not have to be ashamed of its philosophic character, if only it is in a position to give the sufferer the philosophy that he needs, namely, faith in himself."[20] In *Will Therapy* Rank cites Kant about this vision: "You will learn from me not philosophy but to philosophize, not thoughts to be imitated but to think."[21] For Rank, this philosophic attitude became his therapeutic aim: that truth is not static nor is it the expression of universal absolutes; nor can it be confined to a given tenet except momentarily. Following Nietzsche, Rank stressed that truth is as variable as the infinite variety of individuals who strive to express and perpetuate themselves creatively through the psychological birth of innumerable unique selves; and this striving dynamic emanates from the force of life itself, the will.

Nietzsche is held by Rank to be the "first psychologist" because of his philosopher's affirmation of the will in human life, seeing it as a positive force rather than denying it as inordinately negative. According to Rank, the study of the human psyche is the study of the individual's relation to and expression of his natural will.[22] Rank resonated strongly with Nietzsche's attempt to free human psychology from its tendency to become confined to moral absolutes by questioning the *a priori* acceptance by Western society of the moral judgment of the will as evil. He differed strongly with Freud's "making evil" of the will,[23] returning to Nietzsche's insistence that the will to power manifests itself in humans as the primary psychological explanation or motivating force behind all of our actions. However, although he would suggest that Nietzsche freed philosophy and psychology from "the distorting prism of morality," he would quickly add that Nietzsche's emphasis on the birth of the individual overlooked "the deep need in the human being for just that kind of morality."[24]

Despite his differences with Nietzsche, Rank would echo the philosopher's clarion critique of the reductionistic tendencies of Western moral valuation of human nature. As Nancy Seif points out, this kinship to Nietzsche would be most evident in his concern that psychoanalysis was, in fact "a covert moralistic 'philosophy' or ideology (terms which he uses interchangeably) disguised as an objective, logical science."[25] Rank would insist that a scientific psychology founded in unquestionable ideology resembled a negative morality (not unlike Nietzsche's notions of passive nihilism) that undermines the freedom and expression of creative inquiry. As he noted in his later work (1941), "that Freud's psychology did not even permit individuals of the same race and social background to deviate from the accepted type led me beyond these differences in psychologies to a psychology of difference."[26]

One hears Nietzsche's influence in Rank's critique of scientific psychology's claims to hold the key toward assessing objective truth, in light of its devaluing of the affirming character of the will. As Rank stressed, "The individual ego is the temporal representative of the cosmic primal force—the *strength* of this force represented in the individual we call the will."[27] Rank's connection of will to birth is anticipated by Nietzsche's remark that the will "is the womb of all ideal and imaginative phenomena [and has] also brought to light an abundance of strange new beauty and affirmation and perhaps beauty itself."[28] By connecting the will to cosmic origins, Rank is claiming that human psychic life is governed by the same forces that initiate life on a biological level. This

echoes Nietzsche's remark that "life . . . is specifically a will to the accumulation of force . . . nothing wants to preserve itself, everything is to
be added and accumulated."[29] However, as Nathan Oaklander suggests,
Nietzsche underscores that "the really fundamental instinct of life aims
at the expansion of power, and, wishing for that, frequently risks and
even sacrifices self-preservation."[30] Rank would draw from Nietzsche's
notion that will is a striving for difference, a force that pushes us toward
distinction and the discovery of our own unique expressions of life. For
Rank as for Nietzsche, will implies self-realization of the individual in
the fullest sense for it requires the courageous living out of the individual's potentialities in his or her own particular existence. Will is an ontological category, an inseparable aspect of being, not just a mechanism of
aggression or competition in psychological perspectives.[31]

For Nietzsche, power in regard to will can be understood not as a
drive to inflict suffering upon others or to act out one's wishes without
regard for the feelings or concerns of society. Rather, power is *potentia*,
life-force potential, and this is the fundamental drive toward human fulfillment. As Nietzsche maintains, the power harnessed toward hurting
others is actually a *lack of power*: "Certainly the state in which we hurt
others is rarely as agreeable, in an unadulterated way, as that in which
we benefit others; it is a sign that we are still lacking power."[32] Nietzsche stresses, then, that the aim of power is self-overcoming, the overcoming of obstacles that, in the end, are found within.[33] Rank moves in
a related direction when he states that in each of us there is an inner process toward growth and development that, while primal and organic at
first, expresses the life force that subsequently takes on conscious and
psychological structure.

Unlike Freud's structural model, Rank did not think that the child's
development depends upon ego responses torn between instinctual
forces and repressive environmental influences. Instead, Rank stressed
that through the responses and choices a person makes, he or she begins
to make use of both the inner and outer forces for his or her own growth
and development. To these organizing, volitional and choosing processes Rank ascribed the term "will," which he defined as

> an autonomous organizing force in the individual which does not rep-
> resent any particular biological impulse or social drive, but constitutes
> the creative expression of the total personality and distinguishes one
> individual from another. This individual will, as the united and bal-
> ancing force between impulses and inhibition, is the decisive psycho-
> logical factor in human behavior. Its duofold functioning as an impul-
> sive and likewise inhibiting force, accounts for the paradox that the
> will can manifest itself creatively or destructively, depending upon the
> individual's attitude toward himself and life in general.[34]

The balancing forces between impulse and inhibition illustrate a life dilemma that Rank explores throughout his work. Both impulse and inhibition are understood by Rank as initially organic, or present from birth as vital elements of the life process. But Rank is clear in arguing that these instinctual needs for gratification exist in more ways than in a physical sense; rather they depend on *psychosocial* influences as well, that is, our need for response requires social acceptance, affirmation, and attachment. To reflect the interaction between the self and the social world, between the psychological and social aspects of instinct, Rank used the term "impulse." On the other hand, Rank viewed inhibition as a controlling process that operates to guard the self from the destructive effects of uncontrolled instincts. Thus Rank saw this process as derived from inner forces as well as being a response to the external environment. He would view both impulse and inhibition as sources of will, the powerful collective, directing, and organizing force that seeks balance and control. In contrast to psychoanalysis, Rank maintained that this "dynamic dualism operates as a force of balance and not only as a source of conflict."[35]

Impulse and inhibition are opposite in effect but function simultaneously in interrelationships. For instance, the inhibition of certain impulses facilitates an even stronger expression of others. The will utilizes these polar processes, which remain distinct yet interactive in their "mediating, activating, and self-enhancing functions."[36] Thus, the will utilizes both inner forces to stabilize the self's relationship to the outside world as well as to reinforce and strengthen the developing self. Rank would add to this notion the view that "in the growth of the individual, therefore, we have to reckon with the triad *impulse, fear and will*. The dynamic relation, and interaction, of these factors determine the prevalent attitude of the individual toward himself and the world at any given moment; or, after achievement of some kind of balance, his actual type of temperament and character, which in turn determines his social behavior."[37] In the end, Rank rejected Freud's biological, psychological, and social determinism, which he felt denied the personality the very qualities that make our life human: autonomy, responsibility, and conscience.[38]

Rank's writing on impulse and inhibition and the interaction of both is reminiscent of Nietzsche's well-known distinction between and interconnectiveness of the Apollonian, or rational side, and the Dionysian, or passionate side of humanity. According to Nietzsche, a life lived according to a traditional, overrational detachment is not viable, but neither is a life of pure passion. The passions become life-affirming when they initiate us into action, even though they may hinder us from achieving our vision. Addressing a theme that Rank will take up, Nietzsche stresses that the most basic will of the spirit is to continually create a new self by surpassing the old, and this constant growth process, which is called life, in turn has the potential to create a certain type of person—the *overman*—an ideal type who confronts the paradoxical nature of freedom and value.[39] Rank draws from Nietzsche's tendency to use the language of typology with his depiction of the self-becoming person as "the artist, hero, or genius type."[40]

This Apollonian and Dionysian dance, the interaction of the new and the old, is echoed in Rank's view of the will phenomenon as presenting a basic paradox inherent in the life force: We require, indeed must have, closeness, connection and acceptance in order to survive. Yet self-actualization requires separation and differentiation. Hence, too much closeness can impede separateness and the birth of individuality, leading persons to fear the loss of their own distinctiveness necessary to the life development. This can create what Rank calls a "death fear" in regard to the stifling of individuation. However, the fear of death from too much separation is clear from the start of life. The movement toward independence gives rise then to a fear of abandonment, isolation, and destruction. Rank calls this fear of individuation "the life fear." We are caught between the desire for and fear of self-affirmation, and this becomes heightened as we grow to more developed cognitive capacities and notice consequences of our actions as well as the reaction of others. Rank, drawing from Nietzsche's view of will to power, thus asserts that the affirmation of one's difference is a manifestation of the will toward individuation that is expressed in a person's creative expressions. Nietzsche's descriptive images of the organic, growth dynamic capture Rank's thinking that the will originates in the drive for self-actualization that, in turn, introduces the human dilemmas of separation and relatedness.

Rank maintains that willing is always accompanied by a modicum of guilt because not only does it necessitate some aggression in the service of self-assertion, it also means that the individual must separate from the original mother-child empathic bond, and later the experience of the group and the security of collective affirmations. This presupposes an opposition of wills. Rank is clear that our differentiation includes both an identity with the "other" and an experience of separateness. Therein lies a dramatic human struggle: how to live out one's unique expression when it opposes the wishes and needs of another. Rank understood that relatedness is jeopardized by self-assertion, and guilt arises when separation creates a presumption of injury to the other's need for togetherness. He calls this dynamic "ethical guilt," an inner reaction from the fear of hurting the other through separation.

Early expressions of will emerge as counterwill, or negative will—

the oppositional "No's" of the child toward the primary caretakers. As autonomy is expressed, guilt ensues by virtue of the child's departure from the ethical relationship with the mother. By "ethical," Rank means the capacity for relatedness originally experienced when the child and mother were one. In fact, Rank sees guilt as an ethical problem, and in doing so contrasts "ethical" to "moral" connotations, instead referring to the inherent and inevitable relations of self to other. Thus, when we express our will, the empathic response may be charged with the assumption that the "other" does not wish us to separate. Guilt, then, is a natural consequence of the creative urge toward individuality, a byproduct of the experience of separateness. Succinctly put, "Guilt is a confession of the narcissistic origin both of self-assertion through separation and of empathy through union."[41] Thus, Rank adds to Nietzsche's view of guilt as a self-betrayal of individual potential by emphasizing that a source of guilt also includes a person's betrayal of his or her social nature.

Will assertion and its expression particularly as it acts to separate the self can be experienced by the growing child as "bad," especially when he or she discovers that difference leads to inevitable conflicts with individual and social expectations. But Rank, in accounting for the oppositionalism of the child, "differs from Freud in that he does not place the emphasis on a particular phase of libido development—in this case, the anal phase—but rather on the psychological birth of the child as an autonomous self."[42] As both Rank and Nietzsche agreed, will assertions, unfortunately, may be responded to with censure, condemnations, and oppression—implications that the expression of difference is wrong. Excessive guilt for having inclinations toward striving can become threatening to the child's need to grow, impeding a healthy balance of impulse and inhibition. Rank called this kind of guilt "social and moralistic guilt," and argued with the prevalent psychologies of his time that the then definition of resistance often held such value-laden connotations. One hears Nietzsche's call for the revaluation of values concerning good and evil in such a criticism, in particular in light of the vicissitudes of the will phenomenon. In contrast to negative will, Rank coined the term *creative will* to "express a spontaneous and freely arrived at act of will that is uniquely individual and is not predictable by any laws of causality."[43]

Despite the many references to Nietzsche, Rank never fully explores the psychological knowledge he credits to the philosopher. However, in Rank's views of negative will, counterwill and creative will, Nietzsche's genealogical critique of "ascetic values" and active and reactive forces resonates into contemporary psychological language. Nietzsche underscored that all values and their kindred practices or social institutions serve "value-creating powers," and the aim of genealogy is to assess these values and practices in terms of the value-creating powers that they serve and often hide. Nietzsche divides these value-creating powers into two dominant types, "active" and "reactive," and these in turn are designated as "master" and "slave" types, the foundation for his notions of master and slave moralities. Nietzsche suggests that one may look at culture as the hierarchical arrangement of these 'forces' and refers to such patterns as a "will to power." Following these types, the culture is a "negative will to power," or slave morality, when the reactive forces dominate; and an "affirmative will to power," or master morality, when the active forces win out.[44]

In order to illustrate how an "affirmative will to power" is transformed into a "negative will to power," Nietzsche employs the example of the "knightly aristocratic class" and the "priestly aristocratic class" in order to perform a genealogy of the value of "good and evil," which constitute the "ascetic values" that he considers characteristic of Western culture. In doing so, Nietzsche seeks to invert the "value equation" of our views of morality and realign what he considers to be the hierarchies of value-creating forces. This is done through the illustration of the priestly class who are intimidated by the physically powerful knights to the point that they must translate their "*ressentiment*" into a new value code that equates power with evil and the weak with goodness. In introducing these dynamic forces, Nietzsche is suggesting that there are degrees of strength of will. We can detect the dynamic of inversion and reaction in Rank's writing as it is developed in his psychology as the transformation of counterwill from its reactive characteristics to a creative, active will and self-affirming activity. We see a similar view that the will is an integrative and coordinating force with regard to the individual's internal dialectical strivings as manifest in the constant interplay of forces such as action-reaction, impulse and inhibition, and negative and creative will. Both Rank and Nietzsche understood these dialectics within the individual and between individuals and society as responsible for the social and personal history of human life and progress. Indeed, Rank was especially interested in Nietzsche's rejection of the will-as-evil, and his lifelong insistence that human will is the positive source of human potential and creativity became the cornerstone of his therapeutic philosophy.

Although Rank viewed Nietzsche as representing most clearly a "social and ethical reformer,"[45] he was often ambivalent about Nietzsche's overemphasis on the ideal person as amoral and morality as unnatural. Even as Rank was deeply affected by Nietzsche's views concerning the potential destructiveness of objective, moral standards on the creative striving of individuals, he was also critical of what he considered to be Nietzsche's disproportionate leanings toward individualistic efforts at the expense of humanity's natural tendencies toward the fulfillment of social needs. For instance, despite his resonance with Nietzsche's passionate call for the ideal human being to resist "social castration" of his creative life even in the face of condemnation and suffering, Rank pointed out the natural human need for some kind of faith and belief conviction. Even if the Judeo-Christian notions of God produced, as Nietzsche insisted, a "counter-concept of life,"[46] Rank warned that the loss of God threatened humanity with the loss of meaning, and his appreciation of the need for ideologies in regard to the natural development of the human collective and individual psyche remained at odds with Nietzsche's views. As Nancy Seif points out, Rank stressed that "in light of the glaring human dilemma and associated death fears, positive faith, on individual and social bases is the very capacity in man which allows him to create and even live."[47] Rank found that Nietzsche tended to overstress the individual's necessary detachment from society, and, in contrast, believed that our natural will strivings must be understood in the context of our natural proclivities toward others. "There is no I without a Thou," was Rank's response.[48]

Rank regarded Nietzsche as the first theorist to clarify the moral danger in every philosophizing and psychologizing. Such a recognition underscored Rank's own hermeneutical suspicion in the area of psychology, prompting a revaluation of therapeutic methods that he would develop into a critique of "the psychoanalytic cause." Tantamount in spirit to Nietzsche's criticism of "ascetic values," Rank would say, "We are all always far too theoretical and are inclined to think that knowledge alone makes us virtuous."[49] In fact, Rank shared in part with Nietzsche the contention that knowledge and its systems of causality, are interpretations open to interpretation. Nearly echoing Nietzsche verbatim, Rank says "I think we have to break through this vicious circle, but the only way I can see to do that is not with the general cry 'back to facts' that we have heard lately, because there are no facts. The 'facts' are interpretations, and it is with those that we have to deal. If we understand that they are interpretations, then we shall not be fooled by them."[50] However, as Seif reflects, the creatively willing person, which Rank terms the "artist type," will not simply "endure out of superhuman courage and vitality, the loneliness and terror of social exile [like Nietzsche], but will creatively produce manifestation of his own faith, his art, which will unite him with others again and help him cope with both the social (moral) and individual (ethical) judgments directed against his creative will."[51] Despite their differences, both Rank and Nietzsche encouraged in their own ways the rejection of so-called universal norms and moral absolutes where they obstructed the creative life, and "abhorred the moral judgment against individual will as evil and the related devaluation of those who are strong-willed, separate, and different."[52]

Throughout his writing, Rank would stress that a neurotic individual suffers from an inhibition in the ability to will. This inhibition Rank saw as largely the result of the interaction of original endowment with a primary environment that failed to affirm the will of the growing child. Simply put, the task of therapy is to address this developmental deficit in order to support and affirm the patient's will.

Let me illustrate the will dynamic as it is expressed in a brief case example. Terry, an eleven-year-old boy, was referred to me after attempting suicide by hanging. After several weeks in the hospital, he arrived at his first session with me after the suicide attempt. He declared that he did not want to be there, and nothing would change his mind. Each time I responded to him, he would shout "No!," walking around in circles, fist furled. He said he wanted to go and was leaving. My anxiety flared. Where would he go? Would he hurt himself again? How could I stop him? I blocked the door. I was determined to hold onto the "safety" of the therapeutic frame. Stepping back, he drew the blind of the window open and pulled the end of the cord to his neck, then let it fall. "I want to go," he said again.

It was at this point that I realized that the session was becoming more an attempt to allay my own anxieties rather than risk experiencing what Terry was trying to say to me. I was choosing an analytic stance that was in fact keeping Terry from not only leaving the room, but feeling understood as well. I could see quite vividly that my interventions were escalating Terry's imperative to get out, to escape the misattuned response he was experiencing from me. With the cord to his neck Terry was showing me the experience that led him to his suicide attempt. He was recreating the experience of feeling trapped and hopeless, while enacting the attempt to get out, to free himself by the only way he felt he could, through self-destruction.

I opened the door. He visibly calmed and looked at me. I stepped to the side, saying "Got any thoughts about where you want to go?" He responded, "Not really," not yet moving, "Just somewhere outside, just somewhere else." I looked toward the window, asking, "Mind if I come along?" He motioned toward the door. "Follow me," he said, and I followed him.

We went out into the front of the school and sat down on some steps. Some construction paper, abandoned no doubt by a class at recess, lay on one of the stairs. Terry said, "I want to show you something I can do." He took a piece of the colored paper, and began to fold it carefully, reversing the crease, and folding edges under like the process of origami. After about twenty creases he looked up at me as if to ask if I knew what he was making. I was not sure. "It's an airplane—but no ordinary paper plane," he said. He was right. After nearly thirty folds he finished the back wings and added a rudder by a deft tear in the middle.

"Will you show me how you did that?" I asked. "Sure" he said, "Sit down here and I'll walk you through it." We sat. As I followed his direction, tending to a fold, reversing the creases into frames and form, I realized we were sitting together, not in the crucible of angry silences and the ancient cycles of self-pity and repair; rather, we were creating. We were creating in a place beyond compliance and counterwill, in a shared world of life together; and I had become a maker of wings, and he my patient teacher and guide. When I had finished I looked up. Terry was smiling at me and nodding. "Not bad for the first one," he said rising to his feet. "But the test is how they fly. It's in the flight." I was on my feet. "Well, then, let's go fly 'em," I half-shouted, and we jogged to an empty lot at the end of the street.

Terry threw his paper plane first. It looped and soared and lifted high above the broken pavements. It caught an updraft from the river-wind, and carried half-a-block toward the railroad yards and abandoned cars, the empty stores and sagging tenements. In my life I could not remember having seen a paper airplane fly so far. Terry looked back at me and winked. "See what I mean," he called as he ran to retrieve it. I saw.

And then it was my turn. As Terry cheered, I threw the plane as hard as I could, and as I watched it veer and vector high above our gathering cries, I experienced a sudden gratitude for the many flights of feelings both of us had found. Since that day, my work with Terry has found many such instances of a creative will realized. Although he continues to struggle with the many issues his family difficulties bear, he brings them to each session now with a willingness to make of his days what he can.

This case example illustrates well Rank's insight about the therapeutic nature of affirming the will even as it may find its initial expressions in the counterwill dynamic. Nietzsche's spirit resides in this insight as well, for both theorists underscore that human will is the foundational source of our vitality, separation, and creativity, of personal growth and individuation. As evidenced in the interaction with Terry, the will "is the human being's dynamic drive toward *self-formulation and reformulation*, and it opposes directly or indirectly anything which would curb its unique expression and freedom, even paradoxically, itself."[53] According to Nietzsche, and elaborated further in Rank's work, an individual would rather express a "will to nothingness," become "the uncreative average man who wills lifeless righteousness,"[54] than become

completely inert with hopeless guilt. In part, Terry's depression and subsequent suicidal act might be considered this kind of will expression.
Nietzsche believed that even in this righteous aversion to the will,
"rebellion against the most fundamental presuppositions of life . . . is
and remains a will! . . . man would rather will nothingness than not
will."[55] Rank, following Nietzsche, understood well that the counterwill
expression of self-hatred may be preferred by the human being to the
absence of will expression at all. Terry's suicidal act expressed the
cumulative experiences of an unrecognized and unaffirmed creative
spirit, echoing both Rank and Nietzsche's relentless interrogative: without the realization of will, what is the merit of a life? By creating and
flying a paper plane, Terry was showing me not only a wish to be free,
he was also expressing an experience of volitional freedom supported by
the affirming presence of another.

And what of the analyst's own counterwill to leaving the room, to
breaking the frame, and stepping into the unknown? At the beginning
of the session, the more I deferred to preexisting categories of therapeutic intervention and technique, the more I was communicating to Terry
a preconception of what was acceptable and unacceptable in human
relationality. In short, my initial overtures not only recreated the experience of Terry's struggle with his parent in the transference proper,
more importantly it created in the present moment a message to him
that his insistence on freedom and self-assertion were wrong, a therapeutic stance Rank criticized Freud for developing into a psychoanalytic
morality. In the end, in the spirit of Nietzsche and Rank's revaluations
of the will phenomenon, I was able to step aside from the closed door
and give the opportunity for Terry to become his own person, thereby
affirming him as a separate being, to will with passion and to reconstitute the self creatively. In doing so, I engaged my own will to act creatively in a new relationship with Terry. Reversing the crease, from
paper to planes, from counterwill to creative will, Terry claimed his own
self-appointed idiom. In Rank's language, he became no longer "the
artist against his art," but a vital force of creative potential "showing me
what he could do." The notion of the creative force within each person
and between persons resonates with the agency of the life force in us,
and is, as we have seen, ultimately expressed, in the spirit of life and
desire for ethical relationships between the self and others. And as
Menaker says so well, "It is the ability to take experience into oneself,
fashion it so that it will nourish the growth of the self and then to project an expression of the self in a way that may be helpful or enjoyable
to others, that Rank called creative. It is this opportunity that is given
us in the therapeutic situation."[56]

Throughout history, some individuals accomplish an intensity of self-realization in which they may experience life in ways so differentiated from an affirming group that almost each day contains the likelihood of an unbearable sense of alienation and exposure. Ernest Becker remarked, "to live is to stick out, to go beyond safe limits; hence it is to court danger, to be a locus of the possibility of disaster."[57] A truly lived life, then, becomes its own burden, and a willingness to accept this paradox includes a volitional striving to transcend it. Otto Rank achieved such an intensity of individuation, and in so doing experienced the dangers and dilemmas inherent in the singularity of a creative life. As we have seen, what often sustained and nourished his notable achievements was Nietzsche's kindred voice, which Rank said he never "got beyond."[58] Indeed, Nietzsche's emphasis on the creative potential of the will can be discerned in Rank's insistence that no matter how one attempts to deny the difference in himself or others, to make everyone equal and the same, the uniqueness of each life will prevail. With this in mind, it is not enough to say of Rank, as Masud Khan said of Freud, that he became "his own patient."[59] More than that, Rank became his own person, conveying a profound faith in the human capacity to grow and change.

NOTES

1. Esther Menaker, "The Selfobject as Immortal Self," in *The Freedom to Inquire* (Northvale, N.J.: Jason Aronson, 1995), 143. Menaker remarks that "the term *object*, which originated in psychoanalytic theory, is often objected to because of its nonhuman implications. However, we scarcely have a good term. For example, significant other seems self-conscious and is cumbersome. If we think of *object* not as a *thing* but in its grammatical sense as related to a *subject*, it becomes the accusative case of a statement about the self and loses some of its onerous, nonhuman aspects."

2. See Paul Roazen, *Freud and His Followers* (New York: New York University Press, 1984), 391–408. Also, E. James Lieberman, M.D., *Acts of Will: The Life and Work of Otto Rank* (Amherst: University of Massachusetts Press, 1985). Also, Robert D. Stolorow and George E. Atwood. "An Ego-Psychological Analysis of the Work and Life of Otto Rank in the Light of Modern Conceptions of Narcissism," *The International Review of Psychoanalysis* 3 (1976) (pt. 4): 441–59.

3. Jessie Taft, *Otto Rank: A Biographical Study Based on Notebooks, Letters, Collected Writings, Therapeutic Achievements and Personal Associations* (New York: Julian Press, 1958), 15.

4. Esther Menaker, *The Freedom to Inquire*, 106.

5. See M. Khan, *Hidden Selves: Between Theory and Practice* (New York: International Universities Press, 1983), 21. Khan explores the habitual tendency of thinkers like Montaigne, Rousseau, and Freud, who devoted themselves to

self-study with an acute awareness of lived experience as a faithful guide, toward the search for a more authentic being.

6. Taft, *Otto Rank*, 4.

7. Ibid., 13.

8. Ibid., 17.

9. Ibid., 47.

10. Ibid., 34.

11. Otto Rank, *Art and Artist* (New York: Knopf, 1932), 38.

12. See Robert Kramer, ed., *A Psychology of Difference: The American Lectures of Otto Rank* (Princeton: Princeton University Press, 1996), 3–51.

13. Ibid., 10.

14. Ibid., 12.

15. Lieberman, *Acts of Will*, 100.

16. Kramer, *Psychology of Difference*, 20. See also Otto Rank and S. Ferenczi, *The Development of Psychoanalysis* (1924), trans. C. Newton. (New York: Dover, 1956).

17. Esther Menaker, "Some Thoughts on Rank's View of Creativity," paper presented to the American Psychological Association, Spring 1996, p. 5.

18. Kramer, *Psychology of Difference*, xiv.

19. See Esther Menaker, *Otto Rank: A Rediscovered Legacy* (New York: Columbia University Press, 1982). On his mentor's seventieth birthday, Rank's gift to Freud of a 23–volume edition of Nietzsche is evidence not only of the philosopher's powerful influence on both of them, it may have also communicated Rank's ability to differentiate from the psychoanalytic "cause," an act of will in itself. See Kramer, *Psychology of Difference*, 36. The gift of Nietzsche's writing is also discussed in Lieberman, *Acts of Will*, 259. See also Jacques Szaluta, "Sigmund Freud's Philosophical Ego Ideals," in *Psychoanalysis and the Humanities*, ed. Laurie Adams and Jacques Szaluta (New York: Brunner/Mazel, 1996), especially 25n6.

20. Otto Rank, *Will Therapy* (New York, W. W. Norton, 1978), 96.

21. Ibid., 1.

22. See Esther Menaker, "The Concept of Will in the Thinking of Otto Rank and Its Consequences for Clinical Practices," in *Separation, Will, and Creativity* (Northvale, N.J.: Jason Aronson, 1996), 65–80. Rank says it well in *Truth and Reality* (New York: W. W. Norton, 1978): "Nietzsche, who experienced thoroughly the whole tragedy of the creative man and admitted in his amor fati the willingness to pay for it, is in my opinion the first and has been up to now the only psychologist," 18.

23. See Nancy Seif, "*Otto Rank: On Human Evil*," (Ph.D. diss., Yeshiva University, New York, 1980).

24. Otto Rank, *Beyond Psychology* (New York: Dover, 1958), 274.

25. Seif, "Otto Rank," 9.

26. Rank, *Beyond Psychology*, 29.

27. Ibid., 212. See also Esther Menaker, *Separation, Will, and Creativity*, 69, and Rank *Truth and Reality*, 4. Here, Rank says: "Not only is the individual ego naturally the carrier of higher goals, even when they are built on external identifications, it is also the temporal representative of the cosmic primal force no matter whether one calls it sexuality, libido, or id . . . it is the repre-

sentative of this primal force and the strength of this force represented in the individual we call the will."

28. Friedrich Nietzsche, *On the Genealogy of Morals*, trans. Walter Kaufmann (New York: Vintage Books, 1967), II:18.

29. Nietzsche quoted in L. Nathan Oaklander, *Existentialist Philosophy* (Englewood Cliffs, N.J.: Prentice Hall, 1996), 81. This view of Nietzsche's resonates strongly with Rank's notion of "the biological will-to-live of the species," and leads him to say that when the "tendency to perpetual self-maintenance of the species carries over to the individual, there results the powerful will whose manifestations bring with them guilt reactions because they strive for the enrichment of the individual, biologically at the expense of the fellow man." See Rank, *Truth and Reality*, 52.

30. Oaklander, *Existentialist Philosophy*, 81.

31. See Walter Kaufmann, *Nietzsche: Philosopher, Psychologist, Antichrist* (Princeton: Princeton University Press, 1974). The understanding of will as a striving toward self-creation has been misunderstood as a power that seeks to manipulate others only. In his book, Kaufmann debunks the notion that Nietzsche's writing underscores predominate "fascistic" imperatives, and shows the origins of such misreadings of the philosopher's work in detail. Accordingly, in setting the record straight, one can read Kaufmann's research as a response to critics of Rank who misunderstood his writings on will in a similar vein. For example, Erich Fromm's misreading of Rank is clear when he says "the basic trend of Rank's philosophy is akin to Fascist philosophy." See Taft, *Otto Rank*, 258. In fact, Rank's reaction to Fromm's misreading actually anticipates Kaufmann's reassessment of Nietzsche's use of the term "will."

32. Nietzsche quoted in Oaklander, *Existentialist Philosophy*, 82.

33. See ibid.

34. Rank, *Beyond Psychology*, 50. In addition, Rank posits the life force of will in opposition to Freud's notion that humanity is a "a play-ball of the id and super-ego" in *Truth and Reality*, 16.

35. Saul Hofstein, "Will, Choice, and Fate Perspectives on Rankian Thought," in *Journal of the Otto Rank Association* 12 (Summer 1977): 65. See also Otto Rank, "Neurosis: Failure in Creativity," in *A Psychology of Difference*. Rank says "Contrary to the Freudian explanation—on which the idea of self-punishment as a repetition of punishment from without is based—I assumed, from the very beginning, the existence of a self-inhibiting mechanism inherent in the individual. The inhibition of instinct, which operates as a self-preserving protection, I was able later on to define as the individual will," 253.

36. Hofstein, "Rankian Thought," 64.

37. Rank, "Neurosis," in *A Psychology of Difference*, 253.

38. Rank's writing on autonomy, responsibility, and conscience resonates strongly with phenomenological, existential, and humanistic psychologies. For an overview, see Henryk Misiak and Virginia Staudt Sexton, *Phenomenological, Existential, and Humanistic Psychologies: A Historical Survey* (New York and London: Grune and Stratton, 1973).

39. See Fred Evans, *Psychology and Nihilism* (Albany: State University of New York Press, 1994).

40. See Taft, *Otto Rank*, 31. Also in Walter Kaufmann, the introduction to Nietzsche's *The Gay Science* (New York: Vintage Books, 1974), 11. Although Rank contrasts his notions of types to Nietzsche and others, he clearly questions the categorization of individuals when he says in *Will Therapy*, "There are just as many types, or if one prefers, mixture of types, as there are individuals, and also in cases of neurosis that one classifies under the same group . . . the individual differences . . . were even more striking to me and appear more meaningful than the apparent similarity of a ground structure," 107.

41. Menaker, *Otto Rank*, 55.

42. Menaker, *Separation, Will and Creativity*, 70.

43. Menaker, "Some Thoughts on Rank's View of Creativity," 5.

44. See Evans, *Psychology and Nihilism*, 13–15.

45. Rank, *The Trauma of Birth* (New York: Dover, 1958), 110.

46. Friedrich Nietzsche, *Ecce Homo*, trans. Walter Kaufmann (New York: Vintage Books, 1967), "Why I Am a Destiny," sec. 8.

47. Seif, *On Human Evil*, 114.

48. Rank, *Beyond Psychology*, 290. Rank asserts here that "the ego needs the Thou in order to become a Self," and concludes, "the ego needs a Thou to build an assertive self with and against this Thou."

49. Rank, *The Trauma of Birth*, 207. Rank wrote these words when he was still very much aligned to Freudian views, illustrating clearly a growing uneasiness with aspects of psychoanalytic pedagogy.

50. Rank, "The Yale Lectures," in *A Psychology of Difference*, 246.

51. Seif, *On Human Evil*, 114.

52. Ibid. See Also Dennis B. Klein, *Jewish Origins of the Psychoanalytic Movement*, chapter 4.

53. Rank, *Will Therapy*, 187.

54. *GM* III:28.

55. *GM* III:28. In *Will Therapy*, Rank develops Nietzsche's insight concerning the will to nothingness: "For I can conceive of actual self-murder only as an indication, however momentary, of strength of will. Experience also seems to show that it is rather the strong-willed who tend to suicide, yes also to neurosis. At all events we make this assumption tacitly when we are willing to exert ourselves therapeutically. The little that I have seen of cases of suicidal tendencies during treatment, has made me certain that psychologically it concerns a stage in the struggle between the two sides of the personality where it is not merely that one side of the ego has won the upper hand over the other, but that the one side wants to kill the other, will rid himself of it completely. Whether it has to do with the 'old' self which stands in the way of the new development, or with the 'bad' self, which is condemned by the moralistic ego, depends on the individual case. . . . Only when the person wants to live, that is, has strength and courage for it and yet cannot, is he strong enough to kill the sound self that will die rather than accept a living death," 187–88.

56. Esther Menaker, "Some Thoughts on Rank's View of Creativity," 10. In light of our case, Menaker's remarks also remind us of Rank's tendency to correlate the irrational will of self-creation with the activities of play. See *Truth and Reality*, 300. Recalling my initial reactions to Terry in the case example,

and my subsequent therapeutic shift, Rank's words in *Will Therapy* act as a welcomed reminder: "In the ideologic therapy, the analyst is inclined to measure the condition of the patient, his progress or the task still to be done by what has come out in the analysis, while dynamic therapy judges the therapeutic situation at the moment according to what it means to the patient in general and at the present moment in particular; in other words, by what he makes of it," 172.

57. Ernest Becker, *Escape from Evil* (New York: Free Press, 1975), 35.

58. Rank made this remark to Henry Miller. See Lieberman, *Acts of Will*, 329. Also note Rank's homage to Nietzsche in "Neurosis": "Nietzsche not only affirmed his lifelong illness but actually glorified it, because he discovered through his own experience that becoming well is of greater value than being well. . . . Nietzsche not only recognized in himself the usual experience of the artist type who very often seems to be driven by illness and suffering to creative compensation in work; he also sensed the deeper truth that both illness and work are the expression of the creative will in the individual," 255.

59. Khan, *Hidden Selves*, 29.

PART 3

The Psychology of Nietzsche and His Readers (Psychobiography)

CHAPTER 14

Nietzsche's Psychology and Rhetoric of World Redemption: Dionysus versus the Crucified

Claudia Crawford

Let us suppose that my attempt to assassinate two millennia of antinature and desecration of man were to succeed. That new party of life which would tackle the greatest of all tasks, the attempt to raise humanity higher, including the relentless destruction of everything that was degenerating and parasitical, would again make possible that excess of life on earth from which the Dionysian state, too, would have to awaken again.

—*Ecce Homo*

Nietzsche developed the power to do this. He developed the decisive traits of nature to "confront humanity with the most difficult demand ever made of it."[1] He possessed the traits of "the close proximity of the brightest and the most calamitous forces, the will to power as no man ever possessed it, the ruthless courage in matters of the spirit, the unlimited power to learn without damage to the will to act."[2] Power, calamity, demanding, relentless destruction, ruthless courage? In this essay I will maintain that Nietzsche's excessive uses of language in the last quarter of 1888, especially in *Twilight of the Idols, The Antichrist, Ecce Homo, The Case of Wagner,* and in notes and letters from this period, are not symptoms of megalomania and impending madness, rather that Nietzsche was consciously wielding a grand style of agonal rhetorics of prophecy, apocalypse, legislation, and the dithyramb in order to do just what he claimed to be attempting—*to assassinate two millennia of antinature and desecration of man and revive a Dionysian age!*

One man determined to have an effect of this kind? Would this task

271

require a gentle or moderate rhetoric? Wouldn't speaking greatly and immoderately be a first condition? The messages of prophets are usually excessive, full of menaces and reproaches, harsh to the ears and bitter to hear. In fact "severity comes to be a sign that a prophet is genuine."[3] The actions of the prophets were also at times psychologically abnormal and extravagant, and for the ancients this very excessiveness in bearing and speech was a sign . . . of the power of their words, the words that helped to build the power of Christianity.[4] During Nietzsche's time extravagance and excessiveness in bearing and speech was often taken as a sign of degenerate madness. Of course, Nietzsche is the prophet of *antichristianity* and the decline of a Western world that developed under Christianity. Nietzsche is also the prophet of a new time and a new age. It would be a great minimization of Nietzsche's grand agonal language to call it simply prophetic; and this essay aims to demonstrate that Nietzsche's mastery of language and action and his ability to put them to use to instigate a new millennia for humankind, plays out his psychological aim of becoming a redeemer on a par with Jesus and Socrates.

HYPERBOLE

From the time of his earliest childhood, when the "little preacher" Nietzsche spouted off to his young friends, to his discipleship of Wagner who was to redeem German culture, to his own apocalyptic utterances in *Ecce Homo*, and finally, to the act of madness in which Nietzsche becomes the sacrificial god Dionysus, Nietzsche had always displayed as a decisive characteristic the need to revision and redo the world around him, to revalue and redeem humankind. His whole psychology and philosophy led up to a crisis that while making a redeeming demand on humankind, also required the public sacrifice of Nietzsche himself. This is the typical activity of many prophets, redeemers, and new lawgivers.

As we look at Nietzsche's psychology and words, especially at the end of 1888, we have to ask: do they really reflect madness? megalomania? or do they reflect a conscious wielding of a world-redemptive purpose and style?—followed by a world-redemptive act? Let us begin with hyperbole, the trope or figure of exaggeration. Nehamas claims rightly that "Nietzsche's writing is irreducibly hyperbolic. Hyperbole is the most consistent and the most conspicuous feature of his writing."[5] This is true not only of his last writings, which carry hyperbole to mastery, but had always been characteristic of his style. In *The Will to Power* Nietzsche writes: "The spell that fights on our behalf, the eye of Venus that charms and blinds even our opponents, is the magic of the

extreme, the seduction that everything extreme exercises: we immoral-
ists—we are the most extreme."⁶ Nehamas defines hyperbole as "a figure by means of which one says more than is strictly speaking appropriate."⁷ Hyperbole is also defined as exaggeration, extravagance, and
want of due proportion. However, the use of hyperbole is also an excess
that can evoke sublimity, greatness. Thus, excess and impropriety can—
in cases of masterly use—become great, sublime. This is, I maintain, the
case with Nietzsche. Hyperbole is dangerous ("I am no man, I am dynamite"),⁸ untamed ("I am the first immoralist"),⁹ unhegemonic ("I am the
Antichrist"),¹⁰ thus, for Nietzsche's time, mad. I will go a step farther
and claim that Nietzsche also crafted his life as the hyperbolic life, which
stands on a par with the lives of Jesus, Socrates, Moses, and the Old Testament prophets. Whether we speak of the hyperbolic or the prophetic
mode of expression and action, both of which have much in common,
the aim is to impose a sense of urgency on readers and listeners. The
prophet-speaker knows the future, and he knows the present and past as
they control that future. Further, the activity of prophets and redeemers
is to act as mouthpieces for movements and energies that ultimately
transcend them. The problem for the prophetic voice is whether or not
there is an audience who can hear the intent of the words. Nietzsche
opens *The Antichrist*: "How *could* I mistake myself for one of those for
whom there are ears even now? Only the day after tomorrow belongs to
me. Some are born posthumously."¹¹ Because of this "the philosopher-
poet not only puts his gospel forward, but he also proclaims its ultimate
value. He triumphs over recalcitrant members of the audience by envi-
sioning the outcome of the issue in question."¹² Nietzsche: "I am the
bringer of glad tidings like no one before me . . . only beginning with me
are there hopes again."¹³ Because of their hyperbolic power the words
and actions of a prophet and redeemer change the behavior of readers,
the read becomes the acted.

NIETZSCHE'S AGON

Nietzsche held a lifelong agonistics against Socrates and Jesus Christ. He
set up the agon of all agons: "Dionysus versus the Crucified." Dionysus
against the Socratic "logician's instinct." Dionysus against the life-deny-
ing pathos of Christianity. Nietzsche felt that there was a direct line
from Socratic and Platonic idealism to Christian theology.¹⁴ He wanted
to wrestle Christianity and the logician's instinct, "the fact that antinature itself received the highest honors as morality," and all like-thinking
to the ground and he set about this using his "agonistic instinct" in the
ancient Greek sense. In "Homer's Contest," Nietzsche tells us that what

distinguishes the Greek world from ours is that struggle and the joy of victory were a basic value recognized, for example, in the ethical concept of envy:

> Envy spurs men to activity: not to the activity of fights of annihilation but to the activity of fights which are contests. . . . The greater and more sublime a Greek is the brighter the flame of ambition that flares out of him consuming everybody who runs on the same course. . . . Every great Hellene hands on the torch of the contest; every great virtue kindles a new greatness. . . . Every talent must unfold itself in fighting: that is the command of Hellenic popular pedagogy.[15]

Nietzsche writes further that: "Whereas modern man fears nothing in an artist more than the emotion of any personal fight, the Greek knows the artist *only as engaged in a personal fight*."[16] Nehamas writes: "Nietzsche's imagery is directly connected with what, in Blake's words, we might appropriately call 'the mental fight,' the only fight Nietzsche ever seriously envisages and in which he engaged; in fact we might say that the more violent his imagery becomes, the more abstract is the fight in which he is involved."[17] I do not agree with this assessment as will become apparent; Nietzsche's world-historical agonistics involved not only that his rhetoric become more and more apocalyptic, but also that he lay down his life as proof of his words. The enormity of Nietzsche's envy of Socrates and Jesus *in the positive Greek sense* fueled Nietzsche's agonal instinct to set up a world-historical contest in which, through his words and actions, he expected to become the victor in *reality* and not in the form of mad delusions. *Dionysus versus the Crucified.*—He bequeaths this towering juxtapositioning of contestants to posterity for their judgment.

THE PSYCHOLOGY AND RHETORIC
OF THE GREEK GRAND STYLE

> The highest feeling of power and sureness finds expression in a *grand style*. The power which no longer needs any proof, which spurns pleasing, which does not answer lightly, which feels no witness near, which lives oblivious of all opposition to it, which reposes within itself, fatalistically, a law among laws—that speaks of itself as a grand style.[18]

Nietzsche's hyperbolic, prophetic, and agonistic style in word and deed grows out of the Greek grand style. Even as a young philological student and professor of philology, Nietzsche was attracted to the rhetoric of extremes, persuasive power and call to action. In his "Notes on Rhetoric" Nietzsche speaks of the "tripartite division" of rhetorical style that was "appropriate only for the older development of Attic eloquence from Gorgias to Isocrates: *Gravis* [grand], *mediocris* [middle], *extenuata* [simple]."[19] Nietzsche follows the development of the grand style and the ethos of the grand style especially in Gorgias, Thucydides, Lysias, and Demosthenes. In the section of Nietzsche's "Ancient Rhetoric" entitled "Modification of Purity," he discusses the grand style:

> Gorgias . . . became the inventor of the grand and poetic type of speech, which would be perfected, especially by Thucydides. According to Dionysius of Halicarnassus, Thucydides loved the *lexis aperchaiomeme* [style having just become completely ancient] and *glossematike* [(style) fattened with obsolete words]. His language was [such that] it was no longer in use for public discussions in Athens in those days: he held on to what was disappearing, such as the old Attic dialect with its *prasso* [to achieve or accomplish . . . to draw up in order of battle], and so forth.[20]

Prasso, as Nietzsche indicates, is a type of old Attic dialect whose effect apparently was to spur listeners on to action, whether to seek glory in battle or in other service to the polis. The words were to incite or challenge others to achieve something in particular, to accomplish something, to take action. In other words it represents the *old Greek logos*, which Nietzsche adopted as a fundamental of his psychology and thought, wherein words and action were still united as Gorgias expressed it in a notorious funeral oration: "using might of hand and rightness of plan, thinking through the one and acting out the other."[21] Nietzsche's major critique of Socrates and Plato was that they turned to logos and dialogue and away from action. From that point on, Nietzsche felt that all battles were mere word battles that opened the door to idealism and Christian theologizing rather than to relying on the proof of the realities of the body and its deeds.

Dionysius of Halicarnassus further describes Thucydides' style as having the following characteristics: "artificiality of vocabulary, variety of figures, harshness of word-order, rapidity of signification. The special features of his style include compactness and solidity, pungency and severity, vehemence, the ability to disturb and terrify, and above all emotional power."[22] Nietzsche's style, which he had honed to the point of excellence by the time he wrote his last works (in *The Antichrist* and *Ecce Homo* for example), exhibits all these techniques of Thucydides' grand style but intensified. He uses elevated techniques such as unusual construction, superlatives, heightening of tension and exaggerated climax, especially when his subject is of great consequence.

Nietzsche was interested in how the rhetoricians created their ethos. The ethos of the grand style used by Thucydides was distinctive. It displayed the ethos of distance, or what Nietzsche came to call the "pathos of distance." What people often characterize as Nietzsche's self-aggrandizing, aristocratic, esoteric manner is consciously developed by him as the ethos of the grand style. Nietzsche studied Lysias' masterly use of ethos. Here he admired something of the opposite of the distance of Thucydides. Nietzsche admired Lysias' use of ethos in the way it addressed the common man. First, Lysias used *ethopoeia* where a person creates his own persona by using testimony, often testifying to his own worth (*pistis ek tou Biou*) or "proof out of your life."[23] Lysias was often eager to testify to his own courage in battle and generosity as reasons why he should be believed, thus carrying forward the old Greek logos of the correspondence between real action and truth. Second, Lysias often used direct address of the audience to draw them into an agonal bond of confidence that directed suspicion against those outside this bond. Third, he set up a contrast of the ethos of noble persons and base persons in order to praise one and condemn the other. And finally, Lysias often wielded the ethos of indignation and a display of anger with the idea that a person's moral character stands revealed by that which makes him angry.[24] Nietzsche is a master of all of these ethotic techniques both grand and common. For example, his use of a strident and angry tone in *The Antichrist*, cannot be adequately characterized as overly emotional and immoderate—certainly not mad; rather, it is written in the epitome of the grand style as he combines all four of the ethotic techniques above. He directly addresses his readers and aligns them into two opposing camps, those hyperboreans who can follow him into uncharted seas [the noble] and the rest, modern men and Christians who cannot [the base]. "We are Hyperboreans . . . we have found the exit out of the labyrinth of thousands of years. Who *else* has found it? Modern man perhaps? 'I have got lost; I am everything that has got lost,' sighs modern man."[25] Nietzsche often testifies to his character, which is noble and can stand good in reality for the positions he takes and which goes a long way toward making his angry and hyperbolic pronouncements not only believable but a credit to the intensity of his commitment: "I have a subtler sense of smell for the signs of ascent and decline than any other human being before me; I am the teacher *par excellence* for this—I know both, I am both."[26] And then applying indignation of the highest degree for the sense of decline that he feels Christianity reflects, Nietzsche thunders: "I call [Christianity] the one immortal blemish of mankind. And time is reckoned from this *dies nefastus* with which this calamity began—after the *first* day of Christianity! *Why*

not rather after its last day? After today?"[27] Here Nietzsche uses anti-
quated words, vehemence, and *prasso*, a call to action. He uses
prophetic harshness, menace, and hyperbolic excess. About angry
prophets Nietzsche writes:

> The Jews felt differently about anger from the way we do, and called it
> holy: thus they saw the gloomy majesty of the man with whom it
> showed itself associated at an elevation which a European is incapable
> of imagining; they modeled their angry holy Jehovah on their angry
> holy prophets. Measured against these, the great men of wrath among
> Europeans are as it were creations at second hand.[28]

For Nietzsche, alongside Thucydides, Demosthenes was the epitome
of the rhetorician in the grand style. Demosthenes' use of the grand style
absorbed so "much passion and fire" that it became useful for "agonistic delivery."

> It is as if a soldier had first been trained as an athlete and now, in real
> combat, applies his art as it were only unintentionally; everything
> *anankaion* [necessary] will now seem easy, natural, versatile; every-
> thing playful and ostentatious that is contained in all purely epideictic
> art is burned to a crisp by the high earnestness of the cause.[29]

Of Demosthenes, Nietzsche continues: "The stormy air of Athenian
democracy carries his oratory to the heights; just as it in turn makes this
storm more violent and decisive."[30] Again, Nietzsche could just as well
be describing his own style and activity as he harangues and polemicizes
against the idealism, Christianity and nationalism of Germany in *Ecce
Homo, The Case of Wagner,* and in final notes, all with the good of the
polis at heart. Nietzsche frequently asserted that the greatest artist and
philosopher would remain undiscovered unless the times were conducive
to what he had to communicate. Certainly this is true of prophets. In
Daybreak (14), Nietzsche writes of the "proof by madness" of Christian
saints and desert solitaries, some of whom proved themselves by a sort
of fruitful madness and many of whom, having failed to judge the times
correctly, or whom the times had failed to judge correctly, languished in
madhouses. Athens and Demosthenes came together to distinguish each
other and "a man inspired by a great passion of noble rank," was created. Nietzsche is a like man, an orator and prophet in the old sense,
who in *The Antichrist, Twilight of the Idols,* and *Ecce Homo,* takes on
the grand style and wields such weighty rhetorical genres as prophecy,
the legislative, and the apocalyptic, all conceived, as Nietzsche says of
Demosthenes, as "useful for agonistic delivery." For Nietzsche words
become world. Words in the grand style are destroying and creating, legislative, and prophetic: "It is blessedness to write on the will of millennia as on bronze."[31]

ARCHILOCHUS AND PINDAR

Nietzsche also appreciated the rhetorical characteristics and lived life of the grand style perhaps even more when they were exhibited by his favorite poets. Archilochus (seventh century B.C.E.) declared himself to be at once a servitor of the "lord of the battle-cry" and also an expert in the "delightful gift of the muses."[32] Archilochus' poems also represented the two extremes and persistent pressures upon the lives of the ancient Greek citizen: "that of social duty and that of competitive self-realization."[33] He engaged in politics, war, and poetry. He died in battle. As the first lyric poet, Archilochus was famous for his powers of invective; he was a sarcastic reviler in dithyrambs that reflected his turbulent and fierce character. The word dithyramb first appears in Archilochus. He calls it the song of Dionysus that, when under the influence of wine, he sings and leads others to sing, leading forth the "meters" or "dances" of Dionysus.[34]

It is these connections that Nietzsche stresses in his comments on Archilochus in *The Birth of Tragedy*. Nietzsche writes of Archilochus as the "warlike votary of the muses" and emphasizes the identity of Archilochus the lyrist with Dionysian ritual and folk music. "When Archilochus the first Greek lyrist, proclaims to the daughters of Lycambes both his mad love and his contempt, it is not his passion alone that dances before us in orgiastic frenzy: but we see Dionysus and the Maenads."[35] Nietzsche is interested in the surrender of the subjectivity of the lyrist in the Dionysian process. Thus, when the lyrist says "I," he is "the moving center of this world—Dionysus. His self is not the same as that of the waking empirically real man, but the only truly existent and eternal self resting at the basis of things."[36]

Pindar (522–443 B.C.E.) represents for Nietzsche another high point of Greek glory for he combines the highest art of dithyramb and lyric with the grand style. In his victory odes, Pindar reflects the tradition of the older logos where physical actions and words reflect and heighten one another; and this very heightening leads to Dionysian festivity. Pindar was the *exarchon*, the poet who strikes up the lyre and song and leads the dance as Archilochus claimed to have done. The real *komos* (celebration), with its crowning of the victorious athlete with flowers and its procession through the streets, was built up to through the use of futures and vocatives in the ode to heighten expectation. In the odes Pindar's "I" is a "first person indefinite" that is meant to be suitable for adoption both by the chorus that speaks it and the audience that is invited to share in it. Through its hortatory, encouraging tone, the ode actually approximates prophetic language. Nietzsche develops this vocative (future calling) and hortatory tone as early as *The Birth of Tragedy,* and continues it to the very end.[37]

THE DIONYSIAN DITHYRAMB

Archilochus and Pindar are dithyrambists in the old style. A significant aspect of Nietzsche's prophetic and redemptive style and voice is faithful to the old dithyramb in that as a prophet his "I" originates beyond him (as with Archilochus) and is indefinite (empty of ego) inviting others to adopt it as their own (as in Pindar). The fate and style of the Dionysian dithyramb, itself the hyperbolic form of music and poetry, is tied up intimately with Nietzsche's annihilative and redemptive project. In "The Struggle between Science and Wisdom" Nietzsche sets out the "three-part history of the dithyramb":

1. The dithyrambs of Arion, from which the older tragedy proceeds [even before this the dithyramb of Archilochus];
2. The agonistic dithyrambs of the state, parallel to domesticated tragedy;
3. The brilliantly chaotic mimetic dithyrambs.[38]

The original function of the old dithyramb for Nietzsche was to bring real life into a sharper focus. In the old dithyramb Dionysus was not actually present; he was merely imagined as present. In this way the old dithyramb character (of Dionysus) was expanded into an eternal type in which the character was an artistic reflection of a universal law. In the ancients the dithyramb was still completely ordered as in the dithyramb of Pindar and his time, and thus the mythopoetic power of music in the ancient dithyramb was present. In the old dithyramb myth wanted to be experienced vividly as a unique example of a universality and truth that gazed into the infinite.

In the new dithyramb of the state, Nietzsche writes, the popular cult of Dionysus with its primitive, dithyrambic songs was transformed for political ends. In the Greek poetry dithyrambs that were performed at the City Dionysia in Athens, for example, the new dithyrambic chorus was assigned the task of exciting the mood of the listeners to such a degree that, when the character of Dionysus appeared on the stage, they saw a visionary figure born of their own rapture and not experience of the universal. The audience was made to *forget their normal identities in real life* and identify with the actor on stage. The new Attic dithyramb also did away with the universal character of Dionysian music, turning it into a playfully formal and pleasurable imitative counterfeit of phenomena. Thus, for Nietzsche the new Attic dithyramb became un-Dionysian. In the last stage of the development of the "mimetic" dithyramb, Nietzsche writes that the new music became "a wretched copy of phenomena," intensifying tendencies already present in the new Attic dithyramb.[39]

We see that Nietzsche emphasizes the decline of the Greek ancient traditions of dithyramb and the old logos of word and deed that were meant to reinforce in a *participatory and celebratory* mode the reality of the god's traditions of ancestors, family, and polis. And we see him rue their abandonment in favor of what he calls an antinature: a *disregard for reality and a privileging of the power of the persuasion of idealism in word, form, and image.* Nietzsche hoped to bring about a fourth part of the history of the dithyramb through his renewed Dionysian dithyramb. Nietzsche's preferred style, once his grand agonal style had succeeded in propelling us into a new tragic worldview of Dionysian possibility, was to be the dithyramb, the language that Dionysian people speak when they speak to themselves. Nietzsche's praise of the dithyramb in *Ecce Homo*, his claim: "I am the inventor of the dithyramb," and his decision to leave us as his last communication, the Dionysian dithyrambs, are clear evidence of this.[40]

THE LEGISLATOR: NIETZSCHE AND MOSES

Nietzsche writes that by giving new laws:

> the lawgiver may have committed an offense, but by voluntarily accepting punishment he raises himself above his offense, he does not only obliterate his offense through freeheartedness, greatness and imperturbability, he performs a public service as well. —Such would be the criminal of a possible future, who, to be sure also presupposes a future lawgiving—one founded on the idea "I submit only to the law which I myself have given, in great things and in small."[41]

For Nietzsche there are two kinds of philosophers: first, those who make previous values understandable, usable, making past things useful for the future. Second, those who are commanders and legislators: those who say "Thus it shall be!" All knowledge is for them only a means of creation. These philosophers are always close to a "plunge into the abyss."[42] For Nietzsche the lawgiver of new values often must appear to be mad if he is not mad: "All superior men who were irresistibly drawn to throw off the yoke of any kind of morality and to frame new laws had, if they were not actually mad, no alternative but to make themselves or pretend to be mad.—"[43] In these characterizations of future legislators, we see Nietzsche's judgment that voluntary punishment, a plunge into the abyss and the appearance of evil or madness, are conditions of breaking the old law tablets and creating the new. The old Greek congruence of word and deed in the grand style, the hyperbolic style not only in word but followed through in actions; these Nietzsche required of himself as lawgiver.

Another source of Nietzsche's grand style and legislative words and deeds, one apparently valued by him even more than the Greek, was the Old Testament. That Nietzsche admired the Old Testament as a reflection of strong cultures in the grand style, even the ability to "disturb and terrify," is evidenced in several places in his writings: "In the Jewish 'Old Testament,' the book of divine justice, there are human beings, things, and speeches in so *grand a style* that Greek and Indian literature have nothing to compare with it . . . —the taste for the Old Testament is a touchstone for 'great' and 'small.'"[44]

Nietzsche saw in Moses the great prophet and lawgiver of a strong people, the ancient Hebrews, and this admiration for Moses is obvious in that Nietzsche considered himself, in the persona of Zarathustra, as a new Moses, a new lawgiver coming to modern human beings with new tablets. From Nietzsche's perspective Moses combined action, the old logos and the rhetoric of the grand style. He led the Hebrews from bondage and was capable, in great songs to the Lord, of ritual praise of his God and his people in the manner of Thucydides and Demosthenes or of Archilochus and Pindar.

There are many parallels to the Pentateuch and to Moses in particular in Nietzsche's writings, especially in *Zarathustra*. In Exodus, Moses says to God, you yourself warned us to "set limits around the mountain and keep it holy."[45] Zarathustra: "I draw circles around me and sacred boundaries . . . on ever higher mountains."[46] Zarathustra sits on mountains like Moses upon Mount Sinai. When God spoke to Moses upon the mountain there "was thunder and lightning, the sound of the trumpet, and the mountain smoking."[47] Zarathustra's words come as lightning and thunder in "The Seven Seals" as he hangs on mountains as the prophet of the future. Moses dashes sacrificial blood on the people: "See the blood of the covenant that the Lord has made with you in accordance with all these words."[48] Zarathustra says one should write with blood.[49] God says to Moses "come up to the mountain and wait there and I will give you the tablets of stone, with the law and the commandment, which I have written for their instruction."[50] Zarathustra opens "On Old and New Tablets": "Here I sit and wait, surrounded by broken old tablets and new tablets half covered with writing. When will my hour come? The hour of my going down and going under; for I want to go among men once more."[51] And Zarathustra goes on to give humans his new laws in "On Old and New Tablets" in which he revalues, revises or replaces specific Christian laws with his visions of a revaluation of values. Nietzsche admired the dignity of Moses' death. "The Dignity of death and a kind of consecration of passion have perhaps never yet been represented more beautifully . . . than by certain Jews of the Old Testament: to these even the Greek could have gone to school!"[52] Nietzsche was a prophet and lawgiver, who took the position of one who acts to bring about and promises a new land to his descendants though he, like Moses, could not cross over to his promised land for his death was required.

MESSIANIC PROPHET

Nietzsche is one man and so he must take on several voices, positions, and rhetorics to accomplish the unheard of task he has set for himself: to overthrow Jesus and Socrates in order to undo two millennia of occidental heritage and restore a strong age for the future of humans. He must become prophet of the destruction of denatured humanity and herald of a new possibility, he must use the strong rhetorics of ancient cultures and the apocalyptic tone of a new "judgment day" upon which humans, not God, decide their fate. He must become legislator and offer new tablets and he must teach us the dithyramb, a new ability to praise and sing the praises of the bounty that a new Dionysian life will bring before he lays down his life for it.

In addition to the grand style of the Greeks, it is from the Old Testament that Nietzsche takes the language that he uses to curse Christianity! To use the ancient rhetorics and poetry of prophesy and apocalypse is the grand style. Nietzsche turns the language of Christianity against Christianity and is called mad! The great religions of antiquity always had their "inspired" men who claimed to be speaking in the name of god. There is no doubt that Nietzsche admired the prophets of the Old Testament very highly and that he identified himself with them. "Nobody has been more mendacious than holy men—the truth speaks out of me.—"[53] Nietzsche as a new prophet, speaks in the name of the overhuman and one who rejoices in the doctrine of the eternal recurrence. Nietzsche recognizes that he is a new kind of prophet and legislator: "Having no God or 'inspiration' to back up the new law, the lawgiver without God or 'inspiration' is truly in a fearful situation."[54] *In every case then it is Nietzsche himself who speaks and stands good for what he teaches and prophesies.* But Nietzsche's self or "ego" only represents "the nature of things and the future of the nature of things." In Nietzsche's case, it is the will to power that speaks through him not the will of God. "In the end there appears a man, a monster of energy, who demands a monster of a task. For it is our energy that disposes of us; and the wretched spiritual game of goals and intentions and motives is only a foreground—even though weak eyes may take them for the matter itself."[55]

Nietzsche fulfills traditional definitions of prophets to the letter. At some point in their life the prophet receives an irresistible divine call. Nietzsche received this call in August 1881 "6,000 feet beyond man and time." This is when the idea of *Zarathustra* and the eternal recurrence "*overtook*" him.[56]

The divine message comes to prophets in various ways: vision, by hearing, but most often by internal inspiration. "The genuine prophet is fully aware that he is mouthpiece, no more; his words though his own are not his own."[57] Nietzsche's description of inspiration in *Ecce Homo*, one of the most incredible passages in his writings, describes his experience of "divine" inspiration. He describes it as revelation, as a mere becoming medium of overpowering forces, as becoming a mouthpiece with the words provided, and as the feeling of divinity.[58] About this inspiration Nietzsche writes: "This is my experience of inspiration; I do not doubt that one has to go back thousands of years in order to find anyone who could say to me, 'it is mine as well.'"[59] Nietzsche specifically writes that only those prophets and poets of "strong ages" could speak in the way that he and Zarathustra speak. The prophet, like the mystic, is raised to a "supranormal" psychological state by this divine intervention.

Equally various are the methods the prophets use to convey their message: lyrical fragments, prose narratives, in parable or direct speech, curt oracular style or the various literary forms of exhortation, diatribe, sermon, proverb, formal psalms, love songs, satire, funeral lament, as well as other forms.[60] There is often a lack of coherence and logical arrangement, rather random collections or individual units make up the message. The contents of the message are the "prophetic sayings"; these are "oracles," spoken either by God or by the prophet in God's name, or else they are poetic passages conveying some teaching, prediction, threat, or promise. Nietzsche's writings seem to be a paradigm of prophetic style in these senses; his use of aphorisms, poetry, and the non-coherence in any systematic manner of his ideas and proclamations. In much of Nietzsche's writing, but especially in *Zarathustra*, the form is oracular, symbolic, and metaphorical and contains proverbs, exhortations, sermons, songs, and satire. "The prophet was not a writer, he was first and foremost a speaker, a preacher." Zarathustra speaks. Zarathustra was a Persian prophet and thus when Nietzsche recalls him to speak a new message he is by definition a prophet. Prophets end their tracts with, "Thus says the Lord." Nietzsche ends his with, "Thus Spoke Zarathustra." These formulas apply across time and lend authority to what the prophet proclaims.[61] In his last works, notes, and letters where Nietzsche's prophetic and grand agonal voice becomes strongest and vehemently urgent, he predicts, exhorts, uses sharp invective and diatribe, and threatens to herald a new order in the manner of ancient Greek orators and Hebrew prophets to propel himself and Zarathustra into messianic ascendancy.

POLITICAL PROPHET

"In every description of a prophet's call, it is made clear that his mission is to the nation, or, in the case of Jeremiah, to all the nations."[62] All of Nietzsche's admired precursors in the grand style—Archilochus, Pindar, Demosthenes, Thucydides, Moses, Isaiah—were bound up in the fates of their nations. In addition to Nietzsche's messianic mission in *Zarathustra,* in typical prophetic style he pursues concerns for his nation. Nietzsche's declarations concerning the German nation and European politics were prophetic. Ezekiel and Jeremiah proclaimed that because Jerusalem had broken the Covenant and abandoned Yahweh, destruction was coming upon it. Nietzsche was a contemporary Isaiah, a prophet of the concept of a united Europe while castigating the nationalism of Germany. "Part of the meaning and way of my task . . . [is] an attack on the German nation."[63] Just as the prophets harangued against the Israelites for having strayed from Yahweh, Nietzsche's harangue against the growing nationalism of Germany is couched in the extreme language of prophecy and the grand style: "And why should I not go all the way? I like to make a clean sweep of things. It is part of my ambition to be considered a despiser of Germans *par excellence.*"[64] Nietzsche's antinationalistic iconoclasm against the Germans is also completely bound up with his iconoclastic and prophetic castigation of Christians and idealists. In *The Antichrist* he writes:

> They are my enemies, I confess it, these Germans: I despise in them every kind of conceptual and valuational uncleanliness, of *cowardice* before every honest Yes and No. For almost a thousand years they have messed up and confused everything they touched with their fingers; they have on their conscience everything half-hearted—three-eighth's-hearted!—of which Europe is sick; they also have on their conscience the most unclean kind of Christianity that there is, the most incurable, the most irrefutable: Protestantism. If we do not get rid of Christianity, it will be the fault of the *Germans.*[65]

These statements brushed over, thought mad, thought to be megalomania. Why? A "party of life" against the "party of degeneration of life"?

Nietzsche had long written of a noble hierarchy that should rise up to form governments, legislate, and assume the task of revaluing the world. It has been suggested that Nietzsche's desire for a noble rulership, or that he "should rule the world" as impetus for a new hierarchy of "oath-takers" he sought to inspire *through his death*—were only "mad" thoughts of his last days. Yet that dismissal of Nietzsche simply does not take into account many of the overall themes of his critique of European culture and the creation of overhumans. As only one example of how Nietzsche's messianic and political goals come together in his thought, we can look at the following note from some 1885 plans for a *Zarathustra* V:

I. Zarathustra can only *bring good fortune* after the hierarchy has been produced. This must first of all be taught.

II. The hierarchy carried out in a system of world government: ultimately, the Lords of the Earth, a new ruling caste. Springing from them, here and there, an altogether Epicurean god, the overman, who transfigures existence.

III. Overman's conception of the world. Dionysos

IV. Turning back lovingly from this greatest of *alienations* to what is most intimate to him, to the smallest things, Zarathustra blessing all his experiences and, as one who blesses, dying.[66]

Nietzsche was not mad. Megalomania is the wrong word, for this presupposes that one's ego is at the source of one's beliefs and assertions. Nietzsche does not speak for himself, as I have been maintaining, but from the "nature of things." He uses the "I" of Archilochus, of Pindar, of the prophets, which invites those who have ears for what they say to adopt it in a movement toward hope for a future time. In *The Antichrist*, the lightening bolt of the revaluation he is to send into the world "that will make the earth convulse," he announces *Geisteskrieger*, spiritual warfare, "the like of which has never yet been seen."

As only one man bent on the destruction and rebuilding of occidental culture, Nietzsche *can only* try to prevent a politics of domination and further denaturing and "desecration of man" by proposing himself as one who can "rule the world." And how does he do this? How incite *Geisteskrieger*? By proclaiming these things loudly in the grand style of prophetic and apocalyptic language and then dying in the form of "madness." How could Nietzsche instigate wars that were to replace Christianity without actual armies, how could he "undertake the venture of effecting a European revolution without the legions of Caesar or the armies of Napoleon"?[67] By offering *himself* as the perfect example of such a spiritual soldier. One who created himself perfectly, as a warrior of truth in the sense of the old logos, as one who stands stoically in the face of reality and fate, as one proclaiming and praising his future people and his god Dionysus with every fiber of his body and spirit, as a man in the grand style who stands in opposition to 2,000 years of decadence! By making the redemptive move *par excellence* in the grand style; he attempts to "turn every 'it was' into a 'thus I willed it.'"[68] By creating himself as a star glowing on our horizon with our hope on his lips, then by purposely extinguishing himself at the height of his existence, thus dying in battle at the front lines! Nietzsche: "So to die as once I saw him die: victorious, *destroying.*"[69] Nietzsche's act of "madness" was his death; the *deed* he offered to serve as "proof out of his life" [*pistis ek tou Biou*] of his words, his legislative jump into the abyss, the carrying out of his own secret sentence based on his own new law, in order to redeem the world. To create and to die so magnificently in a world historical agon that he himself had created, in order to balance the scales with the dying Socrates and the Crucified so that others, the "oath-takers," would desire nothing more ardently than to take up his words and example to begin creation of a new world.

NIETZSCHE'S APOCALYPSE

> Even when Nietzsche is at his most Nietzschean, spewing out venom in *The Antichrist*—we are tempted to say, indeed, especially then—as he calls for the criminalization of Christianity and the razing of its temples, even then his apocalyptic rhetoric evokes the cadences of St. John at Patmos in the critics' description: "The idea of a new time and a new history."[70]

Prophets typically offer narratives told in the first person: here the prophet relates his own experiences and his own vocation. They recount events in the prophet's life or the conditions in which he worked.[71] Nietzsche's *Ecce Homo* fulfills the first-person narrative of the prophet and serves as his apocalypse as well. The very title refers to Pontius Pilate's designation of Christ before he was to be crucified: "Behold the Man." Nietzsche wants to say in *Ecce Homo*: Behold the new man, the Antichrist, anti-idealist and immoralist, but all out of the great Yes to life and the future overhuman. It is crucial to emphasize that *Ecce Homo* is also a revaluing of the Socratic *Apology*, in which Nietzsche enumerates his life and revaluation, after which he chooses to die publicly for the truth of those values (as did Socrates). In Zarathustra's words: "under their eyes I want to go under; dying, I want to give them my richest gift."[72] Nietzsche's hope was that once his downgoing was recognized as a voluntary redemptive death, the oath-takers would arise to bring on the new Dionysian age.

In the first sentence of *Ecce Homo*, Nietzsche announces that he *must* "confront humanity with the most difficult demand ever made of it." He goes on to say that he is going to wipe his hands of the old world in favor of a future world. This is an apocalyptic claim. He claims that only a few—the chosen ones—will understand what he is about to say. Just as St. John at Patmos writes: "He that hath an ear, let him hear." Nietzsche, in many places writes: "Let those who can, grasp me." He refers to *Zarathustra* as the highest book written and the greatest gift to humankind. It is a book for the most select. In a letter to Paul Deussen, November 26, 1888, Nietzsche writes of his autobiographical *Ecce Homo*: "This book is about me,—I come forth in it with a world historical mission. It is already at the printers—For the first time in this book there is light shed on my *Zarathustra*, the first book of all millennia, the bible of the future, the highest outbreak of human genius, in which the fate of humankind is grasped."[73]

Nietzsche's apocalypse is a vision of the destruction of antinature and the coming of a millennial decision, a turning point in human time. Apocalyptic literature only comes after the rewriting of the Hebraic tradition into the oppositions of good and evil, sin and redemption. The visions of prophets like Ezekiel and Zechariah paved the way, and apocalypse as a literary form was already fully developed by the time of Daniel and in the many apocryphal writings about the time of the beginning of the Christian era. There is only one instance of apocalypse in the New Testament, Revelation. Revelation is first and foremost a tract for the times, like the apocalypse of Daniel that preceded it and on which it draws. Nietzsche's apocalyptical tone speaks for our time and transports a vision of the destruction of denatured and desecrated humans under Christianity and idealism in favor of his Dionysian "party of life," earth, and the future. "The uncovering of Christian morality is an event without parallel, a real catastrophe. He that is enlightened about that is a *force majeure*, a destiny—he breaks the history of mankind in two. One lives before him, or one lives after him."[74]

Apocalyptic rhetoric talks of cosmic events, not just of earthly movements of politics and religious conflict as does prophetic literature. It takes place between heaven and hell where divine power can strike down armies. Nietzsche's prophetic rhetoric ushers in the realities of earthly strife in human increments of time. But his apocalyptic statements go beyond that in the usual definitions of the distinctions between these two types of rhetoric. Apocalyptic literature sets up the cosmic opposites *who must meet in mortal combat*. Christianity not only forms the institutions of Nietzsche's contemporary Europe, but is "a crime against life." Here one moves into the cosmic conflict of life affirmation versus the negation of life, in the apocalyptic literature, the contest between good and evil. Nietzsche:

I contradict as has never been contradicted before and am nevertheless the opposite of a No-saying spirit . . . I am . . . the man of calamity. For when truth enters into a fight with the lies of millennia, we shall have upheavals, a convulsion of earthquakes, a moving of mountains and valleys, the like of which has never been dreamed of. The concept of politics will have merged entirely with a war of spirits; all power structures of the old society will have been exploded—all of them are based on lies: there will be wars the like of which have never yet been seen on earth. It is only beginning with me that the earth knows *great politics*.[75]

Nietzsche sets up the contest between affirmation and the negation of resentment values in line with apocalyptic models, *but he intends to go beyond this duality* in the Dionysian eternal recurrence. This is the very reason for reviving Zarathustra—to destroy the opposites he first created. Apocalyptic literature is more concerned with the "end of history," "last things," than with specific historical circumstances.[76] For Nietzsche there is no end of history or last thing, no final judgment, rather, eternal return. Apocalyptic literature deals with stylized units of time: "weeks" of years, successive kingdoms, or millennia, the present age and the age to come. Nietzsche makes use of all of these units of time but elevated to cosmic proportions in the eternal recurrence. Nietzsche predicts "wars the like of which have never yet been seen on earth," wars for the destruction of Christianity, but these are affirmed as a new moment in the play of eternal recurrence. Nietzsche's *amor fati*, love your fate, is Greek in the old sense. All that comes from the gods is to be met with stoic courage and celebratory strength. From the perspective of *amor fati* and reality, Nietzsche affirms even what Christianity itself has made of us through "the conscience-vivisection and self-torture of millennia,"[77] but only as a moment on the way to something more. This is the overturning of the extreme resentment apocalypse in the Christian sense; no final judgment, rather a promise of more life! "What I am today, where I am today—at a height where I speak no longer with words but with lightning bolts—. . . the great calm in promising, this happy gaze into a future that is not to remain a mere promise!"[78]

After finishing *The Antichrist*, the revaluation of all values, on September 30, 1888, Nietzsche writes: "great victory, seventh day; the leisure of a god walking along the Po river."[79] He has created the vision and possibility of a new world and almost more importantly, from an apocalyptic perspective, the destruction of the old. "Whoever wants to be a creator in good and evil, must first be an annihilator and break values."[80] In his last letter to Jacob Burckhardt of January 6, 1889, Nietzsche expresses the prophetic and redemptive "I" when he writes: "I would much rather be a Basel professor than God; but I have not dared push my private egoism so far as to desist for its sake from the creation of the world."[81]

THE APOCALYPSE OF THE SEVEN SEALS
OR THE YES AND AMEN SONG

By satirizing the Book of Revelation in *Ecce Homo*, Nietzsche is consciously setting up, through the parallel use of apocalyptic language, a new Book of Revelation where not the final judgment of the Christian God is to be awaited, but rather, the revaluation of all values—of those very Christian values themselves. Nietzsche's apocalyptic Book of Revelation, *Ecce Homo*, announces a new Dionysian age with Zarathustra and himself as its instigators. To construct himself as a contestant, literally strong enough not only to herald but to actually begin a millennial change in human life and spirituality, a new rhetoric and way of life must be in place that breaks from the idealistic and resentment forms of Christian rhetoric that Nietzsche adopted only to destroy Christianity. Nietzsche has this in place in the dithyramb. With his newly invented style of dithyramb Nietzsche means to revive the ancient form of dithyramb that led its participants to a direct relation to life and the mysteries of their god. "The Seven Seals or the Yes and Amen Song" in *Zarathustra* is Nietzsche's supreme art of dithyramb in the grand style. It is his new Apocalypse. In it he uses "the art of the *great* rhythm, the *great* style of long periods to express a tremendous up and down of sublime, of superhuman passion." With it he says he "soared a thousand miles beyond what was called poetry hitherto."[82]

In the Old Testament apocalypse of Daniel there is a "sealed book" that contains a divine secret, a message for generations to come. In the New Testament Book of Revelation, John takes the "sealed book" of Daniel: "Then I saw in the right hand of the one seated on the throne a scroll written on the inside and on the back, sealed with seven seals; and I saw a mighty angel proclaiming with a loud voice, 'Who is worthy to open the scroll and break its seals?' And no one in heaven or on earth or under the earth was able to open the scroll or to look into it."[83] Only Jesus can open the seals. As he opens each seal the "wrath of the lamb" is unleashed upon the world. The first four seals release the apocalyptic horsemen who are "to kill by the sword, by famine, by plague and wild beasts." When the sixth seal is opened, "there was a violent earthquake and the sun went as black as coarse sackcloth; the moon turned red as blood all over, and the stars of the sky fell on to the earth like figs dropping from a fig tree when a high wind shakes it; the sky disappeared like a scroll rolling up and all the mountains and islands were shaken from their places."[84] The seventh seal brings not disaster, but seven angels with trumpets setting up seven more actions. More dreadful calamities fall on the earth, but John is not allowed to pass the message of the seventh angel to his readers; it remains unknown and unspoken. Then Jesus says:

> It is done! I am the Alpha and the Omega, the beginning and the end. To the thirsty I will give water as a gift from the spring of the water of life. Those who conquer will inherit these things, and I will be their God and they will be my children. But as for the cowardly, the faithless, the polluted, the murderers, the fornicators, the sorcerers, the idolaters, and all liars, their place will be in the lake that burns with fire and sulfur, which is the second death.[85]

At the end of Revelation there is the "marriage supper of the Lamb" and the bride is the new Jerusalem.

In order to write a new Apocalypse, Nietzsche takes the seventh uncommunicated message of the New Testament Revelation and makes it his own in his dithyramb, "The Seven Seals." Nietzsche's "Seven Seals" is a direct counterpart of the seven seals opened in the Book of Revelation that release destruction on the enemies of God. The Apocalypse of John, which Nietzsche characterizes as "the most wanton of all literary outbursts that vengefulness has on its conscience," is steeped in resentment and unrestrained righteous pleasure in the destruction God brings upon the enemies of Christianity.[86] Nietzsche's "Seven Seals" also speaks of destruction but out of love and eternal affirmation and uses a dithyrambic rhetoric that is a dancing song: light and joyful.

In the "Seven Seals," Nietzsche is a prophet hanging between past and future. He speaks no longer with words, but with prophetic lightening and thunder, and what he speaks and laughs is: Yes! He will kindle the light of the future. It is true that his *wrath* bursts tombs and moves boundary stones, rolls old tablets into steep depths, and that he sits jubilating where old gods lie buried, world blessing, world loving. He loves to sit on broken churches. It was the breath of heavenly need that constrained him to dance such star dances and that constrained him to follow such dances obediently by the long deed of his self-sacrifice. Because he played dice with gods at gods' tables he caused the earth to quake and snort up floods of fire. Out of fragment and accident Nietzsche has created unity and has blended all spices, even the greatest evil, in the draft for the last *foaming over*. The last foaming over is not the last judgment but its opposite, it is the eternal draft of Dionysian wine and celebration! Nietzsche is the agonal contestant. He struggles with life, the sea, and *most fondly* when it contradicts him. He has a seafarer's delight, a warrior's delight and has the courage to go where no one has been. Nietzsche is a Dionysian dancer in golden-emerald delight, filled with sarcasm, laughter, and holy bliss. And then in the sixth verse he writes in direct contradiction to Christ's alpha and omega in John's *Revelation*: "My alpha and omega is that all that is heavy and grave should become light; all that is body, dancer; all that is spirit, bird." The seventh verse and last seal bequeaths to humans the commandment: "Sing, speak no more."[87] All of this while Nietzsche is dancing the marriage pledge with eternity: "Oh, how should I not lust after the nuptial ring of rings, the ring of recurrence. For, I love you, O Eternity!"[88]

The decision is still at hand: the antinature and desecration of man or the new Dionysian party of life! The old Apocalypse of revenge and destruction or the new apocalypse of joy in one's own strength and courage! Nietzsche is the world redeeming *exarchon*; he has struck up the lyre and song; he wants to lead the dithyrambic dance. For this he will need dancers, singers, creators!

NOTES

1. *EH*, preface, 1.
2. *EH*, "The Birth of Tragedy," 4.
3. *Jerusalem Bible* (Garden City, N.Y.: Doubleday, 1966), 1117.
4. *Jerusalem Bible*, 1115–16.
5. Alexander Nehamas, *Nietzsche: Life as Literature* (Cambridge, Mass.: Harvard University Press, 1985), 22.
6. Friedrich Nietzsche, *The Will to Power*, trans. Walter Kaufmann and R. J. Hollingdale (New York: Random House, 1967), 749.
7. Nehamas, *Nietzsche*, 31.
8. *EH*, "Destiny," 1.
9. *EH*, "Destiny," 2.
10. *EH*, "Why I Write Such Good Books," 2.
11. Friedrich Nietzsche, *The Antichrist*, in *The Portable Nietzsche*, trans. Walter Kaufmann (New York: Penguin, 1978), preface.
12. *Nietzsche's Case: Philosophy as/and Literature*, Bernd Magnus, Stanley Stewart, and Jean-Pierre Mileur, (New York: Routledge, 1993), 87.
13. *EH*, "Destiny," 1.
14. See *Twilight of the Idols*, "What I Owe to the Ancients," sec. 2 in *The Portable Nietzsche*.
15. "Homer's Contest," in *Portable Nietzsche*, 35–37.
16. Ibid., 37. See also *TW*, "Ancients," 3.
17. Nehamas, *Nietzsche*, 29.
18. *TW*, "Skirmishes of an Untimely Man," sec. 11.
19. *Friedrich Nietzsche on Rhetoric and Language*, trans. and ed., Sander Gilman, Carole Blair, and David Parent (New York: Oxford University Press, 1989), 91.
20. Ibid., 43.

21. Thomas Cole, *Origins of Rhetoric in Ancient Greece* (Baltimore: Johns Hopkins University Press, 1991), 72.

22. Dionysius of Halicarnassus, *The Critical Essays*, vol. 1, trans. Stephen Usher (Cambridge: Harvard University Press, 1974), 531.

23. Gilman et al., *Rhetoric and Language*, 121–23.

24. Ken Casey, "The Quarrel between Rhetoric and Philosophy: Ethos and the Ethics of Rhetoric" (Ph.D. diss., University of Minnesota, 1992), 85.

25. *AC* 1.

26. *EH*, "Why I Am So Wise," 1.

27. *AC* 62.

28. Friedrich Nietzsche, *Daybreak*, trans. R. J. Hollingdale (Cambridge: Cambridge University Press, 1982), 38.

29. Gilman et al., *Rhetoric and Language*, 229–30

30. Ibid., 231.

31. *TW*, "The Hammer Speaks."

32. H. D. Rankin, *Archilochus of Paros* (Park Ridge, N.J.: Noyes Press, 1977), 16.

33. Ibid., 9.

34. C. A. Trypanis, *Greek Poetry from Homer to Seferis* (Chicago: University of Chicago Press, 1981), 27.

35. Friedrich Nietzsche, *The Birth of Tragedy*, trans. Walter Kaufmann (New York: Random House, 1967), 5, 49.

36. *BT* 5, 52.

37. See *BT* 21, 124. At the end of *Twilight* Nietzsche calls to us to "Become Hard." At the end of *Antichrist* he incites us to create a new time reckoning. At the end of *Ecce Homo* he challenges us to choose between Dionysus and the Crucified.

38. Friedrich Nietzsche, "The Struggle between Science and Wisdom," in *Philosophy and Truth: Selections from Nietzsche's Notebooks of the Early 1870s*, trans. Daniel Breazeale (Atlantic Highlands, N.J.: Humanities Press International, 1979), 133.

39. *BT* 8, 17, 19. I could have gone on to write a section on Nietzsche's admiration of Horace and Rome as a poet and an age that he considered to have written and lived in the grand style. Horace was greatly influenced by Archilochus. To follow up this continuation of his discussions of the grand style in the Roman world, see *Nietzsche on Rhetoric and Language*, 43–47, where he traces certain techniques of the grand style in Roman oratory, his praise of Horace in *TW*, "Ancients," sec. 1, and his anguish at the destruction of the grand style in Roman and Greek life at the hands of Christianity in *AC* 59.

40. *EH*, "Thus Spoke Zarathustra," 7.

41. *D* 187.

42. *WP* 972.

43. *D* 14.

44. Friedrich Nietzsche, *Beyond Good and Evil*, trans. Walter Kaufmann (New York: Random House, 1966), 52.

45. Exodus 19:23.

46. *Thus Spoke Zarathustra,* in *Portable Nietzsche,* pt. III, "On Old and New Tablets, sec. 19.

47. Exodus 24:3, 7.

48. Exodus 24:8.

49. Z I, "On Reading and Writing."

50. Exodus 24:12.

51. Z III, "On Old and New Tablets," 1. See Graham Parkes, "The Dance from Mouth to Hand," in *Nietzsche as Postmodernist,* ed. Clayton Koelb (Albany: State University of New York Press, 1990), where he also explores similarities between Moses and Nietzsche, 130–31.

52. See Walter Kaufmann's preface to *The Antichrist,* in *The Portable Nietzsche,* 565–66.

53. *EH,* "Destiny," 1.

54. *WP* 972.

55. *WP* 995.

56. *EH,* "Thus Spoke Zarathustra," 1.

57. *Jerusalem Bible,* 1116.

58. *EH,* "Zarathustra," 3.

59. *EH,* "Zarathustra," 3.

60. *Jerusalem Bible,* 1116.

61. John Gabel and Charles Wheeler, *The Bible as Literature,* 2nd ed. (London: Oxford University Press, 1990), 106.

62. *Jerusalem Bible,* 1117.

63. *EH,* "The Case of Wagner," 1. Nietzsche's utterances of political vehemence recall Archilochus singing out his "Homeless fellow citizens now grasp my words" and assailing ignorance and public folly. Or he sounds like Horace, who Nietzsche also praises as one who uses the grand style, when Horace harangues the Roman people on the dangers of civil strife in Epode 16: "That is the Rome which we, this race, destroy; We, impious victims of ourselves devoted."

64. *EH,* "Wagner," 4.

65. *AC* 61.

66. At the beginning of *EH,* on the famous interleaf, Nietzsche blesses and is grateful for his whole life, exactly as he represents Zarathustra as doing before his death in section IV of this note, just weeks before orchestrating his own madness. In our books *Postponements: Woman, Sensuality, and Death in Nietzsche* (Bloomington: Indiana University Press, 1986) and *To Nietzsche: Dionysus, I Love You! Ariadne* (Albany: State University of New York Press, 1995), David Farrell Krell and I have shown that one of the world-redemptive models at the heart of Nietzsche's psychology, writing, and life was Empedocles. From 1870 to 1872 Nietzsche was working on notes and sketches for his "Empedocles drama," in which he was writing the very drama, in a prophetic sense, of his own lived life. In the "Empedocles drama" Empedocles ends his life by jumping into the volcano Etna to save the people. The madness and self-sacrifice of Empedocles and the announcement of rebirth before he jumps were depicted by Nietzsche as being necessary for healing the people. Krell shows in many notes and sketches for a "Zarathustra drama" (summer and fall of 1883) and notes

and sketches from the *Zarathustra* period (1883–85), that Nietzsche took these themes up into the character of Zarathustra. In my book (1995), I show that Nietzsche had as a constant psychological perspective the belief that a transforming hero, prophet, legislator must die to transform the world (as did Socrates, Jesus, etc.) and claim that Nietzsche consciously transferred the necessary redeeming death before the eyes of the people (of Empedocles/Zarathustra) to himself in his simulated act of madness.

67. Erich Podach, *The Madness of Nietzsche* (New York: Putnam, 1931), 132–33.

68. *EH*, "Zarathustra," 8.

69. Friedrich Nietzsche, *Dithyrambs of Dionysus*, trans. R. J. Hollingdale (Redding Ridge, Conn.: Black Swan Books, 1984), 39.

70. Magnus et al., *Nietzsche's Case*, 51.

71. Gabel and Wheeler, *Bible as Literature*, 108.

72. Z III, "On Old and New Tablets," 3.

73. *Nietzsche Briefwechsel*, Kritische Gesamtausgabe, 3:6, ed. Giorgio Colli and Mazzino Montinari (Berlin: Walter de Gruyter, 1984), 492.

74. *EH*, "Destiny," 8.

75. *EH*, "Destiny," 1.

76. Gabel and Wheeler, *Bible as Literature*, 132–33.

77. *GM* II:24.

78. *GM* II:16.

79. *EH*, "Twilight," 3.

80. *EH*, "Twilight," 2.

81. Quoted in *Portable Nietzsche*, p. 685.

82. *EH*, "Books," 4.

83. Revelation 5.

84. Revelation 6.

85. Revelation 21:5.

86. *GM* I:16.

87. For just how we are to dance, become light, speak no longer, but sing, see my article "Nietzsche's Dionysian Arts: Dance, Song and Silence," in *Nietzsche, Philosophy and the Arts* (Cambridge University Press, 1998).

88. Z III, "The Seven Seals," sec. 3. See Laurence Lampert, *Nietzsche's Teaching: An Interpretation of Thus Spoke Zarathustra* (New Haven: Yale University Press, 1986), where he also discusses connections between The Book of Revelation and Nietzsche's "Seven Seals," 240–44.

CHAPTER 15

Nietzsche's Secrets

Deborah Hayden

Watch out!—There is nothing we like to show others more than
the seal of secrecy along with what lies under it.
—*The Gay Science*

The philosopher Karl Jaspers wrote that anyone who finds consistency
in Friedrich Nietzsche's work has not read far enough: "*self-contradic-
tion* is the fundamental ingredient in Nietzsche's thought."[1] The same
can be said of his biography. While the linear chronology of his life is
carefully documented, unsolved mysteries and unanswered questions—
of love and death, sex and syphilis, genius and insanity—have yielded so
many different Nietzsches that his contemporary image is more a cubist
painting than a frontal portrait. Each new study off the press adds
another conflicting view, and past interpretations change as new biographical detail is added to the lore. His own life has become the best
illustration of his theory of perspectivism, with prejudices of each successive decade adding complexity to the Nietzsche legend.

Nietzsche was born in the small town of Röcken on October 15,
1844. His father was a Lutheran pastor and his mother a Lutheran pastor's daughter. Pastor Nietzsche died when little Fritz was almost five,
leaving him and his sister Elisabeth to be raised by his mother, two
unmarried aunts, and a grandmother. At fourteen he enrolled on scholarship at the boarding school Pforta. After attending university first at
Bonn and then Leipzig, he was appointed to teach classical philology at
Basel. After ten years there, he obtained a paid medical leave of absence
and spent the next decade traveling and writing, mostly in Italy and
Switzerland. At the start of 1889 he went insane, and after a brief incar-
ceration, he spent the next eleven years in the care of his mother and sister. He died on August 25, 1900.

While each Nietzsche biography uses the well-documented events of his life to tell its own internally consistent story, an overview of the vast literature reveals countless contradictions and scholarly squabbles. Did he have syphilis? If so, when, where and how did he contract it—and was he aware that he was infected? If he was aware, did such knowledge contribute to his self-image as a culture critic and outsider? When did his insanity first manifest? Was it on January 3, 1889, when he fell to the ground in the town square of Turin and rose insane? Or were his last works already showing the effects of dementia? Was he in love with Lou Salomé? (Or Cosima Wagner? Or Paul Rée?) What mysterious "offense" (as he called it) caused his break with Lou? Did he break with Richard Wagner over the religious nature of *Parsifal*—or because Wagner spread dangerous rumors about his sexuality? What did Nietzsche's mother learn that led her to call her son an insult to his father's grave? Had Franziska Nietzsche been both boisterous and overattentive as a young mother, a "wild shoot" in the pious Nietzsche family, or was she stupid and remote? Was Pastor Nietzsche the epitome of the gentle country parson, as Nietzsche recalled, or an evil tyrant who beat the boy and locked him in dark closets?[2]

How these questions are answered shapes the various accounts of Nietzsche's life. The subject—*Nietzsche*—remains the same, but the story unfolds very differently when written by Lou Salomé, Elisabeth Nietzsche, H. L. Mencken, Charles Andler, Erich Podach, Karl Jaspers, Crane Brinton, Walter Kaufmann, R. J. Hollingdale, Curt Paul Janz, or Ronald Hayman.

Contradiction in the biographical literature began with books by Lou Salomé, a woman who was Nietzsche's friend in 1882, and by his sister Elisabeth. Lou's study, published in 1894, was followed a year later by the first of Elisabeth's three volumes (eventually reduced to two—*The Young Nietzsche,* which describes an idyllic childhood, and *The Lonely Nietzsche,* the story of the hermit years). Lou's book traced the development of his thought through various periods of his life. "If the task of the biographer is to explicate the thinker through his person, it applies in an unusual degree to Nietzsche because external intellectual work and a picture of his inner life coalesce completely."[3] By contrast Elisabeth's books contain little about her brother's philosophy but quite a bit about that "miserable compound of cunning and malice"[4]—her enemy, Lou Salomé. Nietzsche's friend and transcriber Peter Gast, who knew Nietzsche's work intimately, marveled that Lou resisted becoming inflamed by Nietzsche and instead retained a cold and observational attitude toward him. To Gast's mind she was a woman whose level of intelligence was seen only five or six times a century. Elisabeth predictably dismissed Lou's effort as "a product of injured feminine vanity revenging itself upon a poor invalid who could no longer defend himself"⁵ and concluded: "Frau Lou Andreas paints a fancy picture, of which one can only say 'It isn't Nietzsche!'"⁶ Nietzsche's friend Franz Overbeck found Elisabeth's book to be the dishonest one: "rarely has the reading public been so duped," he wrote,⁷ as in the book by Nietzsche's dangerous sister.

Lou never answered Elisabeth's various charges against her—despite Sigmund Freud's urging years later. "It has often annoyed me," Freud wrote to her, "to find your relationship to Nietzsche mentioned in a way which was obviously hostile to you and which could not possibly correspond with the facts. You have put up with everything and have been far too decent; I hope that now at last you will defend yourself, even though in the most dignified way."⁸

THE STORY OF NIETZSCHE, LOU, AND ELISABETH

Early in 1882 Nietzsche traveled to Rome with the encouragement of his friend, the philosopher Paul Rée, to meet a young woman from Russia who was traveling in Italy with her mother. Nietzsche spent most of his time in Rome in bed plagued by intense migraines, but he did venture out to meet Lou.

Lou, who had just spent the year studying at the University of Zurich, hoped to find in the spas of Italy a cure for persistent health problems of her own—chronic fever and bleeding lungs. She had met Paul Rée at the salon of Malwida von Meysenbug, idealist and former revolutionary, whose drawing room was one of the cultural centers of Europe. Accompanied by Rée, Lou went to the Basilica of St. Peter to meet Nietzsche. She recorded her first impression of him in her diary:

> I would say that this reserve, this inkling of concealed loneliness, is the first strong impression which makes Nietzsche's appearance so striking. . . . His eyes truly betrayed him. Although half-blind, they showed no trace of the peering and blinking and involuntary intrusiveness of many shortsighted people. They looked much more like guardians of treasures and unspoken secrets which no trespassers should glimpse. This defective vision lent his features a special kind of magic in that instead of reflecting ever-changing, external impressions, they revealed only what he had internalized.⁹

Nietzsche felt he had finally found the long wished-for disciple in Lou. He wrote to Malwida, "This year, which signifies a new crisis in several chapters of my life [epoch is the right word—an intermediate state between two crises, one behind me, one ahead of me] has been made much more beautiful for me by the radiance and charm of this truly heroic soul. I wish to acquire a pupil in her and, if my life should not last much longer, an heir and one who will develop my thoughts."¹⁰ Lou, twenty-one that year, had been raised in a German-speaking community in St. Petersburg where her father was a general in the Czar's military administration. Having come to Europe in pursuit of an intellectual life, she soon made plans to spend the following winter with Nietzsche and Rée in Paris, as part of the lively intellectual circle around the Russian expatriate Ivan Turgenev. When Lou's mentor in Russia, the evangelical preacher Hendrik Gillot, greeted her announcement of the plan with dismay, she replied passionately that she thought he would be singing her praises over how well she had learned her lesson: this was no fantasy but reality involving "individuals you might have selected yourself, filled almost to bursting with spirituality and keenness of mind." She continued with youthful ardor: "I can't live according to some model, and I could never be a model for anyone else; but I intend to shape my life for myself, no matter how it turns out. This is not a matter of some principle I'm following, but something much more wonderful—something that exists inside me, glowing with life itself, something that wants to burst forth with a shout of joy."¹¹

Nietzsche, too, was exuberant. "How could I fear fate," he wrote to Ida Overbeck, "particularly when it confronts me in the wholly unexpected form of Lou? Rée and I feel the same devotion to our courageous, high-minded friend: even on this score he and I have great faith in each other, and we are not of the dumbest or youngest.—So far I have kept strict silence here about all these things."¹² To Peter Gast he wrote that Lou was "amazingly ripe and ready for *my* way of thinking."¹³

Lou spent most of May at Paul Rée's family estate in Stibbe, working on notes for a study of Nietzsche. In July she attended Richard Wagner's summer festival in Bayreuth with Elisabeth but without Nietzsche, who was by then *persona non grata* in the Wagner camp. "As for Bayreuth," Nietzsche wrote to her, "I am satisfied not to *have* to be there, and yet, if I could be near you in a ghostly way, murmuring this and that in your ear, then I would find even the music of *Parsifal* endurable [otherwise it is not endurable]."¹⁴ Lou and Elisabeth had an argument following the festival, and when Elisabeth reported it to Nietzsche he canceled a planned time with Lou, but he soon changed his mind and they spent three weeks together in Tautenburg—with Elisabeth (still angry) staying nearby. There they had their most intense philosophical discussions. Nietzsche later wrote that it was only after meeting Lou that he was ready for his Zarathustra. "If anyone had heard us," Lou wrote in her memoir, "he would have thought two devils were conversing."¹⁵

Elisabeth, apparently, did think just that. From early childhood, she had revered her brother. That summer she discovered he had changed. To her friend Clara Gelzer she wrote:

Do not read my brother's books, they are too frightful for us, our hearts are made for higher things than the self-admiration of egotism. Oh, make no effort or cause yourself any pain by attempting to reconcile these books with earlier Nietzsche works, it is not possible because, my dear dear Clara, and *tell no one*, I have lived through a frightful experience here and I have had to recognize that Fritz has become different, he is just like his books.[16]

Elisabeth blamed Lou for leading her brother astray: "she is the personification of my brother's philosophy with that furious egotism which tears apart everything in its path."[17]

Nietzsche spent October in Leipzig with Lou and Rée, visiting friends and experimenting with the life they planned to live together the following year. But in November without warning he announced to Ida Overbeck that the Trinity was off, and he began to write vicious letters to Lou, blaming her for an unspecified offense. "If I banish you from me now, it is a frightful censure of your whole being. . . . You have caused damage, you have done *harm*—and not only to me but to all the people who have loved me: this sword hangs over you."[18] Lou, whose letters of the period have been lost, apparently defended herself—Nietzsche wrote of her "justification"—but whatever she said failed to reconcile him. "Should Lou be a misunderstood angel?" he asked. "Should I be a misunderstood ass?"[19] And finally, "Adieu, my dear Lou, I shall not see you again."[20]

Lou never did see Nietzsche again. Three times she went to Celerina, a short distance from Sils Maria where Nietzsche spent his summers, but she never made the trip to the white boarding house where he lived. Afterward she lived in a scholarly community as planned with Paul Rée, though in Berlin instead of Paris. In their intellectual circle, which included many of Nietzsche's friends, his absence was felt: "he stood, like a hidden shadow, an invisible figure, in our midst."[21] The sociologist-to-be Ferdinand Tönnies temporarily took Nietzsche's planned place as third housemate. Tönnies, who at first idolized Nietzsche but later came to believe his elitism was dangerous, was sent by Lou on a mission of reconciliation to Sils Maria. "I encountered the hermit frequently and felt the piercing gaze of his feeble eyes upon me," Tönnies wrote, but he found himself unable to speak to Nietzsche: "An alien fate deterred me."[22]

During Nietzsche's insanity Elisabeth took over from her mother the rights of administration of her brother's literary estate and established the Nietzsche Archive at Weimar. Nominated three times for the Nobel Prize for her literary work on Nietzsche's legacy, she enjoyed the fame denied her brother by dementia. She saw herself equal to Cosima Wagner as the guardian of the immortal remains of one of the two greatest men of the nineteenth-century; like Cosima, she claimed the right to edit as she pleased. Her privileged status did not survive the disclosure by Karl Schlechta and others that she had forged and falsified documents, and rewritten or reattributed letters by and to Nietzsche. H. L. Mencken's story of Nietzsche cast Elisabeth as the loving and helpful sister. In the contemporary literature she has been reduced to lurking "malignantly in the footnotes, the undergrowth of history."[23] Ben Macintyre referred to her as nasty, bigoted, ambitious, and bloody-minded. It is a rare subject who can elicit such adjectives from her biographer.

Lou earned her living and established her reputation as a woman of letters in Europe writing novels, stories, essays, and reviews. Beginning at age fifty she trained in psychoanalysis, which she practiced until her death in 1937. She was Sigmund Freud's close friend and confidante.

After her death Ernst Pfeiffer, the executor of her literary estate, published her retrospective memoirs under the title *Looking Back*. Here she stated, as she had previously told others, that Nietzsche and Rée had both proposed marriage to her. For many years Pfeiffer denied access to Lou's archive, with the exception of a few scholars who were restricted to taking notes only when he was present in the room, and at that with some of the material (such as the Anna Freud correspondence) within view—but tantalizingly off limits.

In 1962 H. F. Peters used the material in the archive for a biography of Lou, somewhat in the style of a romantic novel, centering on her troubled friendship with Nietzsche, and in 1968 Rudolph Binion published *Frau Lou: Nietzsche's Wayward Disciple*. If at first Binion had felt no need to "rehash that stale Nietzsche-Lou story,"[24] he soon found Nietzsche (and his rejection of Lou) to be central to the narrative of her life. What began as a psychoanalytic study of a psychoanalyst ended with a repudiation of some of the basic tenets of psychoanalysis, and when Binion finally compiled his thousands of pages of notes into one massive manuscript, he suddenly discovered yet another problem: Lou, it appeared, had invented Nietzsche's proposal of marriage. This surprise led to other unravelings until he "perforce concluded that nothing Lou ever said about herself could be trusted."[25] Faced with yet another rewrite, after his Lou project had already extended years beyond the initial plan, he concluded with a chapter entitled "Beyond *Frau Lou*," in which he acknowledged that the mystery at the base of the story of Lou and Nietzsche was still unsolved. "I am leaving the text discontinuous and inconsistent just so as to underscore its inconclusiveness."[26] In Binion's mind Lou's life is "enchanted,"[27] her writing extraordinary—and her habit of freely fictionalizing her own life irksome to an extreme. Of the many tellings of the tale of Lou and Nietzsche, Binion's remains unique in ending with recognition of the questions that remain unanswered.

While Walter Kaufmann was revising his study of Nietzsche's life, he received the manuscript of *Frau Lou* in the mail. He rewrote his chapter about Lou and Nietzsche based on the new discoveries and concluded:

> The relationships between Nietzsche, Lou, and Rée have been a matter of controversy ever since Nietzsche broke with Lou and Rée. Until 1967 there were mainly two versions: Elisabeth's and Lou's; and those who had discovered Elisabeth's sovereign impatience with the truth, and eventually that she had even tampered with the documents and forged letters, believed in Lou's unquestionable honesty. It was only in a comprehensive study of Lou's life and works published in 1968 that *her* falsification of the record and her tampering with the evidence were proved. Now we know that *both* women are unreliable witnesses.[28]

But Kaufmann's off-handed rejection of the two "unreliable witnesses" was a poor reading of Binion, who had no intention of dismissing Lou so lightly, or of equating her "fabrications" with Elisabeth's "falsifications." Kaufmann ignored Binion's open-ended question of why none of the pieces quite fit together in the story of Lou and Nietzsche: Why *were* both of these women lying? Nietzsche's wish that he and Lou not become the object of European gossip did not come true, and his many invocations to secrecy have only inflamed the curiosity of those who have tried to tell their mysterious story.[29]

Crane Brinton distinguished gentle from tough Nietzscheans. Following Kaufmann most biographers of Nietzsche have been of gentle disposition portraying him as an unlucky lover, chaste but not from choice. Binion's case that Nietzsche's proposal of marriage was Lou's tall tale (whatever her motivation) is lost in the assumption of much of contemporary biography that an infatuated Nietzsche not only proposed to Lou, but that it was her rejection of him that caused his misery at the time of the writing of Zarathustra. Kaufmann, the last person one would expect to accept Elisabeth's word without question, used her correspondence with her friend Clara Gelzer as the source for one of the most inaccurate possible portraits of Lou, stating that "there seems to be no reason to doubt Elisabeth's word"[30] when she promised to tell the whole truth about Lou—warning enough from Elisabeth to be wary of what followed.

In grand soap opera style, various texts have assumed that both Nietzsche and Rée proposed marriage, that Nietzsche had Rée propose on his behalf, that because Rée failed Nietzsche proposed again, and that Nietzsche encouraged Rée to propose. Elisabeth and Ida Overbeck agreed that Nietzsche had no intention of marrying Lou, and Joachim Köhler[31] has suggested that marriage might have been intended as a cover-up for rumors of pederasty[32] circulating around Bayreuth at the time. In all the permutations of marriage possibilities, no one seems to think it strange that two misogynist friends who never before or after had a known erotic relationship would both fall immediately in love with a young woman who expressed a complete disinterest in romantic pursuits.

To sustain this romantic perspective it has often been necessary to contradict Nietzsche. "Dear friend," Nietzsche wrote to Peter Gast, "You'll surely do us both the honor of keeping the notion of a love affair far removed from our relationship. We are *friends,* and I intend to hold this girl and her trust in me sacred."[33] And later, "I myself really do not need to feel ashamed of the whole affair. I have felt the strongest and most genuine emotions for Lou and there was nothing erotic in my love. At most I could have made a god jealous."[34]

While Nietzsche's literary and philosophical reputation has soared, as a man he has always had commentators who have referred to him personally in a demeaning fashion: as "a sport of nature" or "a strange bird" (Jung),[35] "priggish" (Brinton),[36] a "miserable little man" (Nehamas),[37] or a "somewhat pathetic oddball" (Solomon).[38] Similarly, as Lou's stature as a woman of letters has increased with time, speculation about her private life has led to contradictory images that imitate both Nietzsche's high opinion of her in the beginning of their friendship, and his name-calling at the end. (In a letter to Paul Rée's brother he referred to her as "this thin, dirty, evil-smelling little monkey with her false breasts—a fate!")[39] Lou has been described as muse, moral monster, cannibalistic virgin, goddess, cocktease, femme fatale, witch and earth mother. R. J. Hollingdale considered it lucky Nietzsche didn't marry her since she was frigid, while Stanley A. Leavy (editor of her Freud journal) called her compulsively sexual and Victor Emil von Gebsattel (a psychoanalyst and short-term lover) gossiped that she was a nymphomaniac.

QUESTIONS OF SYPHILIS AND SEX
ENTER THE LITERATURE

In 1902 a psychiatrist, P. J. Möbius, published a study that was the result of one of Elisabeth Nietzsche's major miscalculations. Before she granted him access to Nietzsche's medical records at Jena, she might have been warned by his previous books, which included *On the Physiological Weak-Mindedness of Women,* and by his technique, pathography—his other allegedly pathological subjects included Jesus and Shakespeare. He shocked her by revealing the diagnosis of syphilis and by hypothesizing that Nietzsche manifested insanity as early as 1881 (thus before he met Lou). Only the intellectually deaf, Möbius wrote, are unable to hear the undertones of progressive paralysis in Nietzsche's work. He concluded, "If you find pearls do not imagine that it is all one chain of pearls. Be distrustful, for this man has a diseased brain."[40] Möbius wrote that although Nietzsche's attraction for sex had been abnormally weak,[41] he undoubtedly had visited prostitutes; Elisabeth was furious and vehemently denied the possible truth of this allegation. Nonetheless the question of syphilis (and sex) had been raised in print.

To erase the diagnosis of syphilis, Elisabeth tried persuading Franz Overbeck (on his deathbed) to admit that he had given incorrect information when Nietzsche was admitted to the asylum, but Overbeck refused, adding that Nietzsche's doctor, Otto Binswanger, had told him confidentially that he had no doubt of the diagnosis. With word out in the general press, and no help from Overbeck, Elisabeth finally tried at least to control the damage. She commissioned one of Nietzsche's doctors to counter some of the "unsavory" gossip set off by the diagnosis with a hypothesis that Nietzsche might have contracted the disease by smoking a contaminated cigar when he was a military nurse. "How easily a transmission of the poison could have taken place if he ever set down his cigar in order to help a patient in the crowded vehicle!"[42]

A few years after what Elisabeth referred to as Möbius' "disgusting calumny," Ludwig von Scheffler, a student of Nietzsche's at Basel, composed a portrait of his former professor to counter "very bad images" that "distort his features and give a false idea of him"[43] and published it in the *Neue Freie Presse*. Scheffler's portrait, full of homoerotic hints and innuendoes, linked Nietzsche with the poet August von Platen,[44] a royal page in the Bavarian court who escaped to Italy in 1824 to live the rest of his life free of the sexual restrictions of the north. "How great the similarity of the two men's temperaments was, I had been convinced long ago. In Platen's case the evidence is in his memoirs, which say everything. In Nietzsche's case, I learned it from direct experience."[45] That experience was an episode in which Nietzsche invited his student on a vacation in the south, which Scheffler declined in a poignant scene. "Even to this day I cannot speak of it without shyness. Least of all, however, because I fear an uncomprehending reader. Whoever has looked so deeply into Michelangelo's heart and drawn the veil from Platen's confessions will also not stand in timid silence before Nietzsche's mysterious psyche."[46] Nietzsche was quite familiar with Platen's life: he had requested a copy of the biography of the poet for his birthday from his mother when he was at Pforta.

Scheffler described another meeting with Nietzsche, this time in a museum, before Holbein's self-portrait:

I faltered when I came to the mouth. I could see the lips before me. So fully rounded yet so energetically closed! Not avid, yet as if created for pleasure!

"A mouth . . . ," I stammered bewilderedly.

"A mouth to kiss!"

Disconcertedly I looked aside. Truly, it was Nietzsche who had spoken, in an attitude and tone which seemed to contrast most strangely with the mildly sensual coloration of his words. For leaning far back in his armchair, his head bowed onto his chest and his arms hanging limply on the armrests, he seemed to have spoken out of a dream rather than as a comment on my report.[47]

FREUD, JUNG, AND BIOGRAPHICAL GOSSIP

At the April 1, 1908 meeting of the Vienna Psychoanalytic Society, Paul Federn stated: "According to a reliable source, Nietzsche had at certain periods of his life homosexual relations and acquired syphilis in a homosexual brothel." At the second meeting devoted to Nietzsche (a discussion of the recently published *Ecce Homo* on October 28, 1908) Freud revealed, if not the "reliable source" of that rumor, at least the name of the man who brought it to the Freud inner circle. According to Otto Rank's minutes, Freud said: "We just have not succeeded in understanding Nietzsche's personality. One could look at the matter this way: this is an individual about whom we lack some prerequisite information. Some sexual abnormality is certainly present. Jung claims to have learned that Nietzsche acquired syphilis in a homosexual brothel; however, this is immaterial."[48] Freud described Nietzsche as a man who had reached a degree of introspection never before achieved—or likely to be achieved again; due to paresis he was able to penetrate all layers of the psyche and recognize instincts at the base of everything. "Completely cut off from life by illness, he turns to the only object of investigation that is still accessible to him and which, in any event, is close to him as a homosexual, i.e., the ego."[49]

Although Freud's private comments to his Wednesday group of colleagues remained unpublished in Otto Rank's notebook until 1967, he did have one other occasion to reveal Jung's rumor. His friend Arnold Zweig announced a plan to write a comparison between Freud's thought and Nietzsche's. Oddly, after avoiding comparison with Nietzsche all his life, Freud wrote back pleased that such a study would be available—after he was dead and Zweig was haunted by his memory. But Zweig changed his project. Instead he would write a wildly romantic novel following Nietzsche into psychosis—"the dark realm full of magic laws and the wild residues of the psyche,"[50] with Hitler looming in the background, and with Lou and Cosima Wagner as constellations in the sky.

Freud tried to talk him out of this new plan. Unsuccessful, he mentioned Lou as one of the few people alive who knew anything intimate about Nietzsche. "And she is not given to telling it. Certainly she would only do so by word of mouth. She never wanted to tell me about him. For your purposes she would of course be invaluable."[51] Freud wrote to Lou on Zweig's behalf; she responded quickly: "It is absolutely out of the question that I should participate in this in any way. I cannot consider such a thing and the mere thought of it fills me with dismay. Please tell this to your correspondent in the strongest and most final terms—moreover, how right you are to dissuade him altogether from his Nietzsche plan!"[52] Still Zweig would not give up. He said if Lou would not at least give him details about Nietzsche's Saxon dialect or bushy moustache, he could very well just make it up. "Should writers be allowed to weave such a web of fantasy round the crude pathological facts?" Freud queried.[53]

As a last attempt to show Zweig just how far wrong he could go with his project, Freud revealed the rumor that Nietzsche had been a passive homosexual and had acquired syphilis in a male brothel in Genoa, though not citing Jung as the source. "Whether this is true or not—quién sabe?"[54] Zweig never wrote the novel.

When Freud had been a student of Franz Brentano's at the University of Vienna and a member of the study group that corresponded with Nietzsche, the philosopher had been a "remote and noble figure"[55] to him. And when Freud spoke of the heights from which Lou had descended to join the Freud circle, he was perhaps thinking of her association with Nietzsche. As a doctor Freud found Nietzsche to be a case study like none other. By his great introspection Nietzsche "placed his paretic disposition at the service of science"[56]—and by implication, at the service of Freud himself. Freud may or may not have shied away from too much reading of Nietzsche to avoid undue influence, as he claimed at various times. It is clear, however, that he did not shy away from psychological or medical gossip. One of his early personal links to Nietzsche was Josef Paneth, a university friend who spent time with Nietzsche in the winter of 1883–84 and who wrote letters about him to Freud, which Freud subsequently destroyed. Elisabeth quoted from one of Nietzsche's letters to Paneth in her biography: "Fifty years hence, perhaps, a few men [or one man—it would need a genius!] will be able to see what I have done."[57] Freud published his last, and possibly most philosophical, work—*Moses and Monotheism*—exactly fifty years after the onset of Nietzsche's insanity.[58]

If Freud's attitude toward Nietzsche was a cool, clinical detachment,

Jung's was much more emotional and personal. As a native of Basel Jung had the opportunity to learn biographical details from Nietzsche's former colleagues. His research was done less with the techniques of the academic scholar than of the private investigator. At the university he heard many "unflattering tidbits"[59] about Nietzsche, where he only found two people who spoke favorably of him; both were homosexuals, Jung added—one committed suicide, one "ran to seed as a misunderstood genius."[60] Jung was a colleague of Ludwig Binswanger, a member of Freud's Wednesday evening group, whose uncle (Otto Binswanger) had been Nietzsche's doctor in the asylum. He corresponded with Elisabeth Nietzsche about various biographical matters and with one of Nietzsche's early biographers from Basel, Carl Bernoulli.

In the notes on his seminar on *Nietzsche's Zarathustra,* Jung related a dream of Nietzsche's to the diagnosis of syphilis:

> Nietzsche always suffered from the peculiar phobia that when he saw a toad, he felt that he ought to swallow it. And once when he was sitting beside a young woman at a dinner, he told her of a dream he had had, in which he saw his hand with all the anatomical detail, quite translucent, absolutely pure and crystal-like, and then suddenly an ugly toad was sitting upon his hand and he had to swallow it. You know, the toad has always been suspected of being poisonous, so it represents a secret poison hidden in the darkness where such creatures live—they are nocturnal animals. And the extraordinary fact is that it is a parallel to what actually happened to Nietzsche, of all people—that exceedingly sensitive nervous man has a syphilitic infection. That is a historical fact—I know the doctor who took care of him. It was when he was twenty-three years old. I am sure this dream refers to that fatal impression; this absolutely pure system infected by the poison of the darkness.[61]

Perhaps Jung's most fascinating and surprising source of information was Franz Overbeck. "Overbeck always handled Nietzsche with gloves; I knew him. He was a typical, refined historian, a very learned man, and in all his ways exceedingly polite and careful not to touch anything that was hot."[62] What Jung might have discussed with a fellow medical doctor who had treated Nietzsche for syphilis, or with a fellow historical theologian, remains speculation.

Like Freud, Jung wrote that he had long held back from reading Nietzsche, but less from a desire to avoid influence than from "a secret fear that I might perhaps be like him, at least in regard to the 'secret' which had isolated him from his environment."[63] Jung was referring to Nietzsche's "No. 2" personality," his "Zarathustra"— the dangerous part of himself that he fearlessly released into a world that knew nothing of such things. Jung found Nietzsche's hidden personality to be morbid, and the fear that his own second personality was morbid as well filled him with terror. "I must not let myself find out how far I might be like him,"[64] he wrote, though he did in fact find out through self-analysis following his break with Freud many years later. At every step of the way he hit up against "the same psychic material which is the stuff of psychosis and is found in the insane."[65] But Jung felt he was saved by strong ties to the other world—his wife, children, medical career—unlike Nietzsche, the hermit, who "lost the ground under his feet" and was a "blank page whirling about in the winds of the spirit."[66]

THE LONELY, THE TOUGH, THE ROMANTIC NIETZSCHE

One of the most often quoted portraits of Nietzsche as philosopher-hermit comes from biographer and novelist Stefan Zweig:

> Nietzsche's inborn disposition toward an unduly violent reaction to every stimulus was undoubtedly fostered by the fifteen years he spent in a stifling atmosphere of seclusion. Since during the three hundred and sixty-five days of the year nothing corporeal, neither woman nor friend, came into personal contact with him, since he exchanged scarcely a syllable with anyone but himself, he carried on an uninterrupted dialogue with his own nerves.[67]

In writing of Nietzsche's wretched conditions Zweig hoped to counter the image popular at the time of Nietzsche as a Germanic superman, a Prometheus, an archetypal hero—"every feature of this masterful countenance taut with will-power, health, and strength—such is the portrait usually given of him."[68] In its place he created the sick and miserable Nietzsche. He cataloged these complaints: "Headaches so ferocious that all he could do was to collapse onto a couch and groan in agony, stomach troubles culminating in cramps when he would vomit blood, migrainous conditions of every sort, fevers, loss of appetite, exhaustion, hemorrhoids, intestinal stasis, rigors, night-sweats—a gruesome enumeration, indeed."[69] In Zweig's portrait Nietzsche lived in a series of chilly, dowdy rooms lacking flowers, ornaments, books, or letters:

> Wrapped in a loose overcoat, a woolen muffler round his throat—for the miserable stove merely smoked when lighted and gave forth no heat—his fingers stiff with cold, two pairs of spectacles on his nose, which almost touched the paper as he wrote, he scribbled for hours at a stretch, scribbled down words which his eyes were hard put to it to decipher when the work was done. Those poor eyes burned, and watered with fatigue. . . . During all the years of his pilgrimage he never

once put up in friendly and cheerful surroundings, never at night felt the warm body of a woman pressing against his; never did the sun rise to see him famous.[70]

While this portrait of the sick, lonely Nietzsche may have been accurate enough for certain days in his last years of sanity, it is incorrect that he spent fifteen years—from 1873 to 1888 (included here of course is the year of intense social interaction he spent with Lou and Paul Rée)—in such unremitting isolation. That his conditions were often spartan is true, though more from choice than necessity.[71] But his environment was spectacular (Sils Maria for example)—and as to never having "put up in friendly or cheerful surroundings," consider this letter to his mother, written from Florence in November 1885: "The day after tomorrow we [i.e., Herr Lanzky and I] retreat into the wood-, mountain-, and cloister-solitude of Vallombrosa, not at all far from here. The best room is being prepared for me; we'll have quiet; the place is famous: Dante and Milton have glorified it, the latter in his description of Paradise."[72]

Oddly Zweig himself countered the image of the wretched Nietzsche with one ecstatically Dionysian. In a chapter titled "The Discovery of the South," he wrote about Nietzsche's joyous decamping from Germany. This chapter is so contrary to the one about the miserable Nietzsche that Zweig seems to have been creating an entirely different character. In the "sun-intoxicated joy of life" of the south, having left Germany and "patriotic strangulation" for good, Nietzsche discovered a natural style of life. "He wanted to be burned by the sun, not merely to be illuminated by it; clarity must have cruel teeth that bite; joviality must develop into a voluptuous orgasm."[73] Rid of the tentacles of the past, the professorial chrysalis, the restrictions of Christianity and morality, the Germanic fogs and obscurities, Zweig's ecstatic Nietzsche was free to live as an outlawed prince.

The powerful, violent figure that Stefan Zweig had at first countered with his weak and victimized Nietzsche surfaced again in the literature during and after World War II, when Nietzsche's writing was associated with Nazism. This persona lasted until 1950 when Walter Kaufmann published his opinion that Nietzsche, who was anti-anti-semitic and antinationalistic, was not only innocent of ideological association with Nazism, but could be seen as its philosophical antithesis. Biographically that association began with Elisabeth.

In February 1932 Adolf Hitler arrived in Weimar with a phalanx of stormtroopers. In the National Theater, where a play co-authored by Mussolini was being staged, he approached Elisabeth Nietzsche's box and presented her with a huge bouquet of red roses. While at first she was reluctant to befriend the man who was about to lose the next election, Hitler's rise to power eventually resulted in funding for the archive, which she staffed with Nazis. When she died Hitler gave her a state funeral, and placed a laurel wreath on her coffin. "Believe me," she had written, "Fritz would be enchanted by Hitler, who with incredible courage has taken upon himself the entire responsibility for his people."[74] Elisabeth supported the idea that Nietzsche had influenced National Socialism. Hitler might not have read Nietzsche (the pages of the complete Nietzsche given to him by Mussolini remained uncut), but he financed his way into the Nietzsche legend. And he associated himself closely with the Wagner family as well. As "Aunt Elisabeth" had often watched over Richard's and Cosima's children when she and Nietzsche were on intimate terms with Bayreuth, years later Hitler ("Uncle Wolf") was entrusted with the care of Wagner's grandchildren.[75]

QUESTIONS UNANSWERED

Always lurking beneath the surface of Nietzsche's life story is the question of the poison of the darkness, the mystery and myth of syphilis. According to Crane Brinton, "the fact that Nietzsche did have syphilis may be regarded as proved [as certainly as anything of the kind can be proved]."[76] Still the doubt remains. How did this supposedly chaste man become infected with a sexually transmitted disease? Could he have been infected at birth?—a possibility raised by Ronald Hayman.[77] Was he infected in a brothel in Cologne where he was taken (by mistake)? Nietzsche allegedly recounted this event to his friend Paul Deussen: "I stood for a moment speechless. Then I made instinctively for a piano in the room as to the only living thing in that company and struck several cords. They broke the spell and I hurried away."[78] If Nietzsche left in horror, why then is it stated as fact in so many texts that he contracted syphilis in this brothel in Cologne? Thomas Mann recounted the brothel episode in his novel *Doctor Faustus*, which is based in part on Nietzsche's life. But Mann fictionalized a subsequent encounter with a prostitute, who warned the Nietzsche-character that she was infected with the "exhilarating but wasting disease."[79] This leap of logic is motivated by the question: Where else could a young man of the time have contracted syphilis but a brothel?

If a band of ardent scholars were to raid the Röcken cemetery at night to exhume Nietzsche's bones, would they find the telltale scrimshaw marks of the syphilis spirochete? Perhaps. But they might equally well come up with a delicate female bone. There is a rumor that Elisabeth arranged to have her brother's gravestone moved so that it would be over her own grave. This would not have been the first time

Elisabeth exercised her editorial powers over death. She refashioned Nietzsche's death mask to suit her own idea of proper rigor mortis. When her husband preferred strychnine to life with her (and creditors) in the jungles of Paraguay, she bribed an official to issue a death certificate saying "death by nerves." And to avoid hints of familial mental illness, she invented a story that her father died of a concussion after tripping over the family dog.

Freud admonished Arnold Zweig, "First, it is impossible to understand anyone without knowing his sexual constitution, and Nietzsche's is a complete enigma."[80] The various hypotheses and conjectures about Nietzsche's possible loves, as well as about his sexual habits, are often informed by projection, prudery, denial, cover-ups, lies, and wishful thinking. Gossip and misinformation pass from one book to the next, so that in different texts Nietzsche is heterosexual, homosexual, bisexual, a frequenter of prostitutes, incestuous with his sister, oversexed, undersexed, chaste, promiscuous, a compulsive masturbator, sadistic, or masochistic.

If Lou and Elisabeth are not to be trusted to tell the truth, and if the vast biographical literature spins one contradictory tale after another, is Nietzsche's own self-accounting the final source of information about his life? Nietzsche wrote of masks and labyrinths, and what lay beneath the seal of secrecy that protected his own life is anything but clear from his own words. In May 1885 he wrote to Elisabeth:

> I am much too proud as ever to believe that any person could love *me*, namely this requires the precondition that a person knows *who I am*
> . . .
>
> When I have shown you great rage, it is because you forced me to relinquish the last human beings [Lou and Rée] with whom I could speak without Tartuffery. Now—I am alone. With them, I had been able to converse without a mask about things which interested me . . .
>
> Hide this letter from our mother . . .[81]

Whatever Nietzsche might have revealed about himself in these conversations without a mask with Lou Salomé and Paul Rée remains unknown. Rée fell to his death from a cliff without having written his version of Nietzsche's life, and Lou created her own complex literary mask, her own fiction, to protect her privacy, or his, or because she had learned early on (from him?) that one's self-accounting can be as creative as one's fiction, and not the illusion of one fixed historical truth. Might Lou have been thinking of a conversation without the mask in this diary entry? "Cruel people being always masochists also, the whole thing is inseparable from bisexuality. And that has a deep meaning. The first time I ever discussed this theme was with Nietzsche [that sadomasochist unto himself]. And I know that afterward we dared not look at each other."[82]

Philosophers often disregard the person behind the work. Nietzsche argued against this separation, and persistently remained a human presence on his pages. "Gradually, it has become clear to me," he wrote, "that every great philosophy up to the present has been the personal confession of its author and a form of involuntary and unperceived memoir"[83]—an idea he credited to Lou: "My dear Lou, Your idea of reducing philosophical systems to the personal records of their originators is truly an idea arising from a 'brother-sister brain.'"[84]

Who was Friedrich Nietzsche? The answer to that question depends on who is listening to his personal confession—and when, and where. Not content to be a metaphysician alone, he was also a poet, an aesthetician, a culture critic, a theologian, a philologist and perhaps above all a psychologist.

Perhaps Nietzsche *was* merely a sickly philologist whose pathetic life was in sharp contrast to his robust style. Perhaps his only mature passion *did* end in victimization by that vicious Russian adventuress, Lou Salomé. Perhaps he never believed he had syphilis. Mazzino Montinari, the dean of modern Nietzsche scholars,[85] denied the appropriateness of delving into Nietzsche's private life and secrets when he wrote, "I beg the reader's pardon for having once again concerned myself with a pseudo-problem, sickness, sexual relations, chastity, etc., which should no longer interest anyone."[86] Should we *watch out,* and keep the seal of secrecy unbroken over the mysteries of Nietzsche's life? Should we respect his posthumous privacy? Should we believe the story of one biographer over another, subscribe to the interpretive prejudice of one decade more than the next, or read Nietzsche's texts as if they had no author? Nietzsche was the philosopher of questions, not of easy answers, and if mysteries of love and death, sex and syphilis, genius and madness remain unsolved a century after his death, perhaps that was his gift to his readers of the future.

NOTES

1. Karl Jaspers, *Nietzsche: An Introduction to the Understanding of His Philosophical Activity,* trans. Charles F. Wallraff and Frederick H. Schmitz (Tucson: University of Arizona Press, 1966), 10. First published in 1935.

2. With stunning psychohistorical circularity, psychoanalyst Alice Miller inferred this last theory from a reading of *Thus Spoke Zarathustra.* Alice Miller, *The Untouched Key: Tracing Childhood Trauma in Creativity and Destructiveness,* trans. Hildegarde and Hunter Hannum (Garden City, N.Y.: Doubleday, 1990). First published 1988.

3. Lou Salomé, *Nietzsche: The Man in His Works*, ed., trans. and with an introduction by Siegfried Mandel (Redding Ridge, Conn.: Black Swan Books, 1988), 4. First published 1894.

4. Elisabeth Förster-Nietzsche, *The Life of Nietzsche, vol. 2: The Lonely Nietzsche*, trans. Paul V. Cohn (New York: Sturgis and Walton Company, 1915), 143. First published 1914.

5. Ibid., 128.

6. Ibid., 144.

7. H. F. Peters, *Zarathustra's Sister: The Case of Elisabeth and Friedrich Nietzsche* (New York: Markus Wiener Publishing, 1985), 184. First published 1977.

8. Freud to Lou, August 5, 1932. *Sigmund Freud and Lou Andreas-Salomé Letters*, trans. William and Elaine Robson-Scott, ed. Ernst Pfeiffer (New York: Norton, 1972), 198. First published 1966.

9. Lou Andreas Salomé, *Looking Back*, trans. Breon Mitchell, ed. Ernst Pfeiffer (New York: Paragon House, 1991), 167. First published 1951.

10. Nietzsche to Malwida von Meysenbug, July 2, 1882, in Walter Kaufmann, *Nietzsche: Psychologist, Philosopher, Antichrist* (Princeton: Princeton University Press, 1974), 53. First published 1950.

11. Lou to Gillot, March 26, 1882. In Andreas-Salomé, *Looking Back*, 45–46.

12. Nietzsche to Ida Overbeck, May 28, 1882. In Rudolph Binion, *Frau Lou: Nietzsche's Wayward Disciple* (Princeton: Princeton University Press, 1968), 61.

13. Nietzsche to Peter Gast, July 13, 1882. In *Nietzsche: A Self-Portrait from His Letters*, trans. and ed. Peter Fuss and Henry Shapiro (Cambridge: Harvard University Press, 1971), 63.

14. Nietzsche to Lou, July 20, 1882. In *Selected Letters of Friedrich Nietzsche*, trans. and ed. Christopher Middleton (Chicago: The University of Chicago Press, 1969), 188.

15. Andreas-Salomé, *Looking Back*, 50.

16. Elisabeth to Clara Gelzer, October 2, 1882. Trans. by Ruth Treuenfels in *Friedrich Nietzsche, Paul Rée, Lou von Salomé: Die Dokumente ihrer Begegnung*, ed. Ernst Pfeiffer (Frankfurt am Main: Insel Verlag, 1970).

17. Elisabeth to Clara Gelzer, October 2, 1882.

18. Nietzsche to Lou, end of November, 1882. In Angela Livingstone, *Salomé: Her Life and Work* (Mt. Kisco, N.Y.: Moyer Bell, 1984), 53.

19. Nietzsche to Lou, mid-December, 1882. Kaufmann, *Nietzsche*, 59.

20. Nietzsche to Lou, mid-December 1882. Binion, *Frau Lou*, 101.

21. Andreas Salomé, *Looking Back*, 53.

22. Binion, *Frau Lou*, 117.

23. Ben Macintyre, *Forgotten Fatherland: The Search for Elisabeth Nietzsche* (New York: Farrar Straus Giroux, 1992), x.

24. Rudolph Binion, "My Life with *Frau Lou*," in *The Historians Workshop*, ed. L. P. Curtis Jr. (New York: Knopf, 1970), 297.

25. Binion, "My Life with *Frau Lou*," 297.

26. Binion, *Frau Lou*, 493.

27. Binion, *Frau Lou,* 492.

28. Kaufmann, *Nietzsche,* 49.

29. For nonbiographical versions of the story, see Irvin D. Yalom's novel *When Nietzsche Wept (*in which Lou arranges a mutual analysis with Freud's colleague Josef Breuer for Nietzsche in an imaginary thirteenth month added to 1882), Giuseppe Sinopoli's opera *Salomé,* and Liliana Cavani's film *Beyond Good and Evil.*

30. Kaufmann, *Nietzsche,* 54.

31. Joachim Köhler, *Nietzsche's Geheimnis* (Hamburg: Rowohlt Taschenbuch Verlag, 1992). Köhler's biography assumes that Nietzsche was homosexual.

32. Nietzsche thought Wagner himself was in part responsible for these rumors. On April 21, 1883 he wrote to Peter Gast (with instructions to burn the letter immediately), "Wagner is certainly not wanting in malign discoveries; but what do you say to the fact that he exchanged letters [even with my doctors] expressing his *conviction* that my altered way of thinking was the consequence of excesses against nature, leaving it to be understood that it involved pederasty?" In Mazzino Montinari, "Nietzsche and Wagner One Hundred Years Ago: 1980 Addendum," in *Nietzsche in Italy,* ed. Thomas Harrison (Saratoga, Calif.: Anma Libri, 1988), 113–14.

33. Nietzsche to Peter Gast, July 13, 1882. In Fuss and Shapiro, *Nietzsche,* 63.

34. Nietzsche to Peter Gast, middle of December 1882. In H. F. Peters *My Sister My Spouse: A Biography of Lou Andreas-Salomé* (New York: W.W. Norton, 1962), 139.

35. C.G. Jung, *Memories, Dreams, Reflections,* trans. Richard and Clara Winston, ed. Aniela Jaffé (New York: Vintage Books, 1989), 102. First published 1963.

36. Crane Brinton, *Nietzsche* (New York: Harper & Row, 1965), 94. First published 1941.

37. Alexander Nehamas, *Nietzsche: Life as Literature* (Cambridge: Harvard University Press, 1985), 234. Nehamas created a Nietzsche who created himself as a work of art through his writing, a "magnificent character" in contrast to the miserable little man.

38. Robert C. Solomon, "Nietzsche *ad hominem:* Perspectivism, Personality and *Ressentiment,*" in *The Cambridge Companion to Nietzsche,* ed. Bernd Magnus and Kathleen M. Higgins (Cambridge: Cambridge University Press, 1996), 213.

39. Draft of letter to Georg Rée, July 1883 in Peters, *My Sister, My Spouse,* 146.

40. Möbius quoted by Erich F. Podach, *The Madness of Nietzsche,* trans. F. A.Voigt (New York: Putnam, 1931), 61. First published 1930.

41. R. J. Hollingdale disagreed about Nietzsche's low sexual energy: "As many passages in his writings, and especially some in the uninhibited *Ecce Homo,* disclose, Nietzsche was highly sexed and inordinately attracted to women, yet there is no record, or even hint, that he ever went to bed with a woman of his own class and, the documentation of his life being as ample as it is, we may conclude that he never did so. He had many women friends but not

one wife or mistress. The reason may, as has very generally been assumed, be that he suffered from paralyzing inhibition: but might this inhibition, if it really existed, not have originated in his knowledge that he suffered from something else too? something that, seeing he was a man of honour, must for ever keep him 'celibate' in relation to women of his own class?" From the introduction to Friedrich Nietzsche, *Ecce Homo*, trans. and intro. by R. J. Hollingdale (New York: Penguin Books, 1980), 21. First published 1965.

42. Statement by Health Commissioner Vulpius reprinted in *Conversations with Nietzsche: A Life in the Words of His Contemporaries*, ed. Sander L. Gilman, trans. David J. Parent (Oxford: Oxford University Press, 1987), 259.

43. Ludwig von Scheffler, first published in *Neue Freie Presse* (Vienna) August 6 and 7, 1907, reprinted in Gilman, *Conversations with Nietzsche*, 63. Scheffler was Nietzsche's student in 1876.

44. For a discussion of Platen's influence on gay German youth and quotations from his memoirs, see Robert Aldrich, *The Seduction of the Mediterranean: Writing, Art and Homosexual Fantasy* (London: Routledge, 1993): "That homosexuality was at the heart of Platen's poetry was evident to both contemporaries and later commentators," 61.

45. Gilman, *Conversations with Nietzsche*, 75.

46. Ibid., 72.

47. Ibid., 71.

48. *Minutes of the Vienna Psychoanalytic Society, Vol II: 1908–10*, ed. Herman Nunberg and Ernst Federn, trans. M. Nunberg (New York: International Universities Press, 1967), 31.

49. Ibid., 31.

50. Sigmund Freud and Arnold Zweig, *The Letters of Sigmund Freud and Arnold Zweig*, trans. Elaine and William Robson-Scott, ed. Ernst L. Freud (New York: Harcourt, Brace & World, Inc., 1970), 80.

51. Ibid., 76.

52. Ibid., 79.

53. Ibid., 85–86.

54. Ibid., 85.

55. Ibid., 78.

56. Freud, *Minutes*, II, 32.

57. Förster-Nietzsche, *The Life of Nietzsche*, 2:196.

58. For a discussion of the influence of Nietzsche on Freud, and the biographical connections, see Ronald Lehrer, *Nietzsche's Presence in Freud's Life and Thought: On the Origins of a Psychology of Dynamic Unconscious Mental Functioning* (Albany: State University of New York Press, 1995).

59. Jung, *Memories*, 101.

60. Ibid., 103.

61. C. G. Jung, *Nietzsche's Zarathustra: Notes of the Seminar Given in 1934–39*, vol. 1, ed. James L. Jarrett (Princeton: Princeton University Press, 1988), 609. (P. J. Möbius reported corresponding with two doctors who treated Nietzsche for syphilis when he was twenty-three.)

62. Ibid., 635.

63. Ibid., 102.

64. Ibid.

65. Ibid., 188.

66. Ibid., 189.

67. Stefan Zweig, *Master Builders: A Typology of the Spirit*, trans. Eden and Cedar Paul (New York: Viking Press, 1939), 458. First published 1925.

68. Ibid., 448.

69. Ibid., 454.

70. Ibid., 450–51. Contrast this room with von Scheffler's description of Nietzsche's apartment when he was a professor at Basel: "And when one was half sunk into such a gallant armchair, one's gaze fell again on fresh flowers! In glasses, in bowls, on tables, in corners, competing in their discrete mixture of colors with the watercolors on the walls! Everything airy, aromatic and delicate! Lightly curtained windows, filtering the glare of daylight, made one feel like a guest invited not to a professor's house but to a beloved girlfriend's." Gilman, *Conversations with Nietzsche*, 69.

71. See William H. Schaberg, *The Nietzsche Canon: A Publication History and Bibliography* (Chicago: University of Chicago Press, 1995) for an account of Nietzsche's finances. Schaberg estimates that Nietzsche's net worth (partially from inheritance) was 14,000 marks, or four full years of salary, when he left Basel.

72. Nietzsche to Franziska Nietzsche, November 1885 in Kaufmann, *Nietzsche*, 464.

73. Stefan Zweig, *Master Builders*, 504.

74. Elisabeth Nietzsche to Ernest Thiel, 1933, in Peters, *Zarathustra's Sister*, 221.

75. On September 19, 1994 the *New Yorker* published this hearsay in a review of Frederic Spotts' book *Bayreuth: The History of the Wagner Festival* (New Haven: Yale University Press, 1994): "It seems that, besides putting the little Wagners to bed, Hitler sexually abused Wieland. Spotts has revealed this incident—vouchsafed to him by one of Wieland's children—only since the publication of the book; he had omitted it as irrelevant," 110.

76. Brinton, 15n16.

77. Ronald Hayman, *Nietzsche* (New York: Penguin Books, 1982), 24. First published in 1980. Hayman noted that both Nietzsche and his mother had dissimilar sized pupils, a possible indication of syphilis.

78. Paul Deussen, quoted in R. J. Hollingdale, *Nietzsche* (London: Routledge & Kegan, 1985), 33. First published in 1965.

79. A phrase from the dust jacket of the 1948 Knopf edition of *Doctor Faustus*.

80. Freud and Zweig, *Letters*, 85.

81. Nietzsche to Elisabeth, mid-May-1885. In Salomé, *Nietzsche*, lvii–lix.

82. Diary entry May 11, 1913, Lou Andreas-Salomé, *The Freud Journals*, trans. Stanley A. Leavy (New York: Basic Books, 1964), 143.

83. Nietzsche, *Beyond Good and Evil*, 6, quoted in Salomé, *Nietzsche*, 4.

84. Salomé, *Nietzsche*, 3.

85. According to Sander L. Gilman's dedication on the title page of *Conversations with Nietzsche*.

86. Montinari, "Nietzsche and Wagner," 117.

CHAPTER 16

Nietzsche's Readers and
Their "Will to Ignorance"

George Moraitis

The first time I read Nietzsche was in late adolescence. It was shortly after the Second World War, and Goebbels' use of Nietzsche's aphorisms was still ringing in my ears. I was born and raised in Greece, and was introduced to German literature in early childhood. However, my sense of idealization of German culture suffered a severe setback following the four years of German occupation.

At the time I read some of Nietzsche's works, my sister was a graduate student in philosophy and was writing her dissertation on Heidegger and Jaspers. She idealized Nietzsche, and was incensed by the misuse of Nietzsche's ideas by the Nazis. She had the distinct sense that she understood Nietzsche, while I was working hard to convince her of the futility of such an enterprise. Obviously, I had a much easier task than she did, but years later it became evident to me that I had not really won that debate. Nietzsche's ideas had gotten "under my skin" or, more accurately, they had become part of my thinking and, despite my original repudiation of them, I kept debating them in my mind.

During the years I studied medicine, psychiatry, and psychoanalysis, I was under no pressure to return to Nietzsche. Nevertheless, in studying Freud's theories, several of Nietzsche's propositions would come to mind, perhaps more often than I realized at the time. Freud's theories about the instinctual drives, the sublimation of instincts, and the repetition compulsion, for example, seemed to resemble Nietzsche's concepts of the will to power, of self-overcoming, and of eternal recurrence.

I returned to Nietzsche some twenty years ago when I embarked on a project of studying the psychological forces that enter into the work of the biographer, and designed a methodology with which to pursue this project. My first collaborator was a graduate student in history, whose dissertation consisted of a biographical study of Nietzsche, and who was encountering considerable difficulty in completing his work.[1]

I entered the collaboration in the belief that I had no preconceived notions about Nietzsche's ideas and personality. However, my professed "neutrality" was dissipated early during the collaborative process. When I encountered the biographer's intense anger against his subject, I came to Nietzsche's defense with little hesitation, in direct contrast to the role I played during my first reading of Nietzsche in the early years of my life.

This experience made me realize that my responses were the external manifestations of an internal struggle. The reading of Nietzsche's writing produced in my mind a number of diametrically opposed perceptions of the author's contributions and personality that I could not reconcile. I externalized my ambivalence in the hope of producing some level of internal harmony. In subsequent years, introspective data of this nature were very helpful in mastering my emotional responses to Nietzsche's writings and in understanding other readers' creative struggle to come to terms with Nietzsche's philosophical system and its paradoxes.

In this essay, I aim neither to integrate and explicate Nietzsche's philosophy nor to analyze the philosopher's personality, although the reader may draw such inferences from reading this text. It is primarily the readers' response that I will focus upon, and the personal way in which Nietzsche affects his readers.

Generally speaking, Nietzsche's readers may love him or hate him, may idealize or vilify him, may dedicate a lifetime to studying him or refuse to read his writings and question the coherence of his propositions. Nietzsche arouses in his readers a state of "inward tension," a "pathos," as a result of which they cannot remain neutral, detached, and objective. There is nothing accidental about this. In the chapter, "Why I Write Such Good Books" in *Ecce Homo*, Nietzsche explains why he deliberately aimed to make the reading of his books a personal experience for his readers:

> Ultimately nobody can get more out of things, including books, than he already knows. For what one lacks access to from experience one will have no ear.[2]

In the absence of such experience, "there will be the acoustic illusion that where nothing is heard, nothing is there."[3]

This reference to cognitive psychology provides some rationalizations for Nietzsche's philosophizing with the hammer, his tendency to severely attack what the readers are likely to treasure, and his exalting of what the readers are likely to abhor. In doing so, he probably tries to arouse the less conscious aspects of the readers' ambivalence and speak of what the readers did not even dare to think. However, philosophizing with the hammer (or the "tuning fork") is likely to produce in the reader a sense of intrusion that mobilizes powerful psychological forces and the conflicts associated with them.

Such a sense of intrusion is, of course, the inevitable outcome of all important readings. For example, the reading of fiction or the viewing of a play or a film may precipitate the emergence of a wide range of affects and images. In such situations the intrusion is usually welcome, in the sense that the experience of the characters read about in the story reverberates with the readers' memories and experiences. It is, for the most part, a pleasurable process of bringing to mind within the context of a metaphor that which is already known, but temporarily forgotten or set aside.

The reading of a book that challenges the readers' perception of themselves and of the world in which they live is more disturbing than pleasurable. The novel input that such a reading generates is unlikely to reverberate with something already known. More likely, it will address what the readers have struggled to avoid knowing. Accordingly, it will be the readers' censorship that will be challenged and the editing process that is associated with it. Instead of recollections, it is the threatening novelty that must be dealt with and the emerging awareness of the illusionary nature of some of the readers' perceptions. Retaining ignorance and illusions is a condition of life that can partly be reversed only through the individual's great courage and determination.

In *Beyond Good and Evil*, Nietzsche refers to the will to ignorance. He writes:

> From the beginning we have contrived to retain our ignorance in order to enjoy an almost inconceivable freedom, lack of scruple and caution, heartiness, and gaiety of life—in order to enjoy life! And only on this now solid, granite foundation of ignorance could knowledge rise so far—the will to knowledge on the foundation of a far more powerful will: the will to ignorance, to the uncertain, to the untrue! Not as its opposite, but—as its refinement.[4]

Freud's (1915) propositions about the unconscious mental process resonate in many respects with Nietzsche's ideas.[5] What is repressed in the unconscious correlates in some respects to the will to ignorance, to the will not to know. In Freud's propositions, however, ignorance is a relative term. The knowledge presumably exists in the unconscious; the ignorance pertains to consciousness, and is maintained through a number of defenses such as repression, disavowal, denial. Accordingly, Freud's therapeutic goal was originally defined as a process of bringing into consciousness repressed elements of the unconscious.

Although Freud, like Nietzsche, placed the desire to know and the desire not to know on a continuum, Freud, unlike Nietzsche, conceptualized an inevitable conflict and the presence of resistance to knowledge and discovery or, more accurately, rediscovery. Freud's notions about knowledge and ignorance resonate with the Socratian doctrine of recollection, without the metaphysical propositions that pertain to the concept of the soul.

As indicated earlier, Nietzsche's readers are likely to find themselves in a state of ambivalence and conflict between their wish to embrace his ideas and the wish to discard them. Externalizing the conflict may be a convenient way to approach it, but a more effective approach depends on the reader's capacity to arrive at a compromise solution, usually defined as interpretation, with which several readers would hopefully agree. Interpretations are temporary points of arrival that offer the readers a much needed sense of coherence and stability, that enable the readers to make peace with the author and with themselves within the bounds of the culture they live in.

Effective interpretations produce a sense of relatedness that differs substantially from earlier ones generated by direct human contact. Such relatedness is mediated through a world of symbols that have the power to influence large audiences. Only a few of Nietzsche's readers can produce such interpretations, most of them will reach an impasse at some point or other, after which they may embrace the ideas of Nietzsche's interpreters, they may declare Nietzsche incoherent, or learn to tolerate their own sense of ignorance.

In intellectual pursuits there is usually little difficulty in acknowledging the limitations of human knowledge as long as the thinker can identify the source of knowledge on the basis of a given cosmology. Thus the source of knowledge may be presumed to exist in the soul, in God, in science, in nature, in the self, and so on. Depending on how the source is defined, the way to get to it may be morality, faith, rationality, aesthetics, or introspection.

A true sense of ignorance, however, is achieved when thinkers come to the realization not only of their own ignorance, but also of their inability to identify the source of knowledge.

The search for knowledge begins in infancy. Infants search for novelty, but have limited capacity to tolerate frustration. When overstimulated with the novel, they seek the familiar and the comfort it provides. As children mature, however, they become more capable of tolerating frustration, but also more aware of the extent of their ignorance.

The awareness of ignorance gives rise to anxiety because it generates a sense of anarchy and unpredictability. In order to provide for themselves a sense of order and structure, children adopt a simple cosmology according to which the parents know everything. In doing so, they delegate to their parents not only the image of omnipotence, but also the decision of what they should know and what they should remain ignorant of. Later on, this function is assumed more directly by the culture individuals live in, which controls formal education, religion, and, to a great extent, personal relationships.

Culture systematically channels the pursuit of knowledge to areas that are congruent with its values and reinforces the individual's "will to ignorance" for knowledge that conflicts with it.

This filtering process is, in its essence, a censorship that develops gradually, beginning in early childhood, only parts of which are conscious and self-imposed. The purpose of this censorship is to regulate the input of new information so as not to disturb the culturally sanctioned convictions about human nature and the established cosmology associated with it.

In *The Interpretation of Dreams*, Freud (1900) postulated the presence of an unconscious censorship. His propositions, however, pertain to what will be allowed to reach consciousness from the mental contents that already exist within the psychic system. The censorship I postulate pertains to filtering out what is perceived as too novel and unfamiliar, in order to eliminate the threat that such unfamiliarity would create in balancing the existing mental contents. For example, Nietzsche's readers do not necessarily have to understand what Nietzsche said in order to feel threatened by his writings. The enormous novelty of his style and language would suffice in producing an intuitive response of fear and avoidance that can be rationalized in a variety of ways. Such rationalizations may lead to a quick and often false "understanding" of what the author proposed or to labeling the author "incoherent" in order to produce premature closure with which to block further efforts to appreciate the novel input involved.

Scholars dedicate their lives to the pursuit of knowledge and discovery. In order to reach this goal, they must balance the filtering function of both censorships, and rise above pressures generated, on one side, by their need to create a culturally correct product and, on the other, by the whims of their emotions and idiosyncrasies.

How is this to be achieved? The accumulation of a wide range of information and references is only the prelude to becoming a scholar. The development of a professional identity and the capacity to adhere to a code of professional ethics are the sine qua non of all scholarly writings. The basic purpose of the scholarly ethic is to facilitate the scholar's capacity to say it "as it is" and overcome pressures from within and from without to do otherwise.

Given the nature of their task, scholars must limit the area of their endeavors to manageable proportions and create some distance between themselves and their environment. In order to accomplish the first, they join the ranks of a given discipline such as philosophy, psychology, or sociology, and restrict their activities within its bounds. However, given the interdisciplinary nature of all knowledge, such a decision is a double-edged sword. Nietzsche refused to restrain his activities within disciplinary bounds, as a result of which he created some serious difficulties for many of his readers, who must approach his writings not only as philosophical but also as psychological and literary texts.

The scholars' immersion into a solitary activity, on the one hand enhances their capacity to maintain their sense of autonomy, while on the other it creates obstacles in their ability to relate in a person-to-person situation. The process of becoming a scholar precipitates a measure of personality changes. It dramatically increases the individual's capacity to relate within a world of symbols, often at the expense of connectedness in person-to-person situations and the capacity to directly access early life experiences with which it relates. When this occurs, scholars view life experiences through the symbols they have created or embraced and have a sense of the in-depth self-knowledge as a result. Often they do not realize the degree to which their self-knowledge has been shaped by their beliefs and convictions rather than by their experiences. Nietzsche's aphorism, "This is what life taught me," is probably a reference to his world of ideas as well as to his personal experiences.

Young scholars must go through a period of dependence on their mentors before they can, hopefully, mature into autonomous thinkers. This is by far easier when the mentors are not living people and the scholars' relatedness to them is restricted to their writings and symbols. The sense of autonomy is achieved by gradually placing what has been learned into a new conceptual universe of the emerging scholars' own creation.

Nietzsche exemplifies some of these characteristics. His lifestyle and philosophy were a form of the "man apart" quality in scholarly pursuit, which is also associated with the concept of genius, as Pletsch pointed out in his biography of Nietzsche.[6] Nietzsche strongly urged his readers not to become his disciples, but he deliberately made it extremely difficult for them to rise above him as their mentor.

The process of placing a major thinker in context is a process of selectively dealing with the thinker's propositions, accepting some and raising questions about others. Aside from the inherent conceptual difficulties in applying such selectivity to Nietzsche's philosophical system, his highly emotional style mobilizes the reader's personal and idiosyncratic references and the associated affects, producing in the process the need for total acceptance or rejection of the propositions made.

In my collaboration with the historian-biographer, the importance of these issues became immediately evident when we discussed *Ecce Homo*. My collaborator was appalled by Nietzsche's unconventional approach to philosophical writings. Early in his professional career he had idealized Nietzsche, but at the time of our collaboration he was trying to "put Nietzsche behind him"[7] by writing a dissertation on him. His anger at him was motivated by his need to rise above Nietzsche and develop his own professional identity, a goal he accomplished gradually several years later, when he wrote a scholarly biography of Nietzsche.

At the time I approached *Ecce Homo* as Nietzsche's "free associations," and found him colorful and exciting. While my collaborator was trying to "exit" from Nietzsche, I was making a "reentry" with the use of my clinical psychoanalytic tools. As indicated before, I was affected by Nietzsche's ideas early in my life, but their effect upon my thinking did not become evident to me until I entered my collaboration with the biographer.

The reading of *Ecce Homo* and *Thus Spoke Zarathustra* had an enormous impact on me. I believe, however, that I was affected more by the humanity of the author than by his ideas. To use Walter Kaufmann's description, I experienced these readings as the works of an "utterly lonely man"[8] and I felt the need to become his "secret sharer." I was moved by Nietzsche's brief passages about his father in *Ecce Homo*, and directed my attention to Zarathustra's dreams, which I found fascinating.

I sensed that Nietzsche was desperate for recognition and appreciation and took his pleas to his readers to "resist Zarathustra" as protesting too much. I interpreted the dream in "The child with the mirror," in which Zarathustra looks at himself and sees "a devil's grimace and a scornful laughter," as an indication that Zarathustra's loneliness was so deep that it produced a sense of self-estrangement.[9] In order to cure his loneliness, Zarathustra seeks his friends and pleads with them not to be frightened by his "wild wisdom." I wondered who are the anonymous friends he refers to and assumes that they are his readers, the readers who can hopefully understand his pain and soothe it.

As opposed to Narcissus, who looked at his own reflected image and fell in love with it, Zarathustra is appalled by his own reflection. Is this an indication of narcissistic pathology or of his capacity to resist narcissistic self-love? Probably it is neither.

Contemporary psychoanalysis is shifting away from conceptualizing creativity as the product of psychopathology and infantile fantasies. As Gedo (1996) points out: "the creative effort itself cannot be involved in intrapsychic conflict. More often than not, creative persons primarily desire to transmit an artistic (or scientific, or ethical, or scholarly) message that represents the highest ideals in the form of a perfected offering."[10] There are many indications that this was what Nietzsche wanted. He probably assumed that loneliness was the price he had to pay in order to make his offerings.

Nietzsche's "offerings" had a personal meaning for me. This became evident to me when, following the reading of *Ecce Homo* and some of the biographical data about the death of Nietzsche's father my collaborator had furnished me with, I had a dream with images from Erlkönig, Goethe's poem about a father riding through the night holding his dying son.[11] This poem was known to me since childhood, and was associated with affectionate memories of my father and his psychological and philosophical interests. Reading Nietzsche had set in motion a process of recollection through which some personal experiences were illuminated.

Did this facilitate my capacity to understand Nietzsche's works and personality or did it create idiosyncratic notions that interfered with such an understanding? Probably both. On the one side, it increased my capacity to relate in the realm of experience, while on the other it may have directed my attention away from the intellectual realm within which Nietzsche's self-revelations were provided.

Freud introduced the notion that cognition is composed of two fundamentally different mental processes. The "primary" and the "secondary"; the primary being archaic, primitive, chaotic, affect-laden, and irrational, while the secondary is reality-oriented, rational, and organized into coherent gestalt schemata.

More recent studies in psychoanalysis,[12] as well as in language and cognition[13] recognize the presence of two levels of communication, and their findings have been supported by contemporary research in brain function.[14] However, their propositions differed basically from Freud, in the sense that the primary process is recognized not as primitive, but as images of reality that are organized as experiences around self-centered criteria such as wishes, needs, and other experiential states. In contrast, the secondary mode is organized around socially shared and agreed upon symbols that are isolated to whatever extent possible from their emotional and experiential connotations.

When I first read Nietzsche's works, I experienced a sense of intrusion and responded to it in a defensive manner. Yet some of his threatening ideas must have registered subliminally, because my interest in him was not lost.

When, years later, I became reacquainted with Nietzsche's ideas, my defensive stance took another form. I tuned my perceptual instrument to the experiential aspects of my reading by emphasizing primarily the primary mode of cognition. In doing so, I focused on what was personally meaningful to me, to the exclusion of the disagreeable and overwhelming sense of novelty of Nietzsche's philosophical system. This may have enabled me to appreciate Nietzsche's sense of loneliness and sense of mourning under which his life experiences seemed organized, but it provided little information or understanding of his ideas, his symbols, and their power.

My approach is of course consistent with my psychoanalytic background, but it is also consistent with Nietzsche's style of writing, which demands that the reading be introspective. Nietzsche mistrusted the secondary mode of cognition, which he suspected to have been sold out to the culture's "decadent" needs. He warned his readers not to believe the symbols and values of the culture, because they lie to us. Instead, he urged them to turn inward for inspiration and knowledge.

Nietzsche, as Freud did somewhat later, produced his works at a time when the belief in religion and science reigned supreme. Freud considered religion to be an illusion but fully subscribed to the *Weltanschauung* of science. Although the world of science did not embrace Freud, he provided a cultural home for his ideas and their development.

In contrast, Nietzsche denounced both religion and science, as a result of which his ideas remained "homeless" in a cultural sense, until the cultural changes of our time provided for them a new "home."

We live in times in which the distrust of human rationality, objectivity, and capacity to arrive at the truth is part of our cultural paradigm. Some may postulate that it was Nietzsche's pioneering work that precipitated these changes, but this seems too simple an explanation. More likely, Nietzsche was able to anticipate them. There are, however, many parts of Nietzsche's thinking that are still incongruent with the present trends of our culture. His notion of relativism or perspectivism may resonate with the cultural paradigm of our times, but his propositions about "the will to power," "self-overcoming," and the "eternal recurrence" point in a different direction.

Generally speaking, Nietzsche did not find the readership he wanted in his lifetime, but a century later he seems to be finding it at long last. However, Nietzsche was not only a philosopher but a psychologist as well. As such, he was equally suspicious of his friends and admirers as he was of his enemies. He knew that nothing is as it seems. Changes in the climate of an intellectual community do not necessarily represent a shift from ignorance and prejudice to knowledge and open-mindedness.

In some sense, Nietzsche's writings resemble the forbidden scriptures that have come to light after they have broken through a formidable cultural censorship of half a century or more. Nietzsche and his philosophy have become a legend, as a result of it. Under the circumstances, it is important to distinguish between Nietzsche's effect upon his readers as a legend and as a thinker. Those who embrace Nietzsche as a legend celebrate the changes in our culture's paradigms, and not necessarily Nietzsche's ideas.

The changes in the cultural value system have not eliminated the censorship under which Nietzsche is being read; they have simply changed its nature. In contrast to the rejection of the past, many good thinkers in our present intellectual community go to great lengths to illustrate the coherence of Nietzsche's intellectual system and undo the apparent contradictions in the text.

In preparation for this essay, I read some of the works of two well-known interpreters of Nietzsche's ideas: Walter Kaufmann and Alexander Nehamas. I will not attempt to formally review these important publications, but I will selectively refer to them briefly to illustrate how creative interpreters edit the text in order to facilitate the reader's sense of continuity and coherence in Nietzsche's propositions. Furthermore, I will illustrate how the two modes of communication and relatedness, experience and intellectual coherence, are intertwined in order to facilitate the interpreter's objectives.

Walter Kaufmann's *Nietzsche: Philosopher, Psychologist, Antichrist*, is a fascinating intellectual biography, the publication of which played a pivotal role in establishing Nietzsche as a major philosopher in this country. This was precisely the author's intent. There are two stories in the book. The story of Nietzsche's ideas and the story of the man. Kaufmann rejects the notion of strict causality between the life experiences of his subject and his ideas. It is therefore not surprising that the story of Nietzsche's ideas is told lavishly, while the story of the man is only sketchily drawn at strategic points in the book.

Nietzsche's ideas are presented with great clarity and simplicity, which is in direct contrast to the effect the reading of Nietzsche's works produce in many readers. Most contradictions are softened or eliminated, mostly by placing them in a developmental perspective.

There are, however, times when this is not possible, and it is in these passages that Kaufmann abandons his efforts to make Nietzsche's ideas coherent. Instead, he refers the reader to his subject's tortuous life experiences. For example, in reference to "eternal recurrence," Nietzsche's concept that most readers have difficulty with, Kaufmann wonders:

> Why did he [Nietzsche] value this most dubious doctrine which was to have no influence to speak of, so extravagantly? For it is plain that none of his other ideas meant so much to him. The answer must be sought in the fact that the eternal recurrence was to Nietzsche less an idea than an experience—the supreme experience of a life unusually rich in suffering, pain, and agony.[15]

In other words, Kaufmann adduces that Nietzsche's psychological state interfered with his better judgment and creativity. Such suppositions are consistent with Gedo's propositions about the decisive role of the personality of the creative individual "in facilitating or standing in the way of creative ambitions."[16] I too perceived Nietzsche's concept of the eternal recurrence as highly personal and idiosyncratic. It came across to me like a fantasy of life without discontinuities of any kind, a process in which death has no place.

Kaufmann did not further explore his hunches about Nietzsche's psychological state aside from referring to his loneliness and suffering. More specifically, he said nothing about Nietzsche's fits of rage and their effect upon the coherence of his writings. In the chapter on "The master race," where he effectively defends Nietzsche against accusations that he was a racist, he makes no reference to Nietzsche's angry outbursts, as a result of which he (partially) earned this reputation. Also, Kaufmann refers to Nietzsche's slurs against women as being "trivial, hardly pertinent," and "need not greatly concern the philosopher."[17]

Intellectually speaking, the readers are not in doubt that such emotional outbursts are not pertinent, but it is important to keep in mind that Nietzsche based his insight upon experience. Nietzsche's rage is an important part of his experiences and, under the circumstances, it can be neither trivial nor "hardly pertinent."

Alexander Nehamas, in *Nietzsche: Life as Literature*, uses a different strategy in his efforts to achieve greater coherence and continuity in Nietzsche's propositions. He bypasses all biographical references to Nietzsche, and takes at face value Nietzsche's aphorism that "the very notion of an individual is one that essentially refuses to be spelled out in informative terms." Instead, he relies on Nietzsche's efforts to create "an artwork of himself, a literary character who is a philosopher,"[18] in order to bypass the gaps in coherence in Nietzsche's writings.

Nehamas is of course aware that "whatever else we may be tempted to say of Nietzsche's ideas, it is unlikely that we shall describe many of them as sensible."[19] Yet he tries hard to provide for them the appearance of being sensible, by interpreting them not as the products of a cosmology, but as a view of the "self." The term "self," of course, does not pertain to any given individual, which presumably cannot be defined in informative terms, but to the self as portrayed in the fictive literary character of the philosopher that Nietzsche created.

Nehamas does not seem to take seriously into account that, in his writings, Nietzsche made little or no effort to distinguish between himself and the literary character he created, or even between the self and the elusive "cosmos." There is only one distinction that Nietzsche insisted upon: "Hear me! For I am such and such a person. Above all, do not mistake me for someone else."[20]

Nietzsche was probably quite aware of the apparent contradictions of many of his ideas, and the fact that they do not come across as sensible. In his mind, however, there was probably no more need for coherence, constancy, and rationality than there was for justice, shame, and guilt. Accordingly, he did not abide by the established rules of academic writings, as he did not comply with the contingencies of established social and scientific principles and religious beliefs. Nietzsche placed himself into a universe of his own creation that is highly subjective in nature.

Under the circumstances, the "understanding" of Nietzsche's writings cannot be approached simply by logical reasoning and the use of aesthetic and conceptual symbols. Such a level of relatedness may be perfectly sufficient for other philosophical writings, but Nietzsche's writings demand the input of information derived directly from experience. If the readers were to rely exclusively on their own experiences for such an input, they might mobilize references like the ones I did when I dreamt about Erlkönig. Such references, however, are highly idiosyncratic in nature, and probably misleading.

It is therefore essential that Nietzsche's thinking be placed within the context of the author's subjectivity and not simply that of the reader. To those who argue that an individual cannot be defined in "informative terms," I would say that such a definition is as arbitrary as its opposite. Empirically speaking, however, we all go through life constantly defining and redefining ourselves and those who are important to us. How well we perform such tasks depends on the information available and our capacity to rise above our need to define another person's life experiences so that they resonate with our own and with the cultural paradigm of the culture we live in. In other words, defining or understanding an individual and his or her creativity involves a process of "self-overcoming" that takes courage, determination, and the skills to accumulate and process pertinent information. What is being overcome is the anxiety associated with the sense of anarchy that is generated by the input of novelty that disturbs the reader's internal order and structure. The "will to ignorance" is the protection against anything that threatens the internal structure and its delicate balance with the external one.

In contrast, the "will to knowledge" aims for novelty and change, but must be contained within manageable proportions. In my experiences as a psychoanalyst and as a collaborator with biographers, I have been amazed by the determination and perseverance of some of my collaborators in their efforts to move beyond the known and familiar and into the novel and original.

I believe that the study of Nietzsche's thinking mobilizes the readers' "will to knowledge" with unusual intensity by exposing the readers' "will to ignorance." In a sense, Nietzsche operates like an analyst who interprets (unfortunately with the hammer) the analysand's defensive way of thinking. In doing so, he arouses not only the readers' "will to knowledge" but also powerful resistances that are in the service of their "will to ignorance." The crudest way to such ignorance is to burn his books and ridicule his writings. Another crude way to ignorance is to use Nietzsche as the make-believe champion of a political or cultural cause, as the Nazis did.

A more refined approach to obscuring Nietzsche's writings is to link them to one of the prevailing intellectual movements of a given time, such as existentialism, psychoanalysis, constructivism, and deconstructivism, and to perceive him as the forerunner of somebody else's thinking. Although there are important connections between these intellectual movements and Nietzsche's propositions, it is essential not to mistake Nietzsche for someone else.

More commonly, however, the contemporary readers' "will to ignorance" is reflected in their excessive efforts to interpret Nietzsche's propositions as a coherent and integrated whole. It seems to me that such efforts represent the interpreters' efforts to "overcome" Nietzsche rather than themselves. They produce a sense of closure and arrival that reflects more of the interpreters' thinking.

Nietzsche has provided us with enough aphorisms and propositions to confirm or refute most of his interpreters' conclusions, no matter how well thought out they are. In doing so, he also opened the door to his own psyche and invited his readers to enter. Very few have taken that challenge seriously, and those who have are not philosophers themselves. The study of a creative thinker like Nietzsche requires an unusual combination of skills. The investigator must ideally be a philosopher and a biographer-psychologist with extensive experience in studying gifted individuals. The sophisticated work of philosophers like Kaufmann and Nehamas, and many others, can be greatly enhanced by interdisciplinary studies that take into account recent advances in the study of creativity in psychoanalysis and in the field of cognition. Of course, all that investigators can aim for is an approximation. How good this approximation turns out to be, depends on the investigators' capacity to appreciate the interplay between the "will to knowledge" and the "will to ignorance" as it applies to Nietzsche and those who study him.

NOTES

1. George Moraitis, "A Psychoanalyst's Journey into a Historian's World: An Experiment in Collaboration," in *Introspection in Biography*, ed. Samuel Baron and Carl Pletsch (Hillsdale, N.J.: The Analytic Press, 1985), 69–105.

2. Friedrich Nietzsche, *Ecce Homo*, trans. Walter Kaufmann (New York: Vintage, 1967), "Why I Write Such Good Books," sec. 1.

3. Ibid.

4. Friedrich Nietzsche, *Beyond Good and Evil*, trans. Walter Kaufmann (New York: Vintage, 1966), 24.

5. Sigmund Freud, "The Unconscious," in the *Standard Edition of the Complete Psychological Writings of Sigmund Freud* (London: Hogarth Press, 1915), 14:159–209.

6. Carl Pletsch, *Young Nietzsche: Becoming a Genius* (New York: The Free Press, 1991).

7. Carl Pletsch, "Returning to Nietzsche," in *Introspection in Biography*.

8. Editor's preface to *Thus Spoke Zarathustra*, in *The Portable Nietzsche*, trans. Walter Kaufmann (New York: Viking, 1954).

9. *Z* II, "The Child with the Mirror."

10. John Gedo, *The Artist and the Emotional World* (New York: Columbia University Press, 1966), 11.

11. Johann Goethe, *Goethes lyrische und epische Dichtungen*, vol. 1 (Leipzig: Wilhelm Ernst Ausgabe, 1916).

12. Ernst Kris, *Psychoanalytic Explorations in Art* (New York: International Universities Press, 1952); Anton Ehrenzweig, *The Hidden Order of Art* (Berkeley: University of California Press, 1967); P. Noy, "The Psychanalytic Theory of Cognitive Development," in *The Psychoanalytic Study of the Child* (New York: International Universities Press, 1975), 30:169–216; John Gedo, *Portraits of the Artist* (New York: Guilford Press, 1983); L. Sadow "The Modes of Psychoanalytic Thought," in *Psychoanalysis: The Vital Issues*, ed. John Gedo and George Pollock (New York: International Universities Press, 1984), 795–811.

13. Ludwig Wittgenstein, *The Tractatus Logico-Philosophicus*, trans. D. F. Pears and B. F. McGuiness (London: Routledge, 1961); Susanne K. Langer, *Philosophy in a New Key* (Cambridge: Harvard University Press, 1942); Jacob Bronowski, *A Sense of the Future* (Cambridge: MIT Press), 1989.

14. Fred Levin, *Mapping the Mind* (Hillsdale, N.J.: The Analytic Press, 1991); W. Bucci, "The Development of Emotional Meaning in Free Association: A Multiple Code Theory," in *Hierarchical Concepts in Psychoanalysis*, ed. John Gedo and Anton Wilson (New York: Guilford Press, 1993), 3–47.

15. Walter Kaufmann, *Nietzsche: Philosopher, Psychologist, Antichrist* (Princeton: Princeton University Press, 1950), 323.

16. Gedo, *The Artist and the Emotional World*, 226.

17. Kaufmann, *Nietzsche*, 84.

18. Alexander Nehamas, *Nietzsche, Life as Literature* (Cambridge: Harvard University Press, 1985), 8.

19. Ibid., 141.

20. *EH*, "Books," sec. 1.

CHAPTER 17

Nietzsche's Striving

Carl Pletsch

GETTING PERSONAL

In the Winter of 1872–73 Friedrich Nietzsche was writing an essay on *Philosophy in the Tragic Age of the Greeks.*[1] In its early pages he reflected on the importance of the life and personality of philosophers in a way that pertains to Nietzsche himself as much as to the ancient Greeks. The usual histories of philosophy are so dull, he contended, because they catalog ideas and systems but silence the personalities of the philosophers. He insisted, on the contrary, that "the only thing of interest in a refuted system is the personal element. This alone is forever irrefutable."[2] By "the personal element" he apparently meant the aspirations and agonies of the philosophers. "Often we disapprove of their aims, but love them for the ways and means of their striving."[3]

Nietzsche's own career as a philosopher was full of striving, but few of his interpreters have taken up this suggestion to examine his varied writings as the products of his enduring aspirations. The majority of Nietzsche's interpreters have focused upon his ideas, each choosing what seems most salient and attempting to reconcile the rest in one way or another. But Nietzsche's works are anything but systematic, and salient ideas abound in them. What seems most salient, changes with the rhythm of fashion (in recent decades he has been a fashion). Nietzsche's reputation grows, but the credibility of particular interpretations of his works does not. Books with the implied title, "What Nietzsche Means," enjoy brief currency. Yet they sell. Do we want to know what Nietzsche meant so badly that we still hope the next book will really explain him to us? Whatever the case, we seem to be as reluctant to get involved with him personally as we are fascinated by his ideas.

An alternative to ignoring the personal element in Nietzsche is to reverse the order of things and attend to his personality. That is the impetus of psychobiography, which is all too easily diverted into pseudo-psychoanalysis. In the best of cases, psychoanalysis assists individuals in augmenting their self-understanding. It is something very different when a writer's works are used to create a personality profile or even a diagnosis. Psychoanalytic categories may be deployed, but enhanced self-understanding for the writer is out of the question—especially if, like Nietzsche, he happens to be dead. The result is usually a kind of indictment, almost inevitably circular in its reasoning: that is, if Nietzsche wrote books like this, he must have been _____ ; if he was _____ , no wonder he wrote such books. Psychological as this may seem, it does not reveal what Nietzsche alluded to as "the personal element" in philosophy that is "forever irrefutable."

Even as he focused upon "the ways and means of their striving" in his manuscript on the ancient philosophers, Nietzsche was striving to invent his own philosophical persona. He was still in the thrall of his great mentors, Schopenhauer and Wagner, struggling to free himself, not so much by repudiating them as by transcending them. He had just published his brilliantly original book, *The Birth of Tragedy out of the Spirit of Music*. It remains an important work of philosophical aesthetics today, in spite of the fact that it is also a piece of Wagnerian propaganda. But when it appeared in 1872, it was greeted by severe censure from professional philologists. And while Nietzsche was delighted by Wagner's enthusiastic approval, he was dismayed by published criticisms of his book. He responded by undertaking the manuscript of *Philosophy in the Tragic Age of the Greeks* privately. He did not inform the Wagners of his project, and he withheld a visit to them at Christmas. He apparently felt it necessary to work in seclusion, away from the stimulus of Wagner's powerful personality, in order to finish this manuscript.

The obvious inference is that Nietzsche was struggling to free himself from Wagner's influence in order to produce something acceptable to his philological colleagues. But he was also striving toward the more comprehensive intellectual life of an original philosopher. Nietzsche identified with the epoch-making Greek philosophers in his manuscript, with Heraclitus particularly. And as a philosopher affiliated directly with Heraclitus, Nietzsche eventually transcended both classical philology and Wagner. So his allusion to the personal element in philosophy can be read as an affirmation of his own struggle toward an independent perspective, and even as an assertion of himself as a philosopher.

This striving exemplifies the personal element to which Nietzsche referred. He strove to transcend his heroes, their systems, and ultimately the central traditions of his whole civilization. This striving to transcend suffuses Nietzsche's whole career and still sets his writing apart as the asymptote of Western thought a century later. He is the most caustic philosopher so far—perhaps the definitively caustic philosopher. Striving to transcend is the critical reagent in Nietzsche. This characteristic even explains the irreconcilability of many of the positions he adopted: he was not constructing a system of consistent meanings; he was transcending both particular meanings and the very idea of systems of consistent meanings. In fact, Nietzsche's career as a writer seems to be one extended performance of a generalized, philosophical striving to transcend meanings. This may be the irrefutable element in his philosophy.

Nietzsche's books, letters and manuscripts are the tangible evidence of his performance. But the striving that underlies them and the whole production of his philosophy raises many questions. How, for example, did Nietzsche form this ambition to transcend everyone and every thought? And how did he sustain this odd ambition throughout his adult life? To understand Nietzsche's performance one must avoid the concurring temptations to systematize and diagnose, both of which tend to divert from the personal element. A more appropriate approach to Nietzsche may be to emulate his own treatment of the Greek philosophers in the tragic age.

One must get an empathic sense of the person Nietzsche to appreciate the striving to overcome that is so central to his books and ideas. This cannot be conveyed in a short essay. My book *Young Nietzsche, Becoming a Genius* does attempt to convey it.[4] Here I shall point to one important dimension of Nietzsche's striving.

LEARNING TO BE A GENIUS

Nietzsche invented himself by striving and overcoming. He was not predestined to become the premier philosopher of the next century, nor was he born without a first name. In fact, he was christened Friedrich Wilhelm Nietzsche, after a Prussian king, in a conservative gesture intended to curry favor with authorities and perhaps advance his father's career. The father was pastor in a tiny village, but died while the son was a small child. The mother came from a rural parson's family as well; she was barely literate and still in her teens when she married; widowed at an early age, she never remarried, but acquiesced to a role little better than a servant in the household of her mother-in-law and two maiden sisters-in-law. They all moved to the administrative city of Naumburg where the Nietzsches had social connections among the bureaucratic elite. There was nothing liberal in this pious and conservative family. Everyone in Friedrich Wilhelm's early milieu expected him to become a parson like his father and grandfathers before him.

But Nietzsche would ultimately do exactly the opposite.

Nietzsche developed his ideas, wrote his books, and earned his fame and notoriety by transcending his family and the milieu in which he was raised. This was not simply rejection, however. The young Nietzsche aspired to genius. In fact, becoming a genius was the central process of his life. Nietzsche succeeded in overcoming the restrictions of his provincial German upbringing by striving to achieve something great. When he was a child, geniuses like Goethe, Schiller, Mozart, and Beethoven provided examples for him to emulate.

By the time he was fourteen years old, Nietzsche understood what genius was about. Geniuses were cultural heroes to the educated middle class of Germany, the *Bildungsbuergertum*. That Nietzsche aspired to join this pantheon is first demonstrated with certainty by an autobiographical sketch under the title, *Out of My Life (Aus meinem Leben)*, which just happened also to be the title of Goethe's autobiography. Obviously written in emulation of Goethe, it contains the adolescent boy's poems and discussions of his musical compositions. Thus the title, the autobiographical format, and the contents of this little work all give evidence of creative ambition and a growing awareness that he too might become a genius.

In the mid-nineteenth century, when Nietzsche was growing up, cultural and intellectual ambition was commonly framed in terms of genius. Before the mid-eighteenth century, however, genius did not even exist as a cultural category. The Enlightenment prized innovation more highly than innovation had ever been prized in human history before. In retrospect it seems as if the *philosophes* invented the idea of a genius to incorporate innovation and to promote innovators. For example, identifying someone as a genius served the economic function of making innovation profitable. Along with patent and copyright laws (also invented in the eighteenth century) the concept of genius helped assign ownership in intellectual property to individuals. Since the eighteenth century, gifted individuals can hope to be well rewarded for their innovations.

Beyond rewarding innovators in what was becoming the world's first hyperinnovative society, the category of genius fulfilled both social and psychological functions. Labeling an individual as a genius permitted society at large to recognize and accept the distinguished individual's innovations, tolerate his egoism and idiosyncrasy, and even idolize him. Psychologically, thinking of oneself as a genius helped an aspirant to organize his life and marshall his energies to the rigors of a lifelong creative project with no immediate utility. While Nietzsche only achieved the adulation associated with being a genius after his death, he benefited immediately from the self-organizing effects of categorizing himself as a prospective genius, from his fourteenth year at the latest.

Nietzsche had been exposed to many models of genius by the time he entered the university. It was only in his second year at the university, however, that he discovered Arthur Schopenhauer. Schopenhauer instantly became the young Nietzsche's philosophical hero. His writings offered Nietzsche an intellectual foundation for his own creative life's work, not to mention an explicit theory of genius.[5] Schopenhauer enabled Nietzsche to reorganize his ambitions as philosophical ambitions. But, like Goethe and his other adolescent idols, Schopenhauer lived for Nietzsche only in books.

Not long after he became a convert to Schopenhauer, however, Nietzsche met the composer Richard Wagner. Wagner became a tangible force in Nietzsche's life, activating his affinity with genius and giving him a personal exposure to greatness. Wagner's magnetic personality led Nietzsche into the magic circle of genius, as it were, a field of forces in which he saw the creative man drawing to himself the talents of others, working to realize the master's works, the love of an adoring and self-effacing wife, the sycophancy of hangers-on. With Wagner Nietzsche also witnessed the lavish lifestyle, the aura of publicity and scandal, and the true popular adulation that surrounds genius. In Wagner the whole phenomenon of genius was crystallized in the most personal way for Nietzsche. He had finally found a vivacious model of genius to whom he could apprentice himself. Perhaps unintentionally, Wagner enabled Nietzsche to visualize himself in the role.[6]

Nietzsche's intellectual persona changed from the moment he came under Wagner's influence, even as it had when he discovered Schopenhauer. Both encounters energized him remarkably, as if his enthusiasm for these two creative men permitted him to envision greater possibilities for himself. Even as he submitted to their authority, they freed him to create himself. *The Birth of Tragedy*, written in the flush of Wagnerian enthusiasm, reveals how Nietzsche abruptly began to think and write more ambitiously. The book's speculative nature betrays the work of a philosopher rather than simply a precocious young philologist. It is a very partisan book, promoting Wagner as the new Aeschylus, but it conjures up a vision of cultural history in relation to the tragic that was absolutely original to Nietzsche. The book is so speculative, so innovative in fact, that it is difficult to explain. How did Nietzsche go so far and so audaciously beyond the limits of his professional training, even in his first book?

In his mid-twenties, Nietzsche had already become a creative force, an intellectual who knew how to think and express things that no one could have taught him—not his philology professor and *Doktorvater*, Friedrich Ritschl, not his philosophical mentor, Arthur Schopenhauer, and certainly not Richard Wagner. Trying to please Wagner, however, Nietzsche had synthesized his knowledge of the ancient Greeks with an ethical impulse derived from Schopenhauer. In the process he had created an original interpretation of ancient Greek culture and devised a whole new relevance for the ancient Greeks to the modern world. And more to the point of this essay, he had devised—or taught himself—his own way of learning, a method that would permit him to continue to extend his ideas and the range of his thinking throughout his life. This is a primary characteristic of genius. And Nietzsche's deep admiration for his fatherly mentors, especially his desire to please Wagner, was the catalyst of this intellectual leap.

Wagner kept Nietzsche in thrall for another four years after the publication of *The Birth of Tragedy*. Nietzsche remained in the role of disciple and, on occasion, even permitted Wagner to dictate what he should publish. His own susceptibility to fatherly mentors and Wagner's tyrannical nature conspired together. And the culture of genius, which exalted such men as Wagner out of all proportion, foresaw just such feudal relationships. Nietzsche did not become a fully independent force until after his definitive break with Wagner at the first festival of Wagner's *Ring of the Nibelungen* in Bayreuth in 1876. But in that period he learned a great deal more about the role of the genius from Wagner's example. In particular, he learned of the absolute egoism of the genius. Wagner's egotism ultimately repelled Nietzsche. But this and other aspects of genius that he learned from Wagner were essential to Nietzsche's own creative mission. They enabled his transformation from a provincial son of a Lutheran pastor and sometime professor of classical philology into the world-renowned nihilist philosopher.

When Nietzsche finally clarified his creative mission, it turned out to be quite distinct from the concerns of Schopenhauer and Wagner. He would strive for the "transvaluation of all values—*die Umwertung aller Werte*"—overturning culture itself. He would undermine the epistemology, the metaphysics, the morality, the science, and the very logic of Western thought. He tried to discredit the authority of nearly every idealized and heroic figure, starting with Socrates, whose influence he had already decried in *The Birth of Tragedy*, extending even to his own genius mentors, Schopenhauer and, especially, Wagner. Even as he idealized them, he strove to transcend them. And once he had transcended them, there was no genius left but Nietzsche himself.

A genius must have a mission unique to himself, defined by and for himself.[7] Instead of serving others, he must become completely dedicated to himself and to his ambition. The role is psychologically demanding, if for no other reason than because it conflicts with all other social norms that require cooperation and reciprocity from people. To learn this role, Nietzsche submitted to extreme discipline. But now he abandoned all deference and carried the role of genius to an extreme by attacking every received value and pronouncing new values of his own.

Nietzsche's attack was especially radical because he eschewed any systematic alternative to the idols he toppled. He aspired to abolish truth itself. Yet his strategy was not mere iconoclasm. It was an unprecedented, affirmative sort of nihilism, entailing cheerful truthfulness about the impossibility of objective truth. Nietzsche proposed to affirm life after the death of God, when life could have no intrinsic meaning. He attempted to impose values where none were to be found, and he preached a gospel of loving one's fate (*amor fati*). He envisioned a form of moral life without the reassurance of morality. His is perhaps the most drastic assault upon Western thinking that has ever been mounted. It carries to an extreme a certain critical tendency inherent in Western thought, but its effect is to undermine the entire tradition for the first time. Nietzsche against all.

Nietzsche exerted himself at every stage of his life, as he put it, to become what he was. His youth was a struggle against his family's determination that he become a pastor. But his rebellion against family and religion did not free him for a life of hedonism. Quite the contrary, his life developed in almost monastic austerity into a constant striving to overcome. He retained a deep need for a calling in life, but making full use of the category of genius, he transformed the idea of a calling into a life of striving to transcend such ideas. With a strong residual sense of the "Protestant ethic," he worked hard in school and later to fulfill his potential. To the end of his conscious life, he continued to describe his work as his "mission." His Protestant ethic and sense of mission do not indicate a religious proclivity in Nietzsche, nor do they belie his secular accomplishment; they testify to his ability to transform his inheritance into something new. He subjected his liberating mentors to the same revaluation.

Nietzsche did not become a radical thinker easily. But any suggestion that he became who he became as a consequence of mental illness or oedipal rivalry with his chosen mentors would trivialize his achievement. Writing the books that have inscribed the name NIETZSCHE over the doors to the twentieth-century required immense resources, ambition, energy, and above all incredible focus in striving to overcome the world as he found it. How else could he even attempt to topple the whole edifice of Western civilization single-handedly? Is it any wonder he had headaches?

Nietzsche's life demonstrates that genius is not born, but may be made, and by a process far less magical than the romantic ideology of genius may make it seem. Like every other creative individual, he had to

338   THE PSYCHOLOGY OF NIETZSCHE / CARL PLETSCH

make his life in the world as he found it. As Karl Marx wrote, "Men make their own history but not just as they wish; not under circumstances of their own choosing, but under the given and inherited circumstances that directly confront them."[8] Marx's words could be a description of genius, except that in becoming a genius Nietzsche remade himself as he made his own history. Nietzsche created himself in rebellion against the circumstances of his birth. But he was also the beneficiary of those circumstances.

Nietzsche's family background did contribute to his eventual prominence in several ways. In *Young Nietzsche*, I noted several preconditions for the kind of self-creation entailed in becoming a genius: native intelligence, high family expectations, personal ambition and stamina, self-confidence, a good education, and so on. Nietzsche inherited or acquired these enabling qualities well before he encountered the concept of genius, or quite apart from it. But his possession of these traits and advantages in no way contradicts the statement that he invented himself. They made it possible for him to create a unique life and achieve a measure of greatness once he began to imagine himself as a genius. But none of this—not native ability, not education, not family dynamics—could have made him a genius without his characteristic striving to overcome.

GETTING CULTURAL

Many advantages accrued to Nietzsche from being born into an ambitious family that emphasized education. And inheriting great intellectual ability was no disadvantage either. But becoming NIETZSCHE was not as simple as being smart and getting a good education; it was not an option for just anyone born into the German *Bildungsbuergertum*. Even with his advantages, Friedrich Wilhelm Nietzsche had to create himself the peculiar philosopher we know as Nietzsche by channeling his ambition into learning and appropriating the role of genius. He matched his personality to the cultural category by emulating a series of fatherly mentors and ultimately transcending them. This is one dimension of the "personal element" crucial to understanding Nietzsche.

I cannot overemphasize that Nietzsche's striving for genius was an unusual but perfectly healthy process. Within a recognized cultural category, he was ambitious, he emulated models of genius, transcended them, and achieved his own unique outlook. This is not a pathological process in need of diagnosis. There is of course a tendency to associate genius with insanity. That is not surprising, since by ordinary standards geniuses tend to behave oddly. But as I have suggested above, genius is a category that was intended to make allowance for odd behavior, and to protect highly innovative individuals from just this natural reaction, which might otherwise lead to ostracism or worse. Thus it seems to me that the compulsion to diagnose such individuals as Nietzsche is more a symptom of residual ambivalence toward strange innovators than it is an indication of mental imbalance in them. The overwhelming impression of any close look at Nietzsche's career is one of remarkable balance and efficiency in the single-minded pursuit of an ambition that he had defined for himself. His life is marked by unusual autonomy, and his achievement hardly requires emphasis.

I have however emphasized the cultural category of genius in this paper for several reasons. First, and most obviously, because genius empowered Nietzsche. Genius was the mode of self-consciousness that an ambitious young man growing up in the mid-nineteenth century could aspire to, a young man who wanted to achieve something completely new. There is a minor paradox here. A genius must be unique: a genius must create a new frame in which to innovate; a genius must create his very self. Yet genius is a general template for the invention of uniqueness, a framework for the creation of new frameworks. It is within this framework that innovators like Nietzsche—a type—invent themselves. So genius is the established social space in which people like Nietzsche typically become unique innovators. The personal is the cultural.

I have told the story of how Nietzsche did this in *Young Nietzsche*. There I wanted to show how Nietzsche became who he was. But here I have emphasized the cultural category of genius for a second reason also. Acknowledging that the cultural category of genius is the social space in which geniuses make themselves reorients us, setting psychological issues in the historical context of an era where genius had social and economic implications. In one dimension it relates the work of the genius to other social processes of innovation in the modern era, like industrial revolution, social mobility, "progress," and so on. And in another dimension it links the genius to the saints and heroes of other eras. Acknowledging that genius is a historically specific human type puts Nietzsche in a perspective that would otherwise be lacking. As unique as he may be in respect to his creations, he conforms to a type nonetheless. And that type makes a great deal of sense in hyperinnovative modern society.

Psychological processes always unfold in cultural contexts. This may seem less than obvious in discussing modern geniuses, however, for several reasons: The modern context is itself so obvious to us that it may seem natural rather than cultural. Then modern culture defines itself almost exclusively in terms of individuals rather than culturally defined roles. And finally, genius itself is an ideology that emphasizes radical individuality above all else. In fact, it has been one of the primary functions of the ideology of genius to separate geniuses from normal and even very talented individuals (perhaps to encourage innovation while maintaining a certain degree of order in society at large). Individual geniuses are made into myths, to seem even more radically different than they actually are. Thus the cliché that geniuses are born, not made. But the supposedly natural difference (by birth) is itself a cultural feature, inasmuch as it is part of the definition of genius. The context in which individuals like Nietzsche become geniuses is a culture that tends to obscure culture. It emphasizes individuality to the point of excluding cultural categories from our view. I underscore the culture of genius in part to demystify it, but also to temper the psychological tendency in modern criticism with cultural awareness.

If I am right, and genius is the status that Nietzsche was striving for, diagnosing Nietzsche is beside the point for two reasons. First, because his achievement should not be understood as a pathology. And second, because Nietzsche is not just a grown up Friedrich Wilhelm Nietzsche, but NIETZSCHE, a cultural and not a psychological artifact.

What does this analysis infer about Nietzsche's ideas? What is irrefutable about Nietzsche is the particular way he used the role of genius in striving to overcome his background, his mentors, meaning, truth, morality, and all the rest. Whether he was successful—whether his writings are true for us—is less important. For as he noted in his essay *Philosophy in the Tragic Age of the Greeks* mentioned above,

> Philosophical systems are wholly true only for their founders. For all subsequent philosophers they usually seem one great mistake . . . to be repudiated. Thus, many people disapprove of every philosopher, because his goal is not theirs. . . . On the other hand, whoever takes joy in great individuals will also take joy in such systems, even if they are completely erroneous.[9]

This too applies as much to Nietzsche himself as it does to the ancient Greeks.

To study Nietzsche's philosophical performance is to study neither his personality nor his ideas in isolation. It is neither to diagnose nor to obsess about whether his ideas are true or even coherent. It is to study his books and ideas as part of a lifelong project that only emerges to view when taken together, with the current of ambition that connects them.

NOTES

1. He never published it.

2. Friedrich Nietzsche, *Philosophy in the Tragic Age of the Greeks* (Washington, D.C.: Regnery/Gateway, 1962), 25.

3. Ibid.,

4. Carl Pletsch. *Young Nietzsche: Becoming a Genius* (New York: The Free Press, 1991).

5. Cf. ibid., 70–94, and especially 86–89 for Schopenhauer's theory of genius.

6. Cf. ibid., 103–204 on Nietzsche's extended relationship/discipleship with Wagner.

7. My use of the male pronoun in conjunction with the theory of genius is not meant to prejudice women, but to acknowledge that in the nineteenth century heyday of genius it was simply assumed that only men would be geniuses.

8. Karl Marx, *The Eighteenth Brumaire of Louis Bonaparte* (New York: International Publishers, 1963), 15. Translation slightly revised.

9. *Philosophy in the Tragic Age of the Greeks*, 24.

SELECT BIBLIOGRAPHY

Ackerknecht, Erwin H. "Geschichtliches zur Theorie der psychischen Energie." *Schweizer Archiv fur Neurologie, Neurochirurgie und Psychiatrie* 135, no. 2 (1984): 181-185.

Anderson, L. "Freud, Nietzsche." *Salmagundi* 47–48 (Winter-Spring 1980): 3–29.

Andreas-Salomé, L."'Anal' and 'Sexual.'" *Imago* 4, no. 5 (1916): 249-273.

———. "The Dual Orientation of Narcissism." *The Psychoanalytic Quarterly* 31, no. 1 (January 1962 [1921]): 3-30.

———. *The Freud Journal of Lou Andreas-Salomé*, trans. Stanley A. Leavy. New York: Basic Books, 1964.

———. *Looking Back: Memoirs*, ed. Ernst Pfeiffer, trans. Breon Mitchell. New York: Paragon House, 1991.

Ansbacher, H. L. "Adler's 'Striving for Power' in Relation to Nietzsche." *Journal of Individual Psychology* 28 (1972): 12–24.

Assoun, P.-L. *Freud et Nietzsche*. Paris: Presses Universitaires de France, 1980.

Bass, A. "Psychopathology, Metaphysics." *American Imago* 50.2 (Summer 1993): 197–225.

Bassier, W. "Zur Wissenschaftsmethodik der Psychologie: Dilthey, Nietzsche, Jung." *Analytische Psychologie* 13.4 (December 1982): 281–98.

Baudouin, C. "Nietzsche as a Forerunner of Psychoanalysis," in *Contemporary Studies*, trans. Eden & Cedar Paul, London: Allen and Unwin, 1924, pp. 40–43.

Berthold-Bond, D. "Hegel, Nietzsche, and Freud on Madness and the Unconscious." *Journal of Speculative Philosophy* (1991): 193–213.

Bischoff, H. W. "An Exploration into Friedrich Nietzsche's Conception of Saying 'Yes to Life' as Elaborated in *Thus Spoke Zarathustra*." *Journal of Evolutionary Psychology* 7.1–2 (March 1986): 127–36.

Bishop, P. *The Dionysian Self: C. G. Jung's Reception of Friedrich Nietzsche.* Berlin: Walter de Gruyter, 1995.

Blondel, E. *Nietzsche, the Body and Culture*, trans. Sean Hand. Stanford: Stanford University Press, 1991 (1986).

Bolz, N. "Von Nietzsche zu Freud." In *Spiegel und Gleichnis: Festschrift für Jacob Taubes*, ed. Norbert W. Bolz and Wolfgang Hübner, 388–403. Würzburg: Konigshausen and Neumann, 1983.

Brandt, R. "'Freud and Nietzsche: A Comparison.'" *Revue de l'Université d'Ottawa* 25 (1955): 225–34.

Chapelle, D. *Nietzsche and Psychoanalysis*. Albany: State University of New York Press, 1993.

Chapman, A. H. and M. Chapman-Santana. "The Influence of Nietzsche on Freud's Ideas." *British Journal of Psychiatry* 166 (1995): 251–53.

Chessick, R. D. "The Relevance of Nietzsche to the Study of Freud and Kohut." *Contemporary Psychoanalysis* 17 (1981): 359–73.

———. *A Brief Introduction to the Genius of Nietzsche.* New York: University Press of America, 1981.

Clegg, J. S. "Freud and the 'Homeric' Mind." *Inquiry* 17 (Winter 1974): 445–56.

Clowes, E. W. "Self-Laceration and Resentment: The Terms of Moral Psychology in Dostoevsky and Nietzsche: Essays in Honor of Robert Louis Jackson." In *Freedom and Responsibility in Russian Literature*, ed. Elizabeth Cheresh Allen and Gary Saul Morson, 119–33. Evanston, Ill.: Northwestern University Press, 1995.

Corman, L. *Nietzsche: Psychologue des profondeurs.* Paris: Presses Universitaires de France, 1982.

Crawford, C. "Nietzsche's Mnemotechnics, the Theory of *Ressentiment*, and Freud's Topographies of the Psychic Apparatus." *Nietzsche-Studien* 14 (1985): 281–97.

Crookshank, F. G. *Individual Psychology and Nietzsche*, London: C. W. Daniel, 1933.

Danto, A. C. "Philosophical Psychology," ch. 4, and "Religious Psychology," ch. 6. In *Nietzsche as Philosopher.* New York: Columbia University Press, 1965.

Dieckhofer, K. "Human, Overly Human: Toward an Understanding of the Psychology of Nietzsche" (in German). *Zeitschrift für Klinische Psychologie und Psychotherapie* 28.2 (1980): 101–5.

Dimitrov, C. and A. Jablenski. "Nietzsche und Freud." *Zeitschrift für Psychosomatische Med. Psychoanalyse* 13 (1967): 282.

Donnellan, B. "Friedrich Nietzsche and Paul Rée: Cooperation and Conflict." *Journal for the History of Ideas* 43 (1982): 595–612.

Eiland, Howard. "Beyond Psychology: Heidegger on Nietzsche." *The Kenyon Review* 6.1 (Winter 1984): 74–86.

Ellenberger, H. F. *The Discovery of the Unconscious.* New York: Basic Books, 1970.

Emery, E. "A Note on Sandor Ferenczi and the Dionysian Itinerary in Psychoanalysis." *The Psychoanalytic Review* 82.2 (April 1995): 267–71.

Evans, F. *Psychology and Nihilism: A Genealogical Critique of the Computational Model of Mind.* Albany: State University of New York Press, 1993.

Faber, M. D. "Back to a Crossroad: Nietzsche, Freud, and the East." *New Ideas in Psychology* 6.1 (1988): 25–45.

Finken, B. W. "The Early Development of Nietzsche's Philosophy and Psychology." Ph.D. diss., University of Illinois at Urbana, 1993.

Foucault, M. "Nietzsche, Freud, Marx." In *Nietzsche*, Paris: Les Éditions de Minuit, 1967, 183–200.

Fourquet, F. "Libidinal Nietzsche." Trans. S. Guerlac. *Semiotexte* 3.1 (1978): 68–77.

Freschl, Robert. "Friedrich Nietzsche and Individual Psychology." *International Journal of Individual Psychology* 4 (1935): 87–98.

Freud, E. L., ed. *The Letters of Sigmund Freud and Arnold Zweig*, trans. E. and W. Robson-Scott. New York: New York University Press, 1970.

Freud, S. "Discussion of Nietzsche: On the Ascetic Ideal." *Minutes of the Vienna Psychoanalytic Society* (1906–08), ed. Herbert Nunberg and Ernst Federn, trans. M. Nunberg, 1:355–61. New York: International Universities Press, 1962.

———. "Discussion of Nietzsche's *Ecce Homo*," *Minutes of the Vienna Psychoanalytic Society*, 2:25–33. New York: International Universities Press, 1967.

Frey-Rohn, L. *Jenseits der Werte seiner Zeit: Friedrich Nietzsche im Spiegel seiner Werke*. Zurich: Daimon Verlag, 1984. English trans., *Friedrich Nietzsche: A Psychological Approach to His Life and Work*, 1988.

Garcia-Duttmann, A. "'What Is Called Love in All the Languages and Silences of the World': Nietzsche, Genealogy, Contingency." Trans. A. M. Beisswenger and G. Richter. *American Imago* 50.3 (Fall 1993): 277–323.

Gay, P. *Freud, Jews and Other Germans*. Oxford: Oxford University Press, 1978.

Gellner, E. *The Psychoanalytic Movement: The Cunning of Unreason*. Evanston, Ill.: Northwestern University Press, 1996 (1985).

Gillibert, J. "Freud et Nietzsche." *Revue Française de Psychoanalyse* (Paris) 46 (1982): 95–104.

Gilman, S. *Nietzschean Parody: An Introduction to Reading Nietzsche*. Bonn: Bouvier, 1976.

Ginsberg, M. "Nietzschean Psychiatry." In *Nietzsche: A Collection of Critical Essays*, ed. Robert C. Solomon, 293–315. Notre Dame, Ind.: University of Notre Dame Press, 1980.

Godde, G. "Freuds philosophische Diskussionkreise in der Studentenzeit." *Jarbuch der Psychoanalyse* 27 (1991): 73-113. "Wandlungen des Menschenbildes durch Nietzsche und Freud: Eine vergleichende Interpretation aus Philosophiegeschichtlicher Perspektive." *Jahrbuch der Psychoanalyse* 30 (1993): 119–66.

Golomb, J. "Freudian Uses and Misuses of Nietzsche." *American Imago* 37 (1980): 371–85.

———. "Jaspers, Mann and the Nazis on Nietzsche and Freud." *Israel Journal for Psychiatry* 18 (1981): 311–26.

———. "Nietzsche's Early Educational Thought." *Journal of Philosophy of Education* 19 (1985): 99–109.

———. *Nietzsche's Enticing Psychology of Power*. Ames: Iowa State University Press, 1989.

Granier, J. "Le statut de la philosophie selon Nietzsche et Freud." *Revue de Metaphysique et de Morale* 86 (1981): 88-102.

Hagens, J. L. "Jenseits von Nietzsche und Freud: Aktenstucke zweier Psychologen." *Zeitschrift für Klinische Psychologie, Psychopathologie und Psychotherapie* 33.3 (1985): 239–58.

Hans, J. S. *The Origins of the Gods*. Albany: State University of New York Press, 1991.

———. *The Question of Value: Thinking through Nietzsche, Heidegger and Freud*. Carbondale: Southern Illinois University Press, 1989.

Hartley, G. D. "The Centrality of the Concept of Power in Nietzsche, Adler, and May: Implications for Counseling Practice." *Individual Psychology Journal of Adlerian Theory, Research and Practice* 51.4 (December 1995): 346–57.

Heller, P., "Freud in His Relation to Nietzsche." In *Nietzsche and Jewish Culture*, ed. J. Golomb. London and New York: Routledge, 1997.

Hemecker, W. W. *Vor Freud. Philosophie geschichtliche Vor aussetzungen der Psychoanalyse.* Munich: Philosophia Verlag, 1991.

Herrera, R. A. "Freud on Nietzsche—A Fantastic Commentary." *Philosophy Today* 29 (Winter 1985): 339–44.

Howell, T. J. "Early and Late Deconstructions: Nietzsche's Surviving Role in the Philosophy of Literature and Psychology." *Literature and Psychology* 37.3 (1991): 45–58.

Jarmolgch, N. "Nietzche's Concept of Consciousness." *International Studies in Philosophy* 17.2 (1985): 69–75.

Jennings, J. L. "From Philology to Existential Psychology: The Significance of Nietzsche's Early Work." *The Journal of Mind and Behavior* 9.1 (Winter 1988): 57–76.

———. "Aphorisms and the Creative Imagination: Lessons in Creativity, Method, and Communication." *Journal of Mental Imagery* 15.3–4 (Fall-Winter 1991): 111–32.

Kaiser-El-Safti, M. *Der Nachdenker. Die Entstehung der Metapsychologie Freuds in ihrer Abhangigkeit von Schopenhauer und Nietzsche.* Bonn: Bouvier, 1987.

Kant, O. "Nietzsche und die Moderne Psychologie." *Klinische Wochenschrift* 12 (1933): 1416–20.

Kaufmann, W. *Nietzsche: Philosopher, Psychologist, Antichrist.* Princeton: Princeton University Press, 1950.

———. *Discovering the Mind.* Vol. 2: *Nietzsche, Heidegger, and Buber.* New Brunswick, N.J.: Transaction Publishers, 1991 (1980).

———. *Discovering the Mind.* Vol. 3: *Freud, Adler, and Jung.* New Brunswick, N.J.: Transaction Publishers, 1992 (1980).

Kerz, J. P. "Das wiedergefundene 'Es.' Zu Bernd Nitzschkes Aufsatz über die Herkunft des 'Es.'" *Psyche Zeitschrift für Psychoanalyse und ihre Anwendungen* 39.2 (February 1985): 125–43.

Klages, L. *Die Psychologischen Errungenschaften Nietzsches.* Leipzig: Barth, 1926.

Klein, D. B. *Jewish Origins of the Psychoanalytic Movement.* New York: Praeger, 1981.

Kofman, S. "La Femme Narcissique: Freud et Girard." *Revue Française de Psychanalyse* 44.1 (January-February 1980): 195–210.

Krummel, R. F. "Dokumentation: Joseph Paneth über seine Begegnung mit Nietzsche in der Zarathustra-Zeit," *Nietzsche-Studien* 17 (1988): 478–95.

Kuchenhoff, J. "Gross Es oder klein es? Anmerkungen zu dem Artikel von Bernd Nitzschke über die 'Herdunft des Es.'" *Psyche Zeitschrift für Psychoanalyse und ihre Anwendungen* 39.2 (February 1985): 144–49.

Kurz, G. "Nietzsche, Freud, and Kafka." In *Reading Kafka: Prague, Politics, and the Fin de Siècle*, ed. M. Anderson. New York: Schocken, 1988.

Lauret, B. *Schulderfahrung und Gottesfrage bei Nietzsche und Freud*. Munich: Kaiser, 1977.

Leahy, A. J. "Nietzsche interprete par Jung." *Études Nietzscheans* 1.1 (1948): 36–43.

Lehman, H. "Jung Contra Freud: Nietzsche Contra Wagner." *International Review of Psychoanalysis* 13 (1986): 201–9.

Lehrer, R. *Nietzsche's Presence in Freud's Life and Thought*. Albany: State University of New York Press, 1995.

———. "Freud's Relationship to Nietzsche: Some Preliminary Considerations." *The Psychoanalytic Review* 83.3 (June 1996): 363–94.

Lieberman, E. J. *Acts of Will: The Life and Work of Otto Rank*, 2nd ed. Amherst: University of Massachusetts Press, 1993 (1985).

Livingston, N. B. "Darwin, Nietzsche and Freud: The Evolutionary Link between Biology, Philosophy and Psychology." *Journal of Evolutionary Psychology* 15.3–4 (August 1994): 176–83.

Lungstrum, J. "Nietzsche Writing Woman/Woman Writing Nietzsche: The Sexual Dialectic of Palingenesis." In *Nietzsche and the Feminine*, ed. Peter J. Burgard, 135–57. Charlottesville: University Press of Virginia, 1994.

Manuel, F. E. "The Use and Abuse of Psychology in History." *Daedalus* 117.3 (Summer 1988 [1971]): 199–225.

Markert, J. "The Sociology of Friedrich Nietzsche: The Will to Power and Exchange Structuralism." *Cornell Journal of Social Relations* 16.2 (Spring 1981): 70–83.

May, R. "Nietzsche's Contributions to Psychology." *Symposium* 1974 (Spring): 58–73

Mazlish, B. "Freud and Nietzsche." *Psychoanalytic Review* 55 (1968): 360–75.

McGrath, W. J. *Dionysian Art and Populist Politics in Austria*. New Haven: Yale University Press, 1974.

Mette, A. "Nietzsches '*Geburt der Tragödie*' in Psychoanalytischer Beleuchtung," *Imago* (Vienna) 18 (1932): 67–80.

Mittasch, A. *Friedrich Nietzsche als Naturphilosoph*. Stuttgart: Alfred Kroner, 1952.

Moraitis, G. "A Psychoanalyst's Journey into a Historian's World: An Experiment in Collaboration." *Emotions and Behavior Monographs* 4 (1987): 503–53.

Morel, G. "Le Signe et le Nihilisme." *Psychanalystes* 22 (January 1987): 35–67.

Moreno, A. *Jung, God, and Modern Man*. Notre Dame, Ind.: Notre Dame University Press, 1970.

Nash, D. S. "Death or Power: A Reassessment of Human Aggression through an Analysis and Comparison of the Theories of Nietzsche and Freud." Ph.D. diss., University of California at Berkeley, 1984.

Nill, P. "Die Versuchung der Psyche. Selbstwerdung als schöpferisches Prinzip bei Nietzsche und C. G. Jung," *Nietzsche-Studien* 17 (1984): 250–79.

Nitzschke, B. "Zur Herkunft des 'Es': Freud, Groddeck, Nietzsche, Schopenhauer und E.von Hartmann." *Psyche Zeitschrift für Psychoanalyse und ihre Anwendungen* 37.9 (September 1983): 769–804.

Nunberg, H. and E. Federn (eds.). *Minutes of the Vienna Psychoanalytic Soci-*

ety, vols. 1–3, trans. M. Nunberg. New York: International Universities Press, 1962–74.

Parkes, G. "A Cast of Many: Nietzsche and Depth-Psychological Pluralism." *Man and World* 22 (1989): 453–70.

———. *Composing the Soul: Reaches of Nietzsche's Psychology.* Chicago and London: University of Chicago Press, 1994.

Pines, S. "Nietzsche: Psychology vs. Philosophy, and Freedom." In *Nietzsche as Affirmative Thinker*, ed. Y. Yovel, 147–59. Dordrecht: Nijhoff, 1986.

Pletsch, C. "On the Autobiographical Life of Nietzsche." In *Psychoanalytic Studies of Biography*, ed. George Moraitis and George H. Pollock, 405–34. Madison, Conn.: International Universities Press, 1987.

———. *Young Nietzsche.* New York: The Free Press, 1991.

Rattner, J. "Alfred Adler und Friedrich Nietzsche." *Zeitschrift für Individualpsychologie* 7 (1982): 65–75.

Rickels, L. A. "Insurance for and against Women: From Nietzsche to Psychotherapy." In *Nietzsche and the Feminine*, ed. Peter J. Burgard, 257–85. Charlottsville: University Press of Virginia, 1994.

Rider, Le, J. "Les intellectuels juifs viennois et Nietzsche; autour de Sigmund Freud." In *Sils-Maria*, 181–200.

Roazen, P. "Nietzsche and Freud: Two Voices from the Underground." *Psychohistory Review* 19 (1991): 327–48.

———. "Nietzsche, Freud, and the History of Psychoanalysis." In *Returns of the "French Freud": Freud, Lacan, and Beyond*, ed. T. Dufresne, 11–23. New York: Routledge, 1997.

Rudnytsky, P. L. "Nietzsche's Oedipus." *American Imago* 42.4 (Winter 1985): 413–39.

———. *Freud and Oedipus.* New York: Columbia University Press, 1987.

Rudolph, A. "Jung and Zarathustra." *Philosophy Today* 18 (Winter 1974): 312–18.

Russo, L. *Nietzsche, Freud e il paradosso della rapresentazione.* Rome: Istituto della Enciclopedia Italiana, 1986.

Scavio, M. J., A. Cooper, P. Scavio, and P. Clift. "Freud's Devaluation of Nietzsche." *Psychohistory Review* 21.3 (Spring 1993): 295–318.

Schmitt, R. "Nietzsche's Psychological Theory." *Journal of Existentialism* 2 (Summer 1961): 71–92.

Schneider, G. K. "Nietzsche and the Psychology of Self-Deceit." *West Virginia University Philological Papers* 30 (1984): 10–16.

Schrift, A. D. "Between Church and State: Nietzsche, Deleuze and the Genealogy of Psychoanalysis." *International Studies in Philosophy* 24.2 (1992): 41–52.

Schutte, O. "Nietzsche's Psychology of Gender Difference." In *Modern Engendering:Critical Feminist Readings in Modern Western Philosophy*, ed. Bat-Ami Bar On. Albany: State University of New York Press, 1994.

Simon, R. "Freud's Concepts of Comedy and Suffering." *The Psychoanalytic Review* 64.3 (Fall 1977): 391–407.

Smith, J. E. "Freud, Philosophy, and Interpretation." In *The Philosophy of Paul Ricoeur*, ed. Lewis Edwin Hahn. Peru, Ill.: Open Court, 1994.

Soll, I. *"Introduction,"* Nietzsche, Heidegger, and Buber, by Walter Kaufmann, volume 2 of *Discovering the Mind*, 2nd ed. Rutgers, N.J.: Transaction Publishers, 1991.

Sondag, Y. "Nietzsche, Schopenhauer, L'Ascetisme et la Psychanalyse." *Revue Philosophique de la France et de l'Etranger* 96 (1971): 348–59.

Staten, H. *Nietzsche's Voice.* Ithaca, N.Y.: Cornell University Press, 1990.

Thatcher, D. "Nietzsche's Debt to Lubbock." *Journal of the History of Ideas* 39.2 (1983): 293–309.

Thauberger, Patrick C., Sonja A. Ruznisky, and John F. Cleland. "Avoidance of Existential-Ontological Confrontation: A Review of Research." *Psychological Reports* 49.3 (December 1981): 747–64.

Tramer, F. "Friedrich Nietzsche und Sigmund Freud." *Jahrbuch für Psychologie und Psychotherapie* 7 (1960): 325–50.

Treiber, H. "Zurr Logik des Traumes' bei Nietzsche: Anmerkungen zu den Traumaphorismen aus *'Menschiliches, Allzumenschliches'.*" *Nietzsche-Studien* 23 (1994): 1–41.

Trotignon, P. "Le jeu de l'illusion. Reflexions sur Nietzsche et Freud." *Revue Metaphysique Morale* 81 (1976): 171–96.

Tusken, L. W. "Once More with Chutzpah: A Brave Comparison of New Worlds in Nietzsche's *The Genealogy of Morals* and Kafka's *In the Penal Colony.*" *Journal of Evolutionary Psychology* 10.3–4 (August 1989): 342–51.

Valadier, P. "Marx, Nietzsche, Freud et la Bible." *Nouvelle Revue Theologique* 98 (1976): 784–98.

Venturelli, A., "Nietzsche in der Bergasse 19. über die erste Nietzsche-Rezeption in Wien." *Nietzsche-Studien* 13 (1984): 448–80.

Waugaman, R., "The Intellectual Relationship between Nietzsche and Freud." *Psychiatry* 36 (1973): 458–67.

Wehr, G. *Friedrich Nietzsche: Der "Seelen-Errater" als Wegbereiter der Tiefenpsychologie.* Freiburg: Aurum, 1982.

Weissman, K., "Nietzsche and the Anti-Maturism." *American Imago* 20 (1963): 315–29.

Weyland, M. *Una Nueva Imagen del Hombre a Traves de Nietzsche y Freud.* Buenos Aires: Editorial Lasada, 1953.

Will, H. "Freud, Groddeck und die Geschichte des 'Es.'" *Psyche Zeitschrift für Psychoanalyse und ihre Anwendungen* 39.2 (February 1985): 150–69.

Williams, B. "Nietzsche's Minimalist Moral Psychology." In *Nietzsche, Genealogy, Morality*, ed. Richard Schacht, 237–47. Berkeley: University of California Press, 1994.

Wittels, F. *Sigmund Freud: His Personality, His Teaching and His School.* Trans. Cedar Paul. London: Allen & Unwin, 1924.

———. *Freud and His Time.* Trans. Louise Brink. New York: Liveright Publishing, 1931.

———. "Revision of a Biography." *The Psychoanalytic Review* 20 (1933): 361–74.

Wolff, F. "Freud continuateur et correcteur de Nietzsche." *Inform. Psycholog.* 18 (1965): 67–70.

Wyschogrod, E. "Sons without Fathers: A Study in Identity and Culture." *Journal of the American Academy of Psychoanalysis* 6.2 (April 1978): 249–62.
Yalom, I. *When Nietzsche Wept.* New York: Basic Books, 1992.
Yerushalmi, Y. H. "Freud on the 'Historical Novel': From the Manuscript Draft (1934) of *Moses and Monotheism.*" *International Journal of Psychoanalysis* 70 (1989): 370–95.
Yoshizawa, D. "Jaspers's Concern with Nietzsche's Philological Psychology." In *Karl Jaspers*, ed. Richard Wisser. Wurzburg, Germany: Koningshausen, 1993.

INDEX

Ellenberger, Henri, 181, 231
Emotion, 127–143; aroused, 198n33;
    categories of, 131, 137; defense of,
    136; domestication of, 134; in
    ethics, 131; expression of, 130;
    freezing of, 5; hidden, 131;
    language of, 135; and reason, 132;
    role of, 132; as strategy, 130;
    strength of, 137; transparency of,
    131
Empathy, 240, 257
Empedocles, 293n66
Envy, 104, 128, 274
Epicurus, 134
Eros, 127, 178, 210
Esteem, 43
Eternal recurrence, 37–48, 118,
    223–224; as relevant myth, 39, 43;
    as valuation of existence, 39
Ethic(s), 131; character in, 140; in
    Christianity, 155; defining, 14;
    emotion in, 131; idealist, 158;
    philosophical, 14; rational-
    objective, 4; of resentment, 141;
    scholarly, 321; traditional, 14;
    virtue in, 140, 141
Ethos: of distance, 276; of
    indignation, 276
Evolution, 168n37
Executions, 108n43
Existence, 48; affirming, 41;
    devaluation of, 42; and eternal
    return, 39; innocent, 74;
    justification for, 112, 113; and
    original sin, 114; and religion,
    113; slander against, 39; valuation
    of, 39, 117
Experience: affective, 251; anxiety-
    producing, 252; birth, 252;
    cognitive, 111; fantasy, 205; of
    history, 106n12; human, 24, 25,
    32, 34; of illness, 117; imagination
    in, 208; inner, 24, 29; of joy,
    121–125; life, 250; memory of,
    122; of pain, 117; personal, 92,
    115, 119, 322; of pleasure, 115;
    possibilities of, 32, 34; private, 39;

range of, 24; repeated, 37–48; self,
    47; selfobject, 247, 248; of
    separateness, 256, 257; source of,
    106n4; therapeutic, 251; value of,
    48
Exploitation, 8
Expression, free, 2

Faith, 28, 29, 100, 101, 102, 320
Fantasy, 205, 209; activity, 210;
    archetypal, 212; deep-level, 209;
    of empathy, 240; frustration of,
    141; infantile, 323; of revenge,
    141; suspicion of, 208
Fantasy-thinking, 208
Fascism, 83, 103, 308, 309, 317
Fatalism, 57
Fate, love of, 19n42, 41, 43, 48, 139,
    143, 264n22, 288, 337
Fear, 8, 92, 198n33, 252, 256
Fechner, Gustav, 182, 186, 233
Federn, Paul, 304
Ferenczi, Sándor, 202n103, 251
Feuerbach, Ludwig, 184
Fleischl-Marxow, Otto von,
    198n31
Forgetting, 194, 200n58; active, 184;
    intentional, 189; real identities,
    279
Form, and creation, 82
Frankl, Viktor, 241
Freud, Anna, 300
Freud, Sigmund, 9, 18n32, 19n39,
    43, 44, 60, 128, 130, 133, 134,
    150, 151, 161, 164n11, 164n13,
    169n41, 208, 229, 230, 231, 233,
    241, 304, 305, 319, 320, 324; and
    catharsis, 185–189; influence of
    Nietzsche on, 150, 151, 164n11,
    164n13, 171–179, 181–196, 231;
    interest in philosophy, 184; and
    neurosis, 14; on pleasure, 188;
    relations with Rank, 248, 249,
    250, 251, 264n19; and symptom
    formation, 186
Fromm, Erich, 265n31
Fuchs, Carl, 1